Money Chords

A Songwriter's Sourcebook of Popular Chord Progressions

Richard J. Scott

Writers Club Press
San Jose New York Lincoln Shanghai

Money Chords
A Songwriter's Sourcebook of Popular Chord Progressions

All Rights Reserved © 2000 by Richard J. Scott

No part of this book may be reproduced or transmitted in any form or by any means, graphic, electronic, or mechanical, including photocopying, recording, taping, or by any information storage or retrieval system, without the permission in writing from the publisher.

Published by Writers Club Press
an imprint of iUniverse.com, Inc.

For information address:
iUniverse.com, Inc.
620 North 48th Street
Suite 201
Lincoln, NE 68504-3467
www.iuniverse.com

ISBN: 0-595-01039-3

Printed in the United States of America

For Janis

Contents

Preface ...vii
Introduction ...ix
Chord Progressions
    "E" Only Chord Progressions ...3
    "E-F" Chord Progressions ...9
    "E-F#" Chord Progressions ...17
    "E-G" Chord Progressions ...45
    "E-G#" Chord Progressions ...57
    "E-A" Chord Progressions ...81
    "E-A#" Chord Progressions ...151
    "E-B" Chord Progressions ...153
    "E-C" Chord Progressions ...187
    "E-C#" Chord Progressions ...191
    "E-D" Chord Progressions ...219
    "E-D#" Chord Progressions ...233
    "F#" Chord Progressions ...237
    "G" Chord Progressions ...255
    "G#" Chord Progressions ...259
    "A" Chord Progressions ...265
    "A#" Chord Progressions ...289
    "B" Chord Progressions ...291
    "C" Chord Progressions ...303
    "C#" Only Chord Progressions ...305
    "C#-E" Chord Progressions ...309
    "C#-F#" Chord Progressions ...317
    "C#-G#" Chord Progressions ...333
    "C#-A" Chord Progressions ...343
    "C#-B" Chord Progressions ...355
    "C#-D" Chord Progressions ...367
    "C#-D#" Chord Progressions ...369
    "D" Chord Progressions ...373
    "D#" Chord Progressions ...379
Appendix ...381
    The "80" Most Popular Progressions ...381
    Circle of Fifths Progressions ...385
    Ascending Bass Lines ...387

Descending Bass Lines 391
Static Bass Lines 401
Substitute Chord Progressions 411
Turnarounds 413
Endings 417
Transposing 419
Guitar Chord Chart 421

Preface

Money Chords is the result of the compilation and analysis of a large representative sampling of popular chord progressions to gain a more complete understanding of this basic building block of contemporary music. During a period of several years, over two thousand representative examples of popular chord progressions were culled from ten thousand songs reviewed. Next, the individual chord progressions were transposed to the key of "E" to permit easier comparison. The chord progressions were then categorized by chord changes and analyzed for commonalties, trends, and concentrations.

A major finding of the study was the identification of the eighty most popular chord progressions that have been used repeatedly to create hit songs. All eighty progressions are introduced at the beginning of their respective chapters and listed in the Appendix of this book. The study also found that twelve techniques or "tools" were used to create popular chord progressions. Each of the twelve "tools" is discussed in the Introduction.

Chord progressions are categorized both chronologically and by progression type permitting comparison of a large number of similar chord progressions at one time. The chronological listings are helpful for identifying progression types common to a specific time period while the listings by progression type are useful to compare how the best songwriters and performers have utilized similar chord progressions.

Good luck with your new "Tool Box." I hope that you find *Money Chords* to be a good reference source for years to come and that it helps stimulate the creation of many more great songs in the new millenium.

Introduction

The purpose of this book is to provide songwriters, arrangers, performers and other interested persons with a working knowledge of Money Chords. Money Chords are those popular chord progressions that have been used time and again as the basis for writing hit songs that appeal to a wide audience. Twelve "tools" are available to create popular chord progressions. These "tools" include The Circle of Fifths, Ascending/Descending/Static Bass Lines, Chord Substitutions, Chord Quality Changes, The Blues, Borrowed Chords, Partial Progressions, Middle Chords First, The Reverse, and Combinations. For the purposes of this book, all chord progression examples are shown in the key of "E" so that commonalties will be more easily apparent. The Major Scale Notes and Harmonized Chords in the key of "E" are presented below.

Major Scale Notes in the Key of "E"

1	2	3	4	5	6	7
8	9	10	11	12	13	
E	F#	G#	A	B	C#	D#

Harmonized Chords in the Key of "E"

E	F#m	G#m	A	B7	C#m	D#o

Circle of Fifths

The first "tool" available to create popular chord progressions is the Circle of Fifths. The Circle of Fifths shows the most logical, natural movement of one chord to another in Western music. You can start with any chord on the wheel, move in any direction, and use as much or as little as you like to produce new progressions. The Circle of Fifths is shown below.

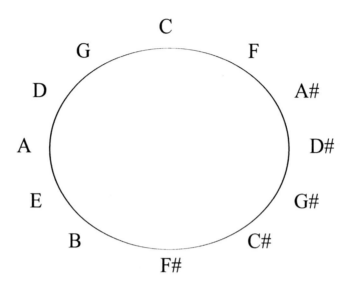

Examples of the most popular progressions that follow the Circle Of Fifths movement are as follows:

Progression Type	Chord Progression (Key of E)
Basic	E-A
Folk	E-B7
Standard	E-C#m-F#m-B7
Ragtime	E-C#7-F#7-B7

The Standard Progression begins with the "E" chord (in the key of "E") and then follows the Circle of Fifths from the "C#" chord through the "B" chord. Chord Quality Changes, that will be discussed later, permit the songwriter to change any chord to its Major, Minor, or Dominant 7th quality. In the Standard Progression above, the "C#" and "F#" chords are changed to their Minor quality and the "B" chord is changed to its Dominant 7th quality. The possible progression combinations that can be created using the Circle of Fifths are almost endless. The Appendix contains a chart of more frequently encountered Circle of Fifths Progressions.

Ascending Bass Lines

The second "tool" available to create popular chord progressions is the Ascending Bass Line. There are three popular Ascending Bass Lines including the "E-F#-G#-A", "E-F#-A-B", and "E-G#-A-B" Bass Lines. A detailed comparison of various Ascending Bass Lines from popular songs is found in the Appendix. Examples of popular progressions that employ these Ascending Bass Lines are as follows:

Bass Line	Chord Progression(Key of E)
E-F#-G#-A	E-F#m-E/G#-A
	E-F#m-G#m-A
E-F#-A-B	E-F#m-A-B7
	E-F#-A-B
E-G#-A-B	E-G#m-A-B7
	E-E/G#-A-B

The "E-F#m-E-A" Progression is transformed into an Ascending "E-F#-G#-A" Bass Line Progression by playing the G# note in the second "E" chord as the bass note creating the "E-F#m-E/G#-A" progression shown above. Numerous opportunities to create interesting Ascending Bass Line Progressions are also detailed in the Progression Type sections of the "E-F#", "E-G#", and "E-A" Chord Progression chapters of this book.

Descending Bass Lines

The third "tool" to produce popular chord progressions is the Descending Bass Line. There are five popular Descending Bass Lines including the "E-D#-C#-A", "E-D#-C#-B", "E-D#-D-C#", "C#-B-A-G#", and "C#-B-A#-A" bass lines. A detailed comparison of Descending Bass Lines used to produce hit songs is found in the Appendix of this book. Below are several examples of popular chord progressions that use Descending Bass Lines:

Bass Line	Chord Progression(Key of E)
E-D#-C#-A	E-B/D#-C#m-A
E-D#-C#-B	E-E/D#-C#m-C#m/B
	E-G#m/D#-C#m-E/B
	E-G#7/D#-C#m-E7/B
	E-B/D#-C#m-G#m/B
E-D#-D-C#	E-G#m/D#-Bm/D-C#7
	E-B/D#-D-A/C#
C#-B-A-G#	C#m-E/B-A-G#
	C#m-G#m/B-AM7-G#11

                    C#m-G#m/B-AM7-G#m
                    C#m-B-A-G#
                    C#m-C#m/B-A7-G#7

C#-B-A#-A   C#m-C#m/B-C#m/A#-AM7

The "E-B-C#m-A" progression is transformed into a Descending "E-D#-C#-A" Bass Line Progression by playing the D# note of the "B" chord as the bass note creating the above "E-B/D#-C#m-A" progression. As with Ascending Bass Lines, numerous opportunities to create interesting Descending Bass Line Progressions are detailed in the Progression Type sections of "E-G#", "E-B", "E-C#, and "C#" Chord Progression chapters of this book.

Static Bass Lines

The fourth "tool" available to create popular cord progressions is the Static Bass Line. There are two ways to create Static Bass Lines. The first is the Chord Quality Substitution. In the Chord Quality Substitution the songwriter or performer employs the General Chord Substitution Rule which allows any chord to be changed to or substituted for its Major, Minor, or Dominant 7th quality. Examples of popular chord progressions that use Chord Quality Substitution to create Static Bass Line Progressions are as follows:

Bass Line   *Chord Progression(Key of E)*

E   E-EM7-E6-EM7
                      E-E+-E6-E7
                      E-Esus
                      E-E11

C#   C#m-C#11
                      C#m-C#m(M7)-C#m7-C#m6

The "E-EM7-E6-EM7" progression uses the "EM7" and "E6" Chord Quality Substitutions to provide a feeling of movement where the "E" chord is used in progressions for more than one or two bars. The other Chord Quality Substitution Static Bass Line Progressions shown above are also commonly used to provide a feeling of movement where the "E" or "C#m" chords are used in progressions for more than one or two bars.

The second way to create Static Bass Lines is to use the same note bass line. Below are examples of popular chord progressions built around the same bass note.

Bass Line	Chord Progression (Key of E)
E	E-F#m/E
	E-G/E
	E-A/E
	E-B/E
C#	C#m-F#/C#
	C#m-A/C#

The "E-F#m7" progression is transformed into the "E-F#m/E" Static Bass Line Progression by playing the E note in the "F#m7" chord as the bass note. A detailed comparison of both Chord Quality Substitutions and Same Bass Note Static Bass Lines used in hit songs is found in the Appendix.

Chord Substitutions

The fifth "tool" available to create popular chord progressions is Chord Substitutions. The general Chord Substitution Rule holds that chords that share two or more notes in common can be readily substituted for each other. A listing of common Chord Substitutions based on this rule for chords in the key of "E" are shown below.

Original Chord	Substitute Chords
E	C#m; G#m; Fo/G#o/Bo/Do
E7	Bm; A#7
F#m	A; D; B7; F#o/Ao/Co/D#o
F#m7	Go/A#o/C#o/Eo
F#7	C#m; C7
G#m	B; E; C#7; G#o/Bo/Do/Fo
G#m7	Ao/Co/D#o/F#o
G#7	D#m; D7
A	F#m; C#m; A#o/C#o/Eo/Go
A7	Em; D#7
B	G#m; D#m; Co/D#o/F#o/Ao
B7	F#m; F7

C#m	E; A; F#7; C#o/Eo/Go/A#o
C#m7	Do/Fo/G#o/Bo
C#7	G#m; G7

Several examples of popular chord progression types created by the use of Chord Substitution are as follows:

Original Progression	*New Progression(Key of E)*
E-A(Basic)	E-F#m [F#m substituted for A.]
	C#m-A [C#m substituted for E.]
	C#m-F#m [C#m substituted for E and F#m substituted for A]
E-C#m-F#m-B7(Standard)	E-G#m-F#m-B7 [G#m substituted for C#m.]
	E-Go-F#m-B7 [Go substituted for C#m.]
	E-C#m-A-B7 [A substituted for F#m.]
E-C#m-A-B7(Rock Ballad)	E-G#m-A-B7 [G#m substituted for C#m.]

Chord Quality Changes

The sixth "tool" to create popular chord progressions is also based on the general Chord Substitution Rule discussed above and holds that any chord can be changed to its Major, Minor, or Dominant 7th quality. These chords would always share two or more notes in common. Below is a representative listing of common Chord Quality Changes for the "E" chord. Any of the Quality Changes may be substituted for each other.

Chord Quality	Quality Changes
Major	E; E5; E6; EM7, EM9; E+; Esus; Eadd9; E6/9
Minor	Em; Em6; Em7; Em(M7); Em11
Dominant 7th	E7; E7sus; E9; E11; E13

In addition to the use of Chord Quality Changes to produce Static Bass Lines discussed earlier, below are examples of how performers have used this tool to create memorable chord progressions from several common chord progressions. Detailed listings are found in the Progression Type sections of this book.

Original Progression	New Progression (Key of E)
E-A (Basic)	E-A6
	E-AM7
	E-A7
	E6-A6
	EM7-A
	EM7-AM7
	EM7-AM7-A6
	EM7-A13
E-B7 (Folk)	E-B+
	E-B7#5
	E-B11
	E-Bm7
	E7-Bm7
E-C#m-F#m-B7 (Standard)	E-C#m7-F#m7-B7
	EM7-C#m7-F#m7-B7b9
	EM9-C#m7-F#m7-B6
E-C#7-F#7-B7 (Ragtime)	E-C#7-F#m7-B7
E-A-B7 (Rock)	E-A-B7b9
	E-A-B11
	E-A6-B
	Eadd9-Aadd9-B7sus

	Em-Am9-B7
E-C#m-A-B7(Rock Ballad)	E-C#m-A-B9
	E-C#m-AM7-B7
	E-C#m-Am-B7
	E-C#m7-A-B11

The Blues

The seventh "tool" available to write popular chord progressions is The Blues. The Classic, Quick Change, and Minor Blues Progressions are widely used as the basis to construct popular songs for not only Blues, but also for Jazz and Rock songs. A detailed list of Blues Chord Progressions can be found in the Progression Type sections of the "E-A" and "C#-F#" Chord Progression chapters of this book. Examples of the three common Blues forms are shown below.

Progression Type	*Chord Progression(Key of E)*
Classic	E7-A7-E7-B7-A7-E7-B7
Quick Change	E7-A7(2x)E7-B7-A7-E7-B7
Minor	C#m-F#m-C#m-G#m-F#m-C#m

Borrowed Chords

Borrowed Chords from other keys is the eighth "tool" to create popular chord progressions. The most popular "Borrowed" chords(in the Key of E)are the "D" and "G" chords that were regularly used in Classic Rock to create an overall Blues feel. Popular examples of Borrowed Chord Progression Types are shown below.

Progression Type	*Chord Progression(Key of E)*
Classic Rock	E-D-A
Classic Rock("D" First)	D-E-A
Classic Rock(Borrowed "D")	E-A-D-A
Classic Rock(Borrowed "G")	E-G-A-E

Detailed listings of Borrowed Chord Progressions are found in the Progression Type sections of the "E-G", "E-A", "E-C", "E-D", and "D" Chord Progression chapters of this book.

Partial Progressions

Partial Progressions is the ninth "tool" available to create popular chord progressions. As the name implies, using just a part of another progression can create new chord progressions. Popular examples of these Partial Progressions are listed below.

Original Progression	*New Progression(Key of E)*
E-A(Basic)	E(One Chord Progression) [First chord only]
E-C#m-F#m-B7(Standard)	E-F#m-B7 [Less C#m chord.]
	F#m-B7 [Last two chords only]
E-C#m-A-B7(Rock Ballad)	E-A-B7 [Less C#m chord]
	E-C#m [First two chords only]
E-D-A(Classic Rock)	E-D [First two chords only]
C#m-B-A-G#(Money Chords)	C#m-B [First two chords only]

Middle Chords First

The tenth "tool" to create popular chord progressions is to play the Middle Chords First. With this technique, you create a new chord progression by selecting another progression and beginning that new progression with the second or third(middle)chord in the progression. Examples of this technique are shown below.

Original Progression	New Progression (Key of E)
E-C#m-F#m-B7 (Standard)	C#m-F#m-B7-E
	F#m-B7-E-C#m
E-C#7-F#7-B7 (Ragtime)	C#7-F#7-B7-E
E-Fo-F#m7-B7 (Fo Cliché)	F#m7-B7-E-Fo
E-A-B7 (Rock)	A-B7-E
	E-B7-A
E-C#m-A-B7 (Rock Ballad)	A-B7-E-C#m

The Reverse

The eleventh "tool" available to create popular chord progressions is The Reverse. Again as the name implies, simply reversing another progression creates new chord progressions. Below are examples of this technique that work best with the two and three chord progressions.

Original Progression	New Progression (Key of E)
E-A (Basic)	A-E
E-B7 (Folk)	B7-E
E-A-B7 (Rock)	B7-A-E

Combinations

The last "tool" available to create popular chord progressions is to combine two or more of the above progressions or techniques into one Combination chord progression. The possible Combinations are virtually endless. A sampling of Combination Progressions are shown below.

Progression Type	Chord Progression (Key of E)
E-A (Basic) & Static "E" Bass Line	E-A/E

Introduction

E-A(Basic)& E-B7(Folk)   E-A-E-B7

E-A-B7(Rock)&
Static "E" Bass Line   E-A/E-B7/E

E-A-B7(Rock)& Ascending
"E-G#-A-B" Bass Line   E-E/G#-A-B

E-G-A-E(Classic Rock
Borrowed G)&
Static "E" Bass Line   E-G/E-A/E-E

C#m-C#m(M7)-C#m7-C#m6
(Minor Cliché)& Descending
"C#-C-B-A#" Bass Line   C#m-C#m/C-C#m/B-C#m/A#

G#m11-C#7b5-F#m11-B7b5
(Circle of Fifths)& Descending
"G#-G-F#-F" Bass Line   G#m11-C#7b5/G-F#m11-B7b5/F

This book is divided into the following three parts: Introduction, Chord Progressions, and Appendix. The Chord Progressions part is divided into twenty-nine chapters(see the complete listing in the Table of Contents). Each chapter discusses popular chord progressions that have verses, choruses, and/or bridges that begin with the referenced chord changes in the Key of "E." A Transposing Chart with instructions on how to use it is included in the Appendix so that you can convert any chord progression to a commonly used key or to a key that best suits your own vocal range.

Each chapter begins with a brief discussion of the most frequent progressions that start with the referenced chord changes followed by a chronological listing of songs with verses, choruses, and/or bridges that begin with the referenced chord sequence. The chronological listing shows repeatedly that nothing succeeds like success. That is to say that the same chord progressions are used repeatedly over long periods of time to create hit songs. The Blues Progression is an excellent example of this concept. The chronology contains the most complete progression listing and is helpful for songwriters trying to create songs from a specific time period. For example, if a songwriter wishes to create a 1930s and 1940s ballad, he or she would review the chronology and, most likely, write a song around the Standard "E-C#m-F#m-B7" Progression. The chronological listing also shows the evolution of various progression types such as the Ragtime(early 1900s), to the Diminished Cliché(1920s & 1930s), to the Standard Changes(1930s & 1940s), to the Rock Ballad(1950s & 1960s), to the Rock(1960s & 1970s).

The letter shown in parenthesis( )after the song title in the chronological listings, indicates the most common key used to play the song. The letters prior to each chord progression, indicate the section of the song for which the chord progression was used. A list of the letters used is as follows:

- I= Intro
- V= Verse
- P/C= PreChorus
- C= Chorus
- T/A= Turnaround
- B= Bridge
- O= Outro

Each chapter ends with a listing of chord progressions grouped by common types. This listing is useful because it allows the reader to compare a large number of similar progressions at one time. You will notice that certain chord substitutions are regularly used with specific progression types or certain time periods. This section also serves as an "Idea Box" to help songwriters develop initial chord progressions to create new hit songs, or to help improve upon existing progressions to songs that are still in the process of being developed.

The last part of this book is the Appendix that includes a listing of Turnarounds/Endings and a Guitar Chord Chart for chords commonly found in the Key of "E."

Chord Progressions

"E" Only Chord Progressions

"E" Only Chord Progressions, as the name implies, use just one chord for an entire verse and/or chorus of a song. These progressions are not very common with only forty or so hit songs employing this technique since the mid-fifties. Songwriters and performers have used various unique bass lines, guitar riffs, and driving rhythms as well as Chord Quality Substitutions to overcome the inevitable boredom of a single chord verse or chorus. The only other chord commonly used for an entire verse is "C#m" which is discussed in a later chapter of this book.

Below is a chronological listing of songs with verses and/or choruses that employ just one chord followed by a listing of chord progressions by type.

Chronological Listing

Date/Song Title	Chord Progression
1955	
Mabellene(Bb)	V=E(Alt. Bass)
Bo Diddley(G)	V=E
1957	
Raunchy(D)	V=E
1961	
Little Sister(E)	V=E7-E
1964	
California Sun(E)	V=E(Riff)

Who Do You Love(Ab)   V=E

It's All Over Now(G)   V=E

1965

Shotgun(Ab)   V=E7

My Generation(G)   V=E-E/D

If I Needed Someone(A)   V=E-E11-E

1966

Land of a Thousand Dances(D)   V=E

Over, Under, Sideways, Down(G)   V=E

Working In The Coal Mine   C=E

Stop, Stop, Stop(D)   V=E7

Tomorrow Never Knows(C)   V=E-E11

1967

You Got To Me(G)   V=E

Soul Man(G)   V=E(Riff)

Western Union(D)   V=E-Esus(6x)

The Beat Goes On(C)   V=E7(Bass Line)

It Takes Two   V=E-E7-E

1968

Jumpin' Jack Flash(B)   V=E(Riff)

Born On The Bayou(E)   V=E7

1969

Proud Mary(D)   V=E

Give Peace A Chance   V=E

New Mother Nature   V=E

Whole Lotta Love(E)   V/C=E(Riff)

1970

Mama Told Me Not to Come V=E7

No Sugar Tonight(F#)   V=E-Esus4/2(8x)

1971

Truckin'   V=E5-E6

1973

Chevy Van   V=E-Esus(7x)E

1974

Midnight Rider(D)   V=E

Rock On(E)   V=E7

Car Wash   V=E7

1975

Black Friday(E)   V=E

Low Rider   V=E7

Shining Star	V=E7#9

1978

Baby Hold On(D)	C=E-E+

1979

Don't Bring Me Down	V=E

1985

Born in the USA(A)	V/C=E-E/A

1987

(I've Had)The Time Of My Life	V=E11-E(4x)

1988

Wild, Wild West	V=E

Listing by Progression Type

Chord Progression   *Song Examples*

"E" Only Chord Progressions

E   Maybellene('55); Bo Diddley('55); Raunchy('57); California Sun('64); Who Do You Love('64); It's All Over Now('64); Land Of A Thousand Dances('66); Over, Under, Sideways, Down('66); Working In The Coal Mine('66);You Got To Me('67); Soul Man('67); Jumpin' Jack Flash('68); Proud Mary('69); Whole Lotta Love('69); Give Peace A Chance('69); New Mother Nature('69); Midnight Rider('74); Black Friday('75); Don't Bring Me Down('79); Wild Wild West('88)

E7	Shotgun('65); Stop, Stop, Stop('66); The Beat Goes On('67); Born On The Bayou('68); Mama Told Me Not To Come('70); Rock On('74); Car Wash('74); Low Rider('75)
E7#9	Shining Star('75)
E-E/A	Born In The USA('85)
E-E/D	My Generation('65)

Static Bass Lines

E5-E6	Truckin'('71)
E-E+	Baby Hold On('78)
E-Esus	Western Union('67); Chevy Van('73)
E-Esus4/2	No Sugar Tonight('70)
E-E7-E	It Takes Two('67)
E7-E	Little Sister('61)
E-E11	Tomorrow Never Knows('66)
E-E11-E	If I Needed Someone('65)
E11-E	(I've Had)The Time Of My Life('87)

"E-F" Chord Progressions

The most frequent progressions that start with the "E" chord and then move to an "F" chord are as follows:

"Fo" Cliché
        E-Fo-F#m7-B7
        E-Fo-F#m7-Go
        E-Fo-B7/F#-B7

The "E-Fo-F#m7-B7" Diminished Cliché was used to write numerous 1920s and 1930s ballads and is similar to the "E-C#m7-F#m7-B7" Standard Changes where the "C#m7" chord has been substituted by the "Fo" chord in order to create an Ascending Bass Line feel. Possibly the most recognizable use of the "E-Fo-F#m7-B7" Diminished Cliché is in the 1933 torch song *Stormy Weather*.

The "E-Fo-F#m7-Go" Diminished Cliché is similar to the "E-Fo-F#m7-B7" Diminished Cliché except that the "Go" chord has been substituted for the "F#m7" chord(which was substituted for the "B7" chord)in order to create an Ascending Bass Line. The 1929 *Ain't Misbehavin'* is the definitive example of this progression.

The "E-Fo-B7/F#-B7" Diminished Cliché is also similar to the "E-Fo-F#m-B7" Diminished Cliché where the "B7/F#" chord is substituted for the "F#m7" chord. A popular example of the "E-Fo-B7/F#-B7" Diminished Cliché is the 1927 song *Ain't She Sweet* which was covered by and a top twenty hit for The Beatles in 1964.

Each of three "Fo" Cliché progressions discussed above have been combined with "6"/"M7" Chord Quality Substitutions to create such popular songs as the 1922 *Carolina In The Morning*, the 1957 Christmas classic *Jingle Bell Rock*, and the 1966 Broadway hit *Mame*.

Below is a chronological listing of songs with verses and/or choruses that begin with the "E-F" chord sequence followed by a listing of chord progressions by type.

Chronological Listing

Date/Song Title　　　　　　　　*Chord Progressions*

1895

America The Beautiful　　　　　V=E-Fo-B7/F#-B7-E

1902

Bill Bailey, Won't You Please
Come Home　　　　　　　　　C=E-Fo-B7/F#-B7-E

1921

Sheik of Araby　　　　　　　　V=E-Fo-F#m7-B9

1922

Carolina In The Morning　　　　V=E-EM7-E6-Fo-B7/F#-B7

1925

If You Knew Suzie　　　　　　V=E-Fo-B7

Yes Sir That's My Baby　　　　V=E-Fo-B7-B11

1927

S'Wonderful　　　　　　　　　V=E6-Fo-F#m7-B13-E6

Ain't She Sweet　　　　　　　V=E-Fo-B7/F#-B7(2x)E-G#7-
　　　　　　　　　　　　　　　C#7-F#7-B7-E

1928

Makin' Whoopee　　　　　　　V=EM7-Fo-F#m7-B7

Baby Face　　　　　　　　　　V=E-Fo-B7-E-F#m7/B-B7

1929

Ain't Misbehavin'   V=E-Fo-F#m7-Go-E/G#-G#7#5-A6-D9-E/G#-C#7-F#m7-B9
T/A=G#7-C#7-F#7-B7

1933

It's Only A Papermoon   V=E-Fo-F#m7-B7-F#m-B7-E-Fo-F#m7-B7-E

Stormy Weather   V=EM7-Fo-F#m7-B7(2x)

1934

Deep Purple   V=E6/9-Fo-[Fm7]-F#m7-B7-G#m7b5-C#7

1938

Winter Wonderland   V=E-Fo-B7/F#-B7-F#9-B7-E6-G#-D#7(2x)G#-B-F#7-B-C#9-F#7-B-Fo-B7/F#

1941

Bewitched   V=E-Fo-F#m7-Go-E/G#-G#7-AM7-A#o-E-F#7-B7-C#7-F#m7-B7

Misirlou(E)   V=E-F(4x)E-Am-G-F

1942

Don't Sit Under The Apple Tree   V=E6-Fo-F#m7-B11-B9

1943

Mairzy Doats   V=E-Fo-F#m7-B7

1948

Once In Love With Amy V=E-Fo-B7/F#-B7(2x)-
E-E7-A-E-F#m7-E-F#7-B7

1950

Orange Colored Sky V=E-Fo-F#m7-Go-E-DM7-C#9-
F#m7-Go-E/G#-C#7-F#m7-
B7-E-Fo-B7/F#

1951

Happy Trails V=E-Fo-B7-B7#5

1952

How Much Is That Doggie In
The Window V=E-Fo-B7/F#-B7#5-
E-Fo-B7

1954

Till There Was You(F) V=E-Fo-F#m7-Am7-
E-G#m7-Gm7-F#m7-B9-
E-F#m7-B9-
I=E-Fo-F#m7-B9(2x)

1956

Que Sera, Sera V=E-Fo-F#m7-B7

1957

Jingle Bell Rock V=E-EM7-E6-EM7-E-Fo-F#m7-
B7

I Remember It Well V=E-EM7-E6-E-Fo-B7-F#m7-B7

1959

High Hopes	V=E6-Fo-F#m7-B7

1962

What Kind Of Fool Am I	V=EM7-Fo-F#m7-B7-G#m7-C#7b9-F#m7-B7b9
Call Me Irresponsible	V=E-E6-Fo-F#m-F#m6-Go-EM7/G#-E/G#-G#7-C#7#5-G#m7b5-C#7

1966

Mame	V=E-E6-EM7-Fo-F#m7-B7-F#m-C#+-F#m7-B7

1967

She's My Girl(E)	V=Em-F-Em-Bm-Em-F-Bb-Esus-G-F#-F-E

1968

For Once In My Life	V=E-E+-E6-Fo-F#m-D-B7

1978

Three Times A Lady	V=E-F/D-C#m-G#7#5/C

Listing By Progression Type

Chord Progression   *Song Examples*

"Fo" Cliché

E-Fo-F#m7-Am7	Till There Was You('54)
E-Fo-F#m7-B7	It's Only A Papermoon('33); Mairzy Doats('43); Que Sera Sera('56)
E-Fo-F#m7-B9	Sheik Of Araby('21)

E6-Fo-F#m7-B7	High Hopes('59)
E6-Fo-F#m7-B11-B9	Don't Sit Under The Apple Tree('42)
E6-Fo-F#m7-B13	S'Wonderful('27)
E6/9-Fo-[Fm7]-F#m7-B7	Deep Purple('34)
EM7-Fo-F#m7-B7	Makin' Whoopee('28); Stormy Weather('33); What Kind Of Fool Am I('62)

The following progression cleverly combine an "E-F-F#-G" Ascending Bass Line with the use of the "Fo" Cliché:

E-Fo-F#m7-Go	Ain't Misbehavin''('29); Bewitched('41); Orange Colored Sky('50)
E-Fo-B7/F#-B7	America The Beautiful(1895); Bill Bailey, Won't You Please Come Home('02); Ain't She Sweet('27); Winter Wonderland('38); Once In Love With Amy('48)
E-Fo-B7/F#-B7#5	How Much Is That Doggie In The Window('52)
E-Fo-B7	If You Knew Suzie('25); Baby Face('28); Happy Trails To You('51)
E-Fo-B7-B11	Yes Sir That's My Baby('25)

Static Bass Lines

The following four progressions combine the use of the "6"/"M7" Chord Quality Substitution with the above "Fo" Cliché:

E-E6-EM7-Fo-F#m7-B7	Mame('66)
E-EM7-E6-EM7-E-Fo-F#m7-B7	Jingle Bell Rock('57)
E-EM7-E6-Fo-B7/F#-B7	Carolina In The Morning('22)
E-EM7-E6-E-Fo-B7	I Remember It Well('57)

The following progression combines the use of the "6"/"M7" Chord Quality Substitution and "E-F-F#-G" Ascending Bass Line with the above "Fo" Cliché.

E-E6-Fo-F#m-F#m6-Go	Call Me Irresponsible('62)

The following progression combines the use of the Augmented Chord Quality Substitution with the above "Fo" Cliché:

E-E+-E6-Fo-F#m-[D]-B7	For Once In My Life('68)

Other "E-F" Progressions

    E-F   Misirlou('41)
    E-F/D-C#m-G#7#5/C   Three Times A Lady('78)–Descending Bass Line
    Em-F-Em-Bm   She's My Girl('67)

"E-F#" Chord Progressions

The most frequent progressions that begin with the "E" chord and then proceed to the "F#" chord are as follows:

Basic("F#m" Substitution)	E-F#m
Partial Standard	E-F#m-B7
Ascending "E-F#-G#-A" Bass Lines	E-F#m-E/G#-A
	E-F#m-G#m-A
Ascending "E-F#-A-B" Bass Lines	E-F#m-A-B7
	E-F#-A-B
Static Bass Lines	E-EM7-E6-EM7
	E-E+-E6-E7
	E-F#m/E

The "E-F#m" Basic("F#m" Substitution) Progression is similar to the "E-A" Basic Progression except that the "F#m" chord has been substituted for the "A" chord. Hit songs that were written around the "E-F#m" Progression include Tommy James & The Shondells' 1969 *Crystal Blue Persuasion*, the Eagles' 1975 number one *The Best Of My Love*, and Ex-Beatle Paul McCartney & Stevie Wonder's 1982 *Ebony And Ivory*.

The "E-F#m-B7" Partial Standard Progression is similar to the "E-C#m-F#m-B7" Standard Changes except that the "C#m" chord has been omitted. Such standards as *I Got Rhythm* and *Try To Remember* were originally written using the "E-F#m-B7" Progression, however, over the years most performers add the missing "C#m" chord to play the more familiar sounding Standard Changes. Examples of hit songs written around this Partial Standard Progression include The Ronettes' 1963 *Be My Baby* and Tom Jones' 1965 breakthrough hit *It's Not Unusual*.

The "E-F#m-E/G#-A" and "E-F#m-G#m-A" Progressions are examples of the use of Ascending "E-F#-G#-A" Bass Lines to create unique and interesting chord progressions. The "E-F#m-E/G#-A"

Progression was used to create such popular songs as the 1949 show tune *I'm Gonna Wash That Man Right Outa My Hair*, Johnny Rivers' 1977 *Slow Dancin'*, and Don Henley's 1990 *Heart Of The Matter*. The "E-F#m-G#m-A" Progression was used to write such classic hits as Bob Dylan's 1965 *Like A Rolling Stone*, The Righteous Brothers' 1965 *You've Lost That Lovin' Feelin'*(which also charted in 1969 & 1980), and Bill Withers' 1972 *Lean On Me*(which was also a number one song for Club Nouveau in 1987).

The "E-F#m-A-B7" and "E-F#-A-B" Progressions are examples of the use of Ascending "E-F#-A-B" Bass Lines to construct forward moving chord progressions. The "E-F#m-A-B7" Progression was used to create hits including The Troggs' 1968 top ten *Love Is All Around*, Don McLean's 1972 *Vincent*, and one hit wonder Bertie Higgins' 1982 *Key Largo*. The definitive "E-F#-A-B" Progression hit is The Rolling Stones' 1966 *As Tears Go By*.

The "E-EM7-E6-EM7" and "E-E+-E6-E7" Static Bass Line Progressions use Chord Quality Substitutions to provide movement where the "E" chord is used in progression for more than one or two bars. A good example of the "E-EM7-E6-EM7" Static Bass Line Progression is Barry Manilow's 1975 number one song *Mandy*. An example of the "E-E+-E6-E7" Static Bass Line Progression is The Dave Clark Five's 1964 hit *Because*.

"E-F#m/E" Same Note Static Bass Line Progressions combine the Basic(F#m Substitution)Progression with a Static "E" Bass Line. The "E-F#m/E" Progression has been used to create memorable hit songs such as the Walker Brothers' 1966 *The Sun Ain't Gonna Shine(Anymore)*and Neil Sedaka's number one 1975 *Laughter In The Rain*.

In addition to the most frequent progressions already discussed, there is a number of other "E-F#" Chord Progressions many of which represent various progression combinations and those that can be transformed into Ascending Bass Line Progressions by playing other chord notes as the bass note.

Below is a chronological listing of songs with verses and/or choruses that use the "E-F#" changes followed by a listing of chord progressions by type.

Chronological Listing

    Date/Song Title   *Chord Progression*

1849

    Oh Susanna   V=E-F#7-B7-E-B7-E

1864

Beautiful Dreamer   V=E-F#m-B7-E-F#m-B7-E

1879

Oh, Dem Golden Slippers   V=E-F#m-B7-E-B-E

1895

The Band Played On   V=E-F#m-B7-E

1899

Hello Ma Baby   V=E-F#7-B7-E/G#-
                                 Go-B7/F#

1904

(I'm A)Yankee Doodle Dandy   C=E-F#-B7-E-C#7-F#m-C#7-F#m

1909

By The Light Of The Silvery
Moon   V=E-F#7-B7-E-
                                 Fo-B7/F#

1921

Second Hand Rose   V=E-F#7-B7-E

Toot, Toot, Tootsie(Good-Bye)   V=E-F#7-B7-E

Ma(He's Makin' Eyes At Me)   V=E-F#7-B7-E

1923

Yes, We Have No Bananas   V=E-F#7-B7-E

1927

I'm Looking Over A Four Leaf Clover   V=E-F#7-B7-E-C#7-F#7-B7

1928

Mack The Knife   V=E6-F#m7-B9-E6

Button Up Your Overcoat   V=E-F#7-B7-E6-B7

1930

Walkin' My Baby Back Home   V=E-E6(EM7-E6)2x F#9-F#m7-B7

1935

Lullaby Of Broadway   V=EM7-F#m7-F#m7/B-F#m/E

My Romance   V=EM7-F#m7-G#m7-Go-F#m7-B7

I'm In The Mood For Love   V=EM7-F#m7-B7-E-[F#m7-Go]-G#m7-Gm7-F#m7-B7-B7+-G#m7

1936

Pennies From Heaven   V=E-F#m7-G#m7-Go-F#m7-B7-F#m7-B7

1939

Friendship   V=E-F#7-B7-E-E7-A-B7-E

1941

Happy Holidays	V=E-F#m7-B7-E-C#m7-F#m7-B7
Chattanooga Choo-Choo	V=E-F#m7-B7-B9-E6-F#m7-B7-B9-E

1942

Don't Get Around Much Anymore	V=E-F#m7-Go-E/G#-E7-D#7-D7-C#7-F#7-B7-E
That Old Black Magic	V=EM7-F#m7-B7-F#m7-B7
White Christmas	V=E-F#m7-B7-A-B7-E-E6-A-B7-E-EM7-E7-A-Am6-E-F#m7-B7

1945

The More I See You	V=E6-F#m11-E/G#-G7-F#m7-C9-B11
If I Loved You	V=E-Eo-E-E+-F#m7-Go-G#m7-G7-F#m-F7

1946

Doin' What Comes Naturally	V=E-F#m7-E/G#-Go-F#m7-B7-E-F#m7-B7-E-B7-E
The Christmas Song	V=E6-F#m7-B7-EM9-F#m7/B-B7b9-E6-Bm7-E7-A-G#7-C#m-Am6-E-A#m7b5-D#7b9-G#-Am7-D7b9-G-F#m-B7

1949

I'm Gonna Wash That Man Right

Outa My Hair   V=E-F#m7-E/G#-A-B7

1951

Getting To Know You   V=E-F#m7-B7-F#m7-B7-E

Hey, Good Lookin'(C)   V=E-F#7-B7-E-B7(2x)

1952

When I Fall In Love   V=E-F#m7-B7-E-B+7-F#m7-B7

1953

That's Amore   V=E-F#m-F#m(M7)-F#m7-F#m6-B7-E-EM7-E6

1955

Venus   V=EM7-F#m7(2x)G#m7-C#7-F#m7-B7

The Great Pretender   V=E-F#m7-B7-E-E7-A-E-E7-A-B7-E-A-F#m7-E-F#m-B7-E

1956

Love Me Tender/ Aura Lee(D)   V=E-F#7-B7-E(2x)

1957

Tonight   V=Eadd9-F#9/E(2x)Eadd9

1959

Bobby Sox To Stockings   V=EM7-E6-F#m7-B7(3x)F#m7-B7-A-G#m-F#m7-B7

1960

Tell Laura I Love Her	V=E-F#m-E-A6-B7-E
Only The Lonely	(F) V=E-F#m-B7-A-E
Itsy Bitsy Teenie Weenie Yellow Polka Dot Bikini	V=E-F#m7-B7-F#m7-B7-E-A-E-F#m7-B7-E
It's Now Or Never	C=E-F#m7-B7-E-Am-E-B7-E

1962

Go Away Little Girl	V=E-F#m7-B7-E

1963

Walk Like A Man	V=E-F#m7(7x)E
Ask Me Why(E)	V=E-F#m-G#m-F#m-E(2x)-G#7-C#m-Am-F#-B
The Patty Duke Theme	V=E-F#m7-G#m7-A-G#m7-F#m7-E-E9-A-G#m7-F#m-G#o-F#7-B7 I=B7b9
Drag City(G)	V=E-F#m-B-E(2x)-[F]-G-C-G-D-C-B
Be My Baby(E)	V=E-F#m-B7(2x)-G#7-C#7-F#-B7
Those Lazy Hazy Crazy Days Of Summer	V=E-F#7-B7-E-E/G#Eo/G-B7F#
Girl From Ipanema	V=EM9-F#13-F#m7-F7b5-EM7-F7 (2x)

1964

P.S. I Love You(G)	V=E-F#m-E-B-C#m-B-C-D-E
Matchmaker	V=E-F#m7-EM9-F#m9
If I Fell(D)	V=E-F#m-G#m-Go-F#m7-B7(2x)-E-Am-B7
Ride The Wild Surf(Ab-A)	V=E-F#m-G#m-B-E-F#m-G#m-B-C#m
Chapel Of Love	V=E-F#m-B7-F#m-B7 C=E-F#m-B-F#m
Suspicion	V=E-F#m-B7sus-E
A Wonderful Day Like Today	V=E-E6-EM7-E6-E-E6-F#m7-B7
People	V=EM7-F#m7-B7-EM7-F#m7-F#m7/B-B7b9-A/E-EM7-C#m7-G#7
Who Can I Turn To	V=EM9-F#m7-B7-F#m7-B7-E-EM7-Bm7-E9
Because(G)	V=E-E+-E6-E7-F#m-B-B+-E-E+-A-Am
I Wanna Be Your Man(E)	C=E7-F#7-B7-E7-C#7-F#7-B7-E

1965

It's The Same Old Song	V=E-F#m7-E/G#-A-B(3x)
Yes, I'm Ready	V=E-F#m-G#m-F#m(2x)-G#m-F#m-G#m-F#m7-G#m-AM7(3x)B7
It Ain't Me Babe(G)	V=E-F#m-G#m-F#m-E(2x)-

Ooo, Baby, Baby(G)	G#m-F#m(4x)A-B V=EM7-F#m7-G#m7-F#m7-B7 C=EM9-F#m7(2x)
Like A Rolling Stone	V=E-F#m-G#m-A-B(2x)A-B
You've Lost That Lovin' Feelin'	V=E11-E(2x)F#m7-G#m7-AM7-B11-B C=E-F#m/E-B7-E-F#m/E-E11-E
My Girl(C)	C=E-F#m-A-B(2x)EM9-F#m7-B7
Eight Days A Week(D)	V=E-F#-A-E(2x) I=Eadd9-F#/E-A6/E-Eadd9
You've Got Your Troubles(A)	V=E-F#7-Am-B-E(2x)
Ticket To Ride(A)	V=E-F#m-B
It's Not Unusual	V=E-F#m7-B7-E-F#m7-G#m-F#m7-B7-E-B7
Tell Her No(E)	V=EM7-E6-F#m9-B13(2x)
Everybody Loves A Clown(D-Eb)	V=E-EM7-E6-E(3x)-F#m-F#m(M7)-B7sus4-B7
California Girls(B)	C=E-F#m7-D-Em7-C-Dm7-E5 O=E-F#m7

1966

Oh How Happy(A)	V=E-F#m/E(6x)
The Sun Ain't Gonna Shine Anymore	V=E-F#m/E(2x)
Lightnin' Strikes(Eb)	V=E-E11-F#m/E(4x)

Poor Side Of Town(E)   V=EM7-F#m7(2x)A-G#m-F#m7-A-E-A-E

Alfie   V=EM9-F#m7/B-EM7-F#m7-G#m7-C#7b9

Here, There, And Everywhere   V=E-F#m7-G#m7-A(2x)-D#m7-G#7(2x)-C#m-F#m-F#m7-B7
I=E-G#m-G-F#m7-B7

And Your Bird Can Sing(E)   V=E-F#m-A-E(2x)

It's My Life   C=E-F#m-A-B(2x)A-B(4x)

As Tears Go By(G)   V=E-F#-A-B(2x)A-B-E-E/D#-C#m-A-B

Elusive Butterfly   V=E-F#m-B7(2x)F#m-B7-E

Sure Gonna Miss Her(E)   V=E-E6-EM7-E6-EM7-E6-F#m7-B

Cherish(F)   V=EM9-F#m7/B-DM9-F#m7/B(2x)G#m-A(3x)

1967

Apples, Peaches, Pumpkin Pie   V=E-F#m7(4x)B-E-B-B7(2x)

Kentucky Woman   V=E-F#m7(2x)B

Groovin'(Eb)   V=E-F#m7-F#m7/B(4x)
C=EM7-F#m7(3x)AM7-B9

You Know What I Mean(E)   V=E-F#(2x)A-D-G-E

Suzanne   V=E-F#m-E-G#m-A(2x)F#m

Carrie Anne(C)   V=E-F#m-E-A-E-AM7

Getting Better(C)	C=E-F#m-G#m-A(2x)
Daydream Believer	V=E-F#m-G#m-A-E-C#m-F#7
Massachusetts(G)	V=E-F#m-A-E(2x)E-A-E-B7-E B7
To Love Somebody(A)	V=E-F#m-A-E-D-E-B-A(2x)
To Sir With Love	V=E-F#-A-E(2x)D#7-G#m(2x)
She'd Rather Be With Me(B-C)	V=E-F#-A-B7(2x)E
Sgt. Pepper's Lonely Hearts Club Band(G)	V=E7-F#7-A7-E7(2x)-F#7-A7-E7-A7-E7
It Must Be Him	V=E-E6-EM7-E6(2x)F#m-B7(3x)EM7-E6
Lazy Day	C=E-EM7-F#m7-B7-E-G-A-B7
All You Need Is Love(G)	C=E-F#7-B7(2x)E-G#7-C#m-C#m7/B-AM7-B7

1968

Lady Willpower	V=E-F#m(2x)G#m7-A-Am-E-B7-C-A-B C=E-F#m-E-B-[C]-C#m-D-C#m-B-A-B
I've Got To Get A Message To You(Bb)	V=E-F#m-F#m7(2x)C#7
Fool On The Hill	V=E6-F#m/E(2x)F#m7-B-E6-C#m-F#m7-B
Young Girl	V=EM7-F#m7(4x)B7-G#7-C#m-F#7-E-B7-C-E7

Stoned Soul Picnic	V=E-F#m7/B-EM7-F#m7/B(2x)-AM7-G#m7-F#m7
Blackbird(G)	V=E-F#m7-E/G#-E-A-A#o-B7-Co-C#m-C-B7-A#o-A-Am-E/G#-F#7-Esus/B-E-A-E/G#-F#7-Esus/B-E
La La Means I Love You(G)	V=EM7-F#m7-G#m7-F#m7/B (2x)
Girl Watcher(A)	V=E-F#m-G#m-A-G#m-F#m-B-E-G#7-C#m-A-D-F#m7/B-E C=E-EM7/B-F#m/E-F#m7/B(3x)-E
Ain't Nothing Like The Real Thing(Eb)	V=E-F#m-G#m-AM7-G#7#5-C#m7sus-C#m7-Bm7-E-A-AM7-E-A
Sexy Sadie(G)	C=E-F#m7-G#m7-AM7-E-F#m7-G#m7-A-F#7-FM7-E
Love Is All Around	V=E-F#m-A-B7(7x)E-F#m-A
The Unicorn Song	V/C=E-F#m-B-E
Gentle On My Mind	V=E-EM7-E6-EM7-F#m-F#m(M7)-F#m7-B7
Honey	V=EM7-E6(2x)F#m7-B7(4x)-E-E6-EM7 C=E-F#m7-B7-F#m7-B7-E-E6-EM7-E6-F#m7-B7-F#m7-B7-E
Words(G)	V=E-F#-B7-A/E-E
Cry Baby Cry(G)	C=E-F#m-D-E-C#m-F#7-D-E

1969

Only The Strong Survive	V=E-F#m/E-F#m(2x)E C=E-F#m/E-F#m-G#m-A-B7
Crystal Blue Persuasion(A)	V=EM7-F#m7(7x)EM7-F#m-A
You've Made Me So Very Happy(Eb)	V=EM7-F#m7(3x)Fm7-F#m7-(3x)Fm7-F#m7/B-Bsus-B7-EM7-C#7
Leaving On A Jet Plane(A)	V=EM7-F#m7/B(2x)EM7-C#m7-B-B7
These Eyes	C=E-EM7(4x)F#-F#-F#M7(4x)G#-G#M7(4x)A#-B
Love(Can Make You Happy)	V=E-F#m-G#m-A- E-F#m-G#m-B7- E-F#m-G#m-A- E-F#m-E-B7
Put A Little Love In Your Heart	C=E-F#m-B(2x)C
Na Na Hey Hey Kiss Him Goodbye	V=E-F#m7-B7-E-G-D-E
More Today Than Yesterday	V=EM7-F#m7-B7(3x)-G#m-AM7-F#m7-B7
Maxwell's Silver Hammer(D)	C=E-F#7-B-F#m7-B7-E

1970

Whipping Post(A)	V=E-F#m/E-G/E-F#m/E
Make It With You(E)	V=EM7-F#m/E(2x)AM7-G#m7-F#m7/B

Ride Captain Ride	V=E-F#-[G-G#]-A-E
No Matter What(A)	V=E-F#m-A-B-A-B-E(2x)
Walk A Mile In My Shoes	V=E-F#-A-B(2x)

1971

Sweet City Woman	V/C=E-F#m(2x)E
Treat Her Like A Lady(A)	C=E-F#m(3x)C#m
Beginnings(A)	V=EM7-F#m/E(4x)G-DM7-G(4x)
Day By Day	V=EM7-F#m/E(2x)AM7-G#m7-F#M7
Never Can Say Goodbye(D)	C=EM7-Em7-F#/E-F/E-E-A(2x)
Temptation Eyes	C=E-F#7/E(x)A-B-Em
Baby, I'm A Want You	V=E-F#m/E-EM7-A-A/G#-F#m7-B11
How Can You Mend A Broken Heart(E)	V=E-EM7-F#m7/B-E-G#7-C#m-F#7-B7
If(A)	V=Eadd9-EM9-E9-F#m/E-F#m7b5/E-E-F#m7b5/A-B7
Old Fashioned Love Song	C=E-F#-A-B-E(2x)
For All We Know	V=E-F#7-F#m-Am-E-G#m7-C#m-E-F#7-BM7-EM7-AM7-B7sus4
Just My Imagination(Running Away With Me)	V/C=E-F#m7(12x)

1972

I Believe In Music	V=E-F#m-B7-[E-A]-E-F#m-B-E C=E-F#m-A-B-E
Hurting Each Other	C=E-F#m/E(3x)E-B/E-A/E-E
You're So Vain	C=E-F#m7-E-C#m-AM7-B7
Precious And Few	V=E-F#m/E-E11-F#m/E-B7-E-F#m/E-E11-F#m/B-B7-AM7
Me And Mrs. Jones	V=EM7-F#m7/B-G#m7/E-F#m7/B-G#m7-[Gm7]-F#m7-F#m9/B-B7+-E6/9-G#7
Lean On Me	V=E-F#m-G#m-A-G#m-F#m-E-F#m-G#m-B7-E
American Pie	V=E-F#m-A-F#m-C#m-B
I'd Love You To Want Me	V=E-F#m-A-B(2x)E C=E-F#m-A-E-F#m-A-B-E
Vincent	V=E-F#m-A-B7(2x)
Stay With Me(A)	V/C=E-F#-A-E
Baby Don't Get Hooked On Me	C=E-F#m-B7-E
I'd Like To Teach The World To Sing	V=E-F#7-B-A-B7-E-F#7-B-A-E(2x)
You Are Everything(Ab)	C=EM7-F#/E-D#m7-G#m7(3x)

1973

Sing	V=E-F#m/E-E-Bm7/E-E7
Living For The City	V=E-F#m/E-Em7-F#m/E(4x)-A-B-B7
And I Love You So	V=E-F#m-F#m7-E-EM7-C#m-F#m7-A-B7
Bad, Bad Leroy Brown(G)	V=E-[F]-F#-[G]-G#-A-B-A-G#-F#-E-B7 C=E-F#-G#-A-B-A-E-B7
Love Train(C)	C=E-F#9-A-AM7/B
Daniel	V=E-F#m-B-G#7-C#m
Just You 'N' Me (Bb)	V=E-F#m7-B-A/E-C#m-A-E-AM9-B6(2x)F#m7-A-B
My Love	V=E-F#m7-B7-G#m7
Say, Has Anybody Seen My Sweet Gypsy Rose	C=E-(F#m7-B7)2x E-E7-A-E-C#m-F#7-B7-A-E
Rocky Mountain High(E)	V=E-F#m7-D-B-E-F#m7-A-B7sus4(2x)

1974

The Best Of My Love(C)	V=E-F#m7(2x)G#m7-F#m7-G#m7-B11
Melissa(E)	V=E-F#m11/E-EM7-F#m11/E-E-F#m11/E-A-B-C#m-D-E-F#m-G#m-A-CM7-B
Rock 'N' Roll Heaven	C=E-F#m/E-A-E-

	E-F#m/E-A-B-E-A-B
You Won't See Me(A)	V=E-F#-A-E(2x)A-Am-E
Billy, Don't Be A Hero	C=E-EM7-F#m7-B7-E
Seasons In The Sun	V=E-F#m-F#m7-F#m7b5-B7-E
Best Thing That Ever Happened To Me	V=EM7-F#m7-B7sus-B7-EM7-E7-AM7-B-EM7
Mandy	V=E-EM7-E6-EM7-F#m-DM7-F#m7

1975

Wildfire(E)	V=E-EM7-F#m(2x)AM7-G#m-(2x)F#m-G#m
Only Women Bleed	V=E-F#/E-F#m/E-E(2x)-E11-A/E-E-G#m-Gm-F#m-B11
Philadelphia Freedom	V=E-F#7-Em6/G-F#m7-E-B7sus-E-F#7-Em6/G-F#m7-E
Must Of Got Lost	C=E-F#m-A-B7-E(2x)
Laughter In The Rain	V=E-F#m/E-B-E(2x)E-C#m7-F#7sus-F#7-B7sus-B7-Am7-Am7/D
I'm Sorry	V=E-F#m-B7-E(2x)
At Seventeen	V=E-F#m7-B7-E(2x)

1976

Afternoon Delight	V=E-F#m7(2x)B7-F#m7-B7

Weekend In New England	C=E-F#m7(3x)C#m-F#7-F#m7-B7-E-F#m7-E
Evergreen	V=E-F#/E-F#m/E-E-E/D#-C#m-G#m7-F#m7-D-B-B7sus-B7
Today's The Day	V=E-F#m7-G#m-F#m7(2x)-G#m7-F#m-G#m-AM7
Nights Are Forever Without You(E)	V=E-F#o/E-F#m-B-E(2x)-F#m-G#m-A-E-F#m-G#m-A-B11
The Boys Are Back In Town	C=E5-F#5-A5(3x)
American Girl(D)	V=E-F#-A-B(2x)

1977

Smoke From A Distant Fire	V=E-F#m7(6x)A-E/G#-F#m7
Feels Like The First Time	V=E-E11-F#m/E(2x)E
Sentimental Lady	C=E-F#m-EM7-E-F#m-EM7-F#m7-EM7-B
Baby, What A Big Surprise	V=E-F#m-E7/G#-A-E/G#-F#m
Slow Dancin'	C=E-F#m7-E/G#-A(4x)
I Like Dreamin'	V=E-F#m-B-F#m-B
After The Lovin'	V=E-EM7-E6-E-F#m-F#m(M7)-B7
New Kid In Town	V=E-(F#m7-B)2x A-B-E
The Things You Do For Love(D)	C=E-E/B(2x)F#m-F#m/E-B/D#-B-C#m-C#m/B-A-F#-B-G#m-C#m-Am

1978

Fire   V=E-F#m7(2x)C#m7-A-B-E

WKRP in Cincinnati   V=EM7-F#m7-F#m7/B(2x)

1979

The Light Is On   C=E-F#/E-F#/G#-G#m7-C#m7-
                              G#m7-GM7-E-F#/E-F#/G#-
                              G#m7-EM7-E/F#

Shadows In The Moonlight   V=E-F#m7-B7-C#m7

Babe   V=E6-F#m7-B11-B(2x)-
                              C#m-AM7-B-AM7-B-B11-B

1980

Don't Ask Me Why(Bb)   E-F#m7-E/G#(2x)-F-B/F#-F#-
                              B-E-A/E-
                              E-F#m7-E/G#(2x)F-B/F#-F#-B-
                              E-G#7-C#m-E7/B-A#m7b5-
                              B11-E-A/E

Longer   V=E-F#m7-EM7/G#-A(3x)

New York, New York   V=E-F#m7-B7-E-E6-F#m7-B7

Never Be The Same   C=E-F#m7-B11-E-B/E
                              E-F#m7-B11-E-B11

1981

All Those Years Ago(D)   V=E-F#m-F#o-E-G#m-F#m-
                              Am-E-C#7-F#m

Woman(D)   V=E-F#m7-E/G#-F#m7-
                              E-C#m-F#m7-Bsus-B-
                              A-F#m-G#m-Bsus-B

1982

Ebony And Ivory   C=E-F#m7(3x)B/F#-B11-B-B/E-E

Key Largo   V=EM9-F#m-A-B11(2x)

1983

Up Town Girl   V=E-F#m-E/G#-A-B

1984

Wake Me Up Before You Go-Go   V/C=E-F#m

Like A Virgin   V=E6-F#m7(2x)C#m7-F#m7
                     C=E6-F#m7-E6

What's Love Got To Do With It   B=E/F#-F#(2x)D-E/D-C#m7-F#

I Just Called To Say I Love You   V=E-F#m-F#m(M7)-F#m-F#m(M7)-F#m7-F#m(M7)-F#m-F#m/B-B-E

To All The Girls I've Loved Before   V=E-F#m7-F#m7/B-B7

1985

Don't Lose My Number   C=E-F#m7-D-A-C#m-B-D(2x)
                        T/A=C#m-G#m7(2x)

Just A Gigolo(Ab)   V=E-EM7-E-F#7-F#m-B7

1988

Don't Worry, Be Happy   V=E-F#m-A-E

1990

Wind of Change   V=E-F#m(2x)C#m7-B

Heart Of The Matter   C=E-F#m(addB)-E/G#-Aadd9-
                               E/B-C#m7-Aadd9-Bsus-B

1991

Every Heartbeat   V=E-F#m7-C#7sus-E6(2x)

Listing By Progression Type

Chord Progression   *Song Examples*

Basic("F#m" Substitution)

E-F#m   Lady Willpower('68); Sweet City Woman('71); Treat Her
                               Like A Lady('71); Wake Me Up Before You Go-Go('84);
                               The Wind Of Change('90)
E-F#m-F#m7   I Got To Get A Message To You('68)
E-F#m7   Walk Like A Man('63); Apples Peaches Pumpkin Pie('67);
                               Kentucky Woman('67); Just My Imagination(Running Away
                               With Me)('71); The Best Of My Love('74); Afternoon
                               Delight('76); Weekend In New England('76); Smoke From A
                               Distant Fire('77); Fire('78); Ebony And Ivory('82)
E-F#m7-F#m7/B   Groovin'('67)–Verse
E-F#   You Know What I Mean('67)
E-EM7-F#m   Wildfire('75)
E-EM7/B-F#m/E-F#m7/B   Girl Watcher('68)
E6-F#m7   Like A Virgin('84)
EM7-F#m7   Venus('55); Poor Side Of Town('66); Groovin'('67)–Chorus;
                               Young Girl('68); You've Made Me So Very Happy('69)

Crystal Blue Persuasion('69)
EM7-F#m7-F#m7/B   WKRP In Cincinnati('78)
EM7-F#m7-F#m7/B-F#m/E   Lullaby Of Broadway('35)
EM9-F#m7   Ooo, Baby, Baby('65)

E-F#m7-E/G#-F#m7   Woman('81)
E-F#m7-EM9-F#m9   Matchmaker('64)
E-F#m7/B-EM7-F#m7/B   Stoned Soul Picnic('68)
EM9-F#m7/B-EM7-F#m7   Alfie('66)

E-F#m-EM7-E	Sentimental Lady('77)
E-F#m-F#m7-E	And I Love You So('73)
E-F#m-F#o-E	All Those Years Ago('81)
E-EM7-F#m7/B-E	How Can You Mend A Broken Heart('71)
E-F#m7-E/G#	Don't Ask Me Why('80)
E-F#m7-E/G#-E	Blackbird('68)
E6-F#m7-E6	Like A Virgin('84)

Partial Standard

E-F#m-B	Ticket To Ride('65); Put A Little Love In Your Heart('69)
E-F#m-B7	Beautiful Dreamer(1864); Be My Baby('63); Elusive Butterfly('66)
E-F#m7-F#m7/B-B7	To All The Girls I've Loved Before('84)
E-F#-B7	Words('68)
E-F#7-B7	All You Need Is Love('67)
E-E/B(2x)F#m-F#m/E-B/D#	The Things You Do For Love('77)
E-EM7-F#m7-B7-E	Billy, Don't Be A Hero('74)
E6-F#m7-B11-B	Babe('79)
EM7-F#m7-B7	People('64); More Than Yesterday('69)
E-F#m-B-E	Drag City('63); The Unicorn Song('68)
E-F#m-B7-E	Oh, Dem Golden Slippers(1879); The Band Played On (1895); I Believe In Music('72); Baby Don't Get Hooked On Me('72); I'm Sorry('75)
E-F#m-B7sus-E	Suspicion('64)
E-F#m7-B7-E	Happy Holidays('41); When I Fall In Love('52); The Great Pretender('55); It's Now Or Never('60); Go Away Little Girl('62); It's Not Unusual('65); Na Na Hey Hey Kiss Him Goodbye('69); At Seventeen('75); New York, New York('80)
E-F#m7-B7-B9-E6	Chattanooga Choo-Choo('41)
E-F#m7-B11-E	Never Be The Same('80)
E-F#-B7-E	(I'm A)Yankee Doodle Dandy('04)
E-F#7-B7-E	Oh Susanna(1849); By The Light On The Silvery Moon ('09); Second Hand Rose('21); Toot, Toot, Tootsie(Good-Bye)('21); Ma(He's Makin' Eyes At Me)('21); Yes, We Have No Bananas('23); I'm Looking Over A Four Leaf Clover('27); Friendship('39); Hey, Good Lookin'('51); Love Me Tender/Aura Lee('56); Those Lazy Hazy Crazy Days Of Summer('63)

E-F#7-B7-E/G#	Hello Ma Baby(1899)
E-F#7-B7-E6	Button Up Your Overcoat('28)
E6-F#m7-B7-EM9	The Christmas Song('46)
E6-F#m7-B9-E6	Mack The Knife('28)
EM7-F#m7-B7-E	I'm In The Mood For Love('35)
EM7-F#m7-B7sus-B7-B7	Best Thing That Ever Happened To Me('74)
E6/9-F#13-Bsus13-B13-E6/9	Girl From Ipanema('63)
E7-F#7-B7-E7	I Wanna Be Your Man('64)

Ascending Bass Lines

E-F#m7-Go-G#m7	Don't Get Around Much Any More('42)
E-F#m-E/G#-A	Up Town Girl('83)
E-F#m-E7/G#-A	Baby, What A Big Surprise('77)
E-F#m7-E/G#-A	I'm Gonna Wash That Man Right Outa My Hair('49); It's The Same Old Song('65); Slow Dancin''77)
E-F#m7-EM7/G#-A	Longer('80)
E-F#m(addB)-E/G#-Aadd9	Heart Of The Matter('90)
E-F#m-G#m-A	Like A Rolling Stone('65); Getting Better('67); Daydream Believer('67); Girl Watcher('68); Love(Can Make You Happy)('69); Lean On Me('72)
E-F#m-G#m-AM7	Ain't Nothing Like The Real Thing('68)
E-F#m7-G#m7-A	The Patty Duke Theme('63); Here, There, And Everywhere ('66)
E-F#m7-G#m7-AM7	Sexy Sadie('68)
E-F#-G#-A	Bad, Bad Leroy Brown('73)
E11-E(2x)F#m7-G#m7-AM7	You've Lost That Lovin' Feelin''('65)
E-F#m-G#m-B	Ride The Wild Surf('64)
EM7-F#m7-G#m7-F#m7/B	La La Means I Love You('68)
E-F#m-A-B	My Girl('65); It's My Life('66); I've Got To Get A Message To You('68); Reach Out In The Darkness('68); No Matter What('70); I'd Love You To Want Me('72); I Believe In Music('72)
E-F#m-A-B7	Love Is All Around('68); Vincent('72); Must Of Got Lost ('75)
E-F#-A-B	As Tears Go By('66); Walk A Mile In My Shoes('70); Old

	Fashioned Love Song('71); American Girl('76)
E-F#-A-B7	She'd Rather Be With Me('67)
E-F#7-Am-B	You've Got Your Troubles('65)
E-F#9-A-AM7/B	Love Train('73)
EM9-F#m-A-B11	Key Largo('82)

Static Bass Lines

E-E6-EM7-E6	It Must Be Him('67)
E-E6-EM7-E6-E-E6	A Wonderful Day Like Today('64)
E-E6-EM7-E6-EM7-E6	Walkin' My Baby Back Home('30); Sure Gonna Miss Her('66)
E-EM7	Lazy Day('67); These Eyes('69)
E-EM7-E	Just A Gigolo('85)
E-EM7-E6-E	Everybody Loves A Clown('65); After The Lovin' ('77)
E-EM7-E6-EM7	Gentle On My Mind('68); Mandy('74)
EM7-E6	Bobby Sox To Stockings('59); Tell Her No('65); Honey('68)
E-E+-E6-E7	Because('64)
E-Eo-E-E+	If I Loved You('45)
F#m-F#m7-F#m7b5	Seasons In The Sun('74)
F#m-F#m(M7)-F#m-F#m(M7)	I Just Called To Say I Love You('84)
F#m-F#m(M7)-F#m7-F#m6	That's Amore('53)
E/F#-F#	What's Love Got To Do With It('84)
E-F#m/E	The Sun Ain't Gonna Shine Anymore('66); Oh How Happy('66); Only The Strong Survive('69); Hurting Each Other('72); Rock 'N' Roll Heaven('74); Laughter In The Rain('75)
E-F#m/E-E-Bm7/E	Sing('73)
E-F#m/E-EM7	Baby, I'm-A Want You('71)
E-F#m/E-E11-F#m/E	Precious And Few('72)
E-F#m/E-Em7-F#m/E	Living In The City('73)
E-F#m/E-G/E-F#m/E	Whipping Post('70)
E-F#m11/E-EM7-F#m11/E	Melissa('74)
E-F#/E	The Lights Are On('79)

E-F#/E-F#m/E-E	Only Women Bleed('75); Evergreen('76)
E-F#7/E	Temptation Eyes('71)
E-F#o/E	Nights Are Forever Without You('76)
E-E11-F#m/E	Lightnin' Strikes('66); Feels Like The First Time ('77)
E6-F#m/E	Fool On The Hill('68)
EM7-F#m/E	Leaving On A Jet Plane('69); Make It With You ('70); Day By Day('71); Beginnings('71)
EM7-F#/E	You Are Everything('72)
EM7-Em7-F#/E-F/E-E	Never Can Say Goodbye('71)
Eadd9-F#/E-A6/E-Eadd9	Eight Days A Week('65)-Intro
Eadd9-F#9/E	Tonight('57)
Eadd9-EM9-E9-F#m/E	If('71)

Other "E-F#m" Progressions

The "E-F#m-E-A" progression is an example of a Basic("F#m" Substitution)& Basic Combination Progression which can be transformed into a Ascending "E-F#-G#-A" progression by playing the G# note in the second "E" chord as the bass note creating the "E-F#m-E/G#-A" progression. The "E-F#m-E-B" progression is an example of a Basic("F#m" Substitution)& Folk Combination progression which, in the same manner as above, can be transformed into the "E-F#m-E/G#-B" progression. Likewise, the "E-F#m7-E/G#-F#m7" progression can be transformed into the "E-F#m7-E/G#-F#m7/A" progrression.

E-F#m-E-G#m	Suzanne('67)
E-F#m-E-A	Carrie Anne('67)
E-F#m-E-A6	Tell Laura I Love Her('60)
E-F#m-E-B	P.S. I Love You('64); Lady Willpower('68)
E-F#m7-E-C#m	You're So Vain('72)
E-F#m7-E/G#-Go	Doin' What Comes Naturally('46)
E-F#7-Em6/G-F#m7	Philadelphia Freedom('75)
E6-F#m11-E/G#-G7	The More I See You('45)

The "E-F#m-G#m-Go" progression can be transformed into an Ascending "E-F#-G#-A#" Bass Line Progression by playing the A# note in the "Go" chord as the bass note creating the "E-F#m-G#m-A#o" progression. In the same manner, the "E-F#m-G#m-F#m" progression can be transformed into the "E-F#m-G#m-F#m/A" progression.

E-F#m-G#m-F#m	Ask Me Why('63); It Ain't Me Babe('65); Yes, I'm Ready ('65)
E-F#m-G#m-Go	If I Fell('64)
E-F#m7-G#m-F#m7	Today's The Day('76)
E-F#m7-G#m7-Go	Pennies From Heaven('36)

EM7-F#m7-G#m7-F#m7	Ooo, Baby, Baby('65)
EM7-F#m7-G#m7-Go	My Romance('35)
EM7-F#m7/B-G#m7/E-F#m7/B	Me And Mrs. Jones('72)

The "E-F#m-A-E" progression can be transformed into an Ascending "E-F#-A-B" Bass Line Progression by playing the B note in the "E" chord as the bass note creating the "E-F#m-A-E/B" progression.

E-F#m-A-E	And Your Bird Can Sing('66); Massachusetts('67); To Love Somebody('67); I'd Love You To Want Me('72); Don't Worry Be Happy('88)
E-F#m-A-F#m	American Pie('72)
E-F#-A-E	Eight Days A Week('65); To Sir With Love('67); Stay With Me('72); You Won't See Me('74)
E-F#-[G-G#]-A-E	Ride Captain Ride('70)
E-F#7-F#m-Am	For All We Know('71)
E5-F#5-A5	The Boys Are Back In Town('76)
E7-F#7-A7-E7	Sgt. Pepper's Lonely Hearts Club Band('67)
E-F#m-B-F#m	Chapel Of Love('64); I Like Dreamin'('77)
E-F#m-B7-F#m	Chapel Of Love('64)
E-F#m7-B-F#m7	New Kid In Town('77)
E-F#m7-B7-F#m7	Getting To Know You('51); Itsy Bitsy Teenie Weenie Yellow Polka Dot Bikini('60); Honey('68); Say Has Anybody Seen My Sweet Gypsy Rose('73)
E-F#7-B-F#m7	Maxwell's Silver Hammer('69)
E-F#m-B-G#7	Daniel('73)
E-F#m7-B7-G#m7	My Love('73)
E-F#m-B7-A	Only The Lonely('60)
E-F#m7-B-A/E	Just You 'N' Me('73)
E-F#m7-B7-A	White Christmas('42)
E-F#-B7-A/E	Words('68)
E-F#7-B-A	I'd Like To Teach The World To Sing('72)
E-F#m7-B7-C#m7	Shadows In The Moonlight('79)
EM7-F#m7-B7-F#m7	That Old Black Magic('42)
EM9-F#m7-B7-F#m7	Who Can I Turn To('64)
E-F#m7-C#7sus-E6	Every Heartbeat('91)

The "E-F#m-D-E" progression can be transformed into an Ascending "E-F#-A-B" Bass Line Progression by playing the A note of the "D" chord as the bass note and the B Note of the "E" chord as the bass note creating the "E-F#m-D/A-E/B" progression.

E-F#m-D-E	Cry Baby Cry('68)
E-F#m7-D-Em7	California Girls('65)
E-F#m7-D-A	Don't Lose My Number('85)
E-F#m7-D-B	Rocky Mountain High('73)
EM9-F#m7/B-DM9-F#m7/B	Cherish('66)

"E-G" Chord Progressions

The most frequent progressions that start with the "E" chord and then move to the "Go" or "G" chords are as follows:

Classic Rock(Borrowed "G")	E-G-A-E
"Go" Cliché	E-Go-F#m7-B7
	E-E/G#-Go-B7/F#-B7
Static Bass Lines	E-G/E

The "E-G-A-E" Classic Rock(Borrowed "G")Progression was used in rock music of the 1960s and 1970s. The sequence, which uses the "G" chord "borrowed" from another key, is generally used without changing chord qualities. Examples of the Classic Rock(Borrowed "G")include Eric Clapton's 1970 *After Midnight* and Harry Chapin's 1974 number one song *Cat's In The Cradle*.

The "E-Go-F#m-B7" Diminished Cliché, like the "Fo" Cliché, was often used to write ballads in the 1920s and 1930s. The progression is similar to the Standard "E-C#m-F#m-B7" Changes, except the "Go" chord has been substituted for the "C#m" chord. The most recognizable use of the "Go" Cliché is Glenn Miller's 1939 swing hit *In the Mood*.

The "E-E/G#-Go-B7/F#-B7" Diminished Cliché, which is similar to the "E-Go-F#m-B7" progression discussed above except the "B7/F#" chord has been substituted for the F#m" chord and the "E/G#" chord is a Chord Quality Change. This Diminished Cliché is often found in Polka music such as the 1934 *The Beer Barrel Polka* and Bobby Vinton's 1974 hit *My Melody Of Love*.

The "E-G/E" Same Note Static Bass Line Progression has been used to create several memorable Classic Rock hits. The definitive example of the use of the "E-G/E" Static Bass Line is The Who's 1967 top ten song *I Can See For Miles* which effectively combined the use of the Classic Rock(Borrowed "G")Progression with a Static "E" Bass Line.

In addition to the most frequent progressions already discussed, there are a number of other "E-G" Chord Progressions that mainly continue to move to the "E", "F#m", "A", and "Borrowed "C" and "D" chords. Although not used as often, the following progression types are also employed:(1)"E-G" Partial Classic Rock(Borrowed "G")and(2)"E-G7-F#m7-B7" Standard("G7" Substitution)Progressions.

Below is a chronological listing of songs with verses and/or choruses that employ the "E-G" sequence followed by a listing of chord progressions by type.

Chronological Listing

Date/Song Title *Chord Progression*

1904

Give My Regards To Broadway   V=E-E/G#-Go-F#m7-B7

1907

School Days   V=E-E/G#-Go-F#m7-B7

1910

Let Me Call You Sweetheart   V=E-Go-E/G#-A-C#7/G#-F#7-
                                  B7-E-Fo-B7/F#-B7

Down By The Old Mill Stream   V=E-Go-B7

1913

You Made Me Love You   V=E-E/G#-Go-B7/F#-B7

1919

How Ya Gonna Keep 'Em Down
On The Farm?   C=E-E/B-E/G#-Go-B7/F#-B7-B+

1928

Embraceable You   V=E6-Go-F#m7-B7

1930

I've Got A Crush On You   V=E-Go-F#m7-B9

Just A Gigolo   V=E-EM7-E6-Go-F#m7-B7

1932

Night And Day   B=E-G(2x)E

1934

Beer Barrel Polka   V=E-E/G#-Go-B7/F#-B7-E(2x)

1937

The Lady Is A Tramp   V=E/G#-G6-F#m7-B7(2x)-
                                  E-EM7-E9-A-D9-
                                  E-E+-A-B7-E-B7

1938

God Bless America   V=E-EM7/G#-Go-B7/F#

1939

Moonlight Serenade   V=E6-Go-F#m7-B7

In The Mood(C)   C=E6-Go-F#m7-B7(3x)-
                                  B7-Bo-B7-C7-B7-E

1943

I'll Be Home For Christmas   V=E-Go-F#m7-B7-E-Bm6/D-C#7-
                                  F#m-G#o-A6-B7-E-C#m-F#7-
                                  B7-B+

1948
Blue Christmas   V=E-Go-B7/F#-B7-F#m-B7-E

1949

Rudolph The Red-Nosed Reindeer   V=E-E/G#-Go-B7/F#

Diamonds Are A Girls Best Friend   V=E-Go-B7-C#7-F#m-C#7-F#-B7

1953

Here Comes That Rainy Day(G)   V=EM7-G13-CM7-FM7-F#m11-B7-EM7-Bm7-E7b9

1954

Young At Heart   V=E-Go-F#m7-B7

1956

(You've Got)The Magic Touch   V=Esus-E-Go-B7-E-B7

1957

Witchcraft   V=E-Go-F#m7-B7-E

Wake Up Little Susie   I/C=E-G/E-A/E-G/E-E(2x)

Seventy-Six Trombones   V=E-Go-B7/F#-E

1959

Let Us Entertain You   C=E-Go-B7/F#-B7-F#m7-B7-E

1962

Green Onions(F)   V=E-G-A(4x)A-C-D(2x)-E-G-A(2x)B-D-E-A-C-D-E-G-A(2x)

1963

It's My Party(A)   V=E-G-E-A-C-E-F#m7-B7

Our Day Will Come	V=E-G7-F#m7-B7(2x)-Bm7-E7-AM7-A6-Am7-G#m7-G7-F#m7-B7
Lazy Hazy Crazy Days Of Summer	V=E-Go-B7-E-F#7-B7

1964

I'm Crying	V=E-G-A-G(4x)A-C-D-C(2x)

1965

What's New Pussy Cat?	V=E-G-F-E-A-G#m7-F#m-B7-G#m7
Liar, Liar(C)	V=E-G-Bm-A

1966

(I Know)I'm Losing You(D)	V=E7-G(2x) C=E-G/E-A/E-G/E(2x)
Magical Mystery Tour(E)	C=E-G-A(4x)
Knock On Wood(E)	I=E-G-A-B-D-B
Hold On! I'm Comin'(Ab)	C=E-G-A5-E
Somewhere My Love	V=E-E/G#-Go-B7sus/F#-B7
Michelle(F)	B=Em-G7-C-B7-Em-Em(M7)-Em7-Em6-CM7/E-B

1967

I Can See For Miles(E)	V=E-G/E-A/E-E(3x)G/E-A/E-C/E-E11-E
I'm Not Your Steppin' Stone	V=E-G-A-C

Gimme Some Lovin'	C=E-G-A-C
I Am The Walrus(A)	V=E-E7-G-A-B11-E-E7-G-A-E
Purple Haze(E)	V=E7#9-G-A-(3x)E
Sgt. Pepper's Lonely Hearts Club Band	C=E7-G7-A7-E7-A7-E7-E7-G7-A7-E7-F#7-B7-A7-E7-F#7-A7-E7

1968

Bend Me, Shape Me	V=E-G-A-D(4x)C#m-B-AM7-C#m-F#m7-G#7
Born To Be Wild(E)	V=E5-E6-E7(4x)G-A-E(4x) B=E7-G-A-G-E-D
On The Road Again(E)	V=E-G-A-E

1969

I Can't Get Next To You	V=E-G(4x)E
I Got A Line On You	V=E-G-A-E-A-G
I'm Free(E)	C=E5-G5-A5-F#5-A5-B5(2x)G-A-D-Dsus-D
Na, Na, Hey, Hey Kiss Him Goodbye	C=E-G-D-E(2x)

1970

No Time(D)	C=E-GM7/E-A/E-E(2x)
Thank You(Falletin Me Be Mice Elf Agin)	V=E-G-A-E-E9

After Midnight(C)	V=E-G-A-E(2x)E-A-B
War	V=Em-G-F#m7/B Em-G-B7(b5/b9)

1971

Temptation Eyes	V=Em-G/D-A7/C#-C-B
Superstar	V=E7-G-A7-E7

1972

Long Cool Woman(E)	V=E-G-A-E(4x)
School's Out(G)	C=Em-G/E-A/E-[D]-Em(3x)
Where Is The Love	V=E-G7-CM7-B7sus(2x)
Old Man(D)	V=E-G-D-A-E-G-D-G-E-G-D-A-E-D-G-D-A

1973

Will It Go Round In Circles	V=E-G-A-E(3x)
La Grange(A)	V=E-G-A-E
Higher Ground	V=E7-G-A-E7

1974

Cat's In The Craddle(F)	V=E-G-A-E(2x)D-D/C#-Bm-Bm/A-G-Bm/F#-E-G-Bm/F#-E
Rock And Roll Hootchie Koo(A)	V=E-G-A(4x)E
Rikki Don't Lose That Number	C=E7-GM7-A-G-D CM7-Em-CM7-D-A-E-

	D-A-E
Doctor Wu(G)	C=EM7-GM7-CM7-Em7-Am7-D11-EM7-G#m7-AM7-EM7-A/D-C#11
My Melody Of Love	C=E-E/G#-Go-B7/F#-B7-E

1976

50 Ways To Leave Your Lover	C=E-G6-A7(2x)E
With Your Love	V=E-EM7-GM7-A-[G-A]-E

1990

Suicide Blonde(E)	V=E-G-A

1992

Bad Wisdom	V=E-G-A7

Listing By Progression Type

Chord Progression *Song Examples*

Classic Rock(Borrowed "G")

E-G-A-E	On The Road Again('68); I Got A Line On You('69); After Midnight('70); Thank you(Falletin Me Be Mice Elf Agin)('70); Long Cool Woman('72); La Grange('73); Will It Go Round In Circles('73); Cat's In The Craddle('74)
E-G-A5-E	Hold On! I'm Comin'('66)
E-EM7-GM7-A-[G-A]-E	With Your Love('76)
E7-G-A-E7	Higher Ground('73)
E7-G-A7-E	Superstar('71)
E7-G7-A7-E7	Sgt. Pepper's Lonely Hearts Club Band('67)

E-G-A	Green Onions('62); Magical Mystery Tour('66); Rock And Roll Hootchie Koo('74); Suicide Blonde('90)
E-G-A7	Bad Wisdom('92)
E-G6-A7	50 Ways To Leave Your Lover('76)
E7#9-G-A	Purple Haze('67)

"Go" Cliché

E-Go-F#m7-B7	I'll Be Home For Christmas('43); Young At Heart('54); Witchcraft('57)
E-Go-F#m7-B9	I've Got A Crush On You('30)
E-E/G#-Go-F#m7-B7	Give My Regards To Broadway('04); School Days('07)
E-EM7-E6-Go-F#m7-B7	Just A Gigolo('30)
E6-Go-F#m7-B7	Embraceable You('28); In The Mood('38); Moonlight Serenade('39)
E-E/G#-Go-B7/F#-B7	You Made Me Love You('13); Beer Barrel Polka('34); My Melody Of Love('74)
E-Go-B7	Down By The Old Mill Stream('10)
E-Go-B7/F#-B7	Blue Christmas('48); Let Us Entertain You('59)
E-E/G#-Go-B7/F#	Rudolph The Red-Nosed Reindeer('49)
E-E/G#-Go-B7sus/F#-B7	Somewhere My Love('66)
E-E/B-E/G#-Go-B7/F#-B7	How Ya Gonna Keep 'Em Down On The Farm?('19)
E-EM7/G#-Go-B7/F#	God Bless America('38)
E-Go-E/G#-A	Let Me Call You Sweetheart('10)
E-Go-B7-E	Lazy Hazy Crazy Days Of Summer('63)
E-Go-B7/F#-E	Seventy-Six Trombones('57)
E-Go-B7-C#7	Diamonds Are A Girls Best Friend('49)
Esus-E-Go-B7	(You've Got)The Magic Touch('56)

Ascending Bass Lines

E-G-A-B	Knock On Wood('66)
E-G-A-C	I'm Not Your Steppin' Stone('67); Gimme Some Lovin'('67)
E-G-A-D	Bend Me, Shape Me('68)
E-E7-G-A-B11	I Am The Walrus('67)

Descending Bass Lines

Em-G/D-A7/C#-C	Temptation Eyes('71)
D-D/C#-Bm-Bm/A	Cat's In The Craddle('74)

Static Bass Lines

E5-E6-E7	Born To Be Wild('68)
Em-Em(M7)-Em7-Em6	Michelle('66)
E-G/E-A/E-E	I Can See For Miles('67)
E-G/E-A/E-G/E	Wake Up Little Susie('57);(I Know)I'm Losing You('66)
E-GM7/E-A/E-E	No Time('70)
Em-G/E-A/E-[D]-Em	School's Out('72)

Other "E-G" Progressions

The "E-G" progression is an example of a Partial Classic Rock(Borrowed "G")Progresson.

E-G	Night And Day('32); I Can't Get Next To You('69)
E7-G	(I Know)I'm Losing You('66)
E-G-E-A	It's My Party('63)
E-G-F-E	What's New Pussy Cat?('65)

The "E-G7-F#m7-B7" progression is an example of a Standard("G7" Substitution)Progression(The "G7 "is a substitution for the "C#7" chord.). This progression can be transformed into an Ascending "E-G-A-B" Bass Line Progression by playing the A note in the "F#m7" chord as the bass note creating the "E-G7-F#m7/A-B7" progression.

E-G7-F#m7-B7	Our Day Will Come('63)
E/G#-G6-F#m7-B7	The Lady Is A Tramp('37)
Em-G-F#m7/B	War('70)

The "E-G-A-G" progression can be transformed into an Ascending "E-G-A-B" Bass Line Progression by playing the B note in the second "G" chord as the bass note creating the "E-G-A-G/B" progression.

E-G-A-G	I'm Crying('64)
E5-G5-A5-F#5	I'm Free('69)
E7-GM7-A-G	Rikki Don't Lose That Number('74)

E-G-Bm-A   Liar, Liar('65)

The following progressions use both the "Borrowed" "G" and "C" chords.

E-G7-CM7-B7sus   Where Is The Love('72)
EM7-GM7-CM7-Em7   Doctor Wu('74)
EM7-G13-CM7-FM7   Here Comes That Rainy Day('53)
Em-G7-C-B7   Michelle('66)

The following progressions use both the "Borrowed" "G" and "D" chords.

E-G-D-E   Na, Na, Hey, Hey Kiss Him Goodbye('69)
E-G-D-A   Old Man('72)

"E-G#" Chord Progressions

The most frequent progressions that begin with the "E" chord and then move to the "G#" chords are as follows:

Rock Ballad ("G#m" Substitution)	E-G#m-A-B7
Standard("G#m" Substitution)	E-G#m-F#m-B7
Five Chord Ragtime	E-G#7-C#7-F#7-B7
Descending "E-D#-C#-B" Bass Lines	E-G#m/D#-C#m-E/B E-G#7/D#-C#m-E7/B
Descending "E-D#-D-C#" Bass Lines	E-G#m/D#-Bm/D-C#7

The "E-G#m-A-B7" Rock Ballad("G#m" Substitution) Progression is similar to the "E-C#m-A-B7" Rock Ballad Progression except the "C#m" chord has been substituted by the "G#m" chord which creates an interesting Ascending Bass Line. The "E-G#m-A-B7" Progression was used in the 1960s and 1970s to create such songs as Peter And Gordon's 1965 top twenty cover of Buddy Holly's *True Love Ways*, Ex-Beatle Paul McCartney's 1973 James Bond film theme hit *Live And Let Die*, and Rod Stewart's 1989 *Have I Told You Lately*.

The "E-G#m-F#m-B7" Standard("G#m" Substitution) Progression is similar to the "E-C#m'F#m-B7" Standard Changes except that the "G#m" chord is substituted for the "C#m" chord. Examples of hit songs based on the Standard("G#m" Substitution) Progression commonly used in 1960s and 1970s include Bobby Vinton's 1963 number one *Blue Velvet*, The Commodores' 1977 top five *Easy*, and Melissa Manchester's 1979 top ten *Don't Cry Out Loud*.

The "E-G#7-C#7-F#7-B7" Five Chord Ragtime Progression follows the Circle of Fifths through four changes was used primarily in the 1920s. Where Blues Progressions tend to be twelve bars, in

Ragtime Progressions various sequence lengths are popular. The most popular examples of Five Chord Ragtime are the 1923 *Charleston* and the 1925 *Five Foot Two, Eyes Of Blue*.

The "E-G#m/D#-C#m-E/B" and "E-G#7/D#-C#m-E7/B" Progressions are examples of the use of descending "E-D#-C#-B" Bass Lines to create memorable chord progressions. The most notable "E-G#m/D#-C#m-E/B" Progression is Billy Joel's 1974 breakthrough hit *Piano Man*. The best example of the "E-G#7/D#-C#m-E7/B" is the 1930 standard *Georgia On My Mind*.

The "E-G#m/D#-Bm/D-C#7" Progression is an example of the use of Descending "E-D#-D-C#" Bass Lines to construct interesting, moving chord progressions. The definitive example of this progression is Frank Sinatra's 1969 *My Way*.

In addition to the most frequent progressions already discussed, there are a number of other "E-G#" Chord Progressions that generally follow the Circle Of Fifths movement to "C#m" and many can be transformed into Descending Bass Line Progressions by playing other chord notes as the bass note.

Below is a chronological listing of songs with verses and/or choruses that use the "E-G#" sequence followed by a listing of chord progressions by type.

Chronological Listing

Date/Song Title   *Chord Progression*

1907

Harrigan   V=E-G#7-C#7-B7-E

1918

Rock-A-Bye Your Baby
With A Dixie Melody   V=E-G#m7-Go-F#m7-B7-B9

1920

My Mammy   V=E-G#m-A-E(4x)F#9-B7

1922

Nobody Knows You When You're

Down And Out(C)	V=E-G#7-C#7-F#m(2x)A-A#o-E-C#7-F#7-B7

1923

Tain't Nobody's Bizness If I Do	V=E-G#7/D#-C#m-E7/B-A-A#o-E-Fo-B7/F#-B7- T/A=E-C#7-F#9-B7
Charleston	V=E-G#7-C#7-F#7-B7-E-B7

1925

Five Foot Two, Eyes Of Blue	V=E-G#7-C#7-F#7-B7-E

1928

You're The Cream In My Coffee	V=E-G#m7-Go-F#m7-B7

1930

Geogia On My Mind	V=E-G#7/D#-C#m-E7/B-A-A#o-E/B-C#7-F#7-B7 T/A=G#o/D-C#m7-F#7-B7

1931

All Of Me	V=E-G#7-C#7-F#m7-C#7

1933

Smoke Gets In Your Eyes	V=E-G#m7-Go-F#m7-B7-E-G#7#5-AM7-A#o-G#m7-C#m7-F#m7-B7 T/A=G#7-C#7-F#m7-B7

1935

I'm Gonna Sit Right Down And
Write Myself A Letter   V=E-EM7-G#7-A-C#7-F#m7-
                                     F#m7/B

1937

Someday My Prince Will Come   V=E-G#7#5-AM7-C#7#5-F#m7-
                                     C#7#5-F#m7-B7

1944

You Always Hurt The One
You Love   V=E-EM7-E6-E-G#m7-Gm7
                                     F#m-C#

1946

Come Rain Or Come Shine   V=EM7-G#7#5b9-C#m7-F#9-B9-
                                     E7

1949

I'm So Lonesome I Could
Cry(G)   V=E-G#m/D#-C#m-B7-
                                     E-G#m/D#-Bm-E7

1952

I Saw Mommy Kissing
Santa Claus   V=E-G#m-C#m-E-B7

1955

Only You   V=E-G#7-C#m7-Bm7-E7-
                                     A-B7-G#7-C#m-F#7-F#m7-B7

1956

Love Me Tender(D) C=E-G#7/D#-C#m-E7/B-A-Am6-E-G#m7b5-C#7-F#7-B7-E

1958

True Love Ways V=E-G#m-A-B7

Twilight Time V=E-G#+-G#7-C#m-E7-A-Am-E-C#9-F#9-F#7-F#m7-B7

Who's Sorry Now? C=E-G#7-C#7-F#7-B7

1959

Sea Of Love V=E-G#7-A-F#7-E-F#7-E-A-E

1960

You're Sixteen V=E-G#7-A-E-F#7-B7-E
T/A=E-C#m7-F#m7-B7sus

1962

I Left My Heart In San Francisco V=E-G#m7-Go-F#m7-F#m7/B-B7#5-E

You Belong To Me V=E-G#m-A-E

Can't Help Falling In Love V=E-G#m-C#m-C#m/B-A-E-B7-A-B7-E-F#m-E-B7-E

Happy Birthday Sweet Sixteen V=E-G#7/D#-C#m-E7/B-A-A#o-E/B-C#7-F#7-B7

The Night Has A Thousand Eyes V=E-G#7-C#7-F#7-F#m7-B7-E6

Sherry V=E-G#7-C#7-F#7-B7

1963

Blue Velvet	V=E-G#m-F#m-B7-E-[G#m-Gm]-F#m-B7
Puff The Magic Dragon(A)	V/C=E-G#m-A-E-A-E-F#7-B7
Green, Green	V=E-G#m-A-E-A-B7-E(2x)
I Will Follow Him	V=E-G#m-C#m-G#m-A-B7-E-C#m-E
Be True To Your School(A)	C=E-G#7-C#m-A-F#7-F#m7-B

1964

My Guy	V=E-(G#m-F#m)4x
Do You Want To Know A Secret(E)	V=E-G#m-[Gm]-F#m-B7(5x)-A-B7-C#m-F#m-B7
Early Mornin' Rain(Bb)	V=E/G#-G#m-F#m-B7/D#-E-Esus-E-E/G#-F#m-B7/D#-E-E-F#m-B7-E-E/G#-G#m-F#m-B7/D#-E-Esus-E
Save It For Me	C=E-G#m-F#m-B-A-B(2x)
I'm Happy Just To Dance With You(E)	V=E-G#m-F#m-B7(2x)A-A6/C#-E-C#m-A-B+-E6-B7
I Feel Fine(G)	C=E-G#m-A-B7(2x)
Mister Lonely	V=E-G#m-A-B7(2x)

A Summer Song(A)	V=E-G#m-A-B(3x)E
Fun, Fun, Fun(Eb)	C=E-G#m-A-B-E-A-G#m-B-E
I Don't Want To See You Again	V=E-G#m-Am-B7(2x)
Any Time At All(D)	V=E-G#m/D#-C#m-Am/C-E/B-B-E
Bad To Me	V=E-G#m-C#m-B7(2x)
World Without Love	V=E-G#7-C#m-E-A6-E
Viva Las Vegas	V=E-G#7-C#m-A-E-A-E
Who Can I Turn To	V=EM7-G#m7-C#7-F#m7-B7-F#m7/B-B7
No Reply(C)	B=E-G#-C#-F#m-A-E(2x)

1965

You're Going To Lose That Girl(E)	V=E-G#m-F#m-B7(2x)
Ferry Cross The Mersey(E)	C=E-G#m-F#m-B7-E-Bm7
Girl(Eb)	C=E-G#m-F#m-B7(2x)
Save Your Heart For Me(D)	V=E-G#m-F#m7-Am6
Let's Hang On(G)	V=E-G#m7-F#m7-B7
Mrs. Brown(C)	V=E-G#m7-F#m7-B7(4x)
Cara Mia	V=E-G#m-A-E-A-Am-E-F#7-B7
A Lover's Concerto	V=E-G#m-A-B7-E-C#m-B7-

	E-C#m-F#m7-B7
I Go To Pieces	V=E-G#m-A-B7(2x)-E-C#m(2x)
Flowers Never Bend With The Rainfall	V=E-G#m7-AM7-E-G#m-AM7-E-A-E
Count Me In(F)	V=E-G#m-B7-E
Stop In The Name Of Love	V=E-G#m-Bm-C#7
Help(A)	V=E-G#m-C#m-A-D-E(2x)
You're Nobody Till Somebody Loves You	V=E-G#7-C#7-F#m-B7-E
Wait(A)	C=E6-G#7-C#m
Tired Of Waiting For You(G)	B=E-G#m-D-B(2x)
It's Only Love(C)	V=E-G#m/D#-D-A-B-B+(2x)

1966

But It's Alright	V=E-G#m-F#m(8x)
Red Rubber Ball(A-Bb)	V=E-G#m-A-E-E-G#m-A-B-A-B-E-C#m-F#m-G#m-A-G#
You Baby(B)	V=E-G#m-A-B(3x)-E-G#m-A-E-G#m-F#m-A-B
You Didn't Have To Be So Nice(E)	V=E-G#m-A-B11(2x)
Green Grass	V=E-G#-A-Am-E-E+-A-Am-E-C#m-A-B7-E-Fo-F#m7-B7
Sign Of The Times	V=E-G#m-C#m-F#m7-B7-F#m7-B7(2x)

What Becomes Of The Broken-Hearted(Bb)	V=E/B-G#m/B-C#m-A/C#-E/B-G#m/B-C#m-G#7/D#-E/D
I Want You	V=E-G#m-C#m-B
That's Life	C=E-G#7-C#m7-[G7]-F#7
Spanish Flea	V=E-G#7-C#7-F#7-B7-E-A-D-G-C-F-B-B7

1967

Silence Is Golden	C=E-G#m-F#m7-B7-E-E-G#m-C#m-F#m7-B7-E
Georgy Girl	V=E-G#m-A-B(2x)-E-G#m-A-D-B7
Different Drum	V=E-G#m-A-B(7x)
Let's Spend The Night Together(G)	V=E-G#m/D#-B7(2x)A-E-B-A-G#
A Whiter Shade Of Pale(C)	V=E-G#m/D#-C#m-E6/B-A-A/G#-F#m-F#m/E-B-B/A-G#m7-B7/F#-E-A-B-A-B7
A Day In The Life(G)	V=E-G#m/D#-C#m-C#m7-A A/G#-F#m9
I Think We're Alone Now	V=E-G#m-C#m-B(2x)
Beautiful People	V=E-G#m-C#m-B7sus-B7(2x)
San Franciscan Nights(C)	V=E-G#m/D#-C#m-B(2x)-

	F#-A-E-F#m-A-E-F#-A-E
There's A Kind Of Hush	V=E-G#7/D#-C#m-E7/B-A-B7-E-B7
Ring Around A Rosy Rag(F)	V/C=E-G#7-C#m-C#m/B-A-A#o-E-F#7-B7

1968

Itchykoo Park(A)	V=E-G#m-E7-A(2x)
A Beautiful Morning(Eb)	V=E-G#m-F#m7-G#m-F#m-E-C#m-E-G#m7-F#m7-G#m-A-B-C#m7-F#m7(2x)G#m7-C#m7-F#m7-F#m7/B
Abraham, Martin, And John	V=E-G#m-F#m7-A-E-G#m7-B6-B7
Grazing In The Grass	V=EM7-G#m7-F#m7-B7sus
The Weight(A)	V=E-G#m-A-E(4x)
Elenore(E)	C=E-G#m-A-E-B7-F#m-F#m(M7)-F#m7-B7-E
Stand By Your Man(A)	C=E-G#7-A-G#m7-F#m7-E-C#7-F#7-B7
Hurdy Gurdy Man	V=E-G#m-A-B7
Woman, Woman	V=E-G#m-A-B C=E-G#m-A-G#m
Dock Of The Bay(G)	V=E-G#-A-[G#-G]-F#(2x)
While My Guitar Gently Weeps(C)	B=E-G#m-C#m-G#m-F#m-B(2x)

Ob-La-Di Ob-La-Da(Bb)	C=E-G#m/B-C#m-E-B7-E

1969

Jean	V=E-G#m-A-B7
Ballad Of Easy Rider(D)	V=E-G#m-A-B7
Build Me Up Butter Cup	C=E-G#7#5-A-B11(2x)
I Started A Joke(G)	V=E-G#m-A-B(4x)
Traces(D-Eb)	V=E-G#m-Bm-C#7
My Way	V=E-G#m/D#-Bm6/D-C#7-F#m-F#m(M7)/F-F#m/E-B7
Goodbye	V=E-G#m-C#m-A-F#m7-B7-E-B7
You Never Give Me Your Money(C)	B=E-G#7-C#m-E7-A-B-E(2x)-D-A-E(2x)
Lay, Lady, Lay	V=E-G#m-D-F#m(4x)

1970

Easy Come, Easy Go	V=E-G#m-E7-A-Am-E-F#m7/B-B7
Gypsy Woman(B)	C=E-G#m-F#m(2x)
Snow Bird	V=E-G#m-F#m-B7-E(2x)
Reflections Of My Life	V=E-G#m-C#m-E7-A-G#m7-F#m7-B7
Didn't I(Blow Your Mind This Time)(A)	V=E-G#7/D#-C#m-E/B-A-E/B-

	A-B11
United We Stand	V=E-G#-C#m-E-A-C#7-F#-B
	C=E-G#-C#m-AM7-E-A-B(2x)

1971

Color My World(F)	V=EM7-G#m-A-DM9-GM7-FM7-C#9-C#7-F#M7-D9-B7 EM7-A-B7-EM7
Sooner Or Later(C-Db)	C=E-G#m7-A-B(2x)
Changes(C)	V=E-G#m7-A-B-A- E-G#m7-A-B- EM7-F#m7-G#m7-Gm7- F#m7-B- EM7-F#m7-G#m7-Gm7- F#m7-B-A I=F#-A7(2x)
Rainy Days And Mondays	V=E-G#m/D#-Bm6/D-C#7-F#m7-G#m7-AM7-G#m7-F#m-AM7-F#m7-E/G#-A-B11 T/A=E/B-F#m7/B(2x)
Another Day	V=E-G#7/D#-C#m-F#m-B7-E-A-E(3x)F#-B7-E

1972

Oh Girl(Bb)	V=E-G#m-A-F#m-B7sus4
Operator(That's Not The Way I Feel)(G)	V=E-G#m-A-G#m-F#m-E
Nice To Be With You	V=E-G#m-A-B(2x)
Ziggie Stardust(G)	V=E-G#m-A-B- E-C#m-F#7-A-

"E-G#" Chord Progressions

	F#m-E-D-E(3x)B-C#
Crocodile Rock(G)	V=E-G#m-A-B(2x)C#m-B(4x)
If You Don't Know Me By Now	C=E-G#m7-AM7-Ao
Rock 'N' Roll Suicide(C)	V=E-G#-A-B- C#m-B-A-B- C#m-B-A-E-B
Until It's Time For You To Go	V=E-G#m/D#-Bm/D-C#7
Doctor My Eyes(F)	V=E-G#m-C#m-A(2x)E
I Wanna Be With You(E)	V=E-G#m-C#m-A-C#m-A6-F#m-B11
Alone Again Naturally	V=EM7-E6-G#m-G#m7b5-C#7- F#m7-F#m7b5-E-E+-E6- A#m7b5-D#7
I'll Be Around	V=EM7-G#m-D#m/F#-G#m

1973

Midnight Train To Georgia	V=E-G#m/D#-F#m/C#-B11(2x)
Pieces Of April	V=E-G#m7-F#m7-B7
Live And Let Die	V=E-G#m-A-B7-B7b9- E-G#m-A-A/B-Am/B- E-G#m-A-F#- B-G-E-A/E-Eo-E7-A/E
We May Never Pass This Way (Again)(E)	V=E-G#m7-AM7-E-Esus-E(2x)- FM9-CM9(3x)FM7-Em-A/D- C#11-C-D-Bm7-Bm9/E(4x)
Goodbye Yellow Brick Road	C=E-G#7-A-E-C#7-F#m-B7-E

Space Oddity(C)   V=E-G#7-A-Am-E-A-Am-E-A
I=E-G#m(2x)C#m-C#m/B-F#

Tie A Yellow Ribbon Round The Ole Oak Tree   V=E-G#m-Bm-C#7-F#m-Am6-C#m-F#7-(Am6-B7)2x-C=E-G#m-Bm-C#7-F#m-Am6-E-G#7-C#m-E-E+-C#m-C#7-F#m-Am6-F#m9-B7-E

Yesterday Once More   V=E-G#m/D#-C#m-C#m/B-AM7-G#m7-F#m7-B/D#-A9/C#-B11

No More Mr. Nice Guy(A)   V=E-G#m-D-F#m-A-B(2x)-C#m-F#m-A-B(2x)A

1974

I'll Have To Say I Love You In A Song(A)   V=EM7-G#m-F#m-B-C#m-D#m

The Way We Were   V=E-G#m7-AM7-C#m7-C#m/B-AM7-G#m7-G#7-C#m-C#m/B-AM7-B

The Air That I Breath   V=E-G#7-A-Am-E(2x)

Piano Man(C)   V=E-G#m/D#-C#m-E/B-A-E/G#-F#7-B-E-G#m/D#-C#m-E/B-A-B11-E
I=E-A/E-EM7-B11
B=C#m-C#m/B-F#7/A#-A

I Like To Live The Love(Bb)   V=E-G#m7-D-C#7-F#m7-C#7/G#-A

1975

Sister Golden Hair(E)   V=E-G#m-A-E-G#m-A-F#m-C#m-G#m-A-F#m-A-E

Love Will Keep Us Together	V=E-G#m7b5-C#7-A-Am
New York State Of Mind	V=E-G#7#9-C#m7-Bm7-E7/B-A-C#7-F#m7-D9

1976

Got To Get You Into My Life(G)	V=E-E11(2x)G#m-G#m(M7)-G#m7-G#m6(2x)A-A/G#-F#m7-B7-E
Today's The Day	C=E-G#m-F#m-B7(2x)
Silly Love Songs	V=E-G#m7-AM7(3x)G#m7-AM7-B
Weekend In New England	V=E-G#m-AM7-B(2x)-A-E/G#-F#m7-B7
The Boys Are Back In Town(A)	V=E-G#m7-A-C#m7-G#m7-C#m7-F#m7-F#m7/B
All By Myself	C=E-G#m/D#-Bm/D-C#7-F#m-F#m7b5-B7
Baby, I Love Your Way	V=E-G#m-C#m-A-D9

1977

Easy	V/C=E-G#m7-F#m7-B11
How Deep Is Your Love(Eb)	V=E-G#m7-F#m7-C#7
Right Time Of The Night	C=E-G#m7-A-B11(3x)
Rich Girl	V=E-G#m7-C#m7-E/B-A-E/G#-F#m7-B11-E-G#m7-C#m7-E/B-A-E/G#-F#m7-E-F#m7-G#m7-AM7-G#m7-F#m7-E/B-C#m7-F#m7-G#m7-C#m7

1978

Emotion	V=EM7-E6-G#m7-Fo-F#m7-B11-EM7
It's A Heartache	V=E-G#m-A-E-B(3x)
Too Much Heaven	C=EM7-G#m7-A-E-B7sus4(2x)
Still The Same	V=EM7-E(2x)EaddF#-G#m-B
We Are The Champions	C=E-G#m-C#m-[A-B]-E-G#m-A-Fo-F#m
Goodbye Girl	V=E-G#m7/D#-C#m7-G#m7-F#m7-C#m7-AM7-B C=E-G#m7-Aadd9-B(2x)

1979

Don't Cry Out Loud	V=E-G#m-F#m-B7sus-E-G#m-F#m-B11
On The Road Again	V=E-G#7-F#m-A-B7-E
Against The Wind	V/C=E-G#m-A-E
Every Time You Go Away(F)	V=E-G#m-A-B(2x)C#m-G#7-A-A#o
It's Still Rock And Roll To Me(C)	V=E-G#m-D-A(2x)

1982

Key Largo	C=E-G#m-A-B11(2x)
Hard To Say I'm Sorry	V=E-G#m7-A-B-C#m-B(2x)

1986

Nikita	V=E-G#m-A-[D/A-A]-E-[A/E-E]-B
Take My Breath Away	V=E-G#m/D#-C#m-G#m/D#(2x)- F#m-A/E-B C=E-G#m/D#-A-B(2x)

1988

What A Wonderful World	V=E-G#m/D#-A/E-G#m/D#- F#m/E-E-G#7/D#-C#m-C- B11-B7-E

1989

Have I Told You Lately(Bb)	V=E-G#m7-A-B11(2x) AM7-G#m7-F#m7-B11-E-B7
If You Don't Know Me By Now	V=E-G#m7-AM7-B7sus- E-G#m7-AM7-F#m7/B C=E-G#m7-AM7-Ao

1990

This Old Heart Of Mine	V=E-G#m7-A(2x)F#m7-B7
All I Want To Do Is Make Love To You(G)	V=E-G#m-A-E- E-G#m-A-B- E-C#m-A-B

1992

Runaway Train(C)	V/C=E-G#m/D#-C#m-B(2x)

1994

Passionate Kisses(E)	C=E-G#m-C#m-A- E-A(3x)E-B-C#m-A

1997

Together Again   V=E-G#m7/D#-G#m7b5/D-C#7b9-
                       C#7-F#m9-B13

Listing By Progression Type

Chord Progression   *Song Examples*

Rock Ballad("G#m" Substitution)

Rock Ballad("G#m" Substitution)Progressions have ascending bass lines, however, they can be transformed into a Descending Bass Line Progressions by playing the D# note of the "G#m" chord as the bass note and by playing the C# note of the "A" chord as the bass note creating the "E-G#m/D#-A/C#-B7" Progression.

Chord Progression	Song Examples
E-G#m-A-B	A Summer Song('64); Fun, Fun, Fun('64); You Baby('66); Different Drum('67); Georgy Girl('67); Woman, Woman('68); I Started A Joke('69); Ziggie Stardust('72); Nice To Be With You('72); Crocodile Rock('72); Every Time You Go Away('79)
E-G#m-A-B7	True Love Ways('58); Mister Lonely('64); I Feel Fine('64); A Lover's Concerto('65); I Go To Pieces('65); Hurdy Gurdy Man('68); Jean('69); Ballad Of Easy Rider('69)
E-G#m-A-B7-B7b9	Live And Let Die('73)
E-G#m-A-B11	You Didn't Have To Be So Nice('66); Key Largo('82)
E-G#m-AM7-B	Weekend In New England('76)
E-G#m-Am-B7	I Don't Want To See You Again("64)
E-G#m/D#-A-B	Take My Breath Away('86)–Chorus
E-G#m7-A-B	Sooner Or Later('71); Changes('71); Hard To Say I'm Sorry('82)
E-G#m7-A-B11	The Right Time Of The Night('77); Have I Told You Lately('89)
E-G#m7-AM7-B7sus	If You Don't Know Me By Now('89)
E-G#m7-Aadd9-B	Goodbye Girl('78)
E-G#-A-B	Rock 'N' Roll Suicide('72)
E-G#7#5-A-B11	Build Me Up Butter Cup('69)

Standard("G#m" Substitution)

The Standard("G#m" Substitution) Progression can be transformed into a Descending "E-D#-C#-B" Bass Line Progression by playing the D# note of the "G#m" chord as the bass note and by playing the C# note of the "F#m" chord as the bass note creating the "E-G#m/D#-F#m/C#-B7" progression. In the same manner, the "E-G#m7-F#m7-B7" progression can be transformed into the Ascending Bass Line "E-G#m7-F#m7/A-B7" Progression.

E-G#m-F#m-B	Save It For Me('64)
E-G#m-F#m-B7	Blue Velvet('63); I'm Happy Just To Dance With You('64); You're Going To Lose That Girl('65); Ferry Cross The Mersey('65); Snow Bird('70); Today's The Day('76)
E-G#m-[Gm]-F#m-B7	Do You Want To Know A Secret('64)
E-G#m-F#m-B7sus	Don't Cry Out Loud('79)
E-G#m-F#m7-B7	Silence Is Golden('67)
E-G#m7-F#m7-B7	Mrs. Brown('65); Let's Hang On('65); Pieces Of April('73)
E-G#m7-F#m7-B11	Easy('77)
E/G#-G#m-F#m-B7/D#	Early Mornin' Rain('64)
EM7-G#m-F#m-B	I'll Have To Say I Love You In A Song('74)
EM7-G#m7-F#m7-B7sus	Grazin' In The Grass('68)

Five Chord Ragtime

E-G#7-C#7-F#7-B7	Charleston('23); Five Foot Two, Eyes Of Blue('25); Who's Sorry Now?('58); Sherry('62); Spanish Flea('66)

Descending Bass Lines

E-G#m/D#-F#m/C#-B11	Midnight Train To Georgia('73)
E-G#m/D#-C#m-E/B	Piano Man('74)
E-G#m/D#-C#m-E6/B	A Whiter Shade Of Pale('67)
E-G#m/D#-C#m-B	San Franciscan Nights('67); Runaway Train('92)
E-G#m/D#-C#m-B7	I'm So Lonesome I Could Cry('49)
E-G#m/D#-C#m-C#m7/B	Yesterday Once More('73)
E-G#7/D#-C#m-E/B	Didn't I(Blow Your Mind This Time)('70)
E-G#7/D#-C#m-E7/B	Tain't Nobody's Bizness If I Do('23); Georgia On My Mind('30); Love Me Tender('56); Happy Birthday Sweet Sixteen('62); There's A Kind Of Hush('67)
E-G#m/D#-C#m-Am/C	Anytime At All('64)

E-G#m/D#-Bm/D-C#7	Until It's Time For You To Go('72); All By Myself('76)
E-G#m/D#-Bm6/D-C#7	My Way('69); Rainy Days And Mondays('71)
E-G#m7/D#-G#m7b5/D-C#7b9	Together Again('97)

Diminished Cliché

EM7-E6-G#m7-Fo-F#m7-B11	Emotion('78)

The following progression is similar to the "E-E/G#-Go-B7/F#-B7" Diminished Cliché except that the "E/G#" chord is substituted by the "G#m7" chord and the "B7/F#" chord is substituted by the "F#m7" chord.

E-G#m7-Go-F#m7-B7	Rock-A-Bye Your Baby With A Dixie Melody('18); You're The Cream In My Coffee('28); Smoke Gets In Your Eyes('31)

The following progression is also similar to the "E-E/G#-Go-B7/F#-B7" Diminished Cliché except that the "E/G#" chord is substituted by the "G#m7", the "B7/F#" chord is substituted by the "F#m7" chord, and the "B7" chord is substituted by the "F#m7/B" chord.

E-G#m7-Go-F#m7-F#m7/B	Left My Heart In San Francisco('62)

Static Bass Lines

E-EM7-E6-E	You Always Hurt The One You Love('44)
EM7-E	Still The Same('78)
EM7-E6	Alone Again Naturally('72); Emotion('78)
E-E11	Got To Get You Into My Life('76)
G#m-G#m(M7)-G#m7-G#m6	Got To Get You Into My Life('76)
E/B-F#m7/B	Rainy Days And Mondays('71)

Other "E-G#" Progressions

Many of the following Other "E-G#" progressions can be transformed into Descending Bass Line Progressions by playing other chord notes as the bass note. Various examples are shown below. The "E-G#m-E7-A" progression can be transformed into a Descending "E-D#-D-C#" Bass Line Progression by playing the D# note of the "G#m" chord as the bass note, by playing the D note of the "E7" chord as the bass note, and by playing the C# note of the "A" chord creating the "E-G#m/D#-E/D-A/C#" progression.

E-G#m-E7-A   Itchykoo Park('68); Easy Come, Easy Go('70)

The "E-G#m-F#m-G#m" progression can be transformed into a Descending "E-D#-C#-B" Bass Line Progression by playing the D# note of the "G#m" chord as the bass note, by playing the C# note of the F#m chord as the bass note, and playing the B note of the G#m chord as the bass note creating the "E-G#m/D#-F#m/C#-G#m/B" progression. The same progression can also be transformed into an Ascending "E-G#-A-B" Bass Line Progression by playing the A note in the "F#m" chord as the bass note and by playing the B note in the "G#m" chord as the bass note creating the "E-G#m-F#mA-G#m/B" progression.

E-G#m-F#m	But It's Alright('66); Gypsy Woman('70)
E-G#m-F#m-G#m	My Guy('64)
E-G#m-F#m7-G#m	A Beautiful Morning('68)
E-G#m-F#m7-A	Abraham, Martin, And John('68)
E-G#m-F#m7-Am6	Save It For Me('65)
E-G#m7-F#m7-C#7	How Deep Is Your Love('77)
E-G#7-F#m-A	On The Road Again('79)

The "E-G#m-A-E" progression can be transformed into a Descending "E-D#-C#-B" Bass Line Progression by playing the D# note of the "G#m" chord as the bass note, by playing the C# note of the "A" chord as the bass note, and by playing the B note of the "E" chord as the bass note creating the "E-G#m/D#-A/C#-E/B" progression. In the same manner, the "E-G#m-A-G#m" progression can be transformed into the "E-G#m/D#-A/C#-G#m/B" progression.

E-G#m-A-Am	Mac Arthur Park('68)
E-G#m-A-E	My Mammy('20); You Belong To Me('62); Green, Green('63); Puff The Magic Dragon('63); Cara Mia('65); Red Rubber Ball('66); Elenore('68); The Weight('68); Sister Golden Hair('75); It's A Heartache('78); Against The Wind('79); All I Want To Do Is Make Love To You('90)
E-G#m-A-[D/A-A]-E	Nikita('86)
E-G#m-A-F#m	Oh Girl('72)
E-G#m-A-G#m	Woman, Woman('68); Operator(That's Not The Way I Feel)('72)
E-G#m-AM7	Silly Love Songs('76)
E-G#m7-A	This Old Heart Of Mine('90)
E-G#m7-AM7-Ao	If You Don't Know Me By Now('89)
E-G#m/D#-A/E-G#m/D#	What A Wonderful World('88)
E-G#m7-A-C#m7	The Boys Are Back In Town('76)
E-G#m7-AM7-E	Flowers Never Bend With The Rainfall('65); We May Never Pass This Way(Again)('73)
E-G#m7-AM7-C#m7	The Way We Were('74)

E-G#-A-[G#-G]-F#	Dock Of The Bay('68)
E-G#-A-Am	Green Grass('66)
E-G#7-AE	You're Sixteen('60); Goodbye Yellow Brick Road('73)
E-G#7-A-F#7	Sea Of Love('59)
E-G#7-A-G#m7	Stand By Your Man('69)
E-G#7-A-Am	Space Oddity('73); The Air That I Breathe('74)
E-G#7#5-AM7-C#7#5	Someday My Prince Will Come('46)
E-EM7-G#7-A-C#7	I'm Gonna Sit Right Down And Write Myself A Letter('35)
EM7-G#m-A-DM9	Color My World('71)
EM7-G#m7-A-E	Too Much Heaven('78)

The "E-G#m-Bm-C#7" progression can be transformed into a Descending "E-D#-D-C#" Bass Line Progression by playing the D# note in the "G#m" chord as the bass note and by playing the D note in the "Bm" chord as the bass note creating the "E-G#m/D#-Bm/D-C#7" progression.

E-G#m-Bm-C#7	Stop In The Name Of Love('65); Traces('69); Tie A Yellow Ribbon Round The Ole Oak Tree('73)
E-G#m-B7	Count Me In('65)
E-G#m/D#-B7	Let's Spend The Night Together('67)

The "E-G#m-C#m-E" progressions can be transformed into a Descending "E-D#-C#-B" Bass Line Progression by playing the "D#" note of the "G#m" chord as the bass note and by playing the B note of the "E" chord as the bass note creating the "E-G#m/D#-C#m-E/B" progression. In the same manner as above, the "E-G#m-C#m-A" progression can be transformed into the Descending Bass Line "E-G#m/D#-C#m-A" progression and the "E-G#m-C#m-B" progression can be transformed into the Descending Bass Line E-G#m/D#-C#m-B" progression.

E-G#m-C#m-E	I Saw Mommy Kissing Santa Claus('52)
E-G#m-C#m-[A-B]-E	We Are The Champions('78)
E-G#m-C#m-E7	Reflections Of My Life('70)
E-G#m-C#m-F#m7	Sign Of The Times('66)
E-G#m-C#m-G#m	I Will Follow Him('63); While My Guitar Gently Weeps('68)
E-G#m-C#m-A	Help('65); Goodbye('69); Doctor My Eyes('72); I Wanna Be With You('72); Baby I Love Your Way('76); Passionate Kisses('94)
E-G#m-C#m-B	I Want You('66); I Think We're Alone Now('67)
E-G#m-C#m-B7	Bad To Me('64)
E-G#m-C#m-B7sus	Beautiful People('67)
E-G#m-C#m-C#m7	A Day In The Life('67)
E-G#m-C#m-C#m/B	Can't Help Falling In Love('62)
E-G#m/B-C#m-E	Ob-La-Di Ob-La-Da('68)

E-G#m/D#-C#m-G#m/D#	Take My Breath Away('86)–Verse
E-G#m/D#-C#m-C#m7	A Day In The Life('67)
E-G#m7-C#m7-E/B	Rich Girl('77)
E-G#m7/D#-C#m7-G#m7	Goodbye Girls('78)
E-G#m7b5-C#7-A	Love Will Keep Us Together('75)
E-G#-C#m-E	United We Stand('70)–Verse
E-G#-C#m-AM7	United We Stand('70)-Chorus
E-G#-C#-F#m	No Reply('64)
E-G#+-G#7-C#m	Twilight Time('58)
E-G#7-C#m-E	World Without Love('64)
E-G#7-C#m-E7	You Never Give Me Your Money('69)
E-G#7-C#m-A	Be True To Your School('63); Viva Las Vegas('64)
E-G#7-C#m-C#m/B	Ring Around A Rosy Rag('67)
E-G#7-C#m7-[G7]-F#7	That's Life('66)
E-G#7-C#m7-Bm7	Only You('55)
E-G#7-C#7-F#m	Nobody Knows You When You're Down And Out('22); You're Nobody Till Somebody Loves You('65)
E-G#7-C#7-F#m7	All Of Me('31)
E-G#7-C#7-F#7	The Night Has A Thousand Eyes('62)
E-G#7-C#7-B7	Harrigan('07)
E-G#7/D#-C#m-F#m	Another Day('71)
E-G#7#9-C#m7-Bm7	New York State Of Mind('75)
E/B-G#m/B-C#m-A/C#	What Becomes Of The Broken-Hearted('66)
E6-G#7-C#m	Wait('65)
EM7-G#m7-C#7-F#m7	Who Can I Turn To('64)
EM7-G#7(#5/b9)-C#m7-F#9	Come Rain Or Come Shine('46)

The following progression can be transformed into a Descending "E-D#-D-C#" Bass Line Progression by playing the D# note of the "G#m" chord as the bass note and by playing the C# note of the "F#m" chord as the bass note creating the "E-G#m/D#-D-F#m/C#" progression. In the same manner, the "E-G#m-D-A" progression can be transformed into the "E-G#m/D#-D-A/C#" progression.

E-G#m-D-F#m	Lay, Lady, Lay('69); No More Mr. Nice Guy('73)
E-G#m-D-A	It's Still Rock And Roll To Me('80)
E-G#m-D-B	Tired Of Waiting For You('65)
E-G#m/D#-D-A	It's Only Love('65)
E-G#m7-D-C#7	I Like To Live The Love('74)
EM7-G#m-D#m/F#-G#m	I'll Be Around

"E-A" Chord Progressions

Chord Progressions that begin with an "E" chord and then progress to an "A" chord are very widely used in all types of popular songs. The most frequent "E-A" chord progressions are as follows:

Basic	E-A
Rock	E-A-B7
Basic & Folk Combination	E-A-E-B7
Blues	E7-A7-E7-B7-A7-E7-B7
	E7-A7(2x)E7-B7-A7-E7-B7
Classic Rock(Borrowed "D")	E-A-D-A
Static Bass Lines	E-E11
	E-A/E

The repeated "E-A" Basic Progression, which follows the Circle Of Fifths movement, is one of the least complex and most popular changes in all popular music with numerous examples found throughout the twentieth century. Keith Richards of the Rolling Stones has made millions of dollars over the years writing and playing hard rock songs with these two basic chords played on an open G tuned electric guitar. Examples of hit songs created around the Basic Progression include the Beatles' 1964 *Love Me Do*, John Denver's 1974 number one *Sunshine On My Shoulders*, and Bruce Springsteen's 1985 *Glory Days*.

The infamous three-chord "E-A-B7" Rock Progression is a staple of Rock 'N' Roll. Whereas the "E-C#m-A-B7" Rock Ballad Progression substituted the harder sounding "A" chord for the softer "F#m" chord in the Standard Changes, the Rock Progression omitted the softer sounding "C#m" chord to create a harder rock sound. Although the quality of the chords in Rock Progressions are not usually changed, sometimes the "A" chord is changed to an "A6" and the "B7" is changed to a "B" or "B11". Common Rock Progression variations include the "E-A-B-E" and "E-A-B-A" Progressions. An inventive combination of the Rock Progression with an Ascending "E-G#-A-B" Bass Line was used to produce Wing's 1978 number one *With A Little Luck* and Billy Joel's 1979 *My Life*.

The "E-A-E-B7" Basic & Folk Combination Progression as the name implies consists of the "E-A" Basic Progression combined with the "E-B7" Folk Progression. One of the oldest songs based on the "E-A-E-B7" is *Amazing Grace* which dates back to 1779. A more recent example of hit songs using the Basic & Folk Combination include Van Morrison's 1967 *Brown Eyed Girl*, Helen Reddy's 1973 *Delta Dawn,* and Natalie Cole's 1988 *Pink Cadillac.*

The Blues Progression, which consists of only three chords, is widely used as the basis for rock, jazz, and blues songs. There are eight, twelve, fourteen, sixteen, and twenty-four bar Blues progressions. The two most common Blues forms are the twelve bar chord progressions shown below. The main difference between the two is that the second progression includes what is known as the "Quick Change" to the "A7" chord in the second bar.

Classic Blues

E7				A7		E7		B7	A7	E7	B7
////	////	////	////	////	////	////	////	////	////	////	////

Quick Change Blues

E7	A7	E7		A7		E7		B7	A7	E7	B7
////	////	////	////	////	////	////	////	////	////	////	////

The "A7" chord change in the tenth bar is sometimes omitted in both Classic and Quick Change Blues progressions. The last two bars of a blues song are referred to as the Turnaround. The Appendix includes a listing of common Blues Turnarounds, each of which can be substituted for the other based on the preference of the songwriter or performer. For a more sophisticated blues progression, take a look at the changes for the 1947 *Call It Stormy Monday.* Chuck Berry's 1958 rock classic *Johnny B. Goode* used the twelve bar Blues Progression without a "Quick Change" or the "A7" chord change in the tenth bar. Like *Johnny B. Goode,* Chuck Berry wrote many of his groundbreaking Rock 'N' Roll songs around Blues Progressions. Other non-blues uses of the Blues Progression include The Andrews Sisters 1941 *Boogie Woogie Bugle Boy*, the 1963 surf instrumental *Wipe Out*, and the Loggins & Messina 1973 *Your Mama Don't Dance.*

The "E-A-D-A" Classic Rock(Borrowed "D")Progression is similar to the "E-D-A" Classic Rock Progression except that the "A" and "D" chords are reversed. Neil Diamond wrote numerous songs early in his career based on the "E-A-D-A" Progression such as his 1966 *Cherry, Cherry* and *I Got The Feelin'(Oh No No)*as well as his 1967 *I Thank The Lord For The Night Time*. The definitive example is The Rolling Stones first big hit in 1965(*I Can't Get No)Satisfaction*. A more recent example would be Guns N' Roses' 1989 *Paradise City.*

The "E-E11" Static Bass Line Progressions use the "E11" Chord Quality Substitution to provide movement where the "E" chord is used in a progression for move than one or two bars. The definitive example of the Static "E-E11" Progression is The Drifters' 1963 hit *On Broadway*.

The "E-A/E" Static Bass Line Progressions combine the "E-A" Basic Progression with a Static "E" Bass Line to create an interesting and memorable progression. Hit songs that employ the "E-A/E" Progression include Sonny & Cher's 1965 breakthrough number one *I Got You Babe*, the Eagles' 1975 *Lyin' Eyes*, and The Rolling Stones' 1981 *Start Me Up*.

In addition to the most frequent progressions already discussed, there are a number of other "E-A" Chord Progressions that continue to move to "E", "F#m", "G#m", "B" and "C#m" as well as the "Borrowed" "G", "C", and "D" chords. Many progressions represent various Combination Progressions.

Below is a chronological listing of songs with verses and/or choruses that employ the "E-A" sequence followed by a listing of chord progressions by type. Dates designated as "N/A" were not available.

Chronological Listing

Date/Song Title	*Chord Progression*
N/A	
Kumbaya	V=E-A(2x)B- E-A(2x)E-B-E
Over The River And Through The Woods	V=E-A-E-B7-E-F#7-B7
We Wish You A Merry Christmas	V=E-A-F#7-B7- G#7-C#m-A-B7-E
No Beer In Heaven	V=E-A-B7-E-A-E-B7-E
1779	
Amazing Grace	V=E-A-E-B(2x)E

1832

Rock Of Ages   V=E-A-E-B

1841

On Top Of Old Smokey   V=E-A-E-B7-E

1857

Jingle Bells   C=E-A-E-F#7-B7

1858

Yellow Rose Of Texas   V=E-A-E-B(2)E

1861

Dixie   V=E-A-E-B7-E(2x)
                           C=E-A-F#7-B7

Battle Hymn Of The Republic   V=E-A-E-B7-E-G#7-C#m-A-E-B7-E
                              C=E-A-E-G#7-C#m-A-F#m-E-B7-E

1869

Little Brown Jug   V=E-A-B(2x)E

1873

Home On The Range   V=E-E7-A-E-F#7-B7-E-E7-A-E-B7-E-B7-E

1880

Twinkle Twinkle Little Star   V=E-A-E-B7-E-B7-E

1881

I've Been Working On The
Railroad   V=E-A-E-C#m-F#7-B7

1884

While Strolling Through The Park   V=E-A-C#7-F#7-B7

1902

In the Good Old Summertime   V=E-E7/G#-A-E-C#m7-F#7-B7

The Entertainer   V=E-E7-A-E-B7-E

1904

Meet Me In St. Louis, Louis   V=E-A-E-B7

Give My Regards To Broadway   C=E-Am6/C-B7-F#m-B7-E

1911

I Want A Girl   V=E-E7-A-A#o-E/B-C#m-F#9-
                                    B9-E

1912   Moonlight Bay   V=E-A(2x)E-B7-E

When Irish Eyes Are Smiling   C=E-E7-A-E-A-
                                    E-C#7-F#7-B7

1919

Swanee   V=E-E+-A-E-C7-B7-E-B7

1924

California, Here I Come   V=E-E+-A-B7-Fo-B7-E

Swing Low, Sweet Chariot	V=E-A-E-B(2x)E

1927

Side By Side	V=E-A/E(3x)E-C#7-F#7-B7-E

1932

Willow Weep for Me(E-F)	V=EM7-A13(2x)-EM7-F#m-G#m-F#m-B7-A9-Am7-F#m7-B7

1934

Santa Claus Is Coming To Town	V=E-E7-A-Am(2x)-E-C#m-F#m7-B7-E7-A(2x)F#7-B-Co-C#m-F#7-B-B+
Corrine, Corrina(D)	V=E-A6-E-B-E

1936

Walkin' Blues(G)	V=E-A-E-B-A-E T/A=E-E7-E6-E+-E5-B
Sweet Home Chicago(E)	V=E-A7(2x)E7-B7-A7-E7-B7
Ramblin' On My Mind(E)	V=E-A7(2x)E-B7-A7-E

1937

Heigh-Ho	V=E-A-F#7-B
Malted Milk(E)	V=E7-A7(2x)E7-B7-A7-E5 T/A=E5-C#7/G#-C7/G-B7
Traveling Riverside Blues(G)	V=E7-A(2x)E7-B7-A7-E7

1938

Good Morning Blues   V=E7-A7-E7-B7-A7-E

Wabash Cannonball   V=E-A-B7-E

1939

In The Mood   V=E-A-E-B7-F#m7
T/A=E-A6-C7-B7-E6

1941

You Are My Sunshine   V=E-E7-A(2x)E-B7-E

God Bless The Child(G)   V=E13-A11(2x)-Bm/E-Bm(M7)/E-Bm7/E-E7b9-AM7-D9+11-G#m7-C#7-F#m7-B7

Boogie Woogie Bugle Boy   V=E-E7-A-E-B7-A7-E

1945

Zip-A-Dee-Doo-Dah   V=E-A(2x)E-F#9-B7

It Might As Well Be Spring   V=E6-A9-G#m7-C#7-F#m7-B7

1946

Let The Good Times Roll   V=E-A7-E-F#m7-B7-E

1947

Move It On Over(E)   V=E-A-E-B-E

Call It Stormy Monday(G)   V=E7-A7-E7-[F7-E7]-A7-E-[F#m7-G#m7-G7]-F#m7-C9
T/A=E7-A7-E7-B+

1948

Tennessee Waltz(F)	V=E-A-E-B-B7
Good Rockin' Tonight(E)	V=E7-A7-E7-A7-B-E-B7

1949

Mona Lisa V=E-A/E-F#m7-B7-F#m-B7-E

1950

Frosty The Snowman V=E-E7-A-E-A-E-B7-E-B7-
E-E7-A-E-A-E-C#m-F#m7-B7-E-
A-E-F#m7-B7-E-
B-Co-C#m7-F#7-B-B7+5

1951

Silver Bells V=E-E7-A-B7-E(2x)
C=E-A-B7(2x)E

Unforgettable V=E-EM7-EoA#-A-AM7-F#9

1952

Some Other Guy(D) V=E7-A7-E7-B7-E7
I=B-D-E7

Your Cheatin' Heart V=E-E7-A-B7-E

1954

That's All Right, Mama(A) V=E-A7-B7-E

1955

I Hear You Knocking(E) V=E-A(2x)B

Ain't That A Shame(Bb) V=E-E6(2x)A-E-A-B7

"E-A" Chord Progressions

Mystery Train(E)	V=E-A/E-A7- E-A/E(4x)A7- E-A/E(4x)B7-A7- E-A/E(4x) I=E-A/E(6x)
I Got A Woman(E)	C=E-A-E-B7-E-A7-E
The Bible Tells Me So	V=E-E7-A-E-B7-E-A-E
Mabellene(Bb)	C=E-A-E-B-E
Rock Around The Clock(A)	V=E-A9-E-B9-E

1956

Don't Be Cruel	V=E-E7-A-E-F#m7-B7-E
Long Tall Sally(G)	V=E-A-E-B7-A7-E-B7
Hound Dog(C)	V=E-A7-E-B7-A7-E
Honey Don't(E)	C=E-A7-E-B7-A7-E
Be Bop A Lula	V=E-A7-E-B7-A7-E
Slippin' And Slidin'(C)	V=E-A7-E-B-A7-E-B
Rip It Up(F)	V=E-A7-E6-A7-E6-B9-E6
Blue Suede Shoes(A)	V=E-A9-E-B9-E
Tutti Fruiti(F)	V=E-E7-A7-E-B7-A7-E
Ready Teddy(C)	V=E7-A9-E-B9-A9-E
Everyday(I Have The Blues)(Bb)	V=E7-A9-E9-B9-A9-E7
Got My Mojo Working(E)	V=E7-A7-E7-B7-A7-E-B

Rollover Beethoven(D)	V=E7-A7(2x)E7-B7-E7-A7-B7-E7
	B=E7-A7-E7-B7-E7
Honky Tonk(E)	V=E7-A7(2x)E7-B7-A7-E7-B7
Heartbreak Hotel(E)	V=E-A7-B7-E7

1957

Peggy Sue(A)	V=E-A(4x)E-B-A
	T/A=E-A-E-B
(Let Me Be Your)Teddy Bear	V=E-A(2x)E-B7-E-A-B7(4x)E
Youngblood	V=E-A(2x)B7#9
I'm Walkin'(Ab)	V=E-A7(2x)E7-B7
Wonderful, Wonderful	V=E6-A6(4x)
Chances Are	V=E7+-A6-E7+-A-Am6-E-G#m7-C#9-C#7
Keep A-Knockin'	V=E-A7-E(2x)
Searchin'(C)	V=E-A-E-B-E
Bony Moronie	V=E-E7-E-A7-E-E7-B-A-B-A-E7-A-E
School Day	V=E-A-E-B-E
	I=B+
Jail House Rock(Eb)	V=E-A7-E-B7-A7-E
	I=D#-E(2x)
Everybody's Trying To Be My Baby(E)	V=E-A-E-B7-A-E
Too Much(A)	V=E-A-E-B7-A7-E

Rock And Roll Music(A)	C=E7-A7-E7-B7-E7-B7-E7 I=B7
Blueberry Hill	V=E7-A-E-B7-E-EM7-E6-E7-A-E-B7-E-D7-E
Lucille(C)	V=E7-A7-E7-B7-A7-E7-B7
Before You Accuse Me(E)	V=E7-A7-E7-B7-A7-E7-B7
I'm A Hoochie Cooche Man	V=E-A-G-E
Words Of Love(A)	V=E-A-B(4x)
Love Is Strange(C)	V=E-A-B
Everyday	V=E-A-B7(2x)E-B7-E-A-E-B7
All Shook Up(Bb)	V=E-A7-B7-E-A7-E I=D#-E
Great Balls Of Fire	V=E-A7-B7-A7-E(2x)
Love Me(F)	V=E-E7-A-B-B7-E-B7
Not Fade Away(E)	V=E-A-D-A-E-A-E(2x)

1958

Lollipop	V=E-A(2x)E-C#m7-F#m7-B7
San Francisco Bay Blues(C)	V=E-A-E-E7-A-E-E7-A-E-C#7-F#7-B7
Johnny B. Goode(Bb)	V=E-A-E-B-E
Rebel 'Rouser(E)	V=E-A-E-B7-E
Good Golly Miss Molly(G)	V=E-A-E-B-A-E O=F9-E9

Oh Boy(A)	V=E-A-E-B7-A-E T/A=E-A-B-E
Dizzy Miss Lizzie(A)	V=E-A-E-B7-A-E-B7
At The Hop	V=E-E7-A-E-B-A-E C=E6-A7-E6-B-A-E O=E-C#m-A-B-E
Rock N' Roll Is Here To Stay	V=E-E7-A-E-B-A-E
Hard Headed Woman(C)	V=E-A7-E-B7-A7-E
The Stroll	V=E6-A7-E6-B7-A7-E6
Rockin' Robin(G)	V=E7-A-E-B9-E I=E-A6-B6
Summertime Blues(E)	V=E-A-B-E
Yakety Yak(G)	V=E-A-B-E
Sixteen Candles	V=E-E7-A-B7-E-B7 I=B7

1959

Lipstick On Your Collar	C=E-A(2x)E-G#7-C#m-G#m-A-E-B7-E
It's Late(A)	V=E-A-E-B
Guitar Boogie Shuffle(E)	V=E-A-E-B7-E
Kansas City(G)	V=E-A-E-B-A-E T/A=E-A-A#-B7 I=E-A9-E-A-A#-B7
Charlie Brown(Bb)	V=E-A-E-B-A-E

Stagger Lee(D)	V=E-A7-E-B-E-B
A Big Hunk O' Love(C)	V=E-E7-A7-E-B7-A7-E
Worried Man Blues	V=E7-A7-E-E7-B7-A7-E
What'd I Say(E)	V=E7-A7-E7-B7-A7-E7-B7
Bad Boy(C)	V=E7-A7-E7-B7-A7-E7-B7
Donna	V=E-A-B(4x)

1960

Teen Angel	V=E-A(3x)B7-E
Theme From "The Andy Griffith Show"	V=E-E/D-A/C#-Am6/C-E-C#m-F#9-B
Chain Gang	V=E-A-E-C#m
New Orleans	V=E-A-E-B7-A7-E
The Twist	V=E7-A7-E-B7-A7-E
Midnight Special(G)	V=E7-A7-E7-B7-A7-E7
The Sky Is Crying	V=E7-A7(2x)E7-B7-A7-E7-B7
Are You Lonesome Tonight?	B=E7-A-F#7-B7

[This is an example of a Tin Pan Ally Commercial Bridge.]

(Meet)The Flintstones	V=EM7-A7-G#m7-C#7b9-F#m7-B11-B7b9
Walking To New Orleans(Db)	V=E-A-B-A-E
Hot Rod Lincoln(E)	V=E7-A7-B7-E7
Will You Love Me Tomorrow	V=E-A-B11-E-B11-G#sus-G#-

	C#m-C#m/C-C#m/B-C#m/A#-A-B11-F#m/E-E

1961

Shop Around	V=E7-A7(4x)F#-B7#9 C=E-A7-E-B
Gee Whiz(F)	V=E-E+/G#-A-Am(2x)-E-C#m-F#m-B(2x)
Michael Row The Boat Ashore	V=E-A-E-G#m-F#m-E-B-E
Cupid	C=E-A-E-B-E-B-E-A-E-B-A7-E
Spanish Harlem	V=E-A-E-B-E
Lion Sleeps Tonight	V=E-A-E-B7(4x) I=E-A-E(2x)
Hello Mary Lou(A)	C=E-A-E-B7-E-G#7-C#m-F#7-B7-E-A-E
I Can't Stop Loving You	C=E7-A-E-B7-E(2x)
Corinna, Corinna	V=E7-A7-E7-B7-E7
Little Sister(E)	C=E-A-E7-B7-C7-B7-E
Crying	V=E-E+-A-Am-E-B
Back Door Man(A)	V=E7-A7-E7-B7-A7-E7
Boys(E)	V=E7-A7-E7-B7-A7-E7-B7
Hideaway(E)	V=E7-A7-E7-B7-A7-E7-B7
I'm Mad(Again)	V=E-A-G-E

"E-A" Chord Progressions

1962

Boom Boom(E)	V=E-A6/E-E(2x)A-D6/A-A-E-A6/E-E-B-E6/B-E-A6-E
Roses Are Red	C=E-E7-A-E-C#m-A-B7-E
The Wanderer(D)	V=E-A-E-B-A-E-B
Let's Go(D)	V=E-A-E-B7-A7-E
Chains(Bb)	V=E-A9-E-B9-A9-E-B
Route 66(A)	V=E6-A9(2x)E6-F#m7-B13-E T/A=E13-D13-B13
Comedy Tonight	V=E-A-B(2x)E-A-D-B7
Surfin' Safari(A)	V=E-A-B(2x)E C=E-A-E-B-A-F#-B
Do You Love Me(D)	V/C=E-A-B7 I=E-A-B7-C#m-B7

1963

Blowin' In The Wind(Bb)	V=E-A(2x)B- E-A-E-C#m-E-A-B- E-A(2x)B
Green Back Dollar	C=E-A(6x)A-B-C#m-B-C#m
Sugar Shack(G)	V=E-A(8x)F#m7-B9(3x)
You Can't Sit Down	V=E-A(2x)E-A7-E-A-E-B7-A7- E-A-E
Walk Like A Man	C=E-A(2x)E-G#m-F#m-B7
Ring Of Fire(G)	V=E-A-E-B-E-A-E-A-E

Little Deuce Coupe(Ab)	V=E-A-E-B-F#m-B-E
Act Naturally(G)	V=E-A-E-B7-E-A-B7-E
You've Really Got A Hold On Me(C)	B=E7-A7-E-B
Green, Green	C=E-A-E-B7(2x)E
Rhythm Of The Rain(E)	V=E-A-E-B(2x)E
Another Saturday Night	V=E-A-E-B(2x)
Dominique	C=E-A-E-B7-E-A-E-A-B-B7-E
It's My Party(A)	C=E-E+-A-Am-E-B7-E
Shut Down(Ab)	V=E-A-E-F#-Am-B-E-B
Surf City(Ab)	C=E-A-E-G-C-D-B
Wipe Out(C)	V=E-A-E-B-A-E-B
Mean Woman Blues	V=E-E7-A7-E-B7-A7-E
Blues With A Feeling(G)	V=E9-A9(2x)E7-B9-A9-E9
Maybe This Time	V=E-E+-E6-E9-A-A+-F#m-A#o-B7
My Boyfriend's Back	V=E-A-B7(6x)
(You're The)Devil In Disguise(F)	V=E-A-B7-E-C#m(4x)A-B-E
If You Want To Be Happy	C=E-E7-A-B7-E-C#m-A-B7-E
Da Doo Ron Run	V=E-A-B-E6(2x)

Ask Me Why(E)	B=E-E+-A-B(2x)E
Louie, Louie(A)	V=E-A-Bm-A
On Broadway	V=E-E11(8x)E-A-A11(3x)A-B

1964

Do Wah Diddy Diddy(E)	V=E-A(4x)E-C#m-A-B
Sha La La(F)	V=E-A(6x)C#m-G#m-F#m-E-C#m-C-B7
Dawn(Go Away)(A)	V=E-A(2x)
There's A Place(E)	V=E-A(2x)E-C#m-B-G#m-A-E-A-C#m
Thank You Girl(D)	V=E-A(2x)E-B7-E-A(3x)E-B7-E-A-B7-A-B7
Glad All Over(D-Eb)	V/C=E-A(8x)
Come A Little Bit Closer(Eb)	V=E-A(3x)B-E-A-B C=E-A-B(2x)A-B
Bread And Butter	V=E-A(6x) C=E-A(5x)E-B7-E
The Way You Do The Things You Do(Eb)	V=E-A(16x)A-D(4)E-A(10x)
I'm Into Something Good(C)	V=E-A(3x)E; A-D(2x)-E-A(2x)B-A-E-A(2x)
Love Me Do(G)	V=E-A(5x)B-A-E(2x)

Bits And Pieces(F)　　　　　V=E-A/C#-E-A-E(7x)

My Boy Lollipop　　　　　　V=E-A6(2x)E-F#m7(2x)B7

Come See About Me　　　　V=E-A6/E(8x)E

She's A Woman(A)　　　　　V=E7-A7(4x)E7-B7-A7-
　　　　　　　　　　　　　E7-A7-E7
　　　　　　　　　　　　　I=B7-A7-E7

Can't They See That She's
Mine(D)　　　　　　　　　V=E7-A7(2x)E7-B7

The Pusher(G)　　　　　　V=E7-E7sus4/6-E7(no3)-
　　　　　　　　　　　　　E7sus4/6-E7(4x)-
　　　　　　　　　　　　　A7-A7sus4/6-A7(no3)-
　　　　　　　　　　　　　A7sus4/6(2x)

The In Crowd　　　　　　　V=E-E11(4x)A-E-
　　　　　　　　　　　　　G#7-C#m-F#7-B-C#m-D

Don't Let The Sun Catch
You Crying(C)　　　　　　V=EM7-AM7(3x)B7

My Bonnie　　　　　　　　V=E-A-E-F#7-B7-
　　　　　　　　　　　　　E-A-E-C#m-F#7-B7-E
　　　　　　　　　　　　　C=E-A-B7-E-A-E-
　　　　　　　　　　　　　E-A-F#7-B7-E-A-E

Dance, Dance, Dance(G)　　C=E-A-E-G#5-A5-B11-B
　　　　　　　　　　　　　V=E-A-B(2x)Riff

Dancing In The Streets(E)　V=E7-A7-E7-G#-C#m7-F#7-
　　　　　　　　　　　　　A-B11-E

Little Children　　　　　　V=E-A-E-D-B7

A Hard Day's Night(G)　　V=E-A-E-Dadd9-D-E(2x)-
　　　　　　　　　　　　　A-B-E-A-E
　　　　　　　　　　　　　I=B7sus4

Song	Progression
Fun, Fun, Fun(Eb)	V=E-A-E-B-E-A
Dead Man's Curve(F#)	V=E-A-E-B-E-A-E-F#m-B-E
Little Old Lady From Pasadena(Eb-F)	V=E-A-E-B-F#7-B-E-C#m-A-F#-D-B C=E-A-E-G-B
Mountain Of Love(E)	V=E-A-E-B7-A-E-B7-E
Nadine(Is That You?)	C=E-A9-E-B7-E V=E-A9-E
If I Fell(D)	B=E9-A-Am-E-B7
Please, Please Me(E)	V=E-A-E-[G-A]-B7-E-A-E-A-F#m-C#m-A-(E-A-B)2x
I Saw Her Standing There(E)	V=E7-A7-E7-B7-E7-A7-C-E7-B7-E7
No Particular Place To Go(G)	V=E-A-E-B-E I=B+
Little Honda(C)	V=E-A-E-B-E-B C=E-A(3x)B
Slow Down(C)	V=E-A-E-B-A-E
GTO	V=E-A-E-B7-A-E-B7
Hi-Heel Sneekers(C)	V=E-A7-E-B7-A7-E
Killing Floor(A)	V=E7-A7-E7-B7-A7-E
Match Box(A)	V=E7-A7-E7-B7-A7-E7
Can't Buy Me Love(C)	V=E7-A7-E7-B7-A7-E7

Money(E)	V=E7-A7-E7-B7-A7-E7-B7
You Can't Do That(G)	V=E7-A7-E7-B7-A7-E7-B7
Hippy Hippy Shake(E)	V=E7-A7-E7-B7-A7-E7-B7
Rock Me Baby(C)	V=E7-A7-E7-B7-A7-E7-B7
Twist And Shout(D)	V=E-A-B7
Time Is On My Side(F)	C=E-A-B(2x)
Dang Me	V=E-A-B(4x)E
Don't Worry Baby(E)	V=E-A-B(2x)F#m-B-G#m-C# I=E-A-B11(2x)
We'll Sing In The Sunshine	V=E-A-B7-F#m-E(2x) C=E-EM7-E7-A-F#m7-B9-E-EM7-E7-A-F#m T/A=E-C#m-F#m-B7
Match Maker	V=E-E+-E6-E+(2x)E-E+-E6-E7-AM7-B11-E-B7b5/9
Goin' Out Of My Head	V=Em7-EM7(2x)AM7-Am7-D9-GM7-Bm7(2x)CM7-D-EM7

1965

Midnight Hour(E)	V=E-A(8x)B-A(2x)
Let's Hang On	C=E-A(3x)D#m-A
Shakin' All Over(E)	V=E-A(2x)E
My Girl(C)	V=E-A6(4x-Riff)
Do You Believe In Magic	V=E-A(4x)F#m7-G#m7-A-B11-E-B11

A Lover's Concerto	V=E-A(2x)B7
Drive My Car(D)	V=E-A(3x)B7
Catch The Wind	V=E-Aadd9(2x)
April Come She Will	V=E-A/E(3x)-E-F#m-C#m-DM7-C#m-A-B-E-C#m-F#m(2x)C#m
I Got You Babe(F-F#)	V=E-A/E-E-A(2x) O=E-A/E-E-B C=E-A/E(3x)
Boy From New York City	V=E-A/E-E7-A/E(4x)-A-D/A-A7-D/A(2x)
I'm Henry VIII I Am(G)	V=E-A-E-F#7-B7
Day Tripper(E)	V=E7(Riff)-A7-E7-F#7-A7-G#7-C#7-B7
On A Clear Day	V=EM7-A9-EM7-G#m7-C#7
All I Really Want To Do	C=E-A-E-C#m-E-A
The Jolly Green Giant	V=E7-A-E7-B7(2x)E7-A-B7
Seventh Son(E)	V=E-A7-E-B-A-E-B7
She's About A Mover	V=E7-A7-E7-B7-[A#7]-A7-E7
One Way Out(A)	V=E7-A7-E7-B7-A7-E7
I Got You(I Feel Good)(D)	V=E7-A7-E7-B7-A7-E9
Wooley Bully(G)	V=E7-A7-E7-B7-A7-E7-B7 I=E7
Seventh Son(E)	V=E-E7-A-E-B7-A-E-B7

Pappa's Got A Brand New Bag(E)	V=E9-A7-E9-B7-A7-E9-B7
Yes It Is(E)	V=E-A-F#m7-B7-E-A-D-B7-C#m-E/B-A-D-C#m-E
Go Now	V=E-EM7-E6-E-AM7-F#m7-B7
I'm Looking Through You(Ab)	V=E-A-F#m7-C#m-B(2x)-C#m-B-F#m-E-A-B-E-A-F#m7-A7-E-A(3x)
I'll Never Find Another You	V=E-A-F#7-B7-E-G#m-A-B
I'm A Man(E)	V=E-A-G-E
Turn, Turn, Turn(D)	I=E-A-G#m-B/F#-E-B7(2x) C=E-A-G#m-B/F#(2x)A-G#m F#m-B7-E
Like A Rolling Stone	C=E-A-B(6x)
It Ain't Me Babe(G)	C=E-A-B(2x)E
King Of The Road	V=E-A-B7(4x)
You Were On My Mind(E)	V=E-A-B(2x)-A-G#m-F#m-B-E-AM7(2x)-E-C#m-A-B
Eve Of Destruction(D)	V=E-A-B(5x) C=E-A-B-E-C#m-A-B-E I=E-Esus-Eadd9
We Gotta Get Out Of This Place(F)	C=E-A-B(3x)C#m-E-D-A-B(4x) V=E-A-B

Song	Progression
It's The Same Old Song(C)	C=E-A-B-F#m-E-B-A(2x)
You've Got To Hide Your Love Away(G)	C=E-A-Bsus-B-Badd9-B(2x)
You're The One(Bb)	C=E-A-B7(2x)E-F#m7
Let's Lock The Door (And Throw Away The Key)	V/C=E-A-B7
Downtown	V=E-EM7-A-B7-E-A-B(2x)-E-C#m(2x)
California Girls(B)	V=E5-E7sus-A5-B5(2x)
Get Off Of My Cloud(E)	V=E-A-B-A(7x)E-A-B C=E-E/G#-A-B-B11(3x)D-B
Down In The Boon Docks	V=E-A-E-C#m-G#7-C#m-F#m7-B7(4x) C=E-A-B-A(2x)G#m-F#m-E
Hang On Sloopy(G)	V=E-A-B-A
Game Of Love	V=E-A-B-A(2x)E-A-F#7-B7
You've Lost That Lovin' Feelin'	B=E-A-B-A-B(4x)E-A-B
I Know A Place	V=E-A6-B6-A6-E-F#-G#-B7 C=E-A-D-B
California Girls(B)	V=E5-E7sus-A5-B5(2x)
(I Can't Get No)Satisfaction(E)	V=E-A/C#-D-A/C#(6x)E C=E-A(2x)E-B7-E-A
Rescue Me(A)	V=E-A-D-Bm(2x)E C=E-A(3x)A-A/G#-A/F#-A/E-B7

Heart Of Stone(C)   V=E-E7-A-[D]-A-F#-B-C#m-A-B-[E]-B

1966

Ain't Too Proud to Beg(C)	V=E-A(3x)E-B11 C=E-A(8x)
Born Free	V=E-A(2x)G#m-F#m7-B7-E
Substitute(D)	V=E-A(2x)F#m-B
Knock On Wood(E)	C=E-A(2x)E-G-A-B-D-B
Rain(G)	V=E-A(3x)E C=E-A/E-E
The Pied Piper(B)	V=E-A(4x)F#m-B C=E-A(2x)E-F#m-B
I Fought The Law(G)	V=E-A-E(2x)E-B7-E
These Boots Are Made For Walkin'	V=E-A-E
She's Just My Style(A)	C=E-A/E(2x)D-B
96 Tears(G)	V=E-A7(18x)C#m-A
Hold On! I'm Comin'(Ab)	V=E7-A7
Season Of The Witch	V=E7-A7(10x)A7-B7-E7(3x)
Last Train To Clarksville	V=E-A7(2x)B-E
Paperback Writer(G)	V=E7-A-E7(2x)
Don't Bring Me Down(C)	V=E7-A7sus4-A7(4x)
19th Nervous Breakdown(E)	V=E-E11(10x)-E-A-E-E11(3x)-E-

"E-A" Chord Progressions

	Bsus-B(2x)-A
I Am A Rock	V=E-A/E-E-F#m-B7-A-E-F#m7-G#m7(2x)F#m-A-B-A C=E-A-B7-E-C#m
She's A Must To Avoid	V=E-A-E-F#m7-B7
What Now My Love	V=E-A6/E-E6-F#m/E-B7-EM7-E6-F#m7/B
You Can't Hurry Love	V=E-A-E-G#m-C#m7-A-B7
Trains And Boats And Planes	V=E-A-E-C#m
Did You Ever Have To Make Up Your Mind	V=E-A-E-C#m-E
I Saw Her Again Last Night(A)	V=E-A-E-C#m-E-A-E-D-C#7-F#-B-E-G#7-C#m-B7b9-E-B I=Bsus
Cabaret	B=E-Am-E-C#m-C#m(M7)-C#m7-F#9-B7
Cheater	V=E-A-E-[F#m-G#m-A]-B(2x)
Cloudy	V=E-AM7-A-E-EM7-Eo-B7 G#m-B-C#m
Mellow Yellow	V=E-A-E-B7-[A#7]-A7-B7
Barbara Ann(F#)	V=E-A-E-B-A-E
Hanky Panky(A)	V=E-A-E-B-A-E-B7
Mean Old World(Bb)	V=E-A-E-A7-E-B7-A-E-B
Barefootin'	V=E-A7-E-B7-A7-E

C.C. Rider(A)	V=E7-A7-E7-B7-A7-E7
Mustang Sally(C)	V=E7-A7-E7-B7-A7-E7-B7
Wouldn't It Be Nice(F)	V=E-A-A/G#-F#m-B7(2x)
Get Ready	V=E-A-G(6x)
Dandy	V=E-A-G#m-F#m
Oh How Happy(A)	C=E-A-G#m-F#m-E-A-G#m F#m-E
The Impossible Dream	V=EM9-E(2x)AM9-A(2x)-G#m-G#m7-A6-F#m-B7
Good Lovin'(D)	V=E-A-B-A(8x)E-A(4x)E-F#-B C=E-A-B-A(4x)E-A-B
Wild Thing(A)	V=E-A-B-A(3x)E-A-B-A11/E-E-A11/E-E(4x)
You Baby(B)	C=E-A-B-A(4x)E
(You're My)Soul And Inspiration	C=E-A-B(3x)C#m7-B-A-E/G#-D/F#-F#m/B-B7-B=E-A-B-A
Reason To Believe(G)	V=E-A-B7-E-F#-B-A-E
Little Girl(E)	V=E-A-D-G-A(2x)
Dirty Water(A)	V=E-A-D-A(4x)A-D-G-A(2x)-E-A-D-A(2x)B7-A#7-A7
Cherry, Cherry	V=E-A-D-A
I Got The Feelin'(Oh No No)(E)	V=E-A-D-A(5x)
Michelle(F)	V=E-Am7-D6-A#o-B-A#o-B(2x)

1967

Darling Be Home Soon	V=E-A(2x)E-A-E-F#m-E
Respect(C)	C=E-A(2x)
Hey Baby(They're Playin' Our Song)	V=E-A(2x)G#m7-F#m7-B7
Pretty Ballerina	V=E-A(3x)E-Bm-A-D-G-B-A-E
Jimmy Mack	V=E-A(3x)
Kentucky Woman	V=E-A(2x)B
Go Where You Wanna Go	V=E-A(7x)E-B-C#m-A-B
Silence Is Golden	V=E-A(2x)B7- E-B7(2x)
Gimme Some Lovin'	V=E-A/E(8x) I=E-E11-A/E-E11-A/E-E7
For What It's Worth(E)	V=E-A-A7(4x)E-D-A-A7
Mercy, Mercy, Mercy(A)	V=E-E7-A7(4x) C=E-A/E-E7-A/E(2x)
Baby, I Need Your Loving(Bb)	V=E-AM7(7x)
Get On Up(A)	V=E-A11(8x)
Lucy In The Sky With Diamonds(A)	V=E-E/D-E/C#-E+/C- E/B-E/D-E/C#-E+/C(2x)- E/B-E/D-E/C#- Am-Am/G-F-G-C-F-G-D-A
Don't You Care(E)	C=E+-A-Am-EM7-F#m7-EM7

98.6	V=E-A-E-F#7-A-B7-E-A-Am-F#m7-B7 C=E-E11(3x)A-Am6-E-E11(3x)A-Am6-E/B-A#o-F#m7-B7 T/A=GM7-CM7-FM7-F#m7-B7
Can't Take My Eyes Off Of You(E)	V=E-EM7-E9-A-Am6-E-F#/E-Am6/E-E
Baby You're A Rich Man(E)	V=E-A/E-E7-E-Dadd9/E-D-E-A
Love Me Two Times(E)	V=E-A-A7-E-D7sus2-C7-G-D7sus2-C7-B7-E
Green Green Grass Of Home	V=E-E7-A-E-B7-F#m7-B7-E-E7-A-G#m7-F#m7-E-B7-F#m-B7-E C=E-E7-A-F#m7-E-B7-F#m7-B7-E-B7
Brown Eyed Girl(G)	V/C=E-A-E-B7
Sunday Will Never Be The Same	C=E-A-E-B7-E-A-D-B7sus-B7
Creeque Alley(B)	V=E7-A7-E7-B7-A7-E7-A7-G7-E7
Shake, Rattle, And Roll(E)	V=E-A-E-B7-A-E
(Your Love Keeps Lifting Me) Higher And Higher(D)	V=E-A/E-F#m/E-E
She'd Rather Be With Me(B-C)	C=E-E7-A-F#-D-B-E-[C7-B7]
Little Bit O' Soul(G)	V=E-A-B-E(8x)
Release Me	V=E-A-B7-E-B7

I Second That Emotion	V=E-A-B7-E
Carrie Anne(C)	C=E-A-B-E-A-B7(2x)
The Tracks Of My Tears(G)	V=E-A-B-E-A-[G#m-F#m]-E(2x) C=E-A-B(3x)E-A(3x)E
Expressway To Your Heart(F#)	V=E-E/G#-A-B(4x)A-A/C#-D-E-(2x)E-E/G#-A-B(2x)- G#m-F#m(3x)G#m-A-B C=E-E/G#-A-B(4x)C#m-C#m/B-C#m/A-C#m/G#(2x)
How Can I Be Sure(D)	V=Em-Em(M7)-Em7-Em6-Am6-B7-Am6-B7(2x)- G#m7-C#m7-F#m7-B7(2x)- GM7-Em-Am7-Am6-E
Lovely Rita(E)	V=E-A-D-G-E-B(2x) T/A=E-C#m-F#m-B
Thank The Lord For The Night Time(E)	V=E-A-D-A(6x)
I Was Made To Love Her(F)	V=E-Am7-D7sus2-C-D-E

1968

Lady Madonna(A)	V=E-A(3x)C-D-E
Revolution(A)	V=E-A(2x)B11- F#m-B-F#m-D-E-C#-B C=E-A(3x)B
I Feel Like I'm Fixin' To Die Rag(E)	V=E-A(2x)F#-Bm-E-A
Master Jack(B)	C=E-A(3x)B-E
Quinn The Eskimo	V=E-A(6x)E-B-A-E

Cry Like A Baby(D)	V=E-A/E(6x)E A-B-A-E-G#
I Wonder What She's Doing Tonight	V=E-A6(7x)D-E C=E-A-D-A-E
On The Way Home	V=E-AM7-E(2x)A-E-A-G#m7- F#m7-B7-D-A-GM7
Itchykoo Park	C=E-E7-A(3x)E-C#m(3x)
Love Child	V=E-E7-A-E-E7-A-E-G#m/D#- E7-A-C-E/B
Tighten Up(F#)	V=EM7-AM9/B
Sky Pilot(Bb)	C=E-A-E(2x)F#m-E(2x)
Dance To The Music	V=E-A-E
Mony, Mony(A)	V=E-A-E(3x)A-B
Both Sides Now(E)	V=E-A/E-E-EM7-A- E-A-F#m7-B
Harper Valley P.T.A.	V=E-EM7-E6-EM7-E7-A7- E-EM7-E6-EM7-E-E7-A7- B7-E
Mac Arthur Park	B=E-EM7-AM7-A6-Ao-E-EM7- AM7-D#m7b5-G#m7-C#7- F#m7-F#m7/B-B7b9-EM7-E- AM7-DM7-F#m7/B-B7
Turn Around, Look At Me	V=E-A-E-F#m7-F#m6-B7
Ain't Nothing Like The Real Thing(Eb)	C=E-EM7-[A-E-F#m-E]- AM7-F#m7(2x)

"E-A" Chord Progressions

	T/A=E-E/D#-C#m7-B11
Hooked On A Feeling	V=E-EM7-E7-A-Am-E-F#m7-B7-E-C#m-E7-A-E-G#m-A-B7-E-G#m-F#m7-B7
Yer Blues(E)	V=E-A7-E-G-B7 T/A=E-A-E/B-B7
Mother Nature's Son(D)	V=E-A/E-E-C#m-C#m7-C#m6-C#m/F#- B-E/B(4x)E-Em7-A/E-E(2x)
Do You Know The Way To San Jose	V=E-A6-E-B7sus-B7
I Wish It Would Rain(Bb)	V=E-A-E-B-A-E-B
Why Don't We Do It In The Road?(D)	V=E7-A7-E7-B7-A7-E7
Paying The Cost To Be The Boss(B)	V=E9-A9(2x)E9-B9-A9-E9-B9
Hey Jude(F)	C=E7-A-A/G#-F#m-F#m/E-B7/D#-B7-E(2x)
Back In The USSR(A)	V=E-A-G-A(2x)E-G-A-E T/A=F#7-B7
Angel Of The Morning	V=E-A-B-A(4x)F#m-A-B(2x) C=E-A-B-A-B
Piece Of My Heart(E)	V=E-A-B-A(2x)E-A-B7- C#m-B-D-B- F#m7-B7(4x) C=E-A-B(3x)A-G#m-F#m-E
Elenore	V=Em-Am9-B7-Em- [C-B7]-Em-Am9-B7-Em

Suzie Q(E)	V=E(riff)-A-C-B-E
This Guy's In Love With You	V=E-AM7-DM7-E-AM7-G#7sus-G#7 B=E-AM7(2x)E

1969

Put A Little Love In Your Heart	V=E-A(2x)E
Get Back(A)	V=E-A(2x)E C=E-E7(2x)A-E-D/E-A/E
And When I Die(A)	V=E-A(6x)B-A-E-(D-A)2x B11-F#m-G#m-A-B-(E-A)4x
Holly Holy	V=E-A(4x)A6-AM7-A-E
Take A Letter Maria	V=E-A(4x)E
You Can't Always Get What You Want(C)	V=E-A(4x) C=E-A(2x)F#-A-(E-A)2x
Sugar, Sugar	V=E-A(3x)B-E-A-B
Every Day People	V=E-A/E
In The Ghetto	V=E-A/E-E(2x)G#m7-A-B-E-A/E-E(2x)
Memories	V=EM7-A-EM7-AM7-EM7-A-EM7-G-GM7-G11-CM7-C6-CM7-Am7-F#m7-B7-EM7-AM7
Take Me To The Pilot	V=E-E11-A/E-E-E/D-[A/C#]-E-E11-A-E7-A/E-G-A-C-Bm-E-D-C-G-E C=E-E7/G#-A-B11-E(4x)

"E-A" Chord Progressions

I Can't Get Next To You	V=E5-A-Am
Honky Tonk Woman(Open G)	V=E-A-Asus-A-E-F#-B- E-A-E5-B-E C=E-B-E- E-B7-E
Polk Salad Annie	V=E-A-(E-G)2x E
Can't Find My Way Back Home(D)	V=E/D-A/C#-Am/C-E/B-G-A-E- (2x)
Lodi(Bb)	V=E-A-E-C#m-A-B
The Worst That Could Happen	V=E-A-E-C#m-A-B7-E-F#m7/B- B7-E-C#m-G-B11 C=E-A-B-A-Am-E-C#m6-D#m7- C#m7-B9-B11-E
Oh Happy Day	V=E-A-E-C#7-F#7- B7-F#7(2x)B7-E
Sweet Caroline(A)	V=E-A-E-B
Someday We'll Be Together	V=E-E7-A-A#o-E-B
Going Up Country(Bb)	V=E-A-E-B-E
Son Of A Preacher Man(E)	V=E-A-E-B7 C=E-A-E(2x)B-A
Ballad Of John And Yoko(E)	V=E-E7-A-E-B7-E
Suite: Judy Blue Eyes (E Modal: Open Tuning)	V=E5-A5-E5-Bsus-A5-A7sus(2x)- E5-Bsus-A5-A7sus-E5-A5-E5 V5=E11-E(3x)A/E-E7(no3)- E11-E6 B=E-Esus(3x)E-A5-A7sus-

	Esus-E(2x)
Crossroads(A)	V=E-A(2x)E-B-A-E
Two Of Us(G)	V=E-A-A/G#-F#m7(2x)-E-B-A(2x)E-A-E
Something(C)	V=E-EM7-E7-A-A/G#-F#7-B-B/D#-C#m-C#m(M7)/C-C#m/B-F#9/A# T/A=A-G-B/F#-E
SWLABR(D)	V=E-E7sus4/6-E-[A-G](3x)
Rain Drops Keep Fallin' On My Head	V=E-EM7-E7-A-(G#m7-C#7)2x-F#m7-B7sus-B
Laughing(A)	V=E-E+-E6-E7-AM7-Am7-G#m7-B
Galveston	V=E-A-B-E-EM7-E7-A-F#m7-B-E-A-F#m7-B-C#m-A-F#m7-E-A-B
Israelite	C=E-A-B-E-G
Dizzy	V=E-A-B-A(3x)
Suspicious Minds	V=E-A-B-A-E-A-E-A-B-A-[B-A-G#m-B7]-A-E-G#m-A-B-C#m-G#m-A-B-B7
Na, Na, Hey, Hey Kiss Him Goodbye(C)	V=E-A6-B(2x)E-C#m-F#m-B-A-G#-C#m-F#-E-A-Am-E
Love(Can Make You Happy)	C=E-A-B7(4x)E-B7
Ruby, Don't Take Your	

Love To Town	V=E-A-B7(2x)A-B7 C=E-A-B7- E-F#m-A(2x)B7
49 Bye-Byes	V=E-A-D-E-E-A-D-A-C#m7-E-B-E
My Cherie Amour(C#)	V=EM7-Asus-DM7-Bsus-B(2x)

1970

Cecilia	V=E-A(2x)E-B- A-E(3x)B
She Came In Through The Bathroom Window(A)	V=E-A(3x)E-Am(2x)- D7-G(2x)E
Montego Bay	V/C=E-A(4x)
Woodstock(G)	V=E5-A(2x)E5
Up On Cripple Creek(A)	V=E-A-E-A-B(2x) C=E-A-B-C#m-D
I've Got A Feeling(A)	V=E-A/E(8x)E7-B-D-A
Bridge Over Troubled Water	V=E-A/E-E-A-D/A-A- E-A(3x)E-B/D#-C#m-B-B9
A Rainy Night In Georgia	V=EM7-A(2x)EM7-C#m-G#m
I Just Can't Help Believin'	V=E-EM7-A6/E-B11-E- E-EM7-Bm/E-A/E-Am/E C=E-A/E(2x)E-AM9/E-Am9/B-E
Love The One You're With(C)	V=E-A/E-E-F#m/E(4x)
All Right Now(A)	V=E5-A/E-E5-Aadd4/E-A/E-E5
The Long And Winding Road(Eb)	B=E/B-A-E/G#-F#m-B7(2x)

Love Grows	V=E-A-E-G#m-C#m-E-A-B
Who'll Stop The Rain	V=E-A-E-G#m-A-E
Teach Your Children(D)	V/C=E-A5-E-B
Spirit In The Sky(A)	V=E-A-E-B I=E-A-G-E-G-A
Solitary Man(G)	C=E-A-E-B-A-E-B-C#m-B-C#m-B
Travelin' Man(F#)	V=E-A-E-B-A-B-E
Hi-De-Ho	V=E-A9-E-B7- E-A7-(E-A9)3xE C=E-A9(8x)
In The Summertime(E)	V=E-E7-A-E-B7-E
One After 909(B)	V=E7-A7-E7-B7-E7
Cracklin' Rosie	V=E-A-F#m-B7
We've Only Just Begun	V=E-AM7-G#m7-C#m7-F#m7- C#m7-F#m7-B11 B=EM7-AM7(2x)
Walk A Mile In My Shoes	C=E-A-B-E
Hitchin' A Ride	V=E-A-B(2x)E- A6-B-E(2x)
Roadhouse Blues(E)	V=E7-A7-B-C-B-E7
Come And Get It(E)	V=E-A-B7(2x)- C-Em-F-Em-B7- E-A-B7-E
Your Song	V=E-AM7-B/D#-G#m- C#m-C#m/B-C#m/A#-A-

	E/B-B-G#/C-C#m- E-F#m7-A-B-Bsus-B I=E-A/E-B/E-A/E
Mama Told Me Not To Come	C=E-E7/G#-A-C(3x)
Tears Of A Clown(C#)	V=E-A-D-A(10x)
Lola(E)	V=E-A-D-E-A(2x)D-C-D-E

1971

Just My Imagination(C)	V=E-A
Do You Know What I Mean	V=E-A(2x)E-B-A-E
I Don't Know How To Love Him	V=E-A(3x)E-B(3x)G#m7-C#m
Day After Day	V=E-A-E(2x)B-F#-A-E-A-E- B-F#-A-E
Domino(A)	V=E-A-E-A6 C=E-A(12x)F#m-B- E-A6(2x)
Baby Don't Get Hooked On Me	V=E-A/E(4x)G#m-G#m7
Tiny Dancer	V=E-A/E(2x)E-A/C#- E-A/E(2x)E-A/C#-EM7/B- AM7-G#m7-C#m7-F#7/A#- F#m7-G#m7-C#m7-B7
The Night They Drove Old Dixie Down(C)	C=E/B-A(4x)E/B-C#m- Bsus-A-E/G#-E
Country Roads(Drop D)	V=E-E11-A/E(2x)- F#m7-B7(3x)C#m7-E11-E-E11-A/E
Imagine(C)	V=Eadd9-EM7-A/E(4x)-

	A/G#-A/F#-A/E-B-E/B-B7
Does Anybody Really Know What Time It Is?	C=EM7-A(4x)
One Toke Over The Line	V=E-E7-A-E-G#m/D#-C#m-F#7-A-B-E(2x)
Brown Sugar(C)	V=E-A-E-D-E
Puppet Man	V=E7-A7-E7-B7-A7-E7-C#b9-F#7-B7b9-E
So Far Away	V=EM9-E6(2x)AM7-A6-F#m7-B11
You've Got A Friend	C=E-EM7-A-F#m7-B7sus4-E-B7sus4-E-EM7-A-F#m7-A-G#m7-F#m7-B7sus4-E-A-B11-E-D#m7-G#7
Changes(C)	C=E-E/D#-E/C#-E/B-A-A/G#-F#-B-A-E-E/D#-E/C#-E/B-A-A/G#-F#-B-A/C#-E/B-D-A-E/G#-B/F#-A/C#-E
Never Can Say Goodbye(D)	V=EM7-E11(3x)AM7-F#m7
Bitch(A)	V=E-A-G
Mr. Big Stuff	C=E-A-B6(2x)
I Am I Said	V=E-A-B7(2x) C=E-A-G#m-F#m-E
Truckin'(E)	C=E-A-B-A-E
Me And You And A Dog Named Boo	V=E-E7-A-Bsus-B
Here Comes The Sun(A)	V=E-A-B7-B7sus4-B7(2x) C=E-A-F#7-E

How Can You Mend A Broken Heart(E)	C=EM7-A/E-(A-B)2x-F#m7-B6-B7-E
Joy To The World(D)	V=[D-D#]-E(3x)-E7-A-C-E-B7-E-A7-B7-E
Ask Me No Questions(A)	V=E7-A7-C7-E-C#7#9-F#m7-B11 T/A=E-E7/G#-A-C/A#-E/B-B7

1972

Anticipation	V=E-A(2x)F#m7-Bsus-B I=E-E7sus-E
Rocket Man	C=E-A(2x)E/G#-F#7-A-E-A
I Can See Clearly Now	V=E-A(2x)B-E-A-E-(D-A-E)2x
Help Me Make It Through The Night	V=E-A(2x)F#m-B7-E-A B=E-A-E-F#7-B7
Bang A Gong(E)	V=E-A(4x)E
Garden Party(D)	V=E-A(2x)-E-E/D#-C#m-C#m/B-A-B
Operator (That's Not The Way I Feel)(G)	C=E-A/E-E-A-B
Feelin' Alright(C)	V=E7-A7
Listen To The Music(E)	V=E-A/E-E-C#m-B-A-A7sus-E B=E-E11-A(2x)
Diary	V=EM7-E11-A6/E-E(2x)
American Pie	C=E-A-E-B(3x)C#m-F#7-C#m-B7

Everything I Own	V=E-E/D#-E/C#-E/B-A-Am-E/B-Bsus-B(2x)F#m-A-B(2x)
Never Been To Spain(G)	V=E-A(2x)E-B-A-E
Reelin' And Rockin'	V/C=E-A7-E-B7-A7-E
Salvation	V=E-EM9-A-G#m-A(2x)
It's Going To Take Some Time	V=E-E11(2x)AM7-G#m7(3x)-C#m-F#m7-B11
Me And Julio Down By The School Yard(A)	V=E-A-B-E I=E-A6-E-B
Brandy(E)	V=E-A-B-C#m7-F#m7-A-D-A-E-A-B-C#m7-F#m7-B11-E
Burning Love	V=E-A-B(4x)E
My Ding A Ling(G)	V/C=E-A-B(2x)E
The Guitar Man	V=E-A-B(2x)C#m-A-C#m-F# AM7-G#m7-F#m7-B
Summer Nights	V=E-A-B-A(2x)E-A-B-C#
You Don't Mess Around With Jim(E)	V=E5-A5-B5-A5-B5-A5-E
Good Time Charlie's Got The Blues	V=E-A6-A-B7-E(2x)F#m-B7-E
Goodbye To Love	V=E-A/E-B/E-E-B/E-A/E-B/E-G#sus4-G#-C#m
Suffragette City(A)	C=E-A-C-G-D(2x)E
Where Is The Love	C=E-E7-A6-D7-G6-CM7-B7sus E-G7-CM7-B7sus-E-G-C-B7sus

1973

Song	Progression
Ramblin' Man(G)	V=E-A(2x)B-A
Loves Me Like A Rock	V=E-A(2x)E-A7-E-A-E
Peaceful Easy Feeling(E)	V=E-A(3x)B7 I=E-Esus(4x)
Walk On The Wild Side(C)	V=E-A6(2x)E-F#-A6
Ramblin' Man(G)	V=E-A6(2x)B6-B-A-E-C#m-A-E-B6-E
You Are The Sunshine Of My Life(B)	C=EM7-A6/9(3x)D#m7b5-G#7(#9/b13)-G#9-C#M7-F#6/9-C#m7-F#9(no3)-B11
Desperado(G)	V=E-E7/9-A-Am6-E-C#m-F#7-B7
Delta Dawn	C=E-A-E-B E-A-E-B-A/E-E
Photograph	V=E-A-E-B-G#-C#m-G#-C#m-B
Stuck In The Middle With You(D)	V=E-A7-E-B7-D-A-E
Steam Roller	V=E-A7(2x)E-B7-A7-E-B7
Your Mama Don't Dance	V=E-A7(2x)E-B7-A7-E
Kodachrome	V=E-EM7-E7-E7#9-A-F#m-B7-E-F#m-B7
Touch Me In The Morning	V=Eadd9-EM7-Aadd9-A-F#m7/B
Rocky Mountain Way(E)	V=E-A-G-E I=E11-E(2x)

Bodhisattva(G)   V=E-A-E-CM7-F#7#5-Bm7-D6-CM7-D6-E

1974

Sunshine On My Shoulders(Bb)   V=E-A(6x)F#m7-B-B7-E-A(8x)-E-F#m7-E/G#-A-E-F#m-G#m-A-E-F#m7-G#m-F#m7-B-B7

Please Come To Boston   V=E-A(2x)B7-E-C#m-A-E-B7-E

Rock Me Gently   V=E-A

Jet(A)   V=E-A/E(2x)E-G#m7-F#m-A6-E

Longfellow Serenade   V=E-A/E-E-A-E-A

Junior's Farm   V=E-A/E-E-D-C#m

You Make Me Feel Brand New(E)   V=E-Am/E(2x)E-C#m9-F#7-F#m7/B-B7

I've Got The Music In Me   V=E7-A7-E(2x)
C=E-A-G-E(2x)

Ease On Down The Road   V=E7#9-A7(3x)

Band On The Run(C)   V=E-AM7(2x)G#m-B-E-G#m-E-C#m-AM7-E-AM7
C=E-AM7(8x)

Tin Man(G)   V=EM7-AM7(4x)-F#m9-EM7(4x)B11-B7
C=EM7-AM7(4x)

The Best Of My Love(C)   V=EM7/B-E(2x)AM7#11-AM7-(2x)EM7-E-A-G#m7-F#m7-G#m7-A-EM7-E-AM7-EM7-

"E-A" Chord Progressions

	E-B-B7-B6-B7
Katmandu	V=E5-A-E5-B
One Hell Of A Woman	V=E7-A-Am-(E-Bm7)2x
Spiders And Snakes	V=E7-A7(2x)E7-B7-A7-E7
I Won't Last A Day Without You	C=E-E11-Aadd9-F#m7-B11
It's Only Rock 'N' Roll (But I Like It)(E)	V=E-A-G-E(2x)
Free Man In Paris(A)	V=Eadd9-A/E-G/D-D-Cadd9(2x)-Eadd9
Then Came You(F)	V=E-A/E-[E-F#-G]-G#m-C#m7-[E/G#-A-B]-A-E/G#-F#m7-F#m7/B-B
Back Home Again(E)	V=E-A-B7-E-E7-A-B7-E
Beach Baby	C=E-A-B(2x)E-B7
The Promised Land(C)	V=E-A-B(3x)E
The Joker(G)	V=E-A-B-A(8x) C=E-A(3x)B-A
I Can Help	V=E-E6(4x)A-A6(2x)E-E6(2x)-B-Dsus4-A-B
Anne's Song(D)	V=E-Esus-A-B-C#m-A-E-G#m/D-C#m-B-A-G#m-F#m-A-B
Laughter In The Rain	V=E-A6/E-B(2x)E-C#m7-F#7sus4-F#7-B7sus4-B7

1975

Feel Like Makin' Love(D)	V=E-A(8x) C=[D]-E-[D]-E-A-E-[D]-E-[D]-E-D-A-E
Send In The Clowns	V=E-A/E(2x)E-AM9-B/E-A/E
Calypso	V=E-A6(2x)E-E11
Wildfire	V=E-EM7-A(2x)AM7-G#m(2x)-F#m-G#m
Another Somebody Done Somebody Wrong Song	V=E-EM7-E7-A-E-F#m-B7-E
Jive Talkin'(C)	V=E-A-E-D-E
Thank God I'm A Country Boy	V=E-A-E-D-B-E-A-E-B-E
Sweet Emotion(A)	V=E5-A-E(7x)E5 C=E-E5
I'll Play For You	V=EM7-A/E(9x)E C=E-EM7-E7-A-E-F#m/B-G#m/B-F#m/B-E
Some Kind Of Wonderful (Eb)	V=E-A7-E-B7-A-E C=E-A(3x)E
Lyin' Eyes(G)	V=E-EM7-A-F#m-B7 C=E-A/E(2x)E-B/D#-C#m-G#m-F#m-B7-E-E11-A-F#7-F#m7-B
Born To Run(E)	V=E-A-B(2X)A-C#m/G#-F#m-C#m/G#-E-E11-A-C#m/G#-F#m-C#m/G#-E-C#m7-E/A-Bsus I=E-Esus-E-A/C#-Bsus(2x)

When Will I Be Loved(B)	V=E-A-B(4x)
Rock 'N' Roll(I Gave You The Best Years Of My Life)	V=E-A-B7(2x)E-C#7-F#m-A-B7
Look In My Eyes Pretty Woman	C=E-A-B-E-G-A-B
Big Yellow Taxi(E)	C=E5-EM7(no3)-E6sus4-E-Eadd9/sus4-E-A-B-E
You Are So Beautiful	V=E-EM7-E7-AM7-D9-E
Good Lovin' Gone Bad	V=E-A-D(2x)E-A
Your Gold Teeth II	V=E-A-D-C#m-G#m-C#m7-F#-A-D-E

1976

You Sexy Thing	V/C=E-A
Don't Go Breaking My Heart	V=E-A/E-E-A-E-B-A-F#7
Take It To The Limit(B)	V=E-A(2x)E-G#7-C#m-B-B/A
Squeeze Box(G)	V=E-A(8x)E- B-Bsus(4x)B- A-Asus(4x)A- B-Bsus(2x)B- A-Asus(2x)A- E-A(4x)E
Dream Weaver	C=E-E7/G#-A(7x)
Tonight's The Night(B)	V=E-AM7(4x) T/A=DM7-B7-A/C#-B/D#
Stand Tall	V=E-E+-E6-E7-AM7-Am-E-A(2x)
All By Myself	V=E-Am/E-E-Bm/D-C#sus-

	C#7-F#m-Am6-E-F#m7b5-B
Theme From Mahogany	V=E-A-F#m-G#7-C#m-C#m/E-F#m6/A-G#7-C#
Slow Ride(A)	C=E-A-G-E
Rock And Roll All Night(G)	C=E-A-B(2x)
Got To Get You Into My Life(G)	C=E-A-B-E
Still The One	V=E-A-B-A-B C=E-A-C#m7-F#7-A-B-E
Closer To You	C=E-A/E-B/E-E-A(3x)-E-A/E-B/E-E-C11
December 1963	V=E-A-B7-E-A-B
More Than A Feeling	C=E-A-C#m-B(3x)-E-A-C-C#m7-F#sus-F#(2x)E-B/D#-C#m7
Still Crazy After All These Years	V=E-E7/G#-A-D7-E-D#o-G#sus-G#7

1977

Car Wash	V=E7-A7
Maybe I'm Amazed(D)	C=E-EM7-E7-A-EaddG(-10)-E-EM7-E7-A-E/G#-Em/G-F#m7-B7
Dancing Queen	V=E-A-E-C#m
How Deep Is Your Love	C=EM7-AM7-Am6-E-Bm/D-C#7-F#m7-Am6-E T/A=G#m7-B11
I Just Want To Make Love	

To You(A)	V=E7-A5-G5(6x)E7-D-D#
Tomorrow(from "Annie")	V=E-EM7-AM7-G#m7-C#m
Blinded By The Light(E)	V=E-A-B7(4x)
Don't Give Up On Us	V=E-E/D#-A-B/A-G#m-C#m7-A-E/G#
Lido Shuffle(G)	V=E-A-B-A-B I=E-[G]-A-[A#]-B-A-[D-G]

1978

Kiss You All Over	V=E-A
Desiree	V=E-A/E(2x)E-B
Lay Down Sally(A)	V=E7-A(2x)B C=E-A-B(2x)E-E7
Hot Blooded(G)	V=E-Esus-E-A-Asus(3x)-B-Bsus(2x)B
Come Sail Away	C=E-A/E-Eadd9-A/E(4x)
I Love The Nightlife	C=E-EM7-E7-A-Am6(2x)
Two Out Of Three Ain't Bad	V=E-EM7-A-E-EM7-C#m-A-B
Hot Leggs(G)	V=E-A-E-B-A-E
Macho Man	V=E-A-E-B7(2x)E
The Gambler	V=E-A/E-E-B-E-A/E C=E-A(2x)
Too Much, Too Little, Too Late	V=E-AM7-G#m7-C#7sus4-C#7
Even Now	V=Eadd9-AM7-G#m7-F#m7-EM7

Sometimes When We Touch	V=E-A/E-B/E-E-G#m-C#m-F#-B
You Needed Me	V=E-A/E-B7/E-E-G#m-Asus-A-F#7-Bsus-B
With A Little Luck(E)	V=E-E/G#-A-B11(2x)C#m7 I=B11-E-B11-A/D-C#m7-B7sus
Short People	V=E-E/D-A/C#-C7
Bluer Than Blue	V=E-E7-A-D11
Hollywood Nights	V/C=E5-A/E-D/E-E5

1979

Lonesome Loser	V=E-A/E-Em7-A/E-E-A/E-Em7-A-C#sus-C#
Forever In Blue Jeans	V=E-A-E-F#m-G#m-B-E
Bad Case Of Loving You	C=E5-A-E5-B7-E5-D5/E-E5
She Believes In Me	V=E-E7/G#-A-[E/G#]-F#m7-B7 B/A-G#m7-C#m7-F#m7-B7sus-B7
My Sharona	V=E5-A-G(2x)E5
Old Time Rock And Roll	V/C=E-A-B-E
My Life(D)	V=E-E/G#-A-B-E-A/E-E
What I Like About You(E)	V/C=E-A-D-A(4x)

1980

I Can't Tell You Why	V=EM7-AM7(2x)G#7sus4
Shining Star	C=E-AM7(4x)B11

Driving My Life Away	V=E-A-E(2x)
You Shook Me All Night Long(G)	C=E5-Aadd9-E/G#-B5-Aadd9-E/G#
Lost In Love	V=Eadd9-E(2x)AM9-A6(2x)-F#m9-F#m7(2x)Eadd9-E(2x)
Déjà vu	V=EM7-A11-G#m7-C#m11
Never Knew Love Like This Before	V=E-A-B/D#-G#m-C#m-F#m7-B11
Hey Nineteen	V=E-A-B7b9-E-A-B
Little Jeannie	V=E-A/E-B/D#-C#m-D/A-A
Hit Me With Your Best Shot(E)	C=E-A-C#m-B(2x)A-B

1981

Watching The Wheels	V=E-A(3x)F#m-B-A-F#m-B
Start Me Up(C)	V=E-A/E(2x)D
Every Woman In The World	V=E-AM7(2x)F#m7-B11-G#m7-C#m-F#m-F#m7-B11 C=EM7-EM7/G#-AM7-F#m7-B11-EM7-EM7/G#-AM7-F#m7-G#7sus-G#7
Wasn't That A Party	V=E-E7-A-E-B7-E
Bad To The Bone(G)	V=E-A-G-E
Endless Love	V=E-A-B11-B(2x)
Her Town Too	C=EM9-AM7-C#m7-G#m7-F#m7-B11-C#11

1982

Even The Nights Are Better	V=E-Am/E(2x)E-B/E-A/E-G-

	F#m-Bm-E
Sad Songs(Say So Much)	C=E-A-[D-A]-B-E-[A-E]
I Love Rock 'N' Roll(E)	C=E5-A5-B5-E5
Up Where We Belong	C=E-E/G#-A-C#m-F#m-E/G#-D-A-B

1983

Islands In The Stream	V=E-E7-A-E-A
Leave A Tender Moment Alone	V=E-AM7-G#m7-F#m7-F#m7/B

1984

Dancing In The Dark(C)	V=E-E6(4x)A-F#m(2x)-E-C#m7(2x)
Footloose	V=E-A/E-E-B-E-A/E C=E-A/E-E-A(3x)
Missing You(G)	V/C=Eadd9-Aadd9-B7sus(4x)-C#m-A-B

1985

Glory Days(A)	V=E-A(4x)B-A(2x)B C=E-A(2x)E-B
One More Night	C=E-A(3x)Bm-E
Rhythm Of The Night	V=E-E11-Asus-A
What About Love(F)	C=E/G#-A5-B5(2x)Bsus-B-E/G#-A-B-A T/A=C#m-C#11-A/C#-C11
I'm On Fire(E)	V=E-A-C#m7-A-B-E

All She Wants To Do Is Dance	V=E7-A-C#m-D
We Built This City	V=E-A/E-D/E-B/E

1986

Like A Rock	V=E-A/E(2x)A-DaddE-A
Next Time I Fall	V=E-A-B-E-A/C#-B/D#-C#m-B/A-A-F#/A#-B/D#
The Greatest Love Of All	V=E-E+-E6-E7-A-A+-A6-A+-G#m-C#m-F#m-B7-G#m-C#m-F#m-B11-B7-E

1987

I Still Haven't Found What I'm Looking For(D)	V=E5-A5-E-A5-E
Keep Your Hands To Yourself(A)	V=E-A-E-B-E
La Bamba(C)	V=E-A-B C=E-A-B-A
Lady In Red	V=E-AM7-B-G#-C#m-B-A C=E-E/G#-A-B-C#m-F#m7-B7
Somewhere Out There	V=Eadd9-EM7/G#-AM7-B11
Shake Down	V=E5-A-D/A-G5/A

1988

Forever Young(E)	V=E-A(2x)E-F#m7-A-C#m7-A-E-A/E-E
Simply Irresistible	V=E5-A(4x)B5-A5-G5
Pink Cadillac(E)	V=E7-A7-E7-B7(2x)E7

Red, Red Wine	V=E-A-F#m-E-A
Got My Mind Set On You	V=E-A-B
Make Me Lose Control	C=E-A-B7(7x)

1989

Angel Of Harlem	V=E-A
Downtown Train(Bb)	C=E-A(3x)F#m7-B
The Living Years	V=E-AM7(2x)D-F#m
The End Of The Innocence	V=Eadd9-Aadd9(2x)B-Eadd9-Aadd9-Eadd9-C#m-A-B
Don't Know Much	V=E-E/G#-A/C#-B/D#
She Drives Me Crazy	C=E-A-C#m-B
Paradise City(G)	C=E-A-D-A-E

1990

Free Fallin'(F)	V=E-Aadd9-E-Bsus
More Than Words(G)	V=E-E/G#-Aadd9-F#m7-A-B-Bsus-E
From A Distance	V=E-A-B7sus(2x)

1991

Baby Baby	V=E-A6-E/A-E-A6-E/B O=E-A6-G/C-F#m/B
She Talks To Angels(Open E)	V=E-A(6/9)/E-E-A(6/9)/E-E(4x)

Look Around	V=E-EM7-AM7-A6-F#m7-B7-E
Smells Like Teen Spirit	V=E5-A5-G5-C5

1992

Lonely Stranger(E)	V=E-A/E-C#m7-F#7-G#7-F#7-B- B/A- E-A/E-C#m7-F#7-D/F#-A- E-A/E-Am6/E-E

1993

Mr. Jones(C)	C=E-A-B(4x)
River Of Dreams	V=E-A-B(2x)C#m-B6- AM7-G#m7(2x)F#-B

1994

Only Wanna Be With You(F#)	V=E-A6/9(no3)(8x)- F#7sus4-Asus2- E-A6/9(no3)(2x)

1995

I'll Be There For You(A)	C=E-A-B(3x)A/C#-D
Secret Garden(C)	V=E-AM7-C#m-AM7-E-AM7

1996

Change The World(E)	V=E-E7sus4/6-E7(no3)-E7sus4/6- E(2x)A-A7sus4/6-A7(no3)- A7sus4/6-A
Give Me One Good Reason(F#)	V=E-A-B
That Thing You Do(E)	V=E-A-B(2x)C#m-F#-D-B- C#m-F#-F#m-Am-B

1997

Candle In The Wind(E)   V=E-A-E/G#-A-Asus-A(2x)

Listing By Progression Type
Chord Progression   *Song Examples*

Basic

E-A   Kumbaya(N/A); Moonlight Bay('12); Zip-A-Dee-Doo-Dah('45); I Hear You Knocking('55); Peggy Sue('57); Let Me Be Your Teddy Bear('57); Young Blood('57); Lollipop('58); Lipstick On Your Collar('59); Teen Angel('60); Sugar Shack('63); You Can't Sit Down('63); Blowin' In The Wind('63); Walk Like A Man('63); Greenback Dollar('63); Do Wah Diddy Diddy('64); Sha La La('64); Dawn(Go Away)('64); Glad All Over('64); Come A Little Bit Closer('64); Bread And Butter('64); The Way You Do The Things You Do('64); I'm Into Something Good('64); Love Me Do('64); Thank You Girl('64); There's A Place('64); Little Honda('64); Midnight Hour('65); Let's Hang On('65); Shakin' All Over "65); Do You Believe In Magic('65); A Lover's Concerto('65); Drive My Car('65);(I Can't Get No)Satisfaction('65); ; Rescue Me('65); The Pied Piper('66); Ain't Too Proud To Beg('66); Born Free('66); Knock On Wood('66); Rain('66); Substitute('66); Respect('67); Darling Be Home Soon('67); Hey Baby They're Playin' Our Song('67); Jimmy Mack('67); Kentucky Woman('67); Pretty Ballerina('67); Silence Is Golden('67); Go Where You Wanna Go('67); Lady Madonna('68); I Feel Like I'm Fixin' To Die Rag('68); Revolution('68); Quinn The Eskimo('68); Master Jack('68); Put A Little Love In Your Heart('69); And When I Die('69); Get Back('69); Holly Holy('69); Take A Letter Maria('69); Sugar Sugar('69); You Can't Always Get What You Want('69); Cecilia('70); Montego Bay('70); She Came In Through The Bathroom Window('70); Up On Cripple Creek('70); Just My Imagination('71); Do You Know What I Mean('71); I Don't Know How To Love Him('71); Domino('71); Anticipation('72); I Can See Clearly Now('72); Bang A Gong('72); Rocket Man('72); Garden Party('72); Help Me Make It Through The Night('72); Loves Me

"E-A" Chord Progressions

	Like A Rock('73); Peaceful Easy Feeling('73); Ramblin' Man('73); Sunshine On My Shoulders('74); Rock Me Gently('74); Please Come To Boston('74); Some Kind Of Wonderful('75); Feel Like Makin' Love('75); You Sexy Thing('76); Take It To The Limit('76); Squeeze Box('76); Kiss You All Over('78);The Gambler('78); Watching The Wheels('81); Glory Days('85); One More Night('85); Forever Young('88); Angel Of Harlem('89); Downtown Train('89)
E-A-A7	For What It's Worth('67)
E-A6	Lollipop('64); My Girl('65); I Wonder What She's Doing Tonight('68); Walk On The Wild Side('73); Ramblin' Man('73); Calypso('75)
E-AM7	Baby, I Need Your Loving('67); This Guy's In Love With You('68); Band On The Run('74); Tonight's The Night('76); Shining Star('80); Every Woman In The World('81); The Living Years('89)
E-Aadd9	Catch The Wind('65)
E-A6/9(no3)	Only Wanna Be With You('94)
E-A7	I'm Walkin''('57); 96 Tears('66); Last Train To Clarksville('66)
E-A9	Hi-De-Ho('70)
E-A11	Get On Up('67)
E-EM7-Eo/A#-A	Unforgettable('51)
E-EM7-AM7-A6	Mac Arthur Park('68); Look Around('91)
E-E+/G#-A-Am	Gee Whiz('61)
E-E7-A	You Are My Sunshine('41); ItchyKoo Park('68)
E-E7-A-Am	Santa Claus Is Coming To Town('34)
E-E7-A-A#o	I Want A Girl('11)
E-E7-A7	Mercy, Mercy, Mercy('67)
E-E7/G#-A	Dream Weaver('76); She Believes In Me('79)
E-E+/G#-A-Am	Gee Whiz('61)
E/B-A	The Night They Drove Old Dixie Down('71)
E5-A	Woodstock('70); Simply Irresistable('88)
E5-A-Am	I Can't Get Next To You('69)
E6-A6	Wonderful Wonderful('57)
EM7-A	A Rainy Night In Georgia('70); Does Anybody Really Know What Time It Is('71)
EM7-AM7	Don't Let The Sun Catch You Crying('64); We've Only Just Begun('70); Tin Man('74); I Can't Tell You Why('80)
EM7-AM9/B	Tighten Up('68)
EM7-A6/9	You Are The Sunshine Of My Life('73)
EM7-A13	Willow Weep For Me('32)
EM7-EM7/G#-AM7	Every Woman In The World('81)

EM7-E7-A6	God Bless The Child('41)
Eadd9-Aadd9	The End Of The Innocence('89)
E7-A	Lay Down Sally('78)
E7-A7	Good Rockin' Tonight('48); Shop Around('61); She's A Woman('64); Can't They See That She's Mine('64); Season Of The Witch('66); Hold On! I'm Comin'('66); Feelin' Alright('72); Car Wash('77)
E7-A7sus-A7	Don't Bring Me Down('66)
E7#9-A7	Ease On Down The Road('74)
E13-A11	God Bless' The Child('41)
E-A-E-E7-A	San Francisco Bay Blues('58)
E-A-E-A6	Domino('71)
E-A-E/G#-A	Candle In The Wind('97)
E-A/C#-E-A	Bits And Pieces('64)
E5-A5-E-A5	I Still Haven't Found What I'm Looking For('87)
EM7-A-EM7-AM7	Memories('69)
E7+-A6-E7+-A	Chances Are('57)
E-A-E	Please, Please Me('64); I Fought The Law('66); These Boots Are Made For Walkin'('66); Dance To The Music('68); Mony, Mony('68); Sky Pilot('68); Son Of A Preacher Man('69); Day After Day('71); Driving My Life Away('80)
E-A6-E/A-E	Baby Baby('91)
E-AM7-E	On The Way Home('68)
E-A7-E	Keep A-Knockin'('57)
E-A9-E	Nadine(Is That You?)('64)
E-EM7-A-E	Ain't Nothing Like The Real Thing('68)
E-E7-A-E	Home On The Range(1873); When Irish Eyes Are Smiling('12); Frosty The Snowman('50);Roses Are Red('62); Itchykoo Park('68); Love Child('68); One Toke Over The Line('71); Island In The Stream('83)
E5-A-E	Sweet Emotion('75)
E7-A-E7	Paperback Writer('66)
E7-A7-E	I've Got The Music In Me('74)

Rock

E-A-B	Little Brow Jug(1869); Words Of Love('57); Love Is Strange('57); Donna('59); Surfin' Safari('62); Comedy Tonight('62); Dance, Dance, Dance('64); Dang Me('64); Don't Worry Baby('64); Time Is

"E-A" Chord Progressions

	On My Side('64); Come A Little Bit Closer('64); Like A Rolling Stone('65); It Ain't Me Babe('65); You Were On My Mind('65);Eve Of Destruction('65); We Gotta Get Out Of This Place('65);(You're My)Soul And Inspiration('66); Carrie Anne('67); The Tracks Of My Tears('67); Piece Of My Heart('68); Hitchin' A Ride('70); Burning Love('72); My Ding A Ling('72);The Guitar Man('72); Beach Baby('74); The Promised Land('74); Born To Run('75); When Will I Be Loved('75); Rock And Roll All Night('76); Lay Down Sally('78); La Bamba('87); Got My Mind Set On You('88); Mr. Jones('93); River Of Dreams('93); I'll Be There For You('95); That Thing You Do('96); Give Me One Good Reason('96)
E-A-B6	Mr. Big Stuff('71)
E-A-Bsus-B-Badd9-B	You've Got To Hide Your Love Away('65)
E-A-B7	Silver Bells('51); Everyday('57); Donna('59); Do You Love Me('62); My Boyfriend's Back('63);(You're The)Devil In Disguise('63); Twist And Shout('64); You're The One('65); Let's Lock The Door(And Throw Away The Key)('65); King Of The Road('65); I Am A Rock('66); Ruby, Don't Take Your Love To Town('69); Love(Can Make You Happy)('69); Come And Get It('70); I Am I Said('71); Rock 'N' Roll(I Gave You The Best Years Of My Life)('75); Blinded By The Light('77); Make Me Lose Control('88)
E-A-B7-B7sus4-B7	Here Comes The Sun('71)
E-A-B7sus	From A Distance('90)
E-A-B7b9	Hey Nineteen('80)
E-A-B11	Don't Worry Baby('64)
E-A-B11-B	Endless Love('81)
E-A6-B	Na, Na, Hey, Hey, Kiss Him Goodbye('69)
E-A6-A-B7	Good Time Charlie's Got The Blues('72)
E-AM7-B/D#	Your Song('70)
E-E/G#-A/C#-B/D#	Don't Know Much('89)
E-EM7/D#-A-B/A	Don't Give Up On Us('77)
E-E+-A-B	Ask Me Why('63)
E-E+-A-B7	California Here I Come('24)
E-Esus-A-B	Annie's Song('74)
E-E7-A-Bsus-B	Me And You And A Dog Named Boo('71)
E/G#-A5-B5	What About Love('85)
E5-E7sus-A5-B5	California Girls('65)
Eadd9-Aadd9-B7sus	Missing You('84)
E7-A7-B	Roadhouse Blues('70)

E-A-B-E	Summertime Blues('58); Yakety Yak('58); Little Bit O' Soul('67); The Tracks Of My Tears('67); Israelite('69); Galveston('69); Walk A Mile In My Shoes('70); Me And Julio Down By The School Yard('72); Look In My Eyes Pretty Woman('75); Got To Get You Into My Life('76); Old Time Rock And Roll('79); Next Time I Fall In Love('86)
E-A-[D-A]-B-E	Sad Songs(Say So Much)('82)
E-A-B-E6	Da Doo Ron Run('63)
E-A-B7-E	Wabash Cannonball('38); No Beer In Heaven(N/A); My Bonnie('64); I Am A Rock('66); Reason To Believe('66); Release Me('67); I Second That Emotion('67); Reason To Believe('71); Back Home Again('74); December 1963('76)
E-A-B11-E	Will You Love Me Tomorrow('60)
E-A6-A-B7-E	Good Time Charlie's Got The Blues('72)
E-A7-B7-E	That's All Right, Mama('54); Heartbreak Hotel('56); All Shook Up('57)
E-EM7-A-B7-E	Downtown('65)
E-E7-A-B7-E	Silver Bells('51); Your Cheatin' Heart('52); Sixteen Candles('58); If You Wanna Be Happy('63)
E-E7-A-B-B7-E	Love Me('57)
E5-A5-B5-E5	I Love Rock And Roll('82)
E7-A7-B7-E7	Hot Rod Lincoln('60)
Em-Am9-B7-Em	Elenore('68)
E-A-B-A	Walking To New Orleans('60); Get Off Of My Cloud('65); Down In The Boon Docks('65); Hang On Sloopy('65); Game Of Love('65); Good Lovin''('66); Wild Thing('66); You Baby('66);(You're My)Soul And Inspiration('66); Angel Of The Morning('68); Piece Of My Heart('68); The Worst That Could Happen('69); Dizzy('69); Suspicious Minds('69); Truckin''('71); Summer Nights('72); The Joker('74); La Bamba('87)
E-A-Bm-A	Louie, Louie('63)
E-A6-B6-A6	I Know A Place('65)
E-A7-B7-A7	Great Balls Of Fire('57)
E-A-B-A-B	You've Lost That Lovin' Feelin''('65); Angel Of The Morning('68)–Chorus; Still The One('76); Lido Shuffle('77)
E5-A5-B5-A5-B5	You Don't Mess Around With Jim('72)

Basic & Folk Combinations

E-A-E-B	Amazing Grace(1779); Rock Of Ages(1832); Yellow Rose Of Texas(1858); Swing Low, Sweet Chariot('25); Move It On Over('47); Tennessee Waltz('48); Searchin'('57); It's Late('59); Cupid('61); Spanish Harlem('61); Surfin' Safari('62); Rhythm Of The Rain('63); Another Saturday Night('63); Little Deuce Coupe('63); Ring Of Fire('63); Fun, Fun, Fun('64); Dead Man's Curve('64); Little Old Lady From Pasadena('64); Sweet Caroline('69); Going Up Country('69); Spirit In The Sky('70); Solitary Man('70); Travelin' Man('70); American Pie('72); Delta Dawn('73); Photograph('73); Hot Legs('78); Keep Your Hands To Yourself('87)
E-A-E-[F#m-G#m-A]-B	Cheater('66)
E-A-E-B7	Over The River And Through The Woods(N/A); On Top Of Old Smokey(1841); Dixie(1861); Battle Hymn Of The Republic(1861); Twinkle Twinkle Little Star(1880); Met Me In St. Louis Louis('04); In The Mood('39); I Got A Woman('55); New Orleans('60); Lion Sleeps Tonight('61); Hello Mary Lou('61); Act Naturally('63); Green, Green('63); Rhythm Of The Rain('63); Dominique('63); Mountain Of Love('64); Mellow Yellow('66); Brow Eyed Girl('67); Sunday Will Never Be The Same('67); Son Of A Preacher Man('69); Macho Man('78); Footloose('84)
E-A-E-[G-A]-B7	Please, Please Me('64)
E-A-E7-B7	Little Sister('61)
E-A5-E-B	Teach Your Children('70)
E-A6-E-B	Me And Julio Down By The School Yard('72)
E-A6-E-B7sus-B7	Do You Know The Way To San Jose
E-Aadd9-E-Bsus	Free Fallin'('90)
E-A7-E-B	Stagger Lee('59); Shop Around('61)
E-A7-E-B7	Stuck In The Middle With You('73)
E-A9-E-B7	Nadine(Is That You?)('64); Hi-De-Ho('70)
E-E+-A-Am-E-B	Crying('61)
E-E+-A-Am-E-B7	It's My Party('63)
E-E7-A-A#o-E-B	Someday We'll Be Together('69)
E-E7-A-E-A7-E-E7-B	Bony Moronie('57)
E-E7-A-E-B7	The Entertainer('02); The Bible Tells Me So('55); Green Green Grass Of Home('67); Ballad Of John And Yoko('69)
E-E7-A-[F#m7]-E-B7	Green Green Grass Of Home('67)
E5-A-E5-B	Katmandu('74)

E5-A-E5-B7	Bad Case Of Loving You('79)
E5-A5-E5-Bsus	Suite: Judy Blue Eyes('69)
E5-Aadd9-E/G#-B5	You Shook Me All Night Long('80)
EM7-AM7-Am6-E-Bm/D	How Deep Is Your Love('77)
E7-A-E-B7	Blueberry Hill('57); I Can't Stop Loving You('62)
E7-A-E7-B7	The Jolly Green Giant('65)
E7-A-Am-E-Bm7	One Hell Of A Woman('74)
E7-A7-E-B	You've Really Got A Hold On Me('63)
E7-A7-E7-B7	Corinna, Corinna('61); I Saw Her Standing There('64); Puppet Man('71); Pink Cadillac('88)
E9-A-Am-E-B7	If I Fell('64)

Classic Blues

E-A-E-B-E	Mabellene('55); School Day('57); Johnny B. Goode('58); No Particular Place To Go('64)
E-A-E-B-E-B	Little Honda('64)
E-A-E-B-A-E	Walkin' Blues('36); Good Golly Miss Molly('58); Kansas City('59); Charlie Brown('59); Slow Down('64); Barbara Ann('66)
E-A-E-B-A-E-B	The Wanderer('62); Wipe Out('63); I Wish It Would Rain('68)
E-A-E-B-A-E-B7	Hanky Panky('66)
E-A-E-B7-E	Rebel 'Rouser('58); Guitar Boogie Shuffle('59)
E-A-E-B7-A-E	Everybody's Trying To Be My Baby('57); Oh Boy('58); Shake, Rattle, And Roll('67)
E-A-E-B7-A-E-B7	Dizzy Miss Lizzie('58); GTO('64)
E-A-E-B7-A7-E	Too Much('57); Let's Go('62)
E-A-E-B7-A7-E-B7	Long Tall Sally('56)
E-A6-E-B-E	Corrina, Corrina('34)
E-A7-E-B-A-E-B7	Seventh Son('65)
E-A7-E-B-A7-E-B	Slippin' And Slidin'('56)
E-A7-E-B7-A-E	Some Kind Of Wonderful('75)
E-A7-E-B7-A7-E	Hound Dog('56); Honey Don't('56); Be Bop A Lula('56); Jail House Rock('57); Hard Headed Woman('58); Hi Heel Sneekers('64); Barefootin'('66); Reelin' And Rockin'('72)
E-A9-E-B9-E	Rock Around The Clock('55); Blue Suede Shoes('56)
E-A9-E-B9-A9-E-B	Chains('62)
E-E7-A-E-B-A-E	Rock N' Roll Is Here To Stay('58); At The Hop('58)-Verse
E-E7-A-E-B7-E	In The Summertime('70); Wasn't That A Party('81)
E-E7-A-E-B7-A-E-B7	Seventh Son('65)
E-E7-A-E-B7-A7-E	Boogie Woogie Bugle Boy('41)

"E-A" Chord Progressions

E-E7-A7-E-B7-A7-E	Tutti Fruiti('56); A Big Hunk O' Love('59); Mean Woman Blues('63)
E6-A7-E6-B-A-E	At The Hop('58)-Chorus
E6-A7-E6-B7-A7-E6	The Stroll('58)
E7-A-E-B9-E	Rockin' Robin('58)
E7-A7-E-B7-A7-E	The Twist('60)
E7-A7-E7-B7-E7	Some Other Guy('52); Rollover Beethoven('56)-Bridge; Rock And Roll Music('57); One After 909('70)
E7-A7-E7-B7-A7-E	Good Morning Blues('38); Killing Floor('64)
E7-A7-E7-B7-A7-E-B	Got My Mojo Working('56)
E7-A7-E7-B7-A7-E7	Midnight Special('60); Back Door Man('61); Match Box('64); Can't Buy Me Love('64); One Way Out('65); C.C. Rider('66); Creeque Alley('67); Why Don't We Do It In The Road ?('68)
E7-A7-E7-B7-A7-E7-B7	Lucille('57); Before You Accuse Me('57); Bad Boy('59); Boys('61); What'd I Say('59); Hideaway('61); Hippy Hippy Shake('64); You Can't Do That('64); Rock Me Baby('64); Money('64); Wooley Bully('65); Mustang Sally('66)
E7-A7-E7-B7-A7-E9	I Got You(I Feel Good)('65)
E7-A9-E-B9-A9-E	Ready Teddy('56)
E7-A9-E9-B9-A9-E7	Everyday(I Have The Blues)('56)
E9-A7-E9-B7-A7-E9-B7	Pappa's Got A Brand New Bag('65)
E7-A7-E-E7-B7-A7-E	Worried Man Blues('59)
E7-A7-E7-B7-[A#7]-A7-E7	She's About A Mover

Quick Change Blues

E-A(2x)E-B-A-E	Crossroads('69); Never Been To Spain('72)
E-A7(2x)E-B7-A7-E	Ramblin' On My Mind('36); Your Mama Don't Dance('73)
E-A7(2x)E-B7-A7-E-B7	Steam Roller('73)
E-A7(2x)E7-B7-A7-E7-B7	Sweet Home Chicago('36)
E7-A(2x)E7-B7-A7-E7	Traveling Riverside Blues('37)
E7-A7(2x)E7-B7-E7	Rollover Beethoven('56)-Verse
E7-A7(2x)E7-B7-A7-E5	Malted Milk('37)
E7-A7(2x)E7-B7-A7-E7	Spiders And Snakes('74)
E7-A7(2x)E7-B7-A7-E7-B7	Honky Tonk('56); Before You Accuse Me('57); The Sky Is Crying('60)
E9-A9(2x)E7-B9-A9-E9	Blues With A Feeling('63)
E9-A9(2x)E9-B9-A9-E9-B9	Paying The Cost To Be The Boss('68)
E-A-E-A7-E-B7-A-E-B	Mean Old World('66)
E-A7-E6-A7-E6-B9-E6	Rip It Up('56)

E6-A9(2x)E6-F#m7-B13-E	Route 66('62)
E7-A7-E7-[F7-E7]-A7-E	Call It Stormy Monday('47)
[F#m7-G#m7-G7]-F#m7-C9	

Classic Rock(Borrowed "D")

E-A-D-A	Not Fade Away('57); Dirty Water('66); Cherry; Cherry('66); I Got The Feelin'(Oh No No)('66); Thank The Lord For The Night Time('67); Tears Of A Clown('70); What I Like About You('79); Paradise City('89)
E-A/C#-D-A/C#	(I Can't Get No)Satisfaction('65)
E-E7-A-[D]-A	Heart Of Stone('65)

Reverse Classic Rock(Borrowed "G")

E-A-G	Get Ready('66); Bitch('71)
E-A-G-E	I'm A Hoochie Cooche Man('57);I'm Mad(Again)('61); I'm A Man('65); Spirit In The Sky('70); Rocky Mountain Way('73); You Got The Music In Me('74); It's Only Rock 'N' Roll(But I Like It)('74); Slow Ride('76); Bad To The Bone('81)
E5-A-G	My Sharona('79)
E7-A5-G5	I Just Want To Make Love To You('77)

Ascending Bass Lines

E-E/G#-A-B	I'll Never Find Another You('65); Expressway To Your Heart('67); My Life('79); Lady In Red('87)
E-E/G#-A-B-B11	Get Off Of My Cloud('65)
E-E/G#-A-B11	With A Little Luck('78)
E-E7/G#-A-B11	Take Me To The Pilot('69)
Eadd9-EM7/G#-AM7-B11	Somewhere Out There('87)
E-F#m7-E/G#-A	Sunshine On My Shoulder('74)
E-E7/G#-A-C/A#	Ask Me No Questions('71)
B7-A/C#-B/D#-E	Tonight's The Night('76)

Descending Bass Lines

E-E/D-E/C#-E+/C	Lucy In The Sky With Diamonds('67)
E-E/D-A/C#-Am6/C	Theme From "The Andy Griffith Show"('60)
E-E/D-A/C#-C7	Short People('78)
E-E/D#-E/C#-E/B	Changes('71); Everthing I Own('72)
E-E/D#-C#m-C#m/B	Garden Party('72)
E-B/D#-C#m-B	Bridge Over Troubled Water('70)
E/B-A-E/G#-F#m	The Long And Winding Road('70)
E/D-A/C#-Am/C-E/B	Can't Find My Way Back Home('69)
A-E/G#-Em/G-F#m7	Maybe I'm Amazed('77)
A-G#m-F#m-E	Oh How Happy('66); Piece Of My Heart('68)
A-A/G#-F#m-F#m/E	Hey Jude('68)
A-A/G#-A/F#-A/E	Resue Me('65)
A/C#-EM7/B-AM7-G#m7	Tiny Dancer('71)
A#m7-A-A/G#-F#m	Sir Duke('77)

The following progressions combine the "C#m" Cliché with the use of a Descending Bass Line.

C#m-C#m/B-C#m/A-C#m/G#	Expressway To Your Heart('67)
C#m-C#m/B-C#m/A#-A	Your Song('70)
C#m-C#m/C-C#m/B-C#m/A#	Will You Love Me Tomorrow('60)
C#m-C#m/C-C#m/B-F#9/A#	Something('69)

Static Bass Lines

E-E6	Ain't That A Shame('55); I Can Help('74); Dancing In The Dark('84)
E-EM7	Lyin' Eyes('75); Wildfire('75); Tomorrow(from "Annie")('77); Two Out Of Three Ain't Bad('78)
E-EM7-E6-E	Go Now('65)
E-EM7-E6-EM7-E7	Harper Valley P.T.A.('68)

E-EM7-E7	We'll Sing In The Sunshine('64); Hooked On A Feeling('68); Raindrops Keep Fallin' On My Head('69); Something('69); I Just Can't Help Believin'('70); You Are So Beautiful('75); Another Somebody Done Somebody Wrong Song('75); I'll Play For You('75); Maybe I'm Amazed('77); I Love The Night Life('78);
E-EM7-E7-E7#9	Kodachrome('73)
E-EM7-E9	Can't Take My Eyes Off Of You('67)
E-EM7-Eo	Cloudy('66)
E-EM9	Salvation('72)
EM7-E	The Best Of My Love('74)
EM9-E	The Impossible Dream('65)
EM9-E6	So Far Away('71)
Em7-EM7	Goin' Out Of My Head('64)
A6-AM7-A	Holly Holy('69)
E-E+	Swanee('19)
E-E+-E6-E+	Match Maker('64)
E-E+-E6-E7	Laughing('69); Stand Tall('76); The Greatest Love Of All('86)
E-E+-E6-E9	Maybe This Time('63)
E-Esus	Suite: Judy Blue Eyes('69); Peaceful Easy Feeling('73); Anne's Song('74)
E-Esus-E	Born To Run('75); Hot Blooded('78)
E-Esus-Eadd9	Eve Of Destruction('65)
E-E7sus-E	Anticipation('72)
E5-EM7(no3)-E6sus4-E	Big Yellow Taxi('75)
Eadd9-E	Lost In Love('80)
Eadd9-EM7	Touch Me In The Morning('73)
E-E7	Get Back('69)
E-E7sus4/6-E	SWLABR('69)
E-E7sus4/6-E7(no3)-E7sus4/6-E	Change The World('96)
E7-E7sus4/6-E7(no3)-E7sus4/6-E7	The Pusher('64)
E-E11	On Broadway('63); The In Crowd('64); 19th Nervous Breakdown('66); 98.6('67); Gimme Some Lovin'('67); Listen To The Music('72); It's Gonna Take Some Time('72); I Won't Last A Day Without You('74); Rhythm Of The Night('85)

E-E11-A/E	Take Me To The Pilot('69); Country Road('71)
EM7-E11	Never Can Say Goodbye('71)
E11-E	Suite: Judy Blue Eyes('69); Rocky Mountain Way('73)
C#m-C#11-A/C#-C#11	What About Love('85)
Em-Em(M7)-Em7-Em6	How Can I Be Sure('67)
Bm/E-Bm(M7)/E-Bm7/E-E7b9	God Bless' The Child('41)
C#m-C#m(M7)-C#m7	Cabaret('66)
E-F#/E-Am6/E-E	Can't Take My Eyes Off Of You('67)
F#m/B-G#m/B-F#m/B	I'll Play For You('75)
E-A/E	Side By Side('27); Mona Lisa('49); Mystery Train('55); April Come She Will('65); I Got You Babe('65); She's Just My Style('66); Gimme Some Lovin''('67); Cry Like A Baby('68); Everyday People('69); I've Got A Feeling('70); I Just Can't Help Believin''('70); Baby Don't Get Hooked On Me('71);Tiny Dancer('71); Jet('74); Then Came You('74); Send In The Clowns('75); Lyin' Eyes('75); Desiree('78); Little Jeannie('80); Start Me Up('81); Like A Rock('86)
E-A/E-E	I Got You Babe('65); I Am A Rock('66); Rain('66); Mother Nature's Son('68); Both Sides Now('68); In The Ghetto('69); Bridge Over Troubled Water('70); Listen To The Music('72); Operator(That's Not The Way I Feel)('72); Longfellow Serenade('74); Junior's Farm('74); Don't Go Breaking My Heart('76); The Gambler('78); Footloose('84); Forever Young('88)
E-A/E-E-F#m/E	Love The One You're With('70)
E-A/E-Eadd9-A/E	Come Sail Away('78)
E-A/E-E7-E	Baby You're A Rich Man('67)
E-A/E-E7-A/E	Boy From New York City('65); Mercy, Mercy, Mercy('67)
E-A/E-Em7-A/E	Lonesome Loser('79)
E-A/E-Am6/E-E	Lonely Stranger('92)
E-A/E-F#m/E-E	(Your Love Keeps Lifting Me)Higher And Higher('67)
E-A/E-B/E-E	Goodbye To Love('72); Closer To You('76); Sometimes When We Touch('78)
E-A/E-B/E-A/E	Your Song('70)
E-A/E-B/E-A/E-Am/E	Up Where We Belong('82)
E-A/E-B7/E-E	You Needed Me('78)
E-A/E-D/E-B/E	We Built This City('85)

E-A6/E	Come See About Me('64); Laughter In The Rain('74)
E-A6/E-E	Boom, Boom('62)
E-A6/E-E6	What Now My Love('66)
E-AM9/E-Am9/E-E	I Just Can't Help Believin''('70)
E-A(6/9)/E	She Talks To Angels('91)
E-Am/E	You Make Me Feel Brand New('74); Even The Nights Are Better('82)
E-Am/E-E	All By Myself('76)
E-EM7-A6/E	I Just Can't Help Believin''('70)
E-Em7-A/E-E	Mother Nature's Son('68)
E5-A/E-E5-Aadd4/E	All Right Now('70)
E5-A/E-D/E-E5	Hollywood Nights('78)
EM7-A/E	How Can You Mend A Broken Heart('71); I'll Play For You('75)
EM7-E11-A6/E-E	Diary('72)
Eadd9-A/E	Free Man In Paris('74)
Eadd9-EM7-A/E	Imagine('71)
A11/E-E	Wild Thing('66)

Other "E-A" Progressions

The "E-A-E-F#m" progression is an example of a Basic & Basic("F#m" Substitution)Combination Progression. The "E-A-E-C#m" progression is an example of a Basic & Partial Rock Ballad Combination Progression. The "E-A-E-D" progression is an example of a Basic & Partial Classic Rock Combination Progression.

E-A-E-F#m	Forever In Blue Jeans('79)
E-A-E-F#m7	She's A Must To Avoid('66); Turn Around, Look At Me('68)
E-A-E-F#	Shut Down('63)
E-A-[Asus]-A-E-F#	Honky Tonk('69)
E-A-E-F#7	Jingle Bells(1857); My Bonnie('64); I'm Henry The VIII I Am('65); 98.6('67); Help Me Make It Through The Night('72)
E-A-E-G	Surf City('63); Little Old Lady From Pasadena('64); Polk Salad Annie('69)
E-A-E-G#m	Michael Row The Boat Ashore('61); You Can't Hurry Love('66); Who'll Stop The Rain('70); Love Grows('70)
E-A-E-G#5	Dance, Dance, Dance('64)
E-A-E-G#7	Battle Hymn Of The Republic(1861)
E-A-E-CM7	Bodhisattva('73)
E-A-E-C#m	I've Been Working On The Railroad(1881); All I Really Want To Do('65); Down In The Boon Docks('65); Trains And

	Boats And Planes('66); Did You Ever Have To Make Up Your Mind('66); I Saw Her Again Last Night('66); Lodi('69); The Worst That Could Happen('69); Dancing Queen('77)
E-A-E-C#	Chain Gang('60)
E-A-E-C#7	Oh Happy Day('69)
E-A-E-D	Little Children('64); Brown Sugar('71); Jive Talkin'('75); Thank God I'm A Country Boy('75)
E-A-E-Dsus-D	A Hard Day's Night('64)
E-A-A7-E-D7sus2	Love Me Two Times('67)
E-A7-E-F#m7	Let The Good Times Roll('46)
E-A7-E-G	Yer Blues('68)
E-Am-E-C#m	Cabaret('66)
E-E7-A-E-F#m7	Don't Be Cruel('56)
E-E7-A-E-F#7	Home On The Range(1873)
E-E7-A-E-C#m	Roses Are Red('62)
E-E7-A-F#	She'd Rather Be With Me('67)
E-E7/G#-A-E-C#m7	In The Good Old Summertime('02)
E-E7/9-A-Am6-E-C#m	Desperado('73)
EM7-A9-EM7-G#m7	On A Clear Day('65)
E+-A-Am-EM7-F#m7	Don't You Care('67)
E7-A7-E7-F#7	Day Tripper('65)
E7-A7-E7-G#	Dancing In The Streets('64)

The "E-A-F#m-B7" progression is an example of a Standard("A" Substitution)Progression. The "E-A-F#7-B7" progression is an example of a Standard("A" & "F#7" Substitution)Progression.

E-A-F#m-E	Red, Red Wine('88)
E-A-F#m-G#7	Theme From Mahogany('76)
E-A-F#m-B7	Cracklin' Rosie('70)
E-A-F#m7-B7	Yes It Is('65)
E-A-F#m7-C#m	I'm Looking Through You('65)
E-A-A/G#-F#m-B7	Wouldn't It Be Nice('66)
E-A-A/G#-F#m7	Two Of Us('69)
E-A-F#7-E	Here Comes The Sun('71)
E-A-F#7-B	Heigh-Ho('37)
E-A-F#7-B7	We Wish You A Merry Christmas(N/A); Dixie(1861); I'll Never Find Another You('65)
E-E/G#-Aadd9-F#m7	More Than Words('90)
E-EM7-A-F#m7	You've Got A Friend('71)
E-E7-A-F#m7	Green Green Grass Of Home('67)

E7-A-F#7	Are You Lonesome Tonight?('60)
E-A-G-A	Back In The USSR('68)
E5-A5-G5-C5	Smells Like Teen Spirit('91)

The "E-AM7-G#m7-C#m7" progression is an example of a Basic & Reverse Minor Folk Combination Progression.

E-A-G#m-F#m	Dandy('66); Oh How Happy('66); I Am I Said('71)
E-A-G#m-B/F#	Turn, Turn, Turn('65)
E-AM7-G#m7-F#m7	Leave A Tender Moment Alone('83)
E-AM7-G#m7-C#m7	We've Only Just Begun('70)
E-AM7-G#m7-C#7sus4	Too Much, Too Little, Too Late('78)
E6-A9-G#m7-C#7	It Might As Well Be Spring('45)
EM7-A7-G#m7-C#7b9	(Meet)The Flintstones('60)
EM7-A11-G#m7-C#m11	Déjà vu('80)
Eadd9-AM7-G#m7-F#m7	Even Now('78)

E-A-B-F#m	It's The Same Old Song('65)
E-A-B-C#m	Up On Cripple Creek('70)
E-A-B-C#m7	Brandy('72)
E-A-B/D#-G#m	Never Knew Love Like This Before('80)
E-A-B7-F#m	We'll Sing In The Sunshine('64)
E-AM7-B-G#	Lady In Red('87)
E-AM7-B/D#-G#m	Your Song('70)
E-Am6/C-B7-F#m	Give My Regards To Broadway('04)
E7-A7-B-C	Roadhouse Blues('70)

E-A-C-G-D	Suffragette City('72)
E-A-C-B	Suzie Q('68)
[D-D#]-E(3x)E7-A-C	Joy To The World('71)
E-E7/G#-A-C	Mama Told Me Not To Come('70)
E7-A7-C7-E	Ask Me No Questions('71)

The "E-A-C#m-B" progression is an example of a Basic & Partial Money Chords Combination Progression. The "E-A-C#m7-A" progression is an example of a Basic & Basic("C#m7" Substitution)Combination Progression.

E-A-C#m-B	More Than A Feeling('76); Hit Me With Your Best Shot('80); She Drives Me Crazy('89)
E-A-C#m7-A	I'm On Fire('85)
E-A-C#m7-F#7	Still The One('76)

E-A-C#7-F#7	While Strolling Through The Park(1884)
E-AM7-C#m-AM7	Secret Garden('95)
E-E/G#-A-C#m	Up Where We Belong('82)
E7-A-C#m-D	All She Wants To Do Is Dance('85)
EM9-AM7-C#m7-G#m7	Her Town Too('81)
E-A-D	Good Lovin' Gone Bad('75)
E-A-D-E	49 Bye-Byes('69); Lola('70)
E-A-D-G	Little Girl('66); Lovely Rita('67)
E-A-D-B	I Know A Place('65)
E-A-D-Bm	Rescue Me('65)
E-A-D-C#m	Your Gold Teeth II('75)
E-AM7-DM7-E	This Guy's In Love With You('68)
E-Am-D7sus2-C	I Was Made To Love Her('67)
E-Am7-D6-A#o	Michelle('66)
E-E7-A-D11	Bluer Than Blue('78)
E-E7-A6-D7-G6	Where Is The Love('72)
E-E7/G#-A-D7-E	Still Crazy After All These Years('76)
E5-A-D/A-G5/A	Shake Down('87)
EM7-Asus-DM7-Bsus	My Cherie Amour('69)

"E-A#" Chord Progressions

Only the three songs shown below were found to have verses that begin with an "E" chord and then move to an "A#" chord.

Chronological Listing

Date/Song Title *Chord Progressions*

1926

Someone To Watch Over Me   V=EM7-A#m7#5-Ao-G#m7#5-Go-B7/F#-Fo-F#m7-C#7/G#-A6-A#m7b5-F#m7-B7
T/A=E-G#7#5-AM7-B7 or
EM7-C#7-F#m9-F7b9

1975

One(from "A Chorus Line")   V=EM7-A#7-EM7-Bm7-C#7

1977

Sir Duke(B)   C=E-A#m7-AM7-F#m7-B11

"E-B" Chord Progressions

The most frequent progressions that start with an "E" chord and then move to a "B" chord are as follows.

Folk	E-B7
Folk & Basic Combination	E-B7-E-A
Reverse Rock("E" First)	E-B-A
Descending "E-D#-C#-A" Bass Lines	E-B/D#-C#m-A
Descending "E-D#-C#-B" Bass Lines	E-B/D#-C#m-G#m/B
Descending "E-D#-D-C#" Bass Lines	E-B/D#-D-A/C#
Static Bass Lines	E-B/E

The "E-B7" Folk Progression, which follows the Circle of Fifths movement, has been employed to write many folk songs dating back over a hundred years. *Camptown Races, Alouette,* and *The Mexican Hat Dance* as well as more recent hits such as The Beatles' 1966 *Yellow Submarine*, Linda Ronstadt's 1977 *Blue Bayou* and Elvis Presley's 1977 *Way Down* were created around the Folk Progression.

The "E-B7-E-A" Folk & Basic Combination Progression consists of the Folk and Basic Progressions, both of which follow the Circle of Fifths movement. This progression has been used since the early 1700s. The most widely recognized version of this progression is the ever popular 1935 *The Birthday Song(Happy Birthday To You)*. Two holiday classics created around the Folk & Basic Combination Progression include the 1711 *Auld Lang Syne* and the 1818 *Silent Night*. More recent examples include The Drifters' 1964 hit *Under The Boardwalk* and Elvis Presley's 1970 *Kentucky Rain*.

The "E-B-A" Reverse Rock("E" First)Progression is similar to the "B-A-E" Reverse Rock Progression where the "E" chord is played first. Common variations of the Reverse Rock("E" First)Progression include the "E-B-A-E" and "E-B-A-B" progressions, both of which can be transformed into Descending Bass Line Progressions by playing other chord notes as the bass note. Examples of hit songs written with the Reverse Rock("E" First)Progression include: Creedence Clearwater Revival's 1969 *Fortunate Son*, The Eagles' 1972 *Take It Easy*, and Fleetwood Mac's 1977 *Go Your Own Way*.

The definitive "E-D#-C#-A" Descending Bass Line Progression is The Beatles' 1970 hit *Let It Be*. The "E-D#-C#-B" Descending Bass Line was used to create such interesting songs as the Everly Brothers' 1960 *Let It Be Me*, The Jackson 5's 1970 *I'll Be There*, Willie Nelson's 1982 *Always On My Mind*, and Eric Clapton's 1992 *Tears In Heaven*. The "E-D#-D-C#" Descending Bass Line was used to write such great songs as The Association's 1967 *Never My Love* and The Commodores' 1978 *Three Times A Lady*.

The "E-B/E Static Bass Line Progressions have been used to create memorable hit songs such as the Who's 1966 *Substitute*, The Electric Light Orchestra's 1975 *Can't Get It Out Of My Head*, and Barbara Streisand & Neil Diamond's 1978 *You Don't Bring Me Flowers*. These songs combined the use of Reverse Rock("E" First)Progression variations with Static "E" Bass Lines.

In addition to the most frequent progressions already discussed, there are a number of other "E-B" progressions that mainly continue to move to the "E", "F#m", "A", "C#m" and "Borrowed" "D" chords. Many of these progressions can be transformed into Descending Bass Line Progressions by playing other chord notes as the bass note.

Below is a chronological listing of songs with verses, bridges, and/or choruses that utilize the "E-B" sequence followed by a listing of chord progressions by type.

Chronological Listing

Date/Song Title	*Chord Progression*
N/A	
Three Blind Mice	V=E-B7
This Train	V=E-B-E-A

1711

Auld Lang Syne						V=E-B7-E-A-E-B7-C#m-F#m7-B7-E

1812

Hail To The Chief					V=E-B7-E-F#7-B7

1814

Star Spangled Banner				V=E-B/D#-C#m-G#/C-C#m-F#7-B-E-B7-E-B-B7-E

1818

Silent Night						V=E-B7-E-A-E-A-E-B7-E-B7-E

1824

Billy Boy						V=E-B7-E-A

1832

Skip To My Lou						V=E-B7(2x)E

1835

Down In The Valley					V=E-B7-E

1848

Blue Tail Fly						C=E-B7-E-A-B7-E

1850

Buffalo Girls						C=E-B7(2x)E

1851

Camptown Races   V=E-B7(2x)E

Old Folks At Home   V=E-B-E-A-
                                   E-B(2x)E-A-E-B-E

1859

The Marine's Hymn   V=E-B7(4x)E-A(2x)E

1870

She'll Be Coming Round
The Mountain   V=E-B7-E-E7-A-E-B7-E

1879

Alouette   V=E-B7(6x)E

1885

Clementine   V/C=E-B7(2x)E

1895

The Band Played On   V=E-B7(2x)

1908

Take Me Out To The Ball Game   V=E-B7(2x)C#7-F#m-F#7-B7

1909

By The Light Of The Silvery Moon   V=E-B7-E-E7-A

1917

Hail, Hail The Gang's All Here   V=E-B7(2x)E

1919

Mexican Hat Dance   V=E-B7(3x)E

1920

America The Beautiful   V=E-B/F#-B-E/B-B7/F#-B7

1921

Careless Love   V=E-B7(2x)E-E7-A7-E-B7(2x)

Ain't We Got Fun   V=E-B7-E-A

1926

When The Red, Red Robin Comes Bob, Bob, Bobbin' Along   V=E-B7(2x)E-E7

1929

Happy Days Are Here Again   V=E-B+(2x)E-B7

1931

Lady Of Spain   C=E-B7-B7#5-E

Roll In My Sweet Baby's Arm   V=E-B-E-A

1935

Happy Birthday   V=E-B7-E-E7-A-E-B7-E

I'm Gonna Sit Right Down And Write Myself A Letter   V=E-EM7-E6-B7#5-EM7-G#7

Top Hat, White Tie and Tails   V=E-B7#5-E6-Fo-B7/F#-B7-E

1944

Sentimental Journey   V=E-E+-E6-E7-E6-B9-C

1945

It Might As Well Be Spring   V=E-EM7-E6-EM7-E-Bm7-E7-
                                  A-Ao-E6-F#m7-B7-EM7

1946

When The Saints Go Marching In   V=E-B7-E-E7-A-E-B7-E

I Got The Sun In The Morning   C=E-B/D#-C#m7-B6(2x)

1950

Jezebel   V=E-Bm7(2x)E-F-E

1952

Singin' In The Rain   V=E6/9-B11-B9-E6/9

1955

Misty   V=EM7-Bm7-E7b9-AM7-A6-
                                  Am7-D9-EM9-C#m7-F#m7-B7b9

Day-O   V=E-B7

1957

Marianne   C=E-B7(3x)

Catch A Falling Star   C=E-B11(7x)

Sea Cruise(C)   V/C=E-B-E

Chances Are   V=E6-B7+-E-Em6-B

1958

He's Got The Whole World In His Hand	C=E-B7(2x)E
Chantilly Lace(E)	C=E-B(2x)E-A-E-B-E
Crying, Waiting, Hoping(A)	C=E-B-E-A-E-B-E-B
Rockin' Around The Christmas Tree	V=E-B7-F#m7-B7-F#m7-B7-E(2x) B=A-G#m-C#m-C#m(M7)-C#m7-F#7-B7
To Know You Is To Love You	V=E-B7-C#m7-A

1959

Do-Re-Mi	V=E-B7(2x)E-E7-A
Red River Rock(C)	V=E-B7-E-E7-A-E-B-E-B7

1960

Save The Last Dance For Me	V=E-B7-E-A-E-B7-E
Teen Angel	C=E-B7-E-A-B7-E-B7-E
Let It Be Me	V=E-B/D#-C#m-G#m/B-A-E/G#-F#m7-B7-E

1961

I Like It Like That	V=E-B7
Wheels(F)	V=E-B7(4x)E
The Watusi	V=E-B7-E-A7-E-B7-A7-E-B7

1962

Jambalaya	V=E-B7(4x)E
A Holly Jolly Christmas	V=E-B7(2x)E-A-G#m-A-E
Limbo Rock	V=E-B7-E(2x)A-E
If I Had A Hammer(D)	V=E-B7-E-E7-B7-E-C#m-A E-A-E-B7(2x)-E-A-E
Bring It On Home To Me	V=E-B7-E7-A
The Alley Cat Song	V=E-B7-F#m7-B7-E(2x)

1963

If You Want To Be Happy	V=E-B7(2x)E
Judy's Turn To Cry(D)	V=E-B7(2x)E-F-A#-B
Detroit City	V=E-B7(2x)E-E7-A-E-F#7-B7
Frankie And Johnny	V=E-B7#5(2x)E-E7-A-E7#5-A-A#o-E/B-C#7
Alberta(C)	V=E-B-E-A-E-B-E-B-E-A-Am-E
Danke Schoen	V=E-B7-E-E7-A
End Of The World	V=E-B/D#-C#m-G#m/B-A-F#m-G#m-C#7-F#m-B7
One Fine Day	V=E-B-C#m-A-E-C#m7-A-B7 T/A=E-C#m-A-Bsus
Don't Think Twice(E)	V=E-B-C#m-A-B-B7-E-B-C#m-F#7-B-B7-E-E7-A-F#9-E-B-C#m-A-E-B-E-B

1964

When I Grow Up
(To Be A Man)(Ab) V=E-B7(2x)E-F#m-B7-G#m-C#m-D9#11-A-G#m-F#m-E-A

Yesterday's Gone V=E-B11(2x)B7-A-E-B7-E-A-E

I'll Cry Instead(G) V=E-B11(6x)B7-A7-E-B11-B7-E-B11(2x)

Tell Me(B) V=E-B(2x)G#-A-B-E-G#-A-F#7-B7

I Should Have Known Better(G) V=E-B(5x)C#m-A-B-E-B(2x)

Ferry Cross The Mersy(E) V=E-Bm7(8x)

Under The Boardwalk V=E-B7-E-A-E-B-E

Crooked Little Man V=E-B7-E-A-B7-E

There, I've Said It Again V=E-Bm7-E7-A-A#o-F#m7-B7-Bm7-C#7-F#7-F#m7-B7
I=B+

Baby's In Black(A) C=E-B-A-B-E-A-E-B

Wishin' And Hopin' C=E-B-A-B-E-B-A-B7

I Feel Fine(G) V=E7-B-B7-A7-E7
I=B7-A7-E7

Surfin' Bird(E) V=E7-B7-A7-E7

Where Did Our Love Go V=E-B-A#-F#m7-B-B/A

I Want To Hold Your Hand(G) V=E-B7-C#m-G#7(2x)A-B7-E-C#m-A-B7-E

	I=A-B(3x)B7
I'm A Loser(G)	V=E-B-Dadd9-E(4x)

1965

Over And Over	V=E-B7
I'm Telling You Now	V=E-B7(3x)F#m7-B7-E-C#m-F#m7-B7-E
Lemon Tree	V=E-B7(4x)E-A-E7(4x)A-A7
Help Me Rhonda(Db)	V=E-B11(2x)E-C#m-A-F#-E-F#m-E
Birds And The Bees	V=E-B7-E(2x)E7-A-E-C#m7
Baby, The Rain Must Fall	V=E-B7-E-A-B-E-E7-A-E-D-B
One, Two, Three	V=E-Bm7-E7-A
I Can't Help Myself(C)	V=E-B-F#m-[G#m]-A-B
Can't You Hear The Fountain Of My Heart Beat(A)	V=E-B-A-E(4x)
The Little Black Egg(A)	V=E-B-A-E(8x)
Everyone's Gone To The Moon	V=EM7-B-A-F#m7-B7(2x)
In My Life(A)	V=E-B-C#m-E/D-A-Am-E(2x)-C#m-A-D-E-C#m-F#-Am-E
I Don't Want To Spoil The Party(G)	V=E-B-C#m-G#7-F#m7-B-E-Dadd9-E
You've Got To Hide	

Your Love Away(G)	V=E-B-D-E-A-D-A(2x)-B-B/A-B/G#-B/F#
I Hear A Symphony(C)	V/C=E-B/D#-D6-F#m-G#m-B7
Stop! In The Name Of Love(C)	V=E-EM7-Bm-C#7(A-B)2x

1966

Yellow Submarine(G)	C=E-B(2x)E
I'm Your Puppet	V=E-B7(8x)
Winchester Cathedral(C)	V=E-B7-E(2x)E-E7-A-F#7-B7
Lies(D)	C=E-B7(2x)C#m-F#7-C#m-F#7 E-A-C#m
(You And Me)Rain On The Roof	V=E-B7(2x)E-F#7-B7
Cabaret	V=E-B7#5(2x)E-EM7-E7-A-A#o-G#m-C#9
Devil With A Blue Dress	V=E-B11
Have You Seen Your Mother Baby, Standing In The Shadows(G)	V=E-B/D#-B(2x)G#-E
Good Vibrations	C=E-Bm7(8x)F#-C#m(4x)-G#-D#m7(4x)
A Groovy Kind Of Love	V=E-B7/E-E-F#m/B-G#m7-F#m7-E-B7/E-E-F#m7/B-B7-E
Did You Ever Have To Make Up Your Mind	V=E-B11-E-C#m-E-C#-E-B-A-B-B11-E
Tijuana Taxi	V=E-B7-E-C#7-F#m-B7-E

Tiny Bubbles	V=E-B7-E-A-E-B7-E
Muddy Water	V/C=E-B7-E-E7-A7-E-B7-E(2x)
Sloop John B(Ab)	V=E-B-E-A-F#m7-E-B-E
Workin' My Way Back To You(G)	V=E-B/D#-A-B(2x)A-Am-E-Eo
Nowhere Man(E)	V=E-B-A-E-F#m7-Am-E-G#m-A(2x)G#m-F#m7-B
Substitute(D)	C/I=E-B/E-A/E-E(4x)
Listen People	V=E-B-C#m-G#7-E-B-A-B7
For No One(B)	V=E-B/D#-C#m-E/B-A-D/F#-E
When A Man Loves A Woman(Db)	V=E-B/D#-C#m-E7/B-A-B11-B-E-B
59th Street Bridge Song	V=E-B/D#-C#m7-B
Homeward Bound	V=E-B/D#-Bm6/D-C#7-F#m/C#-D-E
I'm A Believer	V=E-B-D-E(2x)A-E(3x)B7
Walk Away Renee	V=E-B/D#-D-A/C#-Co-E/B-A-B7

1967

Ruby Tuesday	C=E-B(2x)E-B7-D-A-B-E-B
Come On Down To My Boat	V=E-B C=E-B-A-E(4x)
Pleasant Valley Sunday	V=E-Bm7(2x)G

Ode To Billy Joe	V=E7-Bm7(2x)E7-A7
Fixin' A Hole(F)	V=E-B+-Em7-Em6-(Em7-A7)3x-E-B(3x)E-B-F#(3x)B
You Got What It Takes(G)	V=E-B7-E-F#7
When I'm Sixty Four(C)	V=E-B7-E-E7-A-Am-E-C#-F#-B7-E
With A Little Help From My Friend(E)	V=E-B/D#-F#m/C#-B7-E(2x)
She's Leaving Home(E)	V=E-Bm-F#m7-C#m7-F#7-B7sus4-B9(2x) C=E-Bm6-C#m-F#7-C#m-F#7
To Love Somebody(A)	C=E-B-A-E(2x)
The Letter	C=E-B-A-E-B(2x)G#7
I Think We're Alone Now	C=E-B-A-E(2x)
Here Comes My Baby	V=E-B-A-E-B-A-B-E-A-B
Somebody To Love	C=E-B-C#m-F#(2x)E-B-C#m
Holiday(C)	V=E-B-C#m-G#m-A-E-B-E
All You Need Is Love(G)	V=E-B/D#-C#m(2x)B7/F#-E-B/D#-B/C#-B-B/A-B/G#-B
Strawberry Fields Forever(Bb)	C=E-Bm7-C#7-A-C#7-A-E
(You Make Me Feel Like) A Natural Woman	V=E-B/D#-D-A-[A-E/G#-F#m7]-E-B/D#-D-A-E/G#-F#m7-G#m7(3x)AM7

Never My Love(Db)　　　　　　V=E-B/D#-D-A/C#-E/B-C#m-E-AM7-E

Good Morning Good Morning(A)　V=E-Bm-D-E(2x)A-B

1968

Quinn The Eskimo　　　　　　C=E-B(2x)A-E

Hey Bulldog(B)　　　　　　　V=E-Bm7(2x)D-Bm7-A-A7-Bm7-E

Ob-La-Di Ob-La-Da(Bb)　　　　V=E-B7-E-A-E-B7-E

Hey Jude(F)　　　　　　　　V=E-B-B7-B7sus4-E-A-E-B7-E

Green Tambourine　　　　　　V=E-B-A(4x)Am-E-B-A-G-Dm

(Sittin' On)
The Dock Of The Bay(G)　　　B=E-B-A(3x)E-D-B

The Weight(A)　　　　　　　C=E-B-A(3x)
　　　　　　　　　　　　　T/A=E-B/D#-C#m-G#m/B-A

Bottle Of Wine　　　　　　　V=E-B-A-E-B-E(2x)
　　　　　　　　　　　　　C=E-B-E(2x)

Tuesday Afternoon(F)　　　　V=E-B-A-G#m-C#-B-A-G#m-C#-G7

Tomorrow(E)　　　　　　　　V=E-Bm-A-FM7(2x)

People Got To Be Free(F)　　V=E-B-C#m-G#m-A-E-F#m-B

1969

Down On The Corner(C)　　　V=E-B(2x)E-A-E-B-E

Honky Tonk Woman(G)　　　　C=E-B-E-B7-E

Give Peace A Chance　　　　C=E-B7-E(2x)

Marakesh Express(G)	V=E-Bm(2x)C#m-F#-A-B
Everybody's Talkin'	V=E-E7-B7-E(2x)F#m7-B7-E-E7
Stand By Your Man(A)	V=E-B7-F#m7-B7-E-A-E-F#7-B7
Fortunate Son(G)	C=E-B-A(2x)E
Bad Moon Rising(D)	V=E-B-A-E(4x)
Come Together(D)	V=E-B-A-C#m-C#m/B-A-B
Crimson And Clover(B)	V=E-B-A-B(6x)A
Games People Play	V/C=E-B-A-B
I Guess The Lord Must Be In New York City	V=E-E6(4x)B7-B9(3x)B7-A#o-B7
Oh! Darling(A)	V=E-B-C#m-A F#m-B(2x) T/A=E-A-E-B
Smile A Little Smile For Me	C=E-B-C#m-A-B7(2x)
Build Me Up Butter Cup	V=E-B-D-A-E-F#m-F#m9-B7
Mean Mr. Mustard(E)	V=E7-B7-[C7-C#7]-D7 [C#7-C7]-B7 E7-C7-B7(2x)
Cinnamon Girl(D)	V=E-Bm7-D-A(2x)

1970

Knock Three Times	V=E-B7-E
I Think I Love You	V=Em-B7-E7b9-A-Am-E-Bm-A-E
Kentucky Rain	V=E-B-E-A-E-A-E-E7-

	A-B-E-C#m-F#7-B7
	T/A=AM7
Candida	V=E-B7-F#m7-B7-E-E7
Sweet Jane(D)	V=E-B-A-C#m-B-E
He Ain't Heavy, He's My Brother	V=E-B/D#-A/C#-F#m7/B-B7-C#m-D-F#m7/B-EM7-B/D#-A+2/C#-F#m/B-E-F#m/E-E I=F#m/E
Band Of Gold	V=E-B/D#-B7-A-E/G#-A-E/G#-B11
Signed, Sealed, Delivered I'm Yours(E)	C=E-Bm/D-A7(4x)
Fire And Rain(C)	V=E-Bm7-A-E-B-DM7(2x)
I'll Be There(F)	V=E-B/D#-C#m-G#m/B-A-B11-E-B7sus(2x)
Let It Be(C)	V=E-B/D#-C#m-AM7-A6-E-B/D#-A-A/G#-A/F#-E Break= A-E/G#-B7/F#-E-D-A/C#-B-A-E
Ooh Child(Bb)	C=E-B/D#-C#m7-C#m7/F#(2x)
Lay Down(Candles In The Rain)	C=E-B-D(2x)E
Give Me Just A Little More Time	V=E-B/D#-D6-A-B7
It Don't Matter To Me	V=E-B7/D#-D-Am/C-E/B-F#m7/B-B7/F#-E/G#-G-B7/F#
Let It Rain(D)	V=E-Bm-D-A-E(2x) C=E-Bm(2x)D-A-E

1971

Song	Progression
Have You Ever Seen The Rain(C)	V=E-B(2x)E
If You Could Read My Mind(G)	V=E-Eadd9-Bm/D(2x)
Me And Bobby McGee(G-A)	V=E-B-E-E7-A-E-B
Brand New Key	V=E-B7-E-A-B7-E-A-E
Sunshine(Go Away Today)	V=E-B-E-A(2x)
Joy To The World(D)	C=E-B-E-E7-A-C-E-B7-E
Have You Seen Her(E)	V=E-EM7-E6-E-B7sus4-B7-E
Put Your Hand In The Hand	C=E-B7-F#m-B7-E-A-E-Bm-E7-A-A#o-E-C#m-F#m-B7-E-A-E
Sweet Mary	V=E-B-A-E(2x)E-B(2x)E
Wild World	C=E-B-A-B(2x)-A-E-F#m-G#7-C#m
Wedding Song(There Is Love)(E)	V=E-B/F#-Aadd9-E(2x)-C#m-E-B/F#-Aadd9 T/A=E-F#/E-Aadd9/E-E
Sooner Or Later(C-Db)	V=E-B/D#-A-A/G#-A/F#-A-B
Take Me Home Country Roads(A)	C=E-B-C#m-A-E-B-A-E
What Is Life(E)	V=E-B-C#-F#m-G-D(2x) C=E-B-A-B(4x)D-A/C#-B
Don't Pull Your Love(G)	C=E-B/D#-C#m-G#m/B-A-E/G#-F#m7-B11
It Don't Come Easy(D)	V=E-Bm-D-A-E(2x)-G-A-G-B

1972

Black And White   V=E-B(2x)E-A-B

Rocking Pneumonia And
The Boogie Woogie Flu   V/C=E-B7(2x)

Taxi(D)   V=E-Bm/E(6x)D-C

City Of New Orleans(D)   V=E-B-E-C#m-A-E-
                               E-B-E-C#m-B-E-
                               C#m-G#m-B-F#-
                               C#m-G#m-B7-E

Song Sung Blue   V=E-B-B7-E-E7-A

Old Man   C=E-Bm7-F#m7-A(3x)

Take It Easy(G)   V=E-B-A(2x)E

Stairway To Heaven(C)   V2=E-B/D#-C#m-E-B/D#-AM7-C#m

I Need You(A)   V=E-EM7-Bm-D-G/D(2x)

1973

Drift Away(E)   V=E-B(3x)C#m-E

Cover Of The Rolling Stone   V=E-B7-E-E7-A-B7-E

Tequila Sunrise   V=E-B-F#m-B7-[E-E6-EM7-E6]
                               I=E-E6(4x)F#m-B

Knockin' On Heaven's Door   V=E-B-F#m7-E-B-A

You Are The Sunshine
Of My Life(B)   V=EM9-B/A-G#m7-C#7(b9/b13)-
                               F#m7-B11-EM9-[F#m7-B11]-
                               EM9-B/A-G#m7-C#7(b9/b13)-
                               F#m7-E-[F#m7-B11]

My Maria(E)	V=E-B-A
Top Of The World	V=E-B-A-E-G#m-F#m-B7-E A-B-G#m-C#7-F#m7-B7sus-B7
Give Me Love (Give Me Peace On Earth)(F)	V=E/G#-B/D#-A-B/D#-Am- B/D#-D-A(2x)
I Got A Name	V=E-B/D#-C#m-C#m/B-A-B
Reelin' In The Years(D)	V=E-B/D#-C#m7-B(2x)F#o-Fo- Eo-B/D#-E-B/D#-C#m7-B
Mind Games	V=E-B6/D#-C#m-E/B-AM7- E/G#-F#-F#/E
The Morning After	V=E-Bsus-B7-C#m-C#m/B-AM7
The Most Beautiful Girl(G)	C=E-Bm7-E7-A- C#7-F#7-F#m7-B7- E-Bm7-A-Am- Em-B+/D#-Em7/D-A9/C#-B7-E

1974

The Air That I Breath	C=E-B-E(2x) T/A=B-Bm-A-E-B
Mockingbird	V=E7-B7-E-A7-E-B7-A7-B7
Sundown(E)	V=E5-B7sus-E5-A-D-E5(2x)
Carefree Highway(D)	V=E-B-G#-C#m-C#m/B-A-E- Bsus-B
Already Gone(G)	V/C=E-B-A(4x)
You Ain't Seen Nothin' Yet(A)	C=E-B-A(4x)
W.O.L.D.	C=E-B-C#m-DM9-A-E-B-F#m-

	E-B-C#m-DM9-A-E-B-C#m
When Will I See You Again	V=E-B/D#-C#m-E/B-A-E/G#-F#m7-B7
Beach Baby	V=E-B/D#-C#m-G#/C-A-E-F#m7-B7

1975

Sweet Surrender	V=E-B7(3x)E
Sister Golden Hair(E)	C=E-B-A(2x)F#m-E/G#-A
Island Girl	C=E-B-A-E
The No No Song	V=E-B-A-E-A-E-B-E C=E-B-B7-E
Can't Get It Out Of My Head	C=E-B/E-A/E-B/E(3x)
Free Bird(G)	V=E-B/D#-C#m-D-A-B

1976

Fernando(A)	C=E-B(2x)E
Do You Feel Like We Do(A)	V=E-B(2x)E-A/E-E7(no3)
Let Your Love Flow	V=E-B11(2x)B7
Fly Away	V=E-B7sus4-E-F#m-B7(2x)-E-B7sus4
Stand Tall	C=E-B-A-E
Nights Are Forever Without You(E)	C=E-B-A-B(3x)E-B-A(2x)
New Kid In Town(E)	V=E-B7-Aadd9-B7-E-[Esus]-E-

	E-B7-[A]-Aadd9-A-B7-E-[F#m7sus4/C#-G#sus-G#]
Let Em In	V=EM7-E6(2x)-B7/E-A/E-EM7-E6
Shower The People(F)	V=E-B-C#m-E/B-A-E-B-Co-C#m-E/B-A
Magic Man(Bb)	C=E-B-C#5(2x)
Baby I Love Your Way(G)	V=E-B/D#-C#m-A-Am/D(2x)-G#m7-C#7-F#m7-B C=E-B-F#m-A(3x)

1977

Way Down	C=E-B7(2x)A-E A/C#-E/B-A-E/G#-B7/F#-E
Margaritaville(D)	V=E-Esus-E(2x)B-E-Esus-E-E7
Blue Bayou(F)	V=E-B7-E C=E-B7-E-E7-A-Am-E-B7-E
Main Street	O=E-Bm
Go Your Own Way(F)	V=E-B-A-E
The First Cut Is The Deepest(C)	C=E-B-A-B(3x)E-A-B
It's So Easy(A)	V=E-B-A-B-E-A-B-E-A-E-A-F#-B
Looks Like We Made It	C=E-B/E-A-B-G#m7-C#7-F#m7-B11
Your Smiling Face	V=E-B/D#-C#m7-E/B-A-E/G# F#m-B11-E-C#m7-F#m7-B7sus4-B

Slow Dancing (Swayin' To The Music)	V=E-B/D#-C#m-A-E-B(2x)

1978

Time Passages	V=E-B/E-G#m-A-B-C#m-B-A-(2x)E-B/E-A/E-E-B-C#m-F#-E-B/E-A/E-B-A-G#m-B-E
You Don't Bring Me Flowers	V=E-B/E-A/E-E-A-E/G#-F#m7-AM7-B I=E-B/E-A/E-B11
We've Got Tonight	V=E-B/E-A/E-B/E-E-AM7-A6-E-B
Wonderful Tonight(G)	V=E-B/D#-A/C#-B(2x)
Beast Of Burden	V=E-B/E-C#m-A-B(3x)-A-E/G#(2x)B-Bsus-B
Dust In The Wind(C)	V=E-B/D#-C#m-B-F#m7-C#m-B/D#(2x)
Three Times A Lady	C=E-B/D#-D-A/C#-F#m7-E-B-B/A
Baker Street(A)	V=E-Bm-D-A(2x)Am7-Em7-(2x)G-D-A

1979

Babe	C=E-B/E-A/E-C#m-B-C#m-B-(2x)AM7
We Are Family	V=E-Bm7-A9(8x)
Don't Cry Out Loud	C=E-B/D#-C#m7-F#m7-B11-B7

1980

All Out Of Love	C=E-B/D#-A/C#-A-B(2x)E

September Morn	C=Eadd9-E-Bm7-E9-Aadd9-A-Am9-D9b5
The Rose	V=E-B-A-B-E(2x)
Fire Lake	V=E-B-C#m-B/D#
It's Still Rock And Roll To Me(C)	V=E-B-D-A(2x)G#m-C#m-G#m-F#-B-E-G#m-D-A-C#m-B-E

1981

The One That You Love	V=E-Bm(2x)F#m-D#m7b5-E-Bm6/D-C#7-F#m-F#m/E-B(2x)B/A C=E-B/E-A/E-B/E(2x)A/E
Jessie's Girl	V=E-B-C#m-A-B-E(4x)

1982

Theme From "Cheers"	V=E-B(4x)G#m7b5/D-C#7-F#m-B11
Rock This Town(D) E-B7-E	C=E-B-[C#o-Do-D#o]-E-A-F#7-
Jack And Diane(A)	V=E-B-A-B I=E-B/E(2x)A
Up Where We Belong	V=E-B/E-A/E-Am6/E(3x)E-E7/G#-A-E/G#-F#m7-B7
Hurts So Good(A)	V=E-B-C#m-A(2x)E-B(2x)C#-A-B C=E-B(2x)A-C#m-A-B
Always On My Mind	V=E-B/D#-C#m-E/B-A-B
Blue Eyes	V=E6-B/D#-Bm/D-C#m-A11-

	E/G#-B/F#-B-B7
Man-eater	V=E-B-D-C#-F#m7-B-Co-C#m-G#m7-C#m7

1983

I Guess That's Why They Call It The Blues	C=E-B/D#-A-E-B-A-E-B-C#m-E/G#-A-F#/A#-A-B11-E
Down Under	C=E-B-C#m-A-B(4x)

1984

Karma Chameleon	C=E-B/D#-C#m-F#m7-E-B
Boys Of Summer	C=E-B-A(2x)

1985

Small Town(B)	V=E-B-A-B(3x)F#m-B

1986

All Cried Out	V=E-B/D#-C#11-C#m7-B(2x)
These Dreams	C=E/G#-B/D#-A/C#-E/B-F#m7

1988

Kokomo	V=E-EM7-Bm7-A-Am-E-F#7-B7

1989

Love Shack	V=E7-Bm7
Downtown Train(Bb)	V=E-B-A(4x)A-B(2x)A/C#-B
Right Here Waiting	C=E-B-C#m-A-B(2x)C#m

We Didn't Start The Fire(G)	V=E5-B5-C#5-A5(2x)- C=E/B-B5-C#m-A5- E/B-B5-C#m/G#-A5

1990

Janie's Got A Gun(E)	V=E5-B5(4x)Esus2-E-A5-B5-(2x)
Heart Of The Matter	V=E-B-Aadd9(2x)Bsus- Aadd9(2x)Bsus-B I=E-B7sus4(2x)
How Am I Supposed To Live Without You	V=E-B/D#-A/C#-Am/C-E/B- B/A-E/G#-B/F#
Vision Of Love	V=E-Bm/E-A-G#+-G#7 E-Bm6/E-A-G#+-G#7 G#6-F#7-A-B11-E-E+-E-D13
Love Takes Time	V=E-B/D#-C#m-G#m/B-F#m7 E/G#-Bsus-B

1991

Achy Breaky Heart	V/C=E-B-E
Under The Bridge	V=E-B-C#m-B-A-E-B-C#m-A- (2x)EM7

1992

Tears In Heaven(A)	V=E-B/D#-C#m-C#m/B-A/C#- E/B-B(2x)C#m7-G#/C-E7/B- C#7-F#m7-B11

1994

Passionate Kisses(E)	V=E-B-C#m-A(2x)

Can You Feel The Love Tonight   C=E-B/D#-C#m-A

Listing By Progression Type

Chord Progression   *Song Examples*

Folk

E-B	Chantilly Lace('58); Tell Me('64); I Should Have Known Better('64); Yellow Submarine('66); Come On Down To My Boat('67); Ruby Tuesday('67); Quinn The Eskimo('68); Down On The Corner('69); Have You Ever Seen The Rain('71); Black And White('72); Drift Away('73); Fernando('76); Do You Feel Like We Do('76); Theme From "Cheers"('82); Hurts So Good('82)
E-B/D#-B	Have You Seen Your Mother Baby, Standing In The Shadows('66)
E-B+	Happy Days Are Here Again('29)
E-Bm	Marakesh Express('69);Let It Rain('70); Main Street('77); The One That You Love('81)
E-Bm7	Jezebel('50); Ferry Cross The Mersy('64); Good Vibrations('66); Pleasant Valley Sunday('67); Hey Bulldog('68)
E-B7	Three Blind Mice(N/A); Skip To My Lou(1832); Buffalo Girls(1850); Camptown Races(1851); The Marine's Hymn(1859); Alouette(1879); Clementine(1885); The Band Played On(1895); Take Me Out To The Ball Game('08); Hail, Hail The Gang's All Here('17); Mexican Hat Dance('19); When The Red, Red Robin Comes Bob, Bob Bobbin' Along('26); Day-O('55); Marianne('57); He's Got The Whole World In His Hand('58); Do-Re-Mi('59); Wheels('61); I Like It Like That('61); A Holly Jolly Christmas('62); Jambalaya('62); If You Want To Be Happy('63); Detroit City('63); Judy's Turn To Cry('63); When I Grow Up(To Be A Man)('64); Over And Over('65); Lemon Tree('65); I'm Telling You Now('65); I'm Your Puppet('66); Yellow Submarine('66); Lies('66);(You And Me)Rain On The Roof('66); When I Grow Up(To Be A Man)('66); Rocking Pneumonia And The Boogie Woogie Flu('72); Sweet Surrender('75); Way Down('77)
E-B7#5	Frankie And Johnny('63); Cabaret('66)

E-B11	Catch A Falling Star('57); Yesterday's Gone('64); I'll Cry Instead('64); Help Me Rhonda('65); Devil With A Blue Dress('66); Let Your Love Flow('76)
E-Eadd9-Bm/D	If You Could Read My Mind('71)
E5-B5	Janie's Got A Gun('90)
E7-Bm7	Ode To Billy Joe('67); Love Shack('89)
E-B-E	Sea Cruise('57); Bottle Of Wine('68); The Air That I Breath('74); Achy Breaky Heart('91)
E-B-B7-E	The No No Song('75)
E-B+-Em7-Em6	Fixin' A Hole('67)
E-B7-E	Down In The Valley(1835); Limbo Rock('62); Birds And The Bees('65); Winchester Cathedral('66); Give Peace A Chance('69); Knock Three Times('70); Blue Bayou('77)
E-B7-B7#5-E	Lady Of Spain('31)
E-B7-E-E7	If I Had A Hammer('62)
E-E7-B7-E	Everybody's Talkin''('69)
E-B-E-B7	Honky Tonk Woman('69)
E-B/F#-B-E/B-B7/F#	America The Beautiful('20)

Folk & Basic Combination

E-B-E-A	This Train(N/A); Old Folks At Home(1851); Roll In My Sweet Baby's Arm('31); Crying, Waiting, Hoping('58); Alberta('63); Sloop John B('66); Kentucky Rain('70); Sunshine(Go Away Today)('71)
E-B-[C#o-Do-D#o]-E-A	Rock This Town('82)
E-B-E-E7-A	Joy To The World('71)
E-B-B7-E-E7-A	Song Sung Blue('72)
E-B-B7-B7sus4-E-A	Hey Jude('68)
E-B7-E-A	Auld Lang Syne(1711); Silent Night(1818); Billy Boy(1824); Blue Tail Fly(1848); Ain't We Got Fun('21); Chantilly Lace('58); Save The Last Dance For Me('60); Teen Angel('60); The Watusi('61); Under The Boardwalk('64); Crooked Little Man('64); Baby, The Rain Must Fall('65); Tiny Bubbles('66); Ob-La-Di Ob-la-Da('68); Brand New Key('71)
E-B7-E-E7-A	She'll Be Coming Round The Mountain(1870); By The Light Of The Silvery Moon('09); Happy Birthday('35); When The Saints Go Marching In('46); Red River Rock('59); Danke Schoen('63);

	When I'm Sixty Four('67); Me And Bobby McGee('71); Cover Of The Rolling Stone('73); Blue Bayou('77)
E-B7-E-E7-A7	Muddy Water('66)
E-B7-E7-A	Bring It On Home To Me('62)
E-Bm7-E7-A	One, Two, Three('65); The Most Beautiful Girl('73)
E-Bm7-E7-A-A#o	There, I've Said It Again('64)
E5-B7sus-E5-A	Sundown('74)
EM7-Bm7-E7b9-AM7	Misty('55)
Eadd9-E-Bm7-E9-Aadd9	September Morn('80)
E6/9-B11-B9-E6/9	Singin' In The Rain('52)
E7-B7-E-A7	Mockingbird('74)
Em-B7-E7b9-A	I Think I Love You('70)

Reverse Rock("E" First)

E-B-A	Green Tambourine('68); The Weight('68);(Sittin' On)The Dock Of The Bay('68); Fortunate Son('69); Take It Easy('72); My Maria('73); Already Gone('73); You Ain't Seen Nothin' Yet('74); Already Gone('74); Sister Golden Hair('75); Boys Of Summer('84); Downtown Train('89)
E-B-Aadd9	Heart Of The Matter('90)
E-B-A7	Come Together('69)
E-B/D#-A-A/G#	Sooner Or Later('71)
E-B/D#-B7-A	Band Of Gold('70)
E-Bm/D-A7	Signed, Sealed, Delivered I'm Yours('70)
E-Bm7-A9	We Are Family('79)

The "E-B-A-E" progression can be transformed into a Descending "E-D#-C#-B" Bass Line Progression by playing the D# note of the "B" chord as the bass note, by playing the C# note of the "A" chord as the bass note, and the B note of the "E" chord as the bass note creating the "E-B/D#-A/C#-E/B" progression. In the same manner, the "E-Bm7-A-E" progression can be transformed into the "E-Bm7/D-A/C#-E/B" progression and the "E-EM7-Bm7-A" progression can be transformed into the "E-E/D#-Bm7/D-A/C#" progression.

E-B-A-E	Can't You Hear The Fountain Of My Heart Beat('65); The Little Black Egg('65); Nowhere Man('66); Come On Down To My Boat('67); To Love Somebody('67); The Letter('67); I Think We're Alone Now('67); Here Comes My Baby('67); Bottle Of Wine('68); Bad Moon Rising('69); Sweet Mary('71); Top Of The World('73); The No No Song('75); Island Girl('75); Stand Tall('76); Go Your Own Way('77)

E-B/F#-Aadd9-E	Wedding Song(There Is Love)('71)
E-B/D#-A-E	I Guess That's Why They Call It The Blues('83)
E-B7-A-E	Here Comes My Baby('67)
E-Bm7-A-E	Fire And Rain('70)
E-EM7-Bm7-A-Am-E	Kokomo('88)
E/G#-B/D#-A/C#-E/B	These Dreams('86)
E7-B-B7-A7-E7	I Feel Fine('64)
E7-B7-A7-E7	Surfin' Bird('64)

The "E-B-A-B" progression can be transformed into a Descending "E-D#-C#-B" Bass Line Progression by playing the D# note in the first "B" chord in the bass line and by playing the C# note in the "A" chord as the note creating the "E-B/D#-A/C#-B" progression.

E-B-A-B	Wishin' And Hopin'('64); Baby's In Black('64); Crimson And Clover('69);Games People Play('69); Wild World('71); What Is Life('71); Nights Are Forever Without You('76); It's So Easy('77); The First Cut Is The Deepest('77); The Rose('80); Jack And Diane('82); Small Town('85)
E-B7-Asus2-B7	New Kid In Town('76)
E/G#-B/D#-A-B/D#	Give Me Love(Give Me Peace On Earth)('73)

Descending Bass Lines

E-B/D#-A/C#-A	All Out Of Love('80)
E-B/D#-C#m-A	Baby, I Love Your Way('76); Slow Dancing (Swayin' To The Music)('77); Can You Feel The Love Tonight('94)
E-B/D#-C#m-AM7	Let It Be('70)
E-B/D#-F#m/C#-B7	With A Little Help From My Friends('67)
E-B/D#-A/C#-F#m7/B	He Ain't Heavy, He's My Brother('70)
E-B/D#-A/C#-B	Wonderful Tonight('78)
E-B/D#-C#m-E/B	For No One('66); When Will I See You Again('74); Shower The People('76); Always On My Mind('82)
E-B/D#-C#m-E7/B	When A Man Loves A Woman('66)
E-B/D#-C#m-G#m/B	Let It Be Me('60); End Of The World('63); The Weight('68); I'll Be There('70); Don't Pull Your Love('71); Love Takes Time('90)
E-B/D#-C#m-B	Dust In The Wind('78)
E-B/D#-C#m-C#m/B	I Got A Name('73); Tears In Heaven('92)
E-B/D#-C#m7-E/B	Your Smiling Face('77)
E-B/D#-C#m7-B	59th Street Bridge Song('66); Reelin' In The Years('73)

E-B/D#-C#m7-B6	I Got The Sun In The Morning('46)
E-B/D#-C#11-C#m7-B	All Cried Out('86)
E-B6/D#-C#m-E/B	Mind Games('73)
E-B/D#-A/C#-Am/C	How Am I Supposed To Live Without You('90)
E-B/D#-C#m-G#/C	Star Spangled Banner(1814); Beach Baby('74)
E-B/D#-D-A	(You Make Me Feel Like)A Natural Woman('67)
E-B/D#-D6-A	Give Me Just A Little More Time('70)
E-B7/D#-D-Am/C-E/B	It Don't Matter To Me('70)
E-B/D#-Bm6/D-C#7	Homeward Bound('66)
E-B/D#-D-A/C#	Walk Away Renee('66); Never My Love('67); Three Times A Lady('78)
E6-B/D#-Bm/D-C#m	Blue Eyes('82)

Static Bass Lines

E-E6	I Guess The Lord Must Be In New York City('69)
E-EM7-E6	I'm Gonna Sit Right Down And Write Myself A Letter('35)
E-EM7-E6-E	Have You Seen Her('71)
E-EM7-E6-EM7-E	It Might As Well Be Spring('45)
EM7-E6	Let Em In('76)
E-E+-E6-E7-E6	Sentimental Journey('44)
E-Esus-E	Margaritaville('77)
E-F#/E-Aadd9/E-E	Wedding Song(There Is Love)('71)
E-B/E	Looks Like We Made It('77); Jack And Diane('82)
E-B/E-A/E	Babe('79)
E-B/E-A/E-E	Substitute('66); You Don't Bring Me Flowers('78); Time Passages('78)
E-B/E-A/E-Am6/E	Up Where We Belong('82)
E-B/E-A/E-B/E	Can't Get It Out Of My Head('75); We've Got Tonight('78); The One That You Love('81)
E-Bm/E	Taxi('72); Vision Of Love('90)

Other "E-B" Progressions

Many of the following Other "E-B" progressions can be transformed into Descending Bass Line Progressions by playing other chord notes as the bass note. Various examples are shown below.

E-B-E-C#m	City Of New Orleans('72)
E-B7-E-F#7	Hail To The Chief(1812); You Got What It Takes('67)
E-B7-E-C#7	Tijuanna Taxi('66)
E-B7/E-E-F#m/B	A Groovy Kind Of Love('66)
E-B7sus4-E-F#m	Fly Away('76)
E-B7#5-E6-Fo	Top Hat, White Tie And Tails('35)
E-B11-E-C#m	Did You Ever Have To Make Up Your Mind('66)
E6-B7+-E-Em6-B	Chances Are('57)

The "E-B-F#m-A" progression can be transformed into a Descending "E-D#-C#-A" Bass Line by playing the D# note of the "B" chord as the bass note and the C# note of the F#m chord as the bass note creating the "E-B/D#-F#m/C#-A" progression. In the same manner, the "E-B-F#m-B7" progression can be transformed into the E-B/D#-F#m/C#-B7" progression. Also, the "E-B-F#m7-E" progression can be transformed into the "E-B/D#-F#m7/C#-E/B" progression and the "E-Bm7-F#m7-A" progression can be transformed into the "E-Bm7/D-F#m7/C#-A" progression.

E-B-F#m-A	Baby I Love The Way('76)
E-B-F#m-[G#m]-A	I Can't Help Myself('65)
E-B-F#m-B7	Tequila Sunrise('73)
E-B-F#m7-E	Knockin' On Heaven's Door('73)
E-B7-F#m-B7	Put Your Hand In The Hand('71)
E-B7-F#m7-B7	Rockin' Around The Christmas Tree('58); The Alley Cat Song('62); Stand By Your Man('69); Candida('70)
E-Bm-F#m7-C#m7	She's Leaving Home('67)–Verse
E-Bm7-F#m7-A	Old Man('72)
E-B-G#-C#m	Carefree Highway('74)
EM9-B/A-G#m7-C#7(b9/b13)	You Are The Sunshine Of My Life('73)
E-B-A-G#m	Tuesday Afternoon('68)
E-B-A-C#m	Come Together('69); Sweet Jane('70)
E-Bm-A-FM7	Tomorrow('68)
E-EM7-Bm7-A	Kokomo('88)
EM7-B-A-F#m7	Everyone's Gone To The Moon('65)

E-B-A#-F#m7   Where Did Our Love Go('64)

The "E-B-C#m-A" progression can be transformed into a Descending "E-D#-C#-A" progression by playing the D# note in the "B" chord as the bass note creating the "E-B/D#-C#m-A" progression. In the same manner, the "E-B-C#m-B" progression can be transformed into the "E-B/D#-C#m-B" progression and the "E-B-C#m-E/B" progression can be transformed into the "E-B/D#-C#m-E/B" progression. Also, the "E-B/D#-C#m-F#m7" progression can be transformed into the "E-B/D#-C#m-F#m7/A" progression, the "E-B7-C#m-G#7" progression can be transformed into the "E-B7/D#-C#m-G#7/C" progression, and the "E-EM7-Bm-C#7" progression can be transformed into the "E-E/D#-Bm/D-C#7" progression.

E-B-C#m-E/B	Shower The People('76)
E-B-C#m-E7/D	In My Life('65)
E-B-C#m-F#	Somebody To Love('67)
E-B-C#m-G#m	Holiday('67); People Got To Be Free('68)
E-B-C#m-G#7	I Don't Want To Spoil The Party('65); Listen People('66)
E-B-C#m-A	One Fine Day('63); Don't Think Twice('63); Oh! Darling('69); Smile A Little Smile For Me('69); Take Me Home Country Roads('71); Hurts So Good('82); Theme From "Cheers"('82); Down Under('83); Right Here Waiting('89); Passionate Kisses('94)
E-B-C#m-B	Under The Bridge('91)
E-B-C#m-B/D#	Fire Lake('80)
E-B-C#m-DM9	W.O.L.D.('74)
E-B-C#-F#m	What Is Life('71)
E-B-C#5	Magic Man('76)
E-B/E-C#m-A	Beast Of Burden('78)
E-B/D#-C#m	All You Need Is Love('67)
E-B/D#-C#m-E	Stairway To Heaven('72)
E-B/D#-C#m-F#m7	Karma Chameleon('84)
E-B/D#-C#m-D	Free Bird('75)
E-B/D#-C#m7-F#m7	Don't Cry Out Loud('79)
E-B/D#-C#m7-C#m7/F#	Ooh Child('70)
E-Bsus-B7-C#m	The Morning After('73)
E-B7-C#m-G#7	I Want To Hold Your Hand('64)
E-Bm6-C#m-F#7	She's Leaving Home('67)–Chorus
E-Bm7-C#7-A	Strawberry Fields Forever('67)
E-EM7-Bm-C#7	Stop! In The Name Of Love('65)
E5-B5-C#5-A5	We Didn't Start The Fire('89)

The "E-B-D-E" progression can be transformed into a Descending "E-D#-D-B" Bass Line Progression by playing the D# note of the "B" chord as the bass note and the B note of the "E" chord as the bass note creating the "E-B/D#-D-E/B" progression. In the same manner, the "E-B-D-A" progression can be transformed into the "E-B/D#-D-A/C#" progression, the "E-B/D#-D6-F#m" progression can be transformed into the "E-B/D#-D6-F#m/C#" progression, and the "E-B7-D-Am" progression can be transformed into the "E-B7/D#-D-Am/C" progression.

E-B-D	Lay Down(Candles In The Rain)('70)
E-B-D-E	You've Got To Hide Your Love away('65); I'm A Believer('66)
E-B-D-A	Build Me Up Butter Cup('69); Let It Rain('70); It's Still Rock And Roll To Me('80)
E-B-D-C#	Man-eater('82)
E-B-Dadd9-E	I'm A Loser('64)
E-B/D#-D6-F#m	I Hear A Symphony('65)
E-B7-D-Am	It Don't Matter To Me('70)
E-Bm-D-E	Good Morning Good Morning('67)
E-Bm-D-A	It Don't Come Easy('71); Baker Street('78)
E-Bm7-D-A	Cinnamon Girl('69)
E-EM7-Bm-D	I Need You('72)
E7-B7-[C7-C#7]-D7	Mean Mr. Mustard('69)

"E-C" Chord Progressions

Only a few songs employ the chord sequence of the "E" chord to the "Borrowed" "C" chord. The most frequent "E-C" chord progressions continue to move to the "E", "B", or the "Borrowed" "D" chords. The most notable song is the 1932 standard *Night And Day*.

Below is a chronological listing of songs with verses and/or choruses that begin with the "E-C" chord sequence followed by a listing of chord progressions by type.

Chronological Listing

Date/Song Title	*Chord Progression*
1932	
Night And Day	V=E6-CM7/G-B7/F#-EM7-E6-(2x)A#m7b5-Am7-G#m7-Go-F#m11-B7-EM9-E6
1956	
Honey Don't(E)	V=E-C(2x)B7-E
1957	
Peggy Sue(A)	B=E-C-(E-A)2x B-A-E
1963	
It Won't Be Long(E)	V=E-C(2x)E
1964	
Everybody Knows(C)	V=E-C6-E-F#m7-B7

1965

Gold Finger(E)   V=E-C-Bm-E-A-D#7-B7

She's Just My Style(A)   V=E-C-D-E(2x)

1967

Lazy Day   V=E-C-G-D-F-C-Em-B-E(2x)

She's My Girl(E)   C=E-C-Bm-A-Bm

1968

Honey Pie(G)   V=E-C7-C#7-F#7-B7-E
                             T/A=C7-B7

Dream A Little Dream Of Me   V=E-C9-B9-E-
                             C#7-G#m7b5-C#7

1969

The End(A)   O=E-E11-C-Am7-D7-
                             G-A/G-A#-C-G

1970

Hand Me Down World(B)   V=E-E/D-E/C#-CM7-Bsus-A7-
                             E-E/D-E/C#-CM7-Bsus-A-G

1972

Suffragette City(A)   V=E-C-D(2x)E-F#-A-C-D

1976

Takin' It To The Street(C)   PC=E-E/D-E/C#-C6-B7sus(2x)

1977

Barracuda(E)   V=E5-C(2x)E5
                                      I=E5-F#5-G5-G6

1985

Sunset Grill   V=E/B-C(4x)G-D

1993

All I Wanna Do(E)   V=E-C/G-Dadd9/A

1996

Kiss From A Rose   V/C=E-CM7-D-E

Listing By Progression Type

Chord Progression   *Song Example*

Descending Bass Lines

E-E/D-E/C#-C6	Takin' It To The Street('76)
E-E/D-E/C#-CM7	Hand Me Down World('70)
A#m7b5-Am7-G#m7-Go	Night And Day('32)

Other "E-C" Progressions

E-C	Honey Don't('56); It Won't Be Long('63)
E/B-C	Sunset Grill('85)
E5-C	Barracuda('77)
E-C-E-A	Peggy Sue('57)
E-C6-E-F#m7	Everybody Knows('64)
E-C-G-D	Lazy Day('67)

E-E11-C-Am7	The End('69)
E-C-Bm-E	Gold Finger('65)
E-C-Bm-A	She's My Girl('67)
E-C9-B9-E	Dream A Little Dream Of Me('68)
E6-CM7/G#-B7/F#	Night And Day('32)
E-C7-C#7-F#7	Honey Pie('68)
E-C-D	Suffragette City('72)
E-C-D-E	She's Just My Style('65)
E-C/G-Dadd9/A	All I Wanna Do('93)
E-CM7-D-E	Kiss From A Rose('96)

"E-C#" Chord Progressions

Chord progressions that begin with an "E" chord and then proceed to a "C#m" or "C#7" are widely used in all types of popular songs. The most frequent "E-C#" chord progressions are as follows:

Rock Ballad	E-C#m-A-B7
Partial Rock Ballad	E-C#m
Standard	E-C#m-F#m-B7
Ragtime	E-C#7-F#7-B7
Descending "E-D#-C#-B" Bass Lines	E-E/D#-C#m-C#m/B

The "E-C#m-A-B7" Rock Ballad Progression, which has been a Rock staple since the late 1950s, is closely related to the Standard Changes except the harder sounding "A" chord was substituted for the softer "F#m" chord. Generally, either chord progression can readily be substituted for the other. A great example of this Rock Ballad sequence is Maurice Williams' 1960 classic *Stay*.

The "E-C#m" Partial Rock Ballad Progression consists of the first two chords of the Rock Ballad Progression. Numerous hit songs have been written around these two chords such as Bobby Darin's 1959 *Dream Lover*, the Everly Brothers' 1959 *('Til)I Kissed You*, and Joey Dee & The Starliters' 1962 *Shout*.

The "E-C#m-F#m-B7" Standard Changes follow the Circle of Fifths movement. The Standard Changes were used extensively in songs written in the 1930s and 1940s. The progression was employed for the most frequently played and recognizable piano duet of all time, the 1938 *Heart and Soul*. Due to the pervasiveness of this progression in twentieth century popular songs, songwriters and performers alike have often employed techniques of Chord Substitution in order to disguise or dress up this musical staple. In the Appendix of this book is a list of common chord progressions which can be used in place of the "E-C#m-F#m-B7" progression. Several songs such as the 1930 *I Got Rhythm* and the 1960 *Try To Remember* had verses that were originally written as "E-F#m-B7", however, most performers now add the "missing" "C#m" chord when playing these songs.

The "E-C#7-F#7-B7" Ragtime Progression was popular in the early 1900s. The Ragtime Progression follows the Circle of Fifths movement and is similar to the Standard Changes except the "C#m" and "F#m" chords are substituted for their respective Dominant 7th Chord Qualities to create a harder bouncier sounding progression. Bruce Channel's 1962 hit *Hey! Baby*, the Rooftop Singers' 1963 *Walk Right In*, and Arlo Guthrie's 1967 *Alice's Restaurant* employed this turn of the century chord sequence.

The "E-D#-C#-B" Descending Bass Line was used to write such great songs as Crosby, Stills, Nash & Young's 1970 *Our House* and the Nitty Gritty Dirt Band's 1971 *Mr. Bojangles*.

In addition to the most frequent progressions already discussed, there are a number of other "E-C#" Chord Progressions that mainly continue to move to the "E", "F#m", "G#m", "A", and "B" chords. The "E-C#m-A" and "E-C#m-B" sequences represent Partial Rock Ballad Progressions where the "B" and the "A" chords, respectively, have been omitted.

Below is a chronological listing of songs with verses and/or choruses that employ the "E-C#" sequence followed by a listing of chord progressions by type.

Chronological Listing

Date/Song Title	*Chord Progression*
N/A	
Keep On Truckin' Mama	V=E-C#7-F#7-B7(2x)E-E7-A-C7
1899	
Hello My Baby	V=E-C#7-F#7-B7-E-Go-B7/F#
1918	
After You're Gone	V=EM7-C#m7b9-BM7-G#9-C#9-F#9-BM7-B7
1924	
It Had To Be You	V=E-C#7-F#7-B7

1926

Bye Bye Blackbird　　　V=E-C#7-F#m7-B9-E-E/G#-Go-F#m7-B7

The Blue Room　　　V=E-C#m7-F#m7-B7(2x)

1927

Ol' Man River　　　V=E-C#m7-E-A-E-A-E-C#m7-F#m7-B9(2x)

Can't Help Lovin' Dat Man　　　V=EM7-C#m7-F#m7-B7

1928

When You're Smiling　　　V=E-C#7-F#m-F#m7-B7-B+-E-E7

1929

Tip-Toe Through The Tulips　　　V=E-C#7-F#m-B7-E-G#7-A-Am

1930

I Got Rhythm　　　C=E-C#m-F#m-B7(3x)E-B7-E

1931

Between The Devil And
The Deep Blue Sea　　　V=E-C#m7-F#m7-B7(2x)

1932

Try A Little Tenderness　　　V=E-C#m7-F#m7-B7+5-E-D#+-Bm6/D-C#7-F#7

1934

Blue Moon　　　V=EM7-C#m7-F#m7-B7(7x)

1935

Little Girl Blue	V=E-C#m7-F#m9-B9
Lullaby Of Broadway	V=E-C#7b9-F#m7-B7b9

1936

Let's Call The Whole Thing Off	V=E-C#m7-F#m7-B7(2x)

1938

Heart and Soul	V=E-C#m7-F#m7-B7(4x)
Over The Rainbow	V=E-C#m7-G#m-E7

1940

Polka Dots And Moonbeams	V=EM7-C#m7-F#m7-B7

1943

Have Yourself A Merry Little Christmas	V=E-C#m-F#m7-B7(3x) T/A=G#7-C#7-F#7-B7

1944

Moonlight in Vermont	V=EM7-C#m7-F#m7-B7-EM7-C#m7-D9-F#m7-B11-EM7

1946

(I Love You) For Sentimental Reasons	V=EM7-C#m7-F#m7-B7(2x)

1948

"A" You're Adorable	V=E-C#7-F#7-F#m7-G#m7-C#7

1950

Sleigh Ride | V=E-C#m7-F#m7-B7(8x)-A#m7-D#7-G#-G#6

1952

Love Is A Simple Thing | V=E-C#m-F#m-B9(2x)

When I Fall In Love | V=E-C#7(#5/b9)-F#m7-B7(2x)

1954

Sh Boom(Life Could Be A Dream) | V=E-C#m-F#m7-B7

Hey There | V=E-C#m7-F#m7-B7(2x)

1955

Earth Angel | V=E-C#m-F#m7-B7(7x)

Mickey Mouse March | C=E-C#m-F#7-B7

Love Is A Many-Splendored Thing | V=E-C#m-G#m-Bm7-E7

Unchained Melody | V=E-C#m-AM7-B7-E-C#m-B-B7

1956

I Want You, I Need You, I Love You | V=E-C#m-F#m-B7-E-E7-A-E-G#7-C#7-F#7-Am-B7

Why Do Fools Fall In Love(F) | V=E-C#m7-F#m7-B7(7x)E

Diana | V=E-C#m-F#m7-B7(4x)E7

Silhouettes(C) | V=E-C#m-A-B-A(4x)

You Send Me	V=E-C#m-F#m7-B7
Little Darlin'	V=E6-C#m-F#m7-B7(3x)

1958

Maybe Baby(A)	V=E-C#m(2x)E-A-B-E
Do You Want To Dance	V=E-C#m7-F#m7-B7b9(3x)E-C9-B7
All I Have To Do Is Dream	V=E-C#m-F#m-B7(2x)-E-C#m-A-B7(2x)
Book Of Love	V=E-C#m-F#m7-B7(2x)E-A-E
Lollipop	V=E-C#m-F#m7-B7(3x)E-B7
Poor Little Fool(C)	V=E-C#m-A-B(4x)

1959

Dream Lover	V=E-C#m(2x)E-B7-E-A-E-E-C#m-F#m7-B7-E-B
('Til)I Kissed You(F#)	V=E-C#m(4x)E-A-B
Put Your Head On My Shoulder	V=E-C#m-F#m7-B7
A Teenager In Love	V=E-C#m-A-B7(3x)E-B7
Just Ask Your Heart	V=E-C#m-A-B7(2x)
Since I Don't Have You	V=E-C#m7-Am-B7b9(3x)-F#m7-B7
Lipstick On Your Collar	V=E-C#m-F#m7-B7(2x)-E-E7-A-F#7-B7
Sleep Walker(C)	V=E-C#m-Am-B7

1960

Devil or Angel	V=E-C#m-F#m7-B7(2x)
Sixteen Reasons	V=E-C#m-F#m7-B7(3x)
Are You Lonesome Tonight	C=E-C#7-F#m-B7-E
Try to Remember	V=E-C#m7-F#m7-B7(4x)
Theme From "A Summer Place"	V=EM7-C#m7-F#m7-B9(4x)
Stay(G)	V=E-C#m-A-B(7x)C#m
In The Still Of The Night(Bb)	V=E-C#m-A-B

1961

Travelin' Man(D)	V=E-C#m(2x)E-A-E-B-E-B
Calender Girl	V=E-C#m(2x)A-A#o-E/B-C#7-F#7-B7-E-A6-E C=E-C#m(3x)F#m7-B7-E
His Latest Flame	V=E-C#m(4x)A-B7-E
Cupid	C=E-C#m-E-E7-A-E-B7-E-B7
Sherry	C=E-C#m-F#m-B7(x)E-G-A-E
There's A Moon Out Tonight	V=E-C#m-F#m7-B7
One Summer Night	V=E-C#m-F#m7-B7(5x)
Daddy's Home(Gb)	V=E-C#m7-F#m7-B7(4x)
Where The Boys Are	V=E-C#m-G#m-F#m7-B7-E
Please Mr. Postman(A)	V=E-C#m-A-B

Bristol Stomp	V=E-C#m-A-B(5x)
Pretty Little Angel Eyes	V=E-C#m-A-B7
Runaround Sue(D)	V/C/I=E-C#m-A-B
Stand By Me(A)	V=E-C#m-A-B
Let's Twist Again	V=E-C#m-A-B
Raindrops	V=E-C#m-A-B11
Who Put The Bomp	V=E-C#m-A-B7
Moon River	V=E-C#m-A-E/G#-A-E/G#-D#m7b5-G#7

1962

Shout	V=E-C#m
Johnny Get Angry	C=E-C#m(2x)A-B7-E-A-B7-E
Having A Party	V=E-C#m(3x)E-A-E C=E-C#m-E-A-B-E
Locomotion	V=E-C#m(4x)A-F#m-A
Anna(Go To Him)(D)	V=E-C#m(4x)F#m-B
Johnny Angel	V=E-C#m-F#m7-B7(2x)E-Fo-F#m7-B7
Breaking Up is Hard to Do	V=E-C#m7-F#m7-B7(2x)
Telstar	V=E-C#m7-F#m7-B7(4x)
Big Girls Don't Cry(G)	V=E-C#7-F#m7-B7(7x)

Hey Baby(A)	V=E-C#7-F#7-B7
Return to Sender	V=E-C#m-F#m-B7(2x)E
He's A Rebel	V=E-C#m-A-B7 C=E-C#m-E-B7- A-G#-C#m-A-B7
Duke Of Earl	V=E-C#m-A-B7
Where Have All The Flowers Gone	V=E-C#m-A-B7(3x)A-E-A-B7
Monster Mash	V=E-C#m-A-B
You've Really Got A Hold On Me(C)	V=E-C#m-E7-A7-F#7-B7-E-C#m
Sukiyaki	V=E-C#m(2x)E-G#m-C#m-F#m7
Hello, Dolly	V=E-C#m-EM7/G#-Go-F#m7-B7- F#m7-D/F#-F#m7-B7-G#m7- Go-F#m7-B7

1963

Surf City(Ab)	V=E-C#m(3x)A-F#m-D-B
From Me To You(C)	V=E-C#m-E-B7-A-C#m-E-B7-E
Since I Fell For You	V=E-C#m7-F#m7-Bm7-E-C#m7
More	V=EM7-C#m7-F#m7-B9-B7b9-(2x)
Go Away Little Girl	V=E-C#m-F#m-B7
This Boy(D)	V=E-C#m-F#m-B7(2x)- E-C#m-F#m/E-B7
Two Faces Have I	C=E-C#m7-F#m7-B7(2x)

Be True To Your School(A)	V=E-C#m-F#m-B11-B(2x)
Walk Right In	V=E-C#7-F#7-B7(2x)E-A9-B7
I Call Your Name(E)	V=E7-C#7-F#7-B7-E7-C#7-F#7-A-Am-E7
Just One Look	V=E-C#m-A-B
Judy's Turn To Cry(D)	C=E-C#m-A-B-E-B7 I=B-B+
Be My Baby(E)	C=E-C#m-A-B7
Up On The Roof	V=E-C#m7-A-B11(2x)E-A-A6-AM7-A6-E-C#m-A-F#m7-B9
Surfer Girl(D)	V=E-C#m-A-B7-EM7-E7-A-Am

1964

Pretty Woman(A)	V=E-C#m(2x)A-B7
I Only Want To Be With You(D)	V=E-C#m(2x)A-B7-F#m7-B7
Any Way You Want It(A)	V/C=E-C#m
Needles And Pins(A)	V=E-C#m(3x)A-B
Cry For A Shadow(C)	V=E-C#m(4x)A-B-E-C#m-E
How Do You Do What You Do To Me(A)	V=E-C#m-F#m-B
Tell Me Why(D)	V=E-C#m7-F#m7-B7-E6-F#m7-B7
Today	V=E-C#m-F#m7-B7(2x)-

	E-E7-A-Am- E-C#m-F#m7-B7(2x)
Baby Love(C)	V=E-E/D-C#7-F#m-(E-A6)2x- B-A-E/G#-F#m7-B
I Get Around	C=E-C#7-F#m-D-B7
The Warmth Of The Sun(C)	V=E-C#m-G-Em7-F#m7-B-B+- E-C#m-G-Em7-F#m7-B-G#
She Loves You(G)	V=E-C#m7-G#m-B7(2x)- E-C#m-Am-B7- C#m-F#7-Am-B7- E-C#m-Am-B7-E
Love Me With All Your Heart	V=E-C#m-G#m-A6-F#m6- G#m7b5-C#7
Last Kiss	V=E-C#m-A-B7
Dead Man's Curve(F#)	C=E-C#m-A-B-C-Am-B
Tell Me(B)	C=E-C#5-A-B

1965

Catch Us If You Can(G)	V=E-C#m(2x)E-F#m-G#m-E
Hold Me, Thrill Me, Kiss Me	V=E-C#m-F#m7-B7
You're Going To Lose That Girl(E)	C=E-C#m-F#m-B7
Come Home(D)	V=E-C#m-F#m7-B(2x)
Baby, I'm Yours	V=E-C#7-F#7-B7
Eve Of Destruction(D)	C=E-C#m-A-B

I Can't Explain(E)	B=E-C#m-A-B
I've Just Seen A Face(A)	V=E-C#m-A-B-E-B-A-E-A-E
Wonderful World	V=E-C#m-A-B7(2x)E-A(2x)-E-B7-E
Keep On Dancing	V=E-C#m-A-B7(3x)E-B7
Don't Let Me Be Misunderstood	C=E-C#m-B-A-C#m
Sunshine, Lollipops, And Rainbows	V=E-C#m-B(2x)E-C#m7-F#m7-B7
People Get Ready(Db)	V=E-C#m7-B11-E(3x)

1966

A Well Respected Man(C)	V=E-E/D#-C#m(6x) C=E-E/D#-C#m(4x)-A-G#m-A-F#-B
You Don't Have To Say You Love Me	C=E-C#m-F#m-B7(2x)
Double Shot(Ab)	V=E-C#m-F#m7-B7(4) I=E-C#m(2x)E-B7
Ain't Gonna Lie	V=E-C#m7-F#m7-B7(2x)
Lil' Red Riding Hood	C=E-C#m-F#7-B7(2x)
Flowers On The Wall	V=E-C#m-F#7-B7(2x)
Day Dream	V=E-C#7-F#m7-B7-E-C#7-F#m7-B11-B7
Good Day Sunshine(A)	V=E-C#7-F#7-B7-E(2x)-F#-C#(2x)B7

East West	V=E-C#m-G#m-F#m-G#m-F#m-A-B7
Walk Away Renee	C=E-C#m-A-E-B7-E-C#m-A-E-A-E/G#-F#m7-E

1967

At The Zoo	V=E-C#m(3x)B-B7
Penny Lane(B)	V=E-C#m7-F#m7-B7-E-C#m7-Em7-Em/C#-CM7 B7sus4-B7(2x)
Alice's Restaurant(C)	V=E-C#7-F#7-B7-E(2x)E-E-A#o
Sunday Will Never Be The Same	V=E-C#7-F#m-B7-E-C#m7-F#m-F#7-B7sus-B7
Then You Can Tell Me Goodbye	V=EM7-C#m-F#m7-B7b9-F7#9(2x)E-A(3x) I=E-Fo-F#m7-B7b9-F7#9
Dedicated To The One I Love(G)	V=E-C#m-A-B9(2x)-C#m-G#m-F#m-B7-E I=B7-B9
Hello Goodbye(C)	C=E-E/D#-C#m7-C#m/B-A-C6 E-E/D#-C#m7-C#m/B-A-D9-E
When I Was Young(G)	C=E-C#m-B-C#m-B-C#m
Kind Of A Drag	I=E-E+-C#m-B7
It Must Be Him	V=E-E6-EM7-E6(2x)C#m-B7

1968

Nobody But Me   V=E-C#m(4x)E

(Sittin' On)
The Dock Of The Bay(G)   C=E-C#(2x)E-F#-E-C#

Mrs. Robinson(A)   C=E-C#m(2x)A-A/G#-A/F#-A/E-
                                   B-B/A-B/G#-B/F#

America   V=E-E/D#-C#m-E/B-A

I Will(F)   V=E-C#m-F#m7-B7-
                                   E-C#m-G#m-E7-A-B7-E-A-B7

For Once In My Life(F)   V=E-E+-E6-C#7b9-(F#m-C#+)2x-
                                   F#m-F#m(M7)-F#m7-B7-E-B+-E

My Special Angel   V=E-C#m-G#m-F#m7-B7-
                                   E-Fo-F#m7-B7
                                   E-C#m-F#7-B7

Across The Universe(D)   V=E-C#m-G#m-F#m7-B7

Journey To The
Center Of The Mind(E)   B=E-C#m-A-F#(2x)B

Happiness Is A Warm Gun(C)   C=E-C#m-A-B

I Love How You Love Me   V=E-C#m-A-B7(2x)E

Julia(D)   V=E-C#m-Bm-Bm9-C#7-
                                   A7add9-Am-E-C#m7-G#m-B-E

1969

Smile a Little Smile for Me   V=E-C#m-F#m-B7(2x)C#m-A

Lady Of The Island
(E Open Tuning)   V=Eadd9-Eadd9/D-C#m11-

	F#m7b5/C-(G#m7-F#m11)2x
Maxwell's Silver Hammer(D)	V=E-C#7-F#m-B7-E-B(2x)
Octopus's Garden(E)	V=E-C#m-A-B(3x)C#m-A-B
This Magic Moment	V=E-C#m-A-B7
Something(C)	B=E-E/D#-C#m-C#m/B-A-D-E- E-E/D#-C#m/B-A-D-G
The Boxer(C)	V=E-C#m-B-E

1970

Instant Karma	V=E-C#m(3x)C-D-E- A-F#m(2x)G-Em7-A-B9
El Condor Pasa(G)	V=E-C#m-E-C#m
Evil Woman	V=E-C#-E
Signed, Sealed, Delivered, I'm Yours(E)	V=E-C#m(2x)A-B11
My Sweet Lord(E)	C=E-C#m(2x)E-Fo-G#o-F#m-B
Our House(A)	V=E-E/D#-C#m7-E/B-A-E/G#- F#m7-A/C#-B11
The Wonder of You	V=E-C#m-F#m7-B7(2x)- E-E7-A-B7- E-D7-C#7-F#m7-B7- E-F#m7-B7
Dig A Pony(A)	V=E-C#m-F#m-D7-F#m-D7-B
Ma Belle Amie	V=E-C#m-F#-B(2x)
Give Me Just A Little More Time	C=EM7-C#m7-G#m-A(2x)

One Less Bell To Answer(D)	V=EM7-E6-EM7-C#m9-G#m7(2x)-AM7-D#m7-G#7-C#m9-F#7-F#m7/B-F#m7-G#m7-AM7-AM7/B-EM7
What Have They Done To My Song, Ma	V=E-C#m-A-E-F#-A-E-B7(2x)
Lookin' Out My Back Door(Bb)	V=E-C#m-A-E-B(2x)E
Burn Down The Mission	V=E-C#m-A11-C-E/B-F#/A#-Bsus
Celebrate(A)	V=E-E/D-C#m-Am/C-E/B-F#9/A#-A-E
I'll Never Fall In Love Again	V=E-C#m7-AM7-G#m7-G#m7/C#-C#7-F#m7-B7
Everything Is Beautiful	C=E-C#m-B7sus-F#7-E-B-E-A-E

1971

What's Going On(E)	V=EM7-C#m7(2x)-F#m7-B11-B13 C=EM7-C#m7(2x)
Mr. Bojangles	V=E-E/D#-C#m7-E7/B-A-B7(2x) A-E-G#7-C#m-C#m/B-F#9-B11-B7
Breezin'(D)	V=E-C#m7-F#m7-B11
Mercy, Mercy Me(E)	V=EM7-C#m7-F#m7-B11-B9
If(A)	V=Eadd9-EM9/D#-E9/D-C#m11-Am6/C-E/B-Am6-B7
Take Me Home, Country Roads(A)	V=E-C#m-B-A-E(2x)

1972

Doctor My Eyes(F)   C=E-C#m(2x)B7sus-A/E

All The Young Dudes(D)   V=E-E/D#-C#m-E/B-F#m-B
C=E-E/D#-C#m-Bm-Bm/A-G-D/F#

Without You   V=E-C#m7-F#m7-G#7-
C#m-C#m/B-A-F#m-E-B
C=E-C#m-F#m-B7(2x)

I Believe in Music   V=E-C#m-F#m-B7

Candy Man   V=E-EM7-C#7b9-F#m7-B7-Bm7-E7

(Last Night)
I Didn't Get To Sleep At All   V=E-C#m-G#m-C#m-G#m-AM7-
B7-F#m7/B-B7

Take It Easy(G)   C=E-C#m-A-E-F#m-A-C#m-A-E

Go All The Way(A)   C=E-C#m-A-F#m-B7-
G#m7-C#7-F#m-Am-B(2x)

I Wanna Be With You(E)   C=E-C#m-A-B11(2x)E-E+-A-Am

1973

Aubrey(G)   V=E-E/D#-C#m-EM7/B-A-A/G#-
F#m7-F#m7/B-E-E/D#-C#m-
C+-E/B-A#m7b5-AM7

Who's In The Strawberry Patch
With Sally   V=E-C#7-F#7-A-B7

D'yer Mak'er(C)   V=E-C#m-A-B

1974

Love's Theme   V=E-C#m(2x)F#m7-Am6-

	EM7-C#m-F#m7-F#m7/B
Rock The Boat	V=E-C#m-E-B-F#m
Don't Let The Sun Go Down On Me	C=E-E/D-C#m7-F#7/A#-E/B-B11-B7-E-E/D-A/C#-F#m-E/G#-E/B-B11-E
Mandy	C=E-C#m-A-B-A(2x)

1975

He Don't Love You	C=E-C#m(2x)F#m7-B7-E-EM7-E7-A-Am-E-C#m-F#m7-B7-E
Can't Get It Out Of My Head	V=Eadd9-C#m(2x)AM7-F#m-(2x)B
This Will Be(An Everlasting Love)	V=E-C#m-F#m7-B7(3x)G#m-G-C-B7
Who Loves You(A)	C=E-C#m-F#m7-B11
Lonely People(G)	V=E-C#m-G#m/D#(2x)B
Look In My Eyes Pretty Woman	V=E-C#m-G#m-A-B-B7sus-E-C#m-G#m-A-F#m7-B7-F#m7/C#-B7/D#
Bad Time	C=E-C#m-A-F#m-A-B-F#m-B(4x)
How Sweet It Is (To Be Loved By You)(G)	V=E-C#m-B7-A#7-A7(2x)-E-A7-C#m-A7-A#o-E-A7-E T/A=E-D-C#m-Bm

1976

Strange Magic	V=E-E+(3x)C#m

Fernando	V=E-C#m-F#m-B-E
Happy Days	V=E-C#m-F#m-B-G#-C#m-A-B
If You Leave Me Now(B)	V=E-C#m7-G#m7-C#m7-F#7
Love Hurts	V=E-C#m-A-B7(2x)E-G#7-C#m-E7-A-B7
Only Sixteen	V=E-C#m-A-B7-A-B7-E
Girls Just Want To Have Fun	V=E-C#m-A-C#m-B-A-C#m-B
Show Me The Way(D)	V=E-EM7-C#m-C6-[D]-E-EM7-C#m-C6-B11-A

1977

On And On	V=E-C#m7(addF#)(3x)F#m7-B11
Slip Slidin' Away	C=E-C#m-E-B-A-B-E
Don't It Make My Brown Eyes Blue(E)	V=E-C#m7-F#m7-B7 E-C#m7-D#m7b5-G#7-C#m7 C#m/B-Bm7b5-F#7-A-G#m-A-B11
Handy Man	V=E-[B/D#]-C#m-[B]-A-B- A/C#-B/D#-E-A/E-B- E-B-C#m-F#m7-G#m7-C#m- B-A-B-A/C#-B/D#-E-A/E-B I=E-B-C#m
Sir Duke(B)	V=E-C#m-C7-B7(2x)
We Just Disagree(E)	V=E-C#m-BaddE-A-BaddE-C#m-(2x)E

1978

Can't Smile Without You	V=E-C#m7-F#m7-B7sus(3x)E

Feels Good	V=EM7-C#m-F#m-B-AM7-G#m
Just The Way You Are(D)	V=E-C#m6-AM7-C#m-E7/B-AM7-Am-E/G#-Bm7-E7
Lights(D)	V=E-C#m-D(3x)C#m-D-E-Esus-E

1979

Heartache Tonight	V=E-C#m(2x)E-A-E-B
Heart Of Glass(E)	V=E-C#-C#m(2x)
Reunited	V/C=EM7-C#m7-F#m7-Am7-Am7/D
Goodnight Tonight	V=E-C#m7-F#m7-B7b9-E-C#m9-F#m7-B7b9
You're Only Lonely	V=E-C#m-A-E
Y.M.C.A.	V=E-C#m-A-B-B11-B(2x) C=E-C#m-F#m-F#m(M7)-F#m7-F#m6-B11

1980

(Just Like)Starting Over(A)	V=E-E+-C#m/E-E+-E-B7(2x)
Hungry Heart(C)	V/C=E-C#m7-F#m7-B7sus(2x)
Every Time You Go Away	C=E-C#m-F#m-B(2x)
Do That To Me One More Time	V=E-C#m-A-B7(2x)

1981

Woman	C=EM9-C#m7-F#m7-B6(2x)
Same Old Lang Syne	V=E-C#m7-B(3x)A#m7b5-A-B

1982

Shame On The Moon	V=E-C#m(2x)
Shake It Up	V=E-C#m(3x)D-E-C#m-D
Wasted On The Way(D)	V=E-C#m-A-B-A-E

1983

Memory(from "Cats")	V=E-C#m-A-G#m-F#m-C#m-B7
Making Love Out Of Nothing At All	C=E-C#m-A-B7sus-B7
Every Breath You Take(A)	V=Eadd9-C#madd9-Aadd9-Badd9

1984

Some Guys Have All the Luck	C=E-C#m7-F#m-B7
Girls Just Want To Have Fun	V=E-C#m-A
Purple Rain(Bb)	V=Eadd9-C#m7(add4)-B-Aadd9-Eadd9-C#m7(add4)-B

1985

When The Going Gets Tough, The Tough Get Going(E)	V=E-C#m-E-A(2x) C=E-C#m-B(2x)
Not Enough Love In The World	C=E-E/D#-C#m-A-E-A-B7-E-A-G#m-F#m-B7
Night Shift	V=E-C#m7-A-B-A-Aadd9-A-B
I Want To Know What Love Is	C=E-C#m-B-F#m-C#m-B

1986

A Matter Of Trust(D)	V=E-C#m(2x)G#m-B
Coming Around Again	V=E-C#m7-Aadd9(2x)-E-A-F#m-Dadd9-A

1987

Nothing's Gonna Stop Us Now	V/C=E-C#m7-A-B
I Wanna Dance With Somebody	C=E-C#m7-A-B11
(I've Had)The Time Of My Life	C=E-C#m-D-E-C#m-D

1991

Motown Song(A)	V=E-C#m-B(2x)C#m7-G#m7-C#m7-F#m7-F#m7/B

1995

Fantasy	V=E-C#m
Free As A Bird(A)	V=E-C#m7-CM7-B7-E-C#m-Am-B-E-C#m7-Am-D-G-Em-Bsus-B

Listing By Progression Type

Chord Progression *Song Examples*

Rock Ballad

E-C#m-A-B   Poor Little Fool('58); Stay('60); In The Still Of The Night('60); Please Mr. Postman('61); Bristol Stomp('61); Runaround Sue('61); Stand By Me('61); Let's Twist Again('61); Monster Mash('62); Just One Look('63); Judy's Turn To Cry('63); Dead Man's Curve('64); Eve Of

	Destruction('65); I Can't Explain('65); I've Just Seen A Face('65); Happiness Is A Warm Gun('68); Octopus's Garden('69); D'yer Mak'er('73)
E-C#m-A-B-B11-B	Y.M.C.A.('79)
E-C#m-A-B-A	Silhouettes('57); Mandy('74); Wasted On The Way('82); Night Shift('85)
E-C#m-A-B7	A Teenager In Love('59); Just Ask Your Heart('59); Pretty Little Angel Eyes('61); Who Put The Bomp('61); He's A Rebel('62); Duke Of Earl('62); Where Have All The Flowers Gone('62); Be My Baby('63); Surfer Girl('63); Last Kiss('64); Wonderful World('65); Keep On Dancing('65); I Love How You Love Me('68); This Magic Moment('69); Love Hurts('76); Only Sixteen('76); Do That To Me One More Time('80)
E-C#m-A-B7sus-B7	Making Love Out Of Nothing At All('83)
E-C#m-A-B9	Dedicated To The One I Love('67)
E-C#m-A-B11	Raindrops('61); I Wanna Be With You('72)
E-C#m-AM7-B7	Unchained Melody('55)
E-C#m-Am-B7	Sleep Walker('59)
E-C#m7-A-B	Nothing's Gonna Stop Us Now
E-C#m7-A-B11	Up On The Roof('63); I Wanna Dance With Somebody('87)
E-C#m7-Am-B7b9	Since I Don't Have You('59)
E5-C#5-A-B	Tell Me('64)
Eadd9-C#m(add9)-Aadd9-Badd9	Every Breath You Take('83)

Partial Rock Ballad

E-C#m	Maybe Baby("58); Dream Lover('59); 'Til I Kissed You('59); Travelin' Man('61); Calendar Girl('61); His Latest Flame('61)Shout('62); Locomotion('62); Anna Go To Him('62); Having A Party('62); Johnny Get Angry('62); Surf City('63); Sukiyaki('62); Pretty Woman('64); I Only Want To Be With You('64); Any Way You Want It('64); Needles And Pins('64); Cry For A Shadow('64); Catch Us If You Can('65); At The Zoo('67); Nobody But Me('68); Mrs. Robinson('68); El Condor Pasa('70); My Sweet Lord('70); Signed, Sealed, Delivered I'm Yours('70); Instant Karma('70); Doctor My Eyes('72); Love's Theme('74); He Don't Love You('75); Heartache Tonight('79); Shame On

	The Moon('82); Shake It Up('82); A Matter Of Trust('86); Fantasy('95)
E-C#m7(addF#)	On And On('77)
E-C#	(Sittin' On)The Dock Of The Bay('68)
E-C#-C#m	Heart Of Glass('79)
E-E/D#-C#m	A Well Respected Man('66)
EM7-C#m7	What's Going On('71)
Eadd9-C#m	Can't Get It Out Of My Head('75)

Standard

E-C#m-F#m-B	How Do You Do What You Do To Me('64); Fernando('76); Happy Days('76); Every Time You Go Away('80)
E-C#m-F#m-B7	I Got Rhythm('31); I Want You, I Need You, I Love You('56); All I Have To Do Is Dream('58); Sherry('61); Return To Sender('62); Go Away Little Girl('63); This Boy('63); You're Going To Lose That Girl('65); You Don't Have To Say You Love Me('66); Smile A Little Smile For Me('69); Without You('72); I Believe In Music('72)
E-C#m-F#m-B9	Love Is A Simple Thing('52)
E-C#m-F#m-B11-B	Be True To Your School('63)
E-C#m-F#m7-B	Come Home('65)
E-C#m-F#m7-B7	Have Yourself A Merry Little Christmas('43); Sh Boom('54); Earth Angel('55); Diana('57); You Send Me('57); Book Of Love('58); Lollipop('58); Put Your Head On My Shoulder('59); Lipstick On Your Collar('59); Devil Or Angel('60); Sixteen Reasons('60); One Summer Night('61); There's A Moon Out Tonight('61); Johnny Angel('62); Today('64); Hold Me, Thrill Me, Kiss Me('65); Double Shot('66); I Will('68); The Wonder Of You('70); This Will Be(An Everlasting Love)('75)
E-C#m-F#m7-B11	Who Loves You('75); Can't Smile Without You
E-C#m-F#-B	Ma Belle Amie('70)
E-C#m-F#7-B7	Mickey Mouse March('55); Lil' Red Riding Hood('66); Flowers On The Wall('66)
E-C#m7-F#m-B7	Some Guys Have All The Luck('84)
E-C#m7-F#m7-B7	The Blue Room('26); Between The Devil And The Deep Blue Sea('31); Let's Call The Whole Thing Off('36); Heart And Soul('38); Sleigh Ride('50); Hey There('54); Why Do Fools Fall In Love('56); Try To Remember('60); Daddy's

	Home('61); Telstar('62); Breaking Up Is Hard To Do('62); Two Faces Have I('63); Tell Me Why('64); Ain't Gonna Lie('66); Penny Lane('67)Don't It Make My Brown Eyes Blue('77)
E-C#m7-F#m7-B7sus	Short People('78); Hungry Heart('80)
E-C#m7-F#m7-B7+5	Try A Little Tenderness('32)
E-C#m7-F#m7-B7b9	Do You Want To Dance('58); Goodnight Tonight('79)
E-C#m7-F#m7-B11	Breezin''('71)
E-C#m7-F#m7-Bm7	Since I Fell For You('63)
E-C#m7-F#m9-B9	Little Girl Blue('35)
E6-C#m-F#m7-B7	Little Darlin''('57)
EM7-C#m-F#m-B	Feels Good('78)
EM7-C#m-F#m7-B7b9-[F7#9]	Then You Can Tell Me Goodbye('67)
EM7-C#m7-F#m7-B7	Can't Help Lovin' Dat Man('27); Blue Moon('34); Polka Dots And Moonbeams('40); Moonlight In Vermont('44);(I Love You)For Sentimental Reasons('46)
EM7-C#m7-F#m7-B9	Theme From "A Summer Place"('60)
EM7-C#m7-F#m7-B9-B7b9	More('63)
EM7-C#m7-F#m7-B11-B9	Mercy Mercy Me('71)
EM9-C#m7-F#m7-B6	Woman('81)

Ragtime

E-C#7-F#7-B7	Keep On Truckin' Mama(N/A); Hello My Baby(1899); It Had To Be You('24); Hey Baby('62); Walk Right In('63); I Call Your Name('63); Baby I'm Yours('65); Good Day Sunshine('66); Alice's Restaurant('67)
E-C#7-F#m-B7	Tip-Toe Through The Tulips('29); Are You Lonesome Tonight('60); Sunday Will Never Be The Same('67); Maxwell's Silver Hammer('69)
E-C#7-F#m-F#m7-B7	When You're Smiling('28)
E-C#7-F#m7-B7	Big Girls Don't Cry('62); Day Dream('66)
E-C#7-F#m7-B9	Bye, Bye Blackbird('26)
E-C#7b9-F#m7-B7b9	Lullaby Of Broadway('35)
E-C#7(#5/b9)-F#m7-B7	When I Fall In Love('52)

Ascending Bass Lines

F#m7-G#m7-AM7-AM7/B	One Less Bell To Answer('70)

Descending Bass Lines

E-C#m-C7-B7	Sir Duke('77)
E-C#m7-CM7-B7	Free As A Bird('95)
E-E/D-C#m-Am/C	Celebrate('70)
Eadd9-Eadd9/D-C#m11-F#m7b5/C	Lady Of The Island('69)
E-E/D#-C#m-A	Not Enough Love In The World('85)
E-[B/D#]-C#m-[B]-A-B	Handy Man('77)
E-E/D#-C#m-E/B	America('68); All The Young Dudes('72)-Verse
E-E/D#-C#m-EM7/B	Aubrey('73)
E-E/D#-C#m7-E/B	Our House('70)
E-E/D#-C#m7-E7/B	Mr. Bojangles('71)
E-E/D#-C#m-Bm	All The Young Dudes('72)–Chorus
E-E/D#-C#m-C#m/B	Something('69)
E-E/D#-C#m7-C#m/B	Hello Goodbye('67)
Eadd9-EM9/D#-E9/D-C#m11	If('71)

Static Bass Lines

E-E6-EM7-E6	It Must Be Him('67)
E-E+	Kind Of A Drag('67); Strange Magic('76)
E-E+-E6-C#7b9-F#m	For Once In My Life('68)
F#m-F#m(M7)-F#m7-F#m6	Y.M.C.A.('79)
E-E+-C#m/E-E+-E	(Just Like)Starting Over('80)

Other "E-C#" Progressions

E-C#m-E-E7	Cupid('61)
E-C#m-E-A	When The Going Gets Tough, The Tough Get Going('85)
E-C#m-E-B	Rock The Boat('74); Slip Slidin' Away('77)

E-C#m-E-B7	He's A Rebel('62); From Me To You('63)
E-C#m-EM7/G#-Go	Hello, Dolly('62)
E-C#m-E7-A7	You've Really Got A Hold On Me('62)
E-C#m7-E-A	Ol' Man River('27)
E-C#-E	Evil Woman('70)
E-C#m-F#m-D7	Dig A Pony('70)
E-C#m7-F#m7-G#7	Without You('72)
E-C#7-F#m-D-B7	I Get Around('64)
E-C#7-F#7-F#m7	"A" You're Adorable('48)
E-C#7-F#7-A	Who's In The Strawberry Patch With Sally ('73)
E-EM7-C#7b9-F#m7	Candy Man('72)
E-E/D-C#m7-F#7/A#	Don't Let The Sun Go Down On Me('74)
E-E/D-C#7-F#m	Baby Love('64)
EM7-C#m7-F#m7-Am7	Reunited('79)
E-C#m-G-Em7	The Warmth Of The Sun('64)
E-C#m-G#m/D#	Lonely People('75)
E-C#m-G#m-F#m	East West('66)
E-C#m-G#m-F#m7	Where The Boys Are('61); Across The Universe('68); My Special Angel('68)
E-C#m-G#m-A	Look In My Eyes Pretty Woman('75)
E-C#m-G#m-A6	Love Me With All Your Heart('64)
E-C#m-G#m-Bm7	Love Is A Many-Splendored Thing('55)
E-C#m-G#m-C#m	(Last Night)I Didn't Get To Sleep At All('72)
E-C#m7-G#m-E7	Over The Rainbow('38)
E-C#m7-G#m-B7	She Loves You('64)
E-C#m7-G#m7-C#m7	If You Leave Me Now('76)
EM7-C#m7-G#m-A	Give Me Just A Little More Time('70)

The following progression is an example of a Partial Rock Ballad Progression where the "B7" chord has been omitted.

E-C#m-A	Girls Just Want To Have Fun('84)
E-C#m-Aadd9	Coming Around Again('86)
E-C#m-A-E	Walk Away Renee('66); What Have They Done To My Song, Ma('70); Lookin' Out My Back Door('70); Take It Easy('72); You're Only Lonely('79)
E-C#m-A-E/G#	Moon River('61)
E-C#m-A-F#m	Go All The Way('72); Bad Time('75)

E-C#m-A-F#	Journey To The Center Of The Mind('68)
E-C#m-A-G#m	Memory(from "Cats")('83)
E-C#m-A-C#m	Girls Just Want To Have Fun('76)
E-C#m-A11-C	Burn Down The Mission('70)
E-C#m6-AM7-C#m	Just The Way You Are('78)
E-C#m7-AM7-G#m7	I'll Never Fall In Love Again('70)

The following progression is an example of a Partial Rock Ballad Progression where the "A" chord has been omitted.

E-C#m-B	Sunshine, Lollipops, And Rainbows('65); When The Going Gets Tough The Tough Get Going('85); Motown Song('91)
E-C#m-B-E	The Boxer('69)
E-C#m-B-F#m	I Want To Know What Love Is('85)
E-C#m-B-A	Don't Let Me Be Misunderstood('65); Take Me Home, Country Roads('71)
E-C#m-B-C#m	When I Was Young('67)
E-C#m-BaddE-A	We Disagree('77)
E-C#m-B7-A#7-A7	How Sweet It Is(To Be Loved By You)('75)
E-C#m-B7sus-F#7	Everything Is Beautiful('70)
E-C#m-Bm-Bm9	Julia('68)
E-C#m7-B	Same Old Lang Syne('81)
E-C#m7-B11-E	People Get Ready('65)
EM7-C#m7b9-BM7-G#9	After You're Gone('18)
Eadd9-C#m7(add4)-B-Aadd9	Purple Rain('84)
E-EM7-C#m-C6	Show Me The Way('76)
E-C#m-D	Lights('78)
E-C#m-D-E	(I've Had)The Time Of My Life('87)

"E-D" Chord Progressions

Chord progressions that begin with the "E" chord then move to the "Borrowed D" chord are a staple of Classic Rock of the 1960's through the 1980's. The most frequent "E-D" chord progressions are as follows:

Classic Rock	E-D-A
Partial Classic Rock	E-D
Static Bass Lines	E-Esus

The "E-D-A" Clasic Rock Progression follows the Circle of Fifths movement and the chords are usually played without embellishment. Examples of 1960s and 1970s Classic Rock can be found in The Shadows Of Knight's 1966 *Gloria*, Boston's 1976 *More Than A Feeling*, and Roy Orbison's 1989 *You Got It*.

The "E-D" Partial Classic Rock Progression is comprised of the first two chords of the Classic Rock Progression and was first used in the late 1950s. As the "D" chord can readily be substituted for the "E11" chord, the "E-D" Partial Classic Rock Progression can be used like the "E-E11" Static Bass Line Progression to provide movement where the "E" chord is used in a progression for more than one or two bars. Hit songs created around the "E-D" Progression include The Champs' 1958 *Tequila*, The Kink's 1964 *You Really Got Me*, and Eric Clapton's 1980 *Cocaine*.

The "E-Esus" Static Bass Line Progression uses the "Esus" Chord Quality Substitution to provide movement where the "E" chord is used for one or two bars. The definitive example of the Static "E-Esus" Bass Line Progression is The Mamas And The Papas' 1966 *Monday, Monday*.

In addition to the most frequent progressions already discussed, there are a number of other "E-D" Chord Progressions that mainly continue to move to the "E", "A", "C#m", and the "Borrowed" "G" and "C" chords.

Below is a chronological listing of songs with verses and/or choruses that begin with the "E-D" chord sequence followed by a listing of chord progressions by type.

Chronological Listing

Date/Song Title	Chord Progression

1958

Tequila(F) — V=E-D(16x)A7-E(3x)F#-B7

Rumble(E) — V=E-D(2x)A-D-E-D-B7-E-D

Rock And Roll Is Here To Stay — V=E-D-E-B7

1959

I Only Have Eyes For You(C) — V=E-D

1962

She Cried — V=E-D(C-D)2x

Days Of Wine And Roses — V=EM7-D7-C#7(b5/b9)-C#9

1963

Only In America — V=E-D(3x)E

In My Room(B) — V=E-D-E-C#m7-F#m7-D-B-E-D-E

1964

You Really Got Me(Ab) — V=E-D(16x)F#-E(8x)

Leader Of The Pack — V=E-D-B-A-G#m-B7-E

1965

Five O'Clock World(Ab) — V=E-D(7x)E

Tired Of Waiting(G)	V=E-D(10x)D-A7(3x)
Norwegian Wood(E)	V=E-Dadd9(2x)E-Em-A-Em-F#m7-B
We Can Work It Out(D)	V=E-Esus-E-Esus-Dadd9-E(2x)-A-E-A-B7
Another Girl(A)	V=E-D-E-A7(2x)B7
Baby, The Rain Must Fall	C=E-DM7-E-A-G-A-E-F#m-G#m-C#m-F#m-B7-E-C#m-F#m-B7-E
All Day And All Of The Night(G)	V=E-D-G-E(4x)G-D-F#
Last Time(E)	V=E-D-A(8x)
Nowhere To Run	V/C=E-D/B-A
I Can't Explain(E)	V/C=E-D-A-E
The Night Before(D)	V=E-D-A-B(2x)-C#m-Am6(2x)-E-A7-E-[G-A]

1966

Time Won't Let Me	V=E-D(4x)E-C#m(2x)-F#m-G#m-A-B
Psychotic Reaction(F#)	V=E-D(19x)E
Don't Bring Me Down(C)	C=E-Dsus-D(3x) I=E7-E9-E7sus4-E5-D5-C#5-A5-E5
Uptight(Db)	V=E-D/B
Shapes Of Things(G)	V=E-D/B(3x)D

You Better Run	V=E-D-E-G(8x)F#m-A(2x)-B7
Words Of Love(Ab)	V=E-D-G-F#-B7- E-D-G-F#- Em-D-G-F#-[F]-E-D-C-B
Call Me	V=EM7-Em7-DM7-Dm7-G7- CM7-C6-Am
Monday, Monday(F#)	V=E-Esus(5x)E-D G-G6-GM7-G6-B-E-Esus-E
Gloria(E)	V/C=E-D-A
Just Like Me(C)	V=E-D-A-B
If I Were A Carpenter(D)	V=E-D-A(4x)
Lady Jane(D)	V=E-D-A(2x)E
She Said She Said(Bb)	V=E7-D-A(2x)E7-A- E7-D-A-E(2x)
Taxman(D)	V=E7-E7#9-E7(2x)- D-A7-E7

1967

Talk Talk(F#)	V=E-D(8x)G-C(2x)A-D(2x)- G-A-D-A
Soul Man(G)	C=E-D(2x)E-A-B
Up, Up And Away	V=E-EM7-D-G-GM7-F-A#-A#7- Cm7
Let It Out (Let It All Hang Out)(E)	V=E-D-A B=F#7-A(E-D-A)2x

Lovely Rita(Eb)	C=E-D-A-E-B-C#m-F#-B
Windy(F)	V=E-D-A-B(3x)
Bernadette(Eb)	C=E-Dadd9-C-B-[D]-E-D-C-Am-B

1968

Hello, I Love You(A)	V=E-D(8x) C=E-D-G-E(4x)
Yummy, Yummy, Yummy	V=E-D(2x)E-A-E
Journey To The Center Of The Mind(E)	V=E-D-E
Mony Mony(A)	C=E-D-E(4x)A-G(4x)B
Sunshine Of Your Love(D)	V=E-D-E(4x)A-G-A(2x)-E-D-E(2x)B-D-A(3x)
Magic Bus	V=E-D-A
Hush	V=E-D-A(4x)
Sympathy For The Devil(E)	V=E-D-A-E(4x)
Hey Jude(F)	O=E-D-A-E
Dear Mr. Fantasy	V=E-D-A-E(4x)
Born On The Bayou(E)	C=E7-D-A(3x)E7
Dear Prudence(D)	V=E-E/D-E/C#-E/C(5x)-D-A-E
Tomorrow(E)	C=EM7/B-DM7/A-CM7/G-DM7/A(3x)

1969

Let's Get Together(A)	V=E-D(3x)A-B-E(2x)
Helplessly Hoping(G)	C=E-Dadd9/E(4x)A-E
Ramblin' Gamblin' Man	V=E-D-A
Take A Letter Maria	C=E-D-A-E(2x)
Fortunate Son(G)	V=E-D-A(2x)E
Good Times, Bad Times(E)	V=E-D-A-E(5x)
Gimme Shelter	C=E-D-C(2x)
Pinball Wizard(B)	V=Esus4-E-Dsus4-D-Csus4-C-B7sus4-E-D-G-A(2x)

1970

Whole Lotta Love(E)	V=E-D
I'm Your Captain/ Closer To Home(D)	V=E-Dadd9
Paranoid	V=E5-D5-G5-D5-E5(2x)
Make Me Smile	C=E-D-A(4x)E-C#m-Bsus-B-Asus-A
No Sugar Tonight(F#)	C=E-D-A-E(4x)
All Right Now(A)	V=E-D-A-E(2x)

1971

Here Comes That Rainy Day Feeling Again	V=E-D(2x)A-Am

L.A. Woman(A)	V=E-D(2x)E
Does Anybody Really Know What Time It Is?	V=E-D-GM7-CM7-GM7-CM7-GM7-CM7-B-C#m7-D6-C#m7
Won't Get Fooled Again(A)	V=E-D-A(2x)E-B-A-D

1972

Elected	V=E-D(2x)E
Hold Your Head Up(D)	V=Esus-E-Dsus-D-Esus-E-A-Bm9-Bm
Rock & Roll –Part II	V=E-D-A-B7

1973

Ramblin' Man(G)	C=E-D-E-A-B6-B-A-E-C#m-A-E-B6-E
Saturday Night's Alright For Fighting(G)	V=E-D-A-E(2x)B7#9
China Grove(E)	V/C=E-D-A/C#-A-E
Free Ride(A)	V= E-D-A-D-A-E
We're An American Band(E)	V=E-D-C-D-E-D
Danny's Song(D)	V=E-Dadd9-C#m-F#-B

1974

Junior's Farm	C=E-D(2x)E
Oh My My	V=E-D-E-F#-B C=E-D(2x)E-B-C#m-A-E

Cat's In The Craddle(F)   V=E-D-G-A-E-D-G-Bm/F#-E-G-Bm/F#-E

You Ain't Seen Nothin' Yet(A)   V=E-D-A(4x)

Sweet Home Alabama(D)   V=E-D-A

Takin' Care Of Business(C)   V/C=E-D-A-E(4x/2x)

Carefree Highway(D)   C=E-D-A-B(2x)B-C#m-B-A
                                  E/G#-F#sus-F#-E-D-A-Bsus-B-E

Don't Let The Sun Go Down
On Me   V=E-E7-D-A-D-A

1975

Amie   V=E-D-A(3x)E-(A-G)2x-B
                                  C=E-D-A-E-D-F#m-B

Good Lovin' Gone Bad   C=E-D-A(2x)E-D

1976

Magic Man(G)   V=E5-D5(2x)E5

More Than A Feeling(D)   V=E-D-A(3x)
                                  I=E-Esus-E-Dadd9-A/C#-A

Rock 'N Me(B)   V/C=E-D-A-E

Take The Money And Run(G)   V/C=E-D-A-E

1977

Don't Stop(E)   V/C=E-D-A(3x)B

Main Street   V=E-D-A-F#m

Night Moves   V=E-D-A/E-D(4x)
Peace Of Mind(E)   V=E-D5-A5(2x)B5

1978

What's Your Name(A)   V=E-D-E-B-E-D-A-D-E-B-E

Take Me To The River(E)   V=E-D-A(4x)C-G-A-Asus-G/E
C=E-D-A

1979

Bad Case Of Loving You   V=E5-D5/E(2x)A-B

We Are Family   C=E7-Dadd9-A-D11

1980

Cocaine(E)   V=E-D(4x)C-B

1981

Hold On Loosely(E)   V=E-E/D#-D-D/C#(2x)C-D-
E-E/D#-D-A-[D/D#-D-E]-
E-E/D#-D-A-
F#m-B-F#m-A

Back In Black(E)   V=E5-D-A(2x)B

1982

Southern Cross(A)   V=E-D-A(8x)

Centerfold   V=E-D-A-D-A(3x)
C=E-D-A(4x)

Rosanna   V=E-Dadd9-C#m9-E

Who Can It Be Now   V=E-D-C#m-B(4x)

1983

All Night Long(All Night)   V=E-D-F#m-E(5x)

	C=E-D(2x)E
Pink House	V=E-D-A(2x)

1984

Heart Of Rock And Roll(C)	V=E5-[D#5]-D5-A5-D5-A5-E5

1985

Don't You(Forget About Me)	V/C=E-D-A-D

1986

The Way It Is	C=E-DM7-A-Aadd9(4x)
Addicted To Love(A)	V=E5-D5-A5-E5(2x)

1987

Wanted Dead Or Alive	V=E-D-A-D-A-G-E

1988

The Way You Make Me Feel	V=E-E11-E-DM7/E(3x)

1989

You Got It(A)	V=E-D-A(3x)B-D

1993

Hero	V=Eadd9-D6/9-C#m7-B9sus-B

1995

I'll Be There For You(A)	V=E-D-E-G#m-D-F#m-E-D-A/C#-B

Listing By Progression Type

Chord Progression　　　　　　　　*Song Examples*

Classic Rock

E-D-A	Last Time('65); Gloria('66); If I Were A Carpenter('66); Lady Jane('66); Let It Out(Let It All Hang Out)('67); Magic Bus('68); Hush('68); Ramblin' Gamblin' Man('69); Fortunate Son('69); Make Me Smile('70); Won't Get Fooled Again('71); Free Ride('73); You Ain't Seen Nothin' Yet('74); Sweet Home Alabama('74); Amie('75); Good Lovin' Gone Bad('75); More Than A Feeling('76); Don't Stop('77); Take Me To The River('78); Southern Cross('82); Centerfold('82); Pink House('83); You Got It('89)
E-D-A/C#-A	China Grove('73)
E-D/B-A	Nowhere To Run('65)
E-D5-A5	Peace Of Mind(77)
E-DM7-A-Aadd9	The Way It Is('86)
E-E7-D-A	Don't Let The Sun Go Down On Me('74)
E5-D-A	Back In Black('81)
E5-[D#5]-D5-A5	Heart Of Rock And Roll('84)
E7-D-A	She Said She Said('66); Born On The Bayou('68)
E-D-A-E	I Can't Explain('65); Lovely Rita('67); Hey Jude('68); Dear Mr. Fantasy('68); Sympathy For The Devil('68); Good Times, Bad Times('69); Take A Letter Maria('69); No Sugar Tonight('70); All Right Now('70); Saturday Night's Alright For Fighting('73); Takin' Care Of Business('74); Take The Money And Run('76); Rock 'N' Me('76)
E5-D5-A5-E5	Addicted To Love('86)
E-D-A-D	Centerfold('82); Don't You(Forget About Me)('85); Wanted Dead Or Alive('87)
E-D-A/E-D	Night Moves('77)
E-Dadd9-A-D11	We Are Family('79)

Partial Classic Rock

E-D	Tequila('58); Rumble('58); I Only Have Eyes For You('59); Only In America('63); You Really Got Me('64); Five O'Clock World('65); Tired Of Waiting('65); Time Won't Let Me('66); Psychotic Reaction('66); Talk Talk('67); Soul Man('67); Hello I Love You('68); Yummy, Yummy, Yummy('68); Let's Get Together('69); Whole Lotta Love('70); L.A. Woman('71); Here Comes That Rainy Day Feeling Again('71); Elected('72); Junior's Farm('74); Oh My My('74); Cocaine('80); All Night Long(All Night)('83)
E-D/B	Uptight('66); Shapes Of Things('66)
E-Dsus4-D	Don't Bring Me Down('66)
E-Dadd9	Norwegian Wood('65); I'm Your Captain('70)
E-Dadd9/E	Helplessly Hoping('69)
E5-D5	Magic Man('76)
E5-D5/E	Bad Case Of Loving You('79)
EM7-Em7-DM7-Dm7	Call Me('66)
E-D-E	Journey To The Center Of The Mind('68); Mony Mony('68); Sunshine Of Your Love('68)

Descendng Bass Lines

E-Dadd9-C-B	Bernadette('67)
E-E/D-E/C#-E/C	Dear Prudence('68)
E-E/D#-D-D/C#	Hold On Loosely('81)

Static Bass Lines

E-Esus	We Can Work It Out('65); Monday, Monday('66)
E-Esus-E	More Than A Feeling('76)
Esus-E	Pinball Wizard('69); Hold Your Head Up('72)
E7-E7#9-E7	Taxman('66)
E-D/E-A/E	Get Back('69)
E-E11-E-DM7/E	The Way You Make Me Feel('88)

Other "E-D" Progressions

E-D-E-F#	Oh My My('74)
E-D-E-G	You Better Run('66)
E-D-E-G#m	I'll Be There For You('95)
E-D-E-A	Ramblin' Man('73)
E-D-E-A7	Another Girl('65)
E-D-E-B	What's Your Name('78)
E-D-E-B7	Rock And Roll Is Here To Stay('58)
E-D-E-C#m7	In My Room('63)
E-DM7-E-A	Baby, The Rain Must Fall('65)

The following progression can be transformed into a Descending "E-D-C#-B" Bass Line Progression by playing the C# note of the "F#m" chord as the bass note and by playing the B note of the "E" chord as the bass note creating the "E-D-F#m/C#-E/B" progression.

E-D-F#m-E	All Night Long(All Night)('83)
E-D-G-E	All Day And All Of The Night('65); Hello, I Love You('68)
E-D-G-F#	Words Of Love('66)
E-D-G-A	Cat's In The Craddle('74)
E-D-GM7-CM7	Does Anybody Really Know What Time It Is?('71)
E-EM7-D-G	Up, Up And Away('67)
E5-D5-G5-D5	Paranoid('70)

The "E-D-A-B" progression can be transformed into a Descending "E-D-C#-B" Bass Line Progression by playing the C# note of the "A" chord as the bass note creating the "E-D-A/C#-B" progression.

E-D-A-F#m	Main Street('77)
E-D-A-B	The Night Before('65); Just Like Me('66); Windy('67); Carefree Highway('74)
E-D-A-B7	Rock & Roll –Part II('72)
E-D-B-A	Leader Of The Pack('64)
E-D-C	Gimme Shelter('69)
E-D-C-D	She Cried('62); We're An American Band('73)
EM7/B-DM7/A-CM7/G-DM7/A	Tomorrow('68)
E-D-C#m-B	Who Can It Be Now('82)

E-Dadd9-C#m-F#	Danny's Song('73)
E-Dadd9-C#m9-E	Rosanna('82)
EM7-D7-C#7(b5/b9)-C#9	Days Of Wine And Roses('62)
Eadd9-D6/9-C#m7-B9sus	Hero('93)

"E-D#" Chord Progressions

Although few commonalties are found in this category, many "E-D#" Progressions such as the 1954 *Mr Sandman* and the 1965 *Red Roses For A Blue Lady* follow the Circle of Fifths movement.

Below is a chronological listing of songs with verses and/or choruses that begin with the "E-D#" sequence followed by a listing of chord progressions by type.

Chronological Listing

Date/Song Title   *Chord Progression*

1930

On The Sunny Side Of The Street   V=E-D#m7-G#7-A-D#m7b5-D7-
                                   C#m-F#7-F#m7-B7-E

1954

Mr. Sandman   V=E-D#7-G#7-C#7-F#7-B7-E-C-B9

1960

I'm Sorry   V=E-D#7-E-Fo-F#m7-B7

1963

It Won't Be Long(E)   B=E-D#+-Bm6/D-C#7-Am/C-B7-
                                   F#m7-B7

1965

Yesterday(F)   V=E-D#m-G#7-C#m-C#m/B-A-
                                   B7-E-E/D#-C#m7-F#7-A-E

Red Roses For A Blue Lady   V=E-D#7-G#7-C#9-F#m7-B7

1968

It's Impossible   V=E-E6-EM7-E6-D#m7b5-G#7-C#m-Bm7-E7-G#m7b5-C#7

Sexy Sadie(G)   V=E-D#7-G#m-A-B-
                       E-D#7-A-B-
                       E-D#7-D-B7

I'm So Tired(A)   V=E-D#7-A-B-E-C#m-A-B-
                       E-B+-C#m-Am

1973

Ain't No Woman   C=EM7-D#m7-C#m7(3x)-
                       C#m7/F#

1977

Year Of The Cat   V=EM7-D#m-G#m(3x)C#m7-
                       EM7-F#-G#m

You're In My Heart(E) V=E-D#m-C#m-B(4x)
                       I=EM7/G#-Gm6-F#m7-
                       [B11-C11-C#11]-D11-E

1978

Whenever I Call You Friend   V=E-D#m7b5-G#7-C#m7-Bm7-

1979

She Believes In Me   C=Esus-E(2x)D#m7b5-G#7-
                       C#m-C#m(M7)-C#m7-C#m6-
                       F#m7-B7sus

What You Won't Do For Love(D) V=EM7-D#7#9-G#m9-C#13-
                               EM7-D#7#9-G#m7-C#7-
                               C=EM7-D#7#9-G#m7-B13-
                               B13b9-EM7-A13-G#m9-C#13

1982

    Through The Years   V=E-D#m7-G#7-C#m7-Bm7-E7

Listing By Progression Type

    Chord Progression   *Song Examples*

Descending Bass Lines

    E-D#m-C#m-B   You're In My Heart('77)

    E-D#+-Bm6/D-C#7   It Won't Be Long('63)

Static Bass Lines

    E-E6-EM7-E6   It's Impossible('68)

    Esus-E   She Believes In Me('79)

Other "E-D#" Progressions

    E-D#7-E-Fo   I'm Sorry('60)

    E-D#m-G#7-C#m   Yesterday('65)
    E-D#m7-G#7-A   On The Sunny Side Of The Street('30)
    E-D#m7-G#7-C#m7   Through The Years('82)
    E-D#m7b5-G#7-C#m7   Whenever I Call You Friend('78)
    E-D#7-G#m-A   Sexy Sadie('68)
    E-D#7-G#7-C#7   Mr. Sandman('54)
    E-D#7-G#7-C#9   Red Roses For A Blue Lady('65)
    EM7-D#m-G#m   Year Of The Cat('77)
    EM7-D#7#9-G#m9-C#13   What You Won't Do For Love('79)

    E-D#7-A-B   I'm So Tired('68)

    E-D#m7-C#m7   Ain't No Woman('73)

"F#" Chord Progressions

The most frequent chord progressions that start with an "F#" chord are as follows:

Standard("F#m" First)	F#m-B-E-C#m
Partial Standard("F#m" First)	F#m-B-E
	F#m-B
Standard("A" Substitution /"F#m" First)	F#m-B-E-A
"Fo" Cliché("F#m7" First)	F#m7-B7-E-Fo

The "F#m-B-E-C#m" Standard Changes("F#m" First) are similar to the Standard "E-C#m-F#m-B7" Changes except that it begins with the "F#m" chord instead of the "E" chord. Both progressions follow the Circle of Fifths movement. The Standard Changes("F#m" First) were used to create The Beatles' 1964 *All My Loving*, Roberta Flack's 1972 *First Time Ever I Saw Your Face*, and Debby Boone's 1977 *You Light Up My Life*.

The "F#m-B-E" Partial Standard("F#m" First) Progression is similar to the "E-F#m-B7" Partial Standard Progression except that it begins with the "F#m" chord instead of the "E" chord and also follows the Circle of Fifths movement. Hits written around the "F#m-B-E" Progression include the The Buckinghams' 1967 *Kind Of A Drag*, Lynn Anderson's 1970 *Rose Garden*, and Albert Hammond's 1974 *It Never Rains In Southern California*.

Another Partial Standard(F#m" First) Progression is the "F#m-B" Progression which represents the first two chords of the Standard Changes("F#m" First). Examples of hits created using the "F#m-B" Progression include Ex-Beatle George Harrison's 1970 *My Sweet Lord*.

The "F#m-B-E-A" Standard("A" Substitution/ "F#m" First) Progression is similar to the Standard Changes("F#m" First) except the "A" chord has been substituted for the "C#m" chord. Classic examples of songs written around the "F#m-B-E-A" Progression include Roger Williams 1955 *Autumn Leaves*, Roy Clark's 1969 *Yesterday When I Was Young*, and Roberta Flack's 1973 *Killing Me Softly With His Song*.

The "F#m7-B7-E-Fo" "Fo" Cliché("F#m7" First) is similar to the "E-Fo-F#m-B7" "Fo" Cliche where the last two chords are played first. Elton John put this progression to good use in his 1974 *Bennie And The Jets*. The "Fo" Cliché("F#m" First) was dressed up just a little to produce James Taylor's 1973 *Don't Let Me Be Lonely Tonight* and Frankie Valli's 1975 *My Eyes Adored You*.

In addition to the most frequent progressions already discussed, there are a number of other "F#" Chord Progressions that mainly continue to move to the "E", "G#m", "A", "B", and "C#m" chords. Although not used as frequently as the above progression types, the following progression types are also employed:(1)"F#m-E" Reverse Basic("F#m" Substitution)and(2)"F#m-C#m" Reverse Minor Basic Progression.

Below is a chronological listing of songs with verses and/or choruses begin with the "F#" chord followed by a listing of chord progressions by type.

Chronological Listing

Date/Song Title	*Chord Progression*
1917	
For Me And My Gal	V=F#m7-B7-E(2x)
1924	
Tea For Two	V=F#m7-B7(2x)EM7-E6(2x)
Fascinating Rhythm	V=F#m7-B7(4x)Bm7-E7
1931	
As Time Goes By	V=F#m7-B9-Fo-F#m7-B7-A#m7b5-A13-G#m7-C#m9-F#13-Go-G#m7-C#m7-F#m7-B7 T/A=G#7#5-C#9-F#7#5-B9
1934	
I Get A Kick Out Of You	V=F#m7-B7-E-G#m7

1936

I've Got You Under My Skin   V=F#m7-B7-EM7-C#m7-F#m7-B9

1937

Thanks For The Memory   V=F#m7-B9-EM9-Fo-B7-E6-C#7-F#m7(2x)B7

1947

C'est Si Bon   V=F#m7-B7-E-Em

1953

Satin Doll   V=F#m7-B7(2x)G#m7-C#7(2x)-C#m9-F#9-Cm9-F9
T/A=E-F#m7-G#m7-C#7

Strangers In Paradise   V=F#m7-B9-EM7-E6

1955

Autumn Leaves   V=F#m7-B7-EM7-AM7-D#m7b5-G#7-C#m(2x)

1960

Puppy Love   V=F#m7-B7-E-G#m7-C#m7-F#m7-B7-E

1961

Never On A Sunday   V=F#m7-B7(2x)E

1962

Devil In Her Heart(G)   V=F#m7-B7-E(2x)E7-A-Am-E-E7-A-Am-F#7-B7

Sealed With A Kiss	V=F#-F#m-C#m-F#m-B-E-C#+

1963

Heat Wave(C)	V=F#m7-G#m7-C#m7(2x)-F#m7-G#m7-A6-B7
All My Loving(E)	V=F#m-B-E-C#m-A-F#m-D-B-F#m-B-E-C#m-A-B-E
Little Saint Nick(F#)	V=F#m7-B7(2x)E-EM7-E6-Fo-F#m7-B7(2x)E-EM7-E6-E7-A-F#m7-B7
Fools Rush In	V=F#m7-B7-E-C#m7-F#m7-B7-E

1964

Goin' Out Of My Head	V=F#m7/B-EM7(6x)
Don't Worry Baby(E)	C=F#-G#m-C#(2x)E/B-B-E
I'm A Loser(G)	C=F#m-B(2x)-E-C#m-F#m-D-B
I Get Around	V=F#m7-B7(4x)
Shoop Shoop Song(It's In His Kiss)	V=F#m7-B7(4x)E-C#m7-F#m7-B7-E-A-B7-C#7
The Man With All The Toys	V=F#m7-B7-E-C#7-F#m7-B7-E-C#m7-A-Am6-G#m-C#m-F#7-F#m7-B7
Wives And Lovers	V=F#m7-B7-G#m7-C#9-C#m7-F#7b9-A#m7b5-D#7-EM7-A#m7-D#7

And I Love Her(E)	V=F#m-C#m(3x)A-B7-E6 I=F#m-E6
Things We Said Today(C)	V=F#m-C#m7 B=F#-B7-G#7-C#7- F#-B7-G#7-G-F#
She's Not There(C)	C=F#-F#m-C#m-G#m-C#m- F#-F#m-E-G#7

1965

Hurt So Bad(G)	V=F#m-G#m7(2x)Bm-C#m- F#7-G#M7
Younger Girl	V=F#m7-G#m-A-B7(2x)D-B7
It's My Life(C)	V=F#m-B(4x)F#m-E-D(2x)F#
New York's A Lonely Town	C=F#m7-B7-EM7-C#7- F#m7-B7(3x)GM7-F#m7-B7- EM7-A/E
The Word(C)	V=F#m7-B7-F#m7- C#11-C#-B11-B-F#m7- F#m-E/F#-A/F#-B/F#
Laugh, Laugh(E)	C=F#-B-E-A- D-G-C-B- E-A(4x)
Help(A)	C=F#m-D-B7-E7-E

1966

Black Is Black	V=F#m-E-F#m-B7
Reach Out, I'll Be There(F#)	V=F#m-E/G#-B(5x)E/G#-E- G#7/C-D#o
Turn Down Day(F)	V=F#m7-EM7-F#m7-G#-C#m

	C=F#m7-F#m7/B-EM7-D#m7
(You're My)Soul And Inspiration	V=F#m7-G#m7-AM7-G#m7-F#m7-G#m7-AM7-B11
Lightnin' Striking(Eb)	C=F#m7-G#m7-C#9(2x)
A Place In The Sun	V=F#m7-B7-E-C#m-B7-E
You Don't Have To Say You Love Me	V=F#m-F#m7-B7-E-A-F#m-D#m7b5-G#7-C#m(2x)
See You In September	V=F#m7-B9(2x)F#m7-B7-EM7-E6-C#7-F#m7-B7 C=F#m-B7-EM7-C#7(2x)
What Becomes Of The Broken-Hearted(Bb)	C=F#/C#-A#m/C#-D#m-B/D#-F#/C#-A#m/C#-D#m-F#/C#-A#-[B-C#m-A]
Lady Jane(D)	B=F#7-Bm-E7/G#-A-D-E7/G#-Bm

1967

Gimme Little Sign	V=F#m-E(3x)F#m-G#m-A-B7 C=F#m7-E(4x)
Girl, You'll Be A Woman Soon	V=F#m-E(2x)D C=F#m-B-E(4x)
Pushin' Too Hard(A)	V=F#m-E
By The Time I Get To Phoenix	V=F#m-EM7(2x)AM7-B9 G#m-C#m-F#m7-D-B7
You've Made Me So Very Happy	V=F#m7-EM7(3x)F#m7-G#m7

(You Make Me Feel Like) A Natural Woman	C=F#m7/B(E-A)3x E/G#-E-A-E/G#-F#m7-F#m7/B-E
Rain, The Park And Other Things	V=F#m-G#m-A-E C=F#m-G#m-A-B(2x)
Get On Up(A)	C=F#m-G#m-A-F#m-G#m-B11-A-B11(4x)
Kind Of A Drag	V=F#m-B7-E(2x)E7-A-A+-A6-A7-D-Dm
Tell It Like It Is	V=F#m-B7-E-EM7-E6-C#7-F#m-B7-E-EM7-E6-E
Society's Child	V=F#m7-B(4x)-E-G#7-C#m-A-B

1968

Midnight Confession(F#)	V=F#m-E-G#m-C#m-B-E-B-F#m-B(2x)
Stormy(G)	V=F#m7-EM7(2x)F#m9-EM7-AM7
Tuesday Afternoon	C=F#-E-B
Sky Pilot(Bb)	V=F#m-A(3x)F#m-B
Reach Out In The Darkness	C=F#m-B(4x)F#m-D-E(2x)D-F#m-B
Little Green Apples	V=F#m-F#m7-B7-E-EM7-E6(2x)-E7-A-Am C=F#m7-B7(4x)E-F#m(2x)

1969

These Eyes(C)	V=F#m-EM7-E(2x)C#m-E(3x)-B
Don't Let Me Down(E)	C=F#m7-F#m7/B-E-A/E-E(2x) V=F#m7-EM7-Esus-E(2x)
Helplessly Hoping(G)	V=F#m7-A-E-B(3x)
Yester-me, Yester-you, Yesterday	V=F#m-B7-E(2x)G#7-C#m-F#7-B7-E-A-E
Down By The River(D)	V=F#m7-B(4x)D-C#m(3x)E
Yesterday When I Was Young	V=F#m7-B7-EM7-A-D#m7b5-G#7-C#m(2x)
Aquarius	V=F#m7-B7-C#m(3x)A-B7-E-D-F#m-B7-F#m-E7-A(4x)C#7/G#-F#m-Bm-C#m-Bm-F#m

1970

Kentucky Rain	C=F#7-E-D#m-G#m-C#m-B-A-G#m-A-E-AM7-E-G#m-C#m-G#m-E-C#m-A-B7-E-G#m-A-B7-E
No Time(C)	V=F#5-AM7-B5-F#-F#sus2-F#
My Sweet Lord	V=F#m-B(3x)E-C#m(2x)E-Fo-F#m-B(4x)
Spill The Wine	V=F#m7/B-B7-A6-B7

1971

Wild Horses(G)	C=F#m-A-B-E-D-A-G#m-F#m-A-B-E-D-A
The Story In Your Eyes	V=F#m-B(3x)E

(I Never Promised You A) Rose Garden	C=F#m-B-E(2x)A-A+-F#m-B-E
It's A Family Affair	V=F#m7-B7(9x)C#m-A-F#m7-B7(2x)
For The Good Times	V=F#m7-B7-E-E6-EM7-E6 F#m7-B7-E-E6
Uncle Albert/Admiral Halsey	V=F#m7/B-B(3x)Em7-A-A#-B-Em7-A(4x)A#7-B
Amos Moses	C=F#7-B7-E(2x)B7-G-E

1972

A Horse With No Name(D)	V=F#m-E(6/9)/G#
Hurting Each Other	V=F#m/E-E-Bm7/E-A/E-Am7-Am7/D-EM9-F#/E
Summer Breeze	C=F#m7-G#m7-F#m7-E-Esus-E
It Never Rains (In Southern California)	V=F#m-B-E(2x)A-E C=F#m-B-E(3x)
First Time Ever I Saw Your Face	V=F#m-B7-E-C#m-G#m-A-B-B7-E-D-E-Bm7-E
The Guitar Man	B=F#m-C#+/F#-F#m7-B7-E-E/D#-E/C#-C#7-F#m-C#+/F#-F#m7-B-C#-C#7sus
Don't Let Me Be Lonely Tonight	V=F#m9-B13sus-E-Fo-F#m9-B13sus-G#m7-C#7-AM7-G#m7-C#m7-F#7
You Are Everything(Ab)	V=F#-Bm/F#(2x)F#

1973

Hello It's Me	V=F#m-EM7(2x)D-C#m(2x)-D-AM7
Do It Again	C=F#m7-G#m7-AM7-G#m7-C#m7(2x)G#7sus4
Goodbye Yellow Brick Road	V=F#m-B-E-A-D-B7-E
The Night The Lights Went Out In Georgia	C=F#m-B7-E-C#m(3x)-F#m-B7-Em
My Love	C=F#m7-B7-E-E+-A-B7-E-E+-F#m7-B7-E-E+-A-B7-E-C#m/A#
Killing Me Softly With His Song	V=F#m7-B9 EM7-AM7-F#m7-B9-C#m I=F#m7/B-B9(2x)
Ain't No Woman (Like The One I Got)	V=F#m7-C#m7(3x)F#m7-B-AM7-G#m7-F#m7-D11-C#11-B11
Ridin' The Storm Out	C=F#-C#m(2x)A-B-C#m(4x)
Smoke On The Water	C=F#-D-C#m-F#-D

1974

Pretzel Logic(C)	C=F#/G#-G#/C#-E/F#-F#/B(2x)-F#/G#-G#/C#-E-F#-E-AM7-[B-C#m7]
You Won't See Me(A)	B=F#m-Am-F#o-E-F#-F#m-B7
Whatever Gets You Through	

The Night	V=F#-A-E(2x)
The Night Chicago Died	V=F#m-B7-E
Billy, Don't Be A Hero	V=F#m-B7-E-EM7(2x)
Bennie And The Jets	V=F#m7-B7-E-Fo-F#m7-B-C#m-F#m-G#m-A-E-F#m
Angie Baby	C=F#m7-B7-EM7(2x)
Feel Like Makin' Love	V=F#m9-B13sus-EM7-[D7]-C#7

1975

My Eyes Adore You	V=F#m7-B11-EM7-Fo-F#m7-B11
Attitude Dancing	V=F#-B(4x)E-A(2x)
My Little Town	V=F#-F#m7-F#m7/B-B-E-C#m-Bm-G-D-D+-F#7-B-C#m-F#-B

1976

You're My Best Friend	V=F#m7-E-A-E-F#m-E(3x)B
Kid Charlemagne(C)	C=F#m7-G#m7(3x)A7-B7-E7#9
Shower The People(F)	C=F#m7-B(3x)Co-C#m-G#o-F#m7-B(3x)Co-C#m-D-A
I'd Really Love To See You Tonight	V=F#m7-B7-EM7(2x)G#m7-C#m7-B11-B(2x)
Welcome Back	V=F#m7-F#m7/B-B9-EM7(2x) I=A6-B6-E(2x)

Closer To You   V=F#-B/F#(2x)F#-D#m7-E-
                                   B/D#-C#sus-C#

Wreck Of The Edmund
Fitzgerald(G)   V=F#add9-C#m-E-B-F#add9

1977

I Just Want To Be Your Everything V=F#m-EM7-F#m7-AM7-
                                   E-C#m-F#m7-B9

You Light Up My Life   V=F#m-B-E-C#m-D#m7-G#7-
                                   C#m-C#7-F#m-B-E-B

Torn Between Two Lovers   V=F#m7-B7-E(3x)C#m-F#m
                                   C=F#m-B7-G#m-C#7

1978

Emotion   B=F#m7-EM7(3x)B11-
                                   C#m7-G#m7(2x)A-G#m7-
                                   C#m-B11

We Are The Champions   C=F#5-A#5-D#5 [B5-C#5]

Dust In The Wind(C)   C=F#/A#-B-C#m-C#m/B-F#/A#-
                                   B-C#m-B/D#

Double Vision   C=F#m-C#m(2x)

With A Little Luck(E)   C=F#m-C#7(3x)F#m/C#-C#7-
                                   F#m-C#7-DM7-B11

Stayin' Alive(Ab)   B=F#7-C#m7(2x)

1979

Stumblin' In   V=F#m-B-E-C#m(3x)

1980

Misunderstanding	V=F#m-G#m7-A6-C#m-B-(3)E
Lost In Love	C=F#m7-G#m7-A-E-C#m-F#m7-F#7/A#-A
Fame	C=F#m-B-G#7sus-G#7(2x)-C#m7
Rock With You	C=F#m9-B-C#-F#m9-B-E11

1981

Her Town Too	V=F#m7-B(7x)F#m7-B11
Morning Train(Nine To Five)	V=F#m7-B7(4x)DM7-C#m7
Turn Your Love Around(C)	V=F#m9-B(2x)F#m9-B7sus-EM7

1982

Africa(E)	C=F#m-D-A-E(3x)F#m-D-A-C#m-E-F#m-A-C#m

1986

The Way It Is	V=F#m7-C#m-B-Aadd9-E-B-Aadd9(2x)

1990

Still Got The Blues	V=F#m7-F#m7/B-EM7-AM7-D#m7b5-G#7-C#m
Black Velvet	C=F#m9-B-F#m9-D-A-F#m9-B-A7-G#7sus-C#m

1996

Change The World(E)	C=F#m7-G#7-C#m7-D#m7b5-

G#7-C#m7-D#m7b5-G#7-
C#m7-Cm7-Bm7-A

Listing By Progression Type

Chord Progression   *Song Examples*

Standard ("F#m" First)

The "E6" chord and "C#m7" chords share the same notes.

Chord Progression	Song Examples
F#m-B-E-C#m	All My Loving('63); You Light Up My Life('77); Stumblin' In('79)
F#m-B7-E-C#m	First Time Ever I Saw Your Face('72); The Night The Lights Went Out In Georgia('73)
F#m7-B7-E-E6	For The Good Times('71)
F#m7-B7-E-C#m	A Place In The Sun('66)
F#m7-B7-E-C#m7	Fools Rush In('63); Shoop Shoop Song(It's In His Kiss)('64)
F#m7-B7-E-C#7	The Man With All The Toys('64)
F#m7-B7-EM7-C#m7	I've Got You Under My Skin('36)
F#m7-B7-EM7-C#7	New York's A Lonely Town('65); See You In September('66)
F#m7-B9-EM7-E6	Strangers In Paradise('53)
F#m9-B13sus-EM7-[D7]-C#7	Feel Like Makin' Love('74)

Partial Standard ("F#m" First)

Chord Progression	Song Examples
F#m-B-E	Girl, You'll Be A Woman Soon('67);(I Never Promised You A)Rose Garden('71); It Never Rains In Southern California('72)
F#m-B7-E	Kind Of A Drag('67); Yester-me, Yester-you, Yesterday('69); The Night Chicago Died('74)
F#m-B7-E-EM7	Tell It Like It Is('67); Billy Don't Be A Hero('74)
F#m-F#m7-B7-E	You Don't Have To Say You Love Me('66)
F#m7-B7-E	For Me And My Gal('17); Devil In Her Heart('62); Torn Between Two Lovers('77)
F#m7-B7-E-E+	My Love('73)
F#m7-B7-EM7	Angie Baby('74); I'd Really Love To See You Tonight('76)
F#m7-B7-E-Em	C'est Si Bon('47)
F#7-B7-E	Amos Moses('71)

F#m-B	I'm A Loser('64); It's My Life('65); Reach Out In The Darkness('68); My Sweet Lord('70); The Story In Your Eyes('71)
F#m7-B	Society's Child('67); Down By The River('69); Shower The People('76); Her Town Too('81)
F#m7-B7	Tea For Two('24); Fascinating Rhythm('24); Satin Doll('53); Never On A Sunday('61); Little Saint Nick('63); I Get Around('64); Shoop Shoop Song(It's In His Kiss)('64); Little Green Apples('68); It's A Family Affair('71); Morning Train(Nine To Five)('81)
F#m7-B9	See You In September('66)
F#m9-B	Turn Your Love Around('81)
F#-B	Attitude Dancing('75)

Standard("A" Substitution/"F#m First)

The "F#m7/B" chord has the same notes, except D#, as the B11 chord.

F#m-B-E-A	Goodbye Yellow Brick Road('73)
F#m7-B7-EM7-A	Yesterday When I Was Young('69)
F#m7-B7-EM7-AM7	Autumn Leaves('55)
F#m7-B9-EM7-AM7	Killing Me Softly With His Song('73)
F#m7-F#m7/B-E-A/E	Don't Let Me Down('69)–Chorus
F#m7-F#m7/B-EM7-AM7	Still Got The Blues('90)
F#-B-E-A	Laugh, Laugh('65)
F#7/A#-Bm-E7/G#-A	Lady Jane('66)

"Fo" Cliché("F#m" First)

F#m7-B7-E-Fo	Bennie And The Jets('74)
F#m7-B9-EM9-Fo	Thanks For The Memory('37)
F#m7-B11-EM7-Fo	My Eyes Adore You('75)
F#m9-B13sus-E-Fo	Don't Let Me Be Lonely Tonight('72)

Asdending Bass Lines

F#m-G#m-A-B	Rain, The Park, And Other Things('67)
F#m7-G#m-A-B7	Young Girl('65)
F#m-G#m7-A6-C#m	Misunderstanding('80)

Static Bass Lines

F#m-C#+/F#-F#m7	The Guitar Man('72)
F#m7/E-E-Bm7/E-A/E	Hurting Each Other('72)
F#m-E/F#-A/F#-B/F#	The Word('65)
F#m-F#m7	Little Green Apples('68)
F#-F#m7-F#m7/B-B	My Little Town('75)
F#-F#m	Sealed With A Kiss('62)
F#-F#m	She's Not There('64)
F#-B/F#	Closer To You('76)
F#-Bm/F#	You Are Everything('72)
F#m7/B-B	Uncle Albert/Admiral Halsey('71)
F#m7/B-B7	Spill The Wine('70)
F#m7/B-B9	Welcome Back('76)
F#/C#-A#m/C#	What Becomes Of The Broken-Hearted('66)

Other "F#" Progressions

The "F#m-E" progression is an example of a Reverse Basic("F#m" Substitution)Progression.

F#m-E	Pushin' Too Hard('67); Gimme Little Sign('67); Girl, You'll Be A Woman Soon('67)
F#m-E-F#m-B7	Black Is Black('66)
F#m-E-G#m-C#m	Midnight Confession('68)
F#m-E/G#-B	Reach Out, I'll Be There('66)
F#m-EM7	Hello It's Me('73); By The Time I Get To Phoenix('67)
F#m-EM7-E	These Eyes('69)
F#m-EM7-F#m7-AM7	I Just Want To Be Your Everything('77)
F#m-E(6/9)/G#	A Horse With No Name('72)
F#m7-E	Gimme Little Sign('67)
F#m7-E-A-E	You're My Best Friend('76)
F#m7-EM7	You've Made Me So Very Happy('67); Stormy('68); Emotion('78)
F#m7-EM7-Esus-E	Don't Bring Me Down('69)-Verse
F#m7-EM7-F#m7-G#	Turn Down Day('66)–Verse

F#m7-F#m7/B-EM7-D#m7	Turn Down Day('66)-Chorus
F#m7/B-E-A-E	(You Make Me Feel Like)A Natural Woman('67)
F#m7/B-EM7	Goin' Out Of My Head('64)
F#7-E-D#m-G#m	Kentucky Rain('70)
F#m-G#m-A-E	Rain, The Park And Other Things('67)
F#m-G#m-A-F#m	Get On Up('67)
F#m-G#m7	Hurt So Bad('65)
F#m7-G#m7	Kid Charlemagne('76)
F#m7-G#m7-F#m7-E	Summer Breeze('72)
F#m7-G#m7-A-E	Lost In Love('80)
F#m7-G#m7-AM7-G#m7	(You're My)Soul And Inspiration('66); Do It Again('73)
F#m7-G#m7-C#m7	Heat Wave('63)
F#m7-G#m7-C#9	Lightnin' Striking('66)
F#m7-G#7-C#m7-D#m7b5	Change The World('96)
F#-G#m-C#	Don't Worry Baby('64)
F#m-A	Sky Pilot('68)
F#m-A-B-E	Wild Horses('71)
F#m-Am-F#o-E	You Won't See Me('74)
F#m7-A-E-B	Helplessly Hoping('69)
F#-A-E	Whatever Gets You Through The Night('74)
F#5-AM7-B5-F#	No Time('70)
F#5-A#5-D#5-[B5-C#5]	We Are The Champions('78)
F#m-B-G#7sus-G#7	Fame('80)
F#m-B7-G#m-C#7	Torn Between Two Lovers('77)
F#m7-B7-E-G#m7	I Get A Kick Out Of You('34); Puppy Love('60)
F#m7-B7-F#m7-C#11	The Word('65)
F#m7-B7-G#m7-C#9	Wives And Lovers('63)
F#m7-B7-C#m	Aquarius('69)
F#m7-B9-Fo-F#m7	As Time Goes By('31)
F#m9-B-F#m9-D	Black Velvet('90)
F#m9-B-C#-F#m9	Rock With You('80)
F#-B7-G#7-C#7	Things We Said Today('64)
F#/A#-B-C#m-C#m/B	Dust In The Wind('78)

The "F#m-C#m" progression is an example of a Reverse Minor Basic Progression.

F#m-C#m	And I Love Her('64); Double Vision('78)
F#m-C#m7	Things We Said Today('64)
F#m-C#7	With A Little Luck('78)
F#m7-C#m7	Ain't No Woman(Like The One I Got)('73)
F#m7-C#m-B-Aadd9	The Way It Is('86)
F#-C#m	Ridin' The Storm Out('73)
F#add9-C#m-E-B	Wreck Of The Edmund Fitzgerald('76)
F#7-C#m7	Stayin' Alive('78)
F#m-D-A-E	Africa('82)
F#m-D-B7-E7	Help('65)
F#-D-C#m-F#	Smoke On The Water('73)

"G" Chord Progressions

Only a few songs were found to have verses, choruses, or bridges that start with "G" chords, one of which, *At Seventeen*, was a huge comeback hit for Janis Ian in 1975. Chord Progressions that begin with the "Borrowed G" chord are generally used for choruses and bridges to differentiate and contrast them with corresponding verses using "E" Chord Progressions.

Below is a chronological listing of songs with choruses or bridges that begin with the "G" chord followed by a listing of chord progressions by type.

Chronological Listing

Date/Song Title   *Chord Progression*

1965

This Diamond Ring(Eb)   C=G-Bm/F#-Em-D(2x)

1966

Here, There And Everywhere(G)   B=G-Em-Am-B7-Em-Am-B7

These Boots Are Made
For Walking   C=G-E(3x)

Get Ready(D)   C=G-C-Am-D

1967

Bernadette(Eb)   V=G/D-Em-Am-Dsus(2x)

1968

Words(G)   C=G-D-E-F#-B7

Jumping Jack Flash(B)	C=G-D-A-E(2x)

1969

Two Of Us(G)	B=G-Bm-Em7-F#m-B7

1970

Evil Woman	C=G-D-F-G-D(2x)

1971

That's The Way I Always Heard It Should Be	C=G-F#m-Em7-DM7-G-F#m-B-E

1972

Bang A Gong(E)	C=G-A-E(2x)
Alone Again(Naturally)	B=G-D-F#m7-B7b9-G-C#m7b5-B9-B7
I Can See Clearly Now	B=G-D-G-B-A-G-B

1973

Love Train	B=G-GM7-G6-G-E-E6-EM7-E-G-GM7-G6-G-F#m7/B-B7

1974

Laughter In The Rain	C=GM7-Em7-Am7-Am7/D(2x)-GM7-Em7-CM7-B7sus4-B7

1975

At Seventeen(C)	C=G6-F#m7-B7/D#-Em7-Am7(2x)CM7-B7-Em/B-B7-Em7-Am7-F#m7-B7/D#

Daisy Jane(G)   C=G-A-F#m-Bm(2x)-
                  GM7-F#m7-Esus4-E

1976

Magic Man(G)   C=G-D-E5(2x)D-E-G-A

Listing By Progression Type

Chord Progression   *Song Examples*

Descending Bass Lines

G-Bm/F#-Em-D   This Diamond Ring('65)

Static Bass Lines

E-E6-EM7-E   Love Train('73)
G-GM7-G6-G   Love Train('73)

Other "G" Progressions

G-E   These Boots Are Made For Walking('66)
G-Em-Am-B7   Here, There And Everywhere('66)
G/D-Em-Am-Dsus   Bernadette('67)
GM7-Em7-Am7-Am7/D   Laughter In The Rain('74)

G-F#m-Em7-DM7   That's The Way I Always Heard It Should Be('71)
G6-F#m7-B7/D#-Em7   At Seventeen('75)

G-A-E   Bang A Gong('72)
G-A-F#m-Bm   Daisy Jane('75)

G-BmEm7-F#m   Two Of Us('69)

G-C-Am-D   Get Ready('66)

The "G-D-A-E" progression follows the Circle of Fifths movement.

G-D-E5   Magic Man('76)
G-D-E-F#   Words('68)
G-D-F-G   Evil Woman('70)

G-D-F#m7-B7b9	Alone Again (Naturally) ('72)
G-D-G-B	I Can See Clearly Now ('72)
G-D-A-E	Jumping Jack Flash ('68)

"G#" Chord Progressions

Although few commonalties are found in this category, many "G#" Chord Progressions follow the Circle Of Fifths movement such as the "G#7-C#7-F#7-B7" Progression which is similar to the "E-G#7-C#7-F#7-B7" Five-Chord Ragtime Progression except the "E" chord has been omitted. The most often cited example of a "G#7-C#7-F#7-B7" Progression is the bridge from the 1930 Gershwin standard *I Got Rhythm*.

Below is a chronological listing of songs with verses, choruses, and bridges that begin with the "G#" chord followed by a listing of chord progressions by type.

Chronological Listing

Date/Song Title   *Chord Progression*

N/A

Havah Nagilah   V=G#7-C#m(2x)G#7-
                           F#m-G#7(2x)

1930

I Got Rhythm   B=G#7-C#7-F#7-B7

1946

Anniversary Song   V=G#7-C#m-F#m-C#m-
                           G#7-C#m

1961

One Note Samba(Bb)   V=G#m11-C#7b5/G-F#m11-
                           B7b5/F(2x)-
                           Bm11-E7b5/A#-AM7-A6-

	G#m11-C#7b5/G-F#m11-B7b5/F-E

1964

I'll Cry Instead(G)	B=G#m-F#7-B-C#m-F#7-B7
A Hard Day's Night(G)	B=G#m-C#m-G#m-E-C#m-A-B
Can't Buy Me Love(C)	C=G#m-C#m-E7-G#m-C#m-F#m7-B6
She's A Woman(A)	C=G#m-C#-G#m-A-B
Walk On By	V=G#m7-C#(3x)F#m7-G#m7
You Can't Do That(G)	B=G#7-C#m-F#m-G#m-E7-G#7-C#m-F#m-G#m-B7

1965

Laugh, Laugh(E)	V=G#m-C#m(3x)B-E-A-B-E
What The World Needs Now	V=G#m7-C#m7(2x)A6-A-G#m-B7
Yesterday(F)	B=G#7sus4-G#7-C#m-B-A-C#m/G#-F#m6-B7(2x)

1966

Listen People	C=G#m7-F#m7(3x)A-B7
And Your Bird Can Sing(E)	B=G#m-G#m(M7)-G#m7-C#/F-E-F#m-B
Nowhere Man(E)	B=G#m-A(2x)G#m-F#m7-B
Secret Agent Man(G)	C=G#m-C#m(2x)A7-G#7-C#m

Mr. Dieingly Sad(Bb)	V=G#M7-G#m7-C#7-F#M7-F#m7-B7-EM7-C#9

1967

People Are Strange(G)	C=G#7-E(2x)G#7
Never My Love(Db)	C=G#7sus4-G#7-C#m-F#7-BM7-EM7-AM7-A6-G#m-C#m

1968

Like To Get To Know You(C)	V=G#m7-Bm6-AM7-D7b9/#11-C#m-AM7(2x) C=G#m7-F#m7-F#m7/B(2x) O=G#m7-AM7-B7#5

1971

Wild Horses(G: Open Tuning)	V=G#m-E-Esus-E(2x)-F#m-A-B-E- E-B-A
Cross Eyed Mary(C)	V=G#m-A-B-F#(2x)
If You Really Love Me	C=G#m-C#m7-F#m7(4x)A-E-F#m7-E-G#m-F#o

1973

I Got A Name	C=G#m7-A-G#m-C#7-A-B-D

1974

I Shot The Sheriff	V=G#m-C#m-G#m(2x)-EM7-D#m7-G#m
Wishing You Were Here	V=G#-C#-G#-C#m-F#m7-B7-C#m-A-B- G#-C#-G#-C#m-F#m7-B7-

                                C#m-
                                E/C#-D#/C#-D/C#-C#m(2x)-
                                A-B

1975

Listen To What The Man Said   V=G#m-AM7-G#m7-C#7sus4-
                               [C#-G#m]-F#m-G#m-AM7-E

1976

Silly Love Songs   B=G#m7-C#m-F#m7-E-G#m7-
                               C#m-F#m7-[E]-F#m7-E/C#-
                               F#m7-F#m7/B

Listing By Progression Type

Chord Progression   *Song Examples*

Descending Bass Lines

The following progression combines the use of a Descending Bass Line with a Circle of Fifths chord movement.

G#m11-C#7b5/G-F#m11-B7b5/F   One Note Samba('61)

Static Bass Lines

G#m-G#m(M7)-G#m7   And Your Bird Can Sing('66)
E/C#-D#/C#/D/C#-C#m   Wishing You Were Here('74)

Other "G#" Progressions

G#m-E-Esus-E   Wild Horses('71)
G#7-E   People Are Strange('67)

The "G#m-F#m" progression is an example of a Basic("G#m" & "F#m" Substitution)Progression.

G#m-F#7-B-C#m   I'll Cry Instead('64)
G#m7-F#m7   Listen People('66)
G#m7-F#m7-F#m7/B   Like To Get To Know You('68)

The following progression is an example of a Basic("G#m" Substitution)Progression.

G#m-A	Nowhere Man('66)
G#m-A-B-F#	Cross Eyed Mary('71)
G#m-AM7-G#m7-C#7sus4	Listen To What The Man Said('75)
G#m7-A-G#m-C#7	I Got A Name('73)
G#m7-AM7-B7#5	Like To Get To Know You('68)
G#m7-Bm6-AM7-D7b9/#11	Like To Get To Know You('68)

The "G#m-C#m-F#m" progression follows the Circle of Fifths movement. *Never My Love* follows the Circle of Fifths through five changes and *Mr. Dieingly Sad* follows the Circle of Fifths through four changes. The *I Got Rhythm* bridge follows the Circle of Fifths through three changes.

G#m-C#m	Laugh, Laugh('65); Secret Agent Man('66)
G#m-C#m-E7-G#m	Can't Buy Me Love('64)
G#m-C#m-G#m	I Shot The Sheriff('74)
G#m-C#m-G#m-E	A Hard Day's Night('64)
G#m-C#-G#m-A	She's A Woman('64)
G#m7-C#m-F#m7-E	Silly Love Songs('76)
G#m7-C#m7	What The World Needs Now('65)
G#m7-C#m7-F#m7	If You Really Love Me('71)
G#m7-C#	Walk On By('64)
G#-C#-G#-C#m	Wishing You Were Here('74)
G#M7-G#m7-C#7-F#M7	Mr. Dieingly Sad('66)
G#7-C#m	Havah Nagilah(N/A)
G#7-C#m-F#m-G#m	You Can't Do That('64)
G#7-C#m-F#m-C#m	Anniversary Song('46)
G#7-C#7-F#7-B7	I Got Rhythm('30)
G#7sus4-G#7-C#m-F#7	Never My Love('67)
G#7sus4-G#7-C#m-B	Yesterday('65)

"A" Chord Progressions

Sometimes songwriters will begin a verse, chorus, or bridge with an "A" Chord Progression to differentiate and contrast it with a corresponding verse, chorus, or bridge that is built around an "E" Chord Progression.

The most frequent progressions that begin with an "A" chord are as follows:

Reverse Basic	A-E
Rock("A" First)	A-B-E
Rock Ballad("A" First)	A-B-E-C#m

The "A-E" Reverse Basic Progression is the reverse of the ever-popular Basic "E-A" Progression, both of which follow the Circle of Fifths movement. The Reverse Basic Progression was used to create choruses for Buddy Holly's 1957 *That'll Be The Day*, The Everly Brothers' 1957 *Bye Bye Love*, and The Eagles' 1976 *Take It To The Limit*.

The "A-B-E" Rock("A" First)is similar to the "E-A-B"Rock Progression except it also starts with the "A" chord instead of the "E" chord. The Rock("A" First)Progression was used to create Rod Stewart's 1972 *You Wear It Well*, Paul Simon's 1972 *Mother And Child Reunion*, and Jimmy Buffett's 1978 *Cheeseburger In Paradise.*

The "A-B-E-C#m" Rock Ballad("A" First)Progression is similar to the "E-C#m-A-B7" Rock Ballad Progression except that it begins with the "A" chord instead of the "E" chord. Examples of hit songs written around the Rock Ballad("A" First)Progression include Creedence Clearwater Revival's 1971 *Have You Ever Seen The Rain*, Ex-Beatle John Lennon's 1981 *Watching The Wheels* and Marc Cohn's 1991 *Walking In Memphis*.

In addition to the most frequent progressions already discussed, there are a number of other "A" Chord Progressions that mainly continue to move to the "E", "F#m", "G#m", "B", "C#m", and the "Borrowed D" chords. Although not used as frequently as the above progressions, the following seven progression types are also employed:(1)"A-E-A-B" Reverse Basic & Partial Rock Combination;(2)"A-E-B" Reverse Rock("A" First);(3)"A-B" Partial Rock;(4)"A-B-C#m" Reverse

Partial Money Chords;(5)"A-C#m" Reverse Basic("C#m" Substitution);(6)"A-D-A-E" Reverse Classic Rock(Borrowed "D"); and(7)"A-D" Partial Reverse Classic Rock(Borrowed "D").

Below is a chronological listing of songs with verses and/or choruses that use a progression starting with an "A" chord followed by a listing of chord progressions by type.

Chronological Listing

Date/Song Title	Chord Progression
1849	
Oh Susanna	C=A-E-B7-E-B7-E
1918	
After You've Gone	V=AM7-Am6-E-C#7-F#9-B9-E
1927	
Ain't She Sweet	B=A7-E(2x)B7
1929	
Stardust	V=A6-Am6-E-G#m-C#7-F#m7-C#7-F#m7-Am-B7 I=E7#5
1932	
Willow Weep For Me(E-F)	C=Am-F-Em-E-Am-G-F-E7
1947	
Almost Like Being In Love	V=AM7-B7-G#m7-C#m7-F#m7
1954	
Till There Was You(F)	B=A-Am-E-C#9-F#m-F#m(M7)-

"A" Chord Progressions

F#m7-F#7-B-B9-B+

1955

Unchained Melody   B=A-B-A-G-A-B-E

1956

What Ever Will Be, Will Be
(Que Sera, Sera)   C=A-E-B7-E-B7-E

Don't Be Cruel   C=A-B7(2x)E

1957

That'll Be The Day(A)   V=A-E(3x)F#-B7
                        C=A-E(2x)B-E

Bye, Bye Love(A)   C=A-E(3x)B7-E-E7

Wake Up Little Susie   V=A-E7(5x)A-B(2x)

Whole Lotta Shakin' Goin' On   V=A7-E(2x)B7-E

Chances Are   V=A6-E7+5-A-Am6-E-G#m7

1959

Dream Lover   B=A-E-F#7-B7

1961

Travelin' Man(D)   C=A-G#m-A-E-A-G#m-F#-B

1962

Baby It's You(G)   V=A-E(2x)C#m-F#m-
                        E-C#m-A-B7-
                        E-C#m(2x)

Chains(Bb)	B=A9-E-E7-A9-B
I Can't Stop Loving You(B)	C=A-E-B-E-E7-A-E-B-E-A-E
Return To Sender	C=A-B7(3x)E-E7-A-B7(2x)F#7-B7

1963

Blue On Blue	C=A6/E-E(3x)A6/E-A-B7-E
This Boy(D)	B=A-G#7-C#m-E7-A-F#7-B7
Blowin' In The Wind(Bb)	C=A-B-E-C#m-A-B-E
I Call Your Name(E)	B=A7-C#m-F#7-C7-B7
Walk Like A Man(Bb)	C=A-D(2x)

1964

P.S. I Love You(D)	C=A-E(3x)E-B-E I=A-Co-E(3x)E-B-E
Do You Want To Know A Secret(E)	B=A-F#m-C#m-Bm(2x)F#m-B7
Please Please Me(E)	B=A-B-E(3x)A-B
A Summer Song(A)	B=A-B-E-C#m- A-B-C#m- E-G#7-C#m-G#m-F#m- C#m-B(2x)
Ride The Wild Surf(Ab-A)	C=A-B-A-E-C#m-A-F#-G#- [B-C]
You Don't Own Me	V=Am-B7-Am-B7#5-B7-Em
Tell Me Why(D)	B=A7-B7-C#m-F#m7-B7-E

1965

All I Really Want To Do	V=A-E-B-E(4x)
Ticket To Ride(A)	B=A-B(2x)
Let Me Be(A)	V=A-B(3x)E
No Reply(C)	V=A-B-E(2x)-C#m-G#m-AM7-G#m-F#m7-B-E
How Sweet It Is(C)	C=A-B11-E(2x)
You're The One(Bb)	V=A-C#m-F#m-C#m-B7-E-C#m-F#7-B7
Five O'Clock World(Ab)	C=A-D(6x)A-E
The Last Time(E)	C=A-D-A-E-D-A(2x)

1966

Knock On Wood(E)	V=A-E7-A
You Didn't Have To Be So Nice	C=A-AM7-A6-AM7-E(2x)B
Shapes Of Things(G)	C=A-G(3x)B
I'm A Man	C=A-G#-G-F#m7
Mother's Little Helper(G)	C=A-B-E-A-B-C#m
Guantanamera	V=A6-B7-E-A6-B7 C=A6-B7-E-A-B7
You Don't Have To Say You Love Me	V=Am-Am7-D7-G-C

1967

Hello Goodbye(C)	V=A6-E-B7-C#m-B7(2x)-B7-E/B-B7-A/G
Darling Be Home Soon	C=Asus-A(2x)E
Jimmy Mack	C=A-F#m7-EM7-A(2x)B
Ain't No Mountain High Enough(D)	C=AM7-F#m7-G#m7-C#m(3x)-F#-G#-A
It Takes Two	C=A-B7-E(2x)
Standing In The Shadows Of Love(Db)	V=A-Bm-E(4x)
Come Back When You Grow Up	V=A-B7-E-(F#m7-B7)4x E
Light My Fire(D)	C=A-B-E-Esus-E-A-B-E-C#-A-E-F#-F#7
Wear Your Love Like Heaven	V=AM7-B-E-B
Daydream Believer	C=A-B7-C#m(2x)A-E(2x)-C#m-F#7-B7

1968

She's A Rainbow(Bb)	C=A(Esus-E)3x-A-E-B7-E
Back In The U.S.S.R.(A)	B=A7-E-E7-A-A/G#-A/G-F#7 B7-A7-E-F#7-B7
People Got To Be Free(F)	C=A-E-B7-E(4x)E-B7(2x)
Love Is All Around	B=A-F#m-A-E-F#m-B

Young Girl	C=A-G#m(2x)F#m7-B7-D-C
Journey To The Center Of The Mind(E)	C=A-C-[C-B-Bb](2x)-A-C-B-Bb-B
Lady Madonna(A)	C=Am7-D7-G-Em7-Am7-D7-G-F#m7-B7sus4-B7

1969

Laughing(A)	C=A-E-F#m(2x)A-B-E
Marakesh Express(G)	C=A-E-F#m-E-A-E-C#m7-F#-A-B-E
Wichita Lineman	V=AM7-E6/9-F#m7-C#m-G#m-F#-C#-B-F#-F#m-C#-B-A-G#m-A
Down By The River(D)	C=A-E-B(3x)F#m7-B(2x)
Down On The Corner(C)	C=A-E-B-E(2x)
Bad Moon Rising(D)	C=A-E-B-A-E
Easy To Be Hard	B=A-Em(4x)F#m-B7(3x)E
Wedding Bell Blues	V=AM7-G#m7-F#m7-B11-EM7-C#m7-F#m7-B7-E-G#7-C#m-AM7-G#m7
Nature's Way(E)	V=Aadd9-G#sus-G#(2x)-C#m-A-B(2x)E-B-A
Good Morning Star Shine	V=A-B(6x)E-B7-E-A-B(3x)A-G#7-C#m-E7-A-G7-F#7-B11-E
Ballad Of John And Yoko(E)	B=A-B7
Undun(G)	C=A(b5)-G#(3x)

Pinball Wizard(B)	C=A-B-E(3x)C-G-Gsus-G
My Cherie Amour(C#)	C=AM9-Bsus-B-D7#11-C#7-F#9-B13-B7-EM7-B7b9
Oh! Darling(A)	B=A-C-E-F#-E-C-B-C

1970

Oh Me Oh My	V=A-E(2x)A-B7 C=A-B7-E-C#m(3x)F#m-A-B7
Candida	C=A-E-B7-E-E7
Knock Three Times	C=A-E-B7-E-E7
No Time(D)	V=A-E-Bm-E(2x)D-C#m(4x)
Fire And Rain(C)	C=A-A/G#-F#m7 B11-E(3x)-D-A/C#-Bm7-Bm/E
Hey There Lonely Girl	V=AM7-G#m7-F#m7-EM7
Woodstock(G)	C=A-E-A-G-D-A-E
Close To You	V=AM7-G#7sus-G#7-G#m7 C#m7-A-E6-EM7 B=A-G#m-D9sus-D9-D7-Aadd9-A
Mississippi Queen(A)	V=A5-B5(4x)D5-E5(2x)-A5-B5(2x)E5-F#5(2x)B

1971

Sunshine(Go Away Today)	C=A-E(3x)D-B-B7
Won't Get Fooled Again(A)	C=A-E(6x)D-B(2x)D-A(2x)
Signs(G)	V=A-E/G#-B/F#-E-B-F#-E-F#

Me And Bobby McGee(G-A)	C=A-E-B-E(2x)
Uncle Albert/Admiral Halsey	C=A-F#m-Bm-E7-[D-F-G]-A
Superstar	C=A-G#m-F#m-E(3x)D-AM7-C#m
Have You Ever Seen The Rain(C)	C=A-B-E-E/D#-C#m-C#m/B(2x)-A-B-E
Imagine(C)	C=A-B-E-G#7(3x)-A-B-E
Me And You And A Dog Named Boo	C=A-B-Esus-E-A-B-E

1972

Nice To Be With You	C=A-E(2x)B-A-E
You Don't Mess Around With Jim(E)	C=A7-E7(2x) A5-B5-E5-B5
Ventura Highway(D)	V=A6-EM7(4x) C=A6-EM7(3x)G#m11
Anticipation	C=A-EM7-F#m7-B-F#m7-B
You Wear It Well(A)	V=A-B-E(2x)B-F#m-E/G#-A-B
Mother And Child Reunion	V=A-B-E(3x)C#m-F#m-E-B
Everybody Plays The Fool Sometime	V=A-B-E-G#+(3x)
City Of New Orleans(D)	C=A-B-E-C#m-A-E-B7-E B-C#m-C#m/B-F#/A#-D-D/C#-B-E
(If Loving You Is Wrong) I Don't Want To Be Right(G)	C=A-C#m(2x)

1973

Peaceful Easy Feeling(E)   C=A-E-A-F#7add4-B7-E-F#m-A-B7-E

Rocky Mountain Way (E)   C=A-E-A-B

Raised On Robbery(C)   V=A-E-B-A-E-A-D-B-E

Stuck In The Middle With You(D)   B=A7-E(2x)F#m7/B-E

Live And Let Die   B=A9-E7-B7-C#m-D

Wildflower(F)   C=AM7-F#m7/B-EM7-A-G#7-C#m-C#m/B-AM7-G#m7-F#m7-F#m7/B-B7-EM7

Saturday Night's Alright For Fighting(G)   C=A-G-D-A(2x)-E

Ain't No Woman (Like The One I Got)   C=AM7-G#m7-F#m7(4x)-F#m7/B

My Love   V=AM7-G#m7-C#9-F#m7 G#m7-AM7-C#m/A#-E-F#m7-A-E

Reelin' In The Years(D)   C=Aadd9-Badd9(3x)

Rocky Mountain High(E)   C=A-B-E(3x)A-E-F#m7-A-B7sus4(2x)

Kodachrome   C=A-C#7-F#7-Bm-E-A-D-B

1974

It's Only Rock "N" Roll (But I Like It)(E)   C=A-E(2x)D-A-E-A-E-A-D-A-D-A-E

Come Monday(A)   C=A-E-A-B

                                                    E-G#m7-A-B
                                                    A-B-E

If You Love Me(Let Me Know)	C=A-E-B7-E-E7-A-E
Radar Love(A)	C=A-E-B-C#-A-E-B
Let It Ride(A)	C=A/E-E-B-C#m7-F#m7-C#m7(2x)
Best Thing That Ever Happened To Me	C=AM7-F#m7-B
Then Came You(F)	C=AM7-G#m7/C#-F#m7-E/G#-A-C#m7-E/G#
Rikki Don't Lose That Number	B=AM7-G#m7-AM7-C#m7-F#m7-A-B7#9
I'll Have To Say I Love You In A Song(A)	C=A-A#o-G#7-C#m-A-EM7-B
Rebel Rebel(A)	V/C=A-B(4x) I=Aadd9-[E]-B
Rock The Boat	C=A-B6(2x)E-A(2x)E-Gsus-D
Back Home Again(E)	C=A-B7-E(3x) B=A-B7-E-A-F#m-B7-E-E7-A-B7-E-A-F#m-A-B7
You Ain't Seen Nothin' Yet(A)	P/C=A-C/A-D/A-E-G#m7-C#m7-F#m7-B11
Wishing You Were Here	B=A-B-C#m-B-A-E-A/E(2x)E

1975

Calypso	C=A-E(2x)B-E

Philadelphia Freedom	C=A-E(2x)D-C#7-F#m7-D7-C#7-C-A
Daisy Jane(G)	V=AM7-EM7(3x)D
Someone Saved My Life Tonight	C=A-E/G#-F#m7(2x)
I'm Not In Love(E)	V=A-Am-E/G#-G#7-C#m-C#m7-(2x)A-B9sus4-E-A/E-G/E-A/E B=Am-D7-G-Em-Am-D7-E11-E-E11-E
Big Yellow Taxi(E)	V=A-E-A-B-E
Listen To What The Man Said	C=A6-E-A6-EM7-E7-A-E-A6-EM7-A-E-A6-EM7-A-E
One Of These Nights(G)	C=AM7-EM7-AM7-F#m-G#m-B
Black Friday(E)	C=A-G6-F#7-G6-D#m7-DM9-B11-E
Wild Fire	C=AM7-G#m(3x)F#m-B-AM7
How Sweet It Is (To Be Loved By You)(G)	C=AM7-G#m7-F#m7-B11-E-D-C#m-Bm-AM7-G#m7-F#m7-B11-E-F#m7-B11
I'm Sorry	C=A-B7-E(3x)B7-C#m-A-F#m-B7-E
Wish You Were Here(G)	V=A/E-B/D#-F#m-F#m/C#-F#m-E-A/E-F#m/C#-E C=A/E-B/D#-F#m-E
When Will I Be Loved(B)	B=A-B-A-E-A-B(2x)

Shining Star	C=A7-D9-G13-C9(2x)E7#9

1976

Take It To The Limit(B)	C=A-E(2x)A-B-E
She's Gone	C=A-E/G#-F#m7-B11(2x)
Kid Charlemagne(C)	O=AM7-G#m7-F#m7-EM7
Let Your Love Flow	C=A-B7-E-A-E
I'd Really Love To See You Tonight	C=AM7-B/A-G#m7(2x)C#m7-AM7-B/A-G#m7-C#m7-B11-E
Takin' It To The Streets(C)	V=Am/B-B11-E/B-F#7/B-B7sus
Do You Feel Like We Do(A)	C=A-Cadd9-Gadd9-D-A(2x)

1977

Hotel California(D)	C=A-E-G#7-C#m-A-E-F#m-G#7
Changes In Latitudes(D)	C=A-E-B-E-A-E-B-A-E/G#-F#m-E
Year Of The Cat	V=AM7-G#m7-C#m7(3x)F#m-B T/A=AM7-B6-C#m-B6
It's Sad To Belong	C=AM7-G#m7-C#m7-F#m7-B11-E(2x)B11
Sentimental Lady	V=A-B(2x)C#m
Dreams(C)	V=AM7-B C=AM7-B13
Blinded By The Light(E)	C=A-B-E(2x) A-B-C#m-B7-A-E-A-E-C#m

Margaritaville(D)	C=A-B-E-Esus-E7(2x)-A-B-E-B/D#-A/C#-B-E
We Just Disagree(E)	C=A-BaddE-E(2x)-A-BaddE-E/G#-A
I Just Want To Be Your Everything	C=AM7-B7-EM7-C#7-F#m7-B7sus4-B7-EM7-E+
Just Remember I Love You(C)	V=AM7-B6-AM7-G#m-AM7-B6
That Smell	V/C=A-C#m
You're In My Heart(E)	C=A-D(4x)C#m-Bm7-A-Ao
Do You Want To Make Love	V=A-D-A-E-B11-E-E/B-B-A/C#-B/D#-E-B11

1978

Running On Empty(A)	V=A/E-E(6x)A-E/G#-B C=A/E-E(3x)C#m
Only The Good Die Young	V=A-E/B-C#m-A-B-E
How Much I Feel	V=AM7-F#m7-B11-EM7-E6 C=AM7-B11-EM7(2x)AM7-G#7sus4-G#7-C#m-B6
Peg(G)	V=AM7-G#m7#5(6x)DM7-C#m7#5(2x)AM7-G#m7#5(2x)EM7-D#m7#5-DM7-C#m7#5-AM7-G#m7#5(2x) C=AM7-G#m7#5-F#m11-C#7sus/G#(2x)A#m7#5-A6/9-E-D#7-G#m7-C#7#9-F#m7-B11
Magnet And Steel	V=A-B(10x)Cm

Cheeseburger In Paradise(D)	C=A-B-E(3x)A-E-B-E
Too Much, Too Little, Too Late	C=AM7-B/A-G#m7-G#m7/C#
Prove It All Night(A)	C=A-B-C#m-A-Bsus-G#m-C#m-A-B-C#m-A-B
Reminiscing	B=AM7-Am9-C#9-AM7-C9-E-F#m/E-E
What's Your Name(A)	C=[G-G#] A [C-B] A [C#] D

1979

Don't Bring Me Down	C=A-E-G-D-A-E
Heart Of Glass(E)	B=A-E-A-F#-B
Heartache Tonight	C=A7-E7-A7-F#-B
Rock 'N' Roll Fantasy	C=A5-F#5-E5-B5-F#5(2x)-C#m(no 3rd)
Here Comes My Girl(E)	V=A-B/A(8x)
Cruel To Be Kind(C)	C=A-B-G#m-C#m(3x)A-B

1980

Boulevard(A)	V=A/E-E(7x)B-C#m(2x)
You'll Accompany Me	V=A-E5-A/E-E5
Late In The Evening	V=A-E-A-B-E
All Out Of Love	V=A/E-E(2x)A/E-B/D#-A/C#-AM7-B7sus
Sailing	V=Aadd9(add D#)-AaddB(2x)-C#9-C#m7(addF#)(2x)-B/A-E/A(2x) B/E-E(2x)

1981

Watching The Wheels   C=A-B-E-C#m-A-C#m/G#-F#m7-F#m/E-B-B/A-C#m-C#m/B-A#m7b5-A-C6-E

Arthur's Theme   V=Am7-D7-G-C-F-B7sus-B7-E
C=AM7-B/A-A-EM7-F#m7-E/F#-F#m7-E-E/G#
T/A=B/E-E-E/G#

1982

Caught Up In You   C=A-E/G#-F#m7-C#m-E(2x)-A-E/G#-F#m7-E/G#-A-F#/A#-B5

Heart Light   C=AM7-EM7-B7sus-B-EM7
AM7-C#7sus-C#7-F#m7-EM7
EM9-AM7-G#m7-F#m7-B11-B-B11

Wasted On The Way(D)   C=A-B-E-C#m-A-B-G#m-E7-A-B-E-C#m-A-B-A-E

Somebody's Baby(D)   V=A-B-C#m-B/D#-E-B/A-A-B(2x)

Even The Nights Are Better   C=Am7-D7-GM7-Em7-Am7-D7-E

1983

Maniac(F)   C=AM7-B-C#m7(3x)B-AM7-B-F#m7

1984

Purple Rain(Bb)   C=Aadd9-Eadd9-C#m7(add4)-B-B5

Leave A Tender Moment Alone   V=AM7-G#m7-F#m7-F#m7/B-E-(2x)

1985

Forever Man(F) V=A-B-C#m(3x)F#m

1988

Fast Car V=AM7-E5-C#m-Badd4

1989

Save The Best For Last V=A-B-E/G#-A-B-C#m

1990

How Am I Supposed To Live Without You C=AM7-B/A-G#m7-C#m7

1991

November Rain V=AM7-F#m9-E-Esus-E(2x)

Walking In Memphis V/C=A-B-E-C#m(8x)

1993

Round Here V=Aadd9-Bsus-C#m7-E(4x)
C=A-B-C#m-E(2x)

1995

You Were Meant For Me(Gb) V=Aadd9-E6/G#-A-C#m-
Aadd9-E6/G#-A-B
C=A-B-E-E5/D#-C#m(2x)-
A-B-C#m

Listing By Progression Type

Chord Progression *Song Examples*

Reverse Basic

A-E	That'll Be The Day('57); Bye, Bye Love('57); Baby It's You('62); P.S. I Love You('64); Oh Me Oh My('70); Sunshine Go Away Today('71); Won't Get Fooled Again('71); Nice To Be With You('72); It's Only Rock "N" Roll(But I Like It)('74); Calypso('75); Philadelphia Freedom('75); Take It To The Limit('76)
A-E7	Wake Up Little Susie('57)
A-Em	Easy To Be Hard('69)
A6-EM7	Ventura Highway('72)
AM7-EM7	Daisy Jane('75)
A7-E	Ain't She Sweet('27); Whole Lotta Shakin' Goin' On('57); Stuck In The Middle With You('73)
A7-E7	You Don't Mess Around With Jim('72)
A-E5-A/E-E5	You'll Accompany Me('80)
A6-E-A6-EM7	Listen To What The Man Said('75)
A-E7-A	Knock On Wood('66)
A6-E7+-A-Am6	Chances Are('57)
A7-E-E7-A	Back In The USSR('68)
A9-E-E7-A9	Chains('62)

Rock("A" First)

A-B-E	Please Please Me('64); No Reply('65); Pinball Wizard('69); You Wear It Well('72); Mother And Child Reunion('72); Rocky Mountain High('73); Blinded By The Light('77); Cheeseburger In Paradise('78)
A-B-E-Esus-E	Light My Fire('67)
A-B-E-Esus-E7	Margaritaville('77)
A-B-Esus-E	Me And You And A Dog Named Boo('71)
A-BaddE-E	We Just Disagree('77)
A-B7-E	It Takes Two('67); Back Home Again('74); I'm Sorry('75)
A-B11-E	How Sweet It Is('65)

"A" Chord Progressions

A-Bm-E	Standing In The Shadows Of Love('67)
AM7-B11-EM7	How Much I Feel('78)
A-B-E-A	Mother's Little Helper('66)
A-B-E/G#-A	Save The Best For Last('89)
A-B7-E-A	Let Your Love Flow('76)
A6-B7-E-A6	Guantanamera('66)

Rock Ballad("A" First)

A-B-E-C#m	Blowin' In The Wind('63); A Summer Song('64); City Of New Orleans('72); Watching The Wheels('81); Wasted On The Way('82); Walking In Memphis('91)
A-B-E-E/D#-C#m	Have You Ever Seen The Rain('71)
A-B7-E-C#m	Oh Me Oh My('70)

Ascending Bass Lines

A-B-C#m-B/D#	Somebody's Baby('82)

Descending Bass Lines

A-E/G#-B/F#-E	Signs('71)
A-G#m-F#m-E	Superstar('71)
AM7-G#m7-F#m7-EM7	Hey There Lonely Girl('70); Kid Charlemagne('76)
A-G#-G-F#m7	I'm A Man('66)
A-A/G#-A/G-F#7	Back In The USSR('68)

Static Bass Lines

A-AM7-A6-AM7	You Didn't Have To Be So Nice('66)
Esus-E	She's A Rainbow('68)
Asus-A	Darling Be Home Soon('67)
Aadd9(add D#)-Aadd9	Sailing('80)

A/E-E	Running On Empty('78); All Out Of Love('80); Boulevard('80)
A6/E-E	Blue On Blue('63)
A-C/A-D/A	You Ain't Seen Nothin' Yet('74)

Other "A" Progressions

The "A-E-A-B" progression is an example of a Reverse Basic and Partial Rock Combination Progression.

A-E-F#m	Laughing('69)
A-E-F#m-E	Marakesh Express('69)
A-E-F#7-B7	Dream Lover('59)
A-E-G-D	Don't Bring Me Down('79)
A-E-G#7-C#m	Hotel California('77)
A-E-A-F#	Heart Of Glass('79)
A-E-A-F#7add4	Peaceful Easy Feeling('73)
A-E-A-G	Woodstock('70)
A-E-A-B	Come Monday('74); Big Yellow Taxi('75); Late In The Evening('80)

The "A-E-B" and "A-E-B-E" progressions are examples of a Reverse Rock("A" First)Progression.

A-E-B	Down By The River('69); Up Around The Bend('70)
A-E-B-E	I Can't Stop Loving You('62); All I Really Want To Do('65); Down On The Corner('69); Me And Bobby McGee('71); Changes In Latitudes('77)
A-E-B7-E	Oh Susanna(1849); What Ever Will Be, Will Be(Que Sera Sera)('56); People Got To Be Free('68); Candida('70)Knock Three Times('70); If You Love Me(Let Me Know)('74)
A-E-Bm-E	No Time('70)
A-E-B-C#	Radar Love('74)
A-E/G#-F#m7	Someone Saved My Life Tonight('75)
A-E/G#-F#m7-B11	She's Gone('76)
A-E/G#-F#m7-C#m	Caught Up In You('82)
A-E/B-C#m-A	Only The Good Die Young('78)
A-EM7-F#m7-B	Anticipation('72)
A-Am-E/G#-G#7	I'm Not In Love('75)
A/E-E-B-C#m7	Let It Ride('74)
A6-E-B7-C#m	Hello Goodbye('67)

"A" Chord Progressions

A6-Am6-E/B-G#m	Stardust('29)
AM7-E5-C#m-Badd4	Fast Car('88)
AM7-EM7-AM7-F#m	Wild Fire('75)
AM7-EM7-B7sus-B	Heart Light('82)
AM7-E6/9-F#m7-C#m	Wichita Lineman('69)
AM7-Am6-E-C#7	After You're Gone('18)
Aadd9-Eadd9-C#m7(add4)-B	Purple Rain('84)
A7-E7-A7-F#	Heartache Tonight('79)
A9-E7-B7-C#m	Live And Let Die('73)
Am-F-Em-E	Willow Weep For Me('32)
A-F#m-A-E	Love Is All Around('68)
A-F#m-Bm-E7	Uncle Albert/Admiral Halsey('71)
A-F#m-C#m-Bm	Do You Want To Know A Secret('64)
A-F#m7-EM7-A	Jimmy Mack('67)
A-A/G#-F#m7-B11	Fire And Rain('70)
A5-F#5-E5-F#5	Rock 'N' Roll Fantasy('79)
AM7-F#m7-G#m7-C#m	Ain't No Mountain High Enough('67)
AM7-F#m7-B	Best Thing That Ever Happened To Me('74)
AM7-F#m7-B11-EM7	How Much I Feel('78)
AM7-F#m7/B-EM7-A	Wild Flower('73)
AM7-F#m9-E-Esus	November Rain('91)
A-G	Shapes Of Things('66)
A-G-D-A	Saturday Night's Alright For Fighting('73)
A-G6-F#7-G6	Black Friday('75)
A-G#m	Young Girl('68)
A-G#m-A-E	Travelin' Man('61)
A-G#m-D9sus-D9	Close To You('70)
A-G#7-C#m-E7	This Boy('63)
Aadd9-G#sus-G#	Nature's Way('69)
A(b5)-G#	Undun('69)
AM7-G#m	Wild Fire('75)
AM7-G#m7-F#m7	Ain't No Woman(Like The One I Got)('73)
AM7-G#m7-F#m7-F#m7/B	Leave A Tender Moment Alone('84)
AM7-G#m7-F#m7-B11	Wedding Bell Blues('66); How Sweet It Is(To Be Loved By You)('75)
AM7-G#m7-AM7-C#m7	Rikki Don't Lose That Number('74)

AM7-G#m7-C#m7	Year Of The Cat('77)
AM7-G#m7-C#m7-F#m7	It's Sad To Belong('77)
AM7-G#m7-C#9-F#m7	My Love('73)
AM7-G#m7/C#-F#m7-E/G#	Then Came You('74)
AM7-G#m7#5	Peg('78)-Verse
AM7-G#m7#5-F#m11-C#sus/G#	Peg('78)-Chorus
AM7-G#7sus-G#7-G#m7	Close To You('70)
A-A#o-G#7-C#m	I'll Have To Say I Love You In A Song('74)

The "A-B" and "A-B7" progressions are examples of a Partial Rock Progression. The "A-B-C#m" progression is an example of a Reverse Partial Money Chords Progression.

A-B	Ticket To Ride('65); Let Me Be('65); Good Morning Star Shine('69); Rebel Rebel('74); Sentimental Lady('77); Magnet And Steel('78)
A-B6	Rock The Boat('74)
A-B7	Don't Be Cruel('56); Return To Sender('62); Ballad Of John And Yoko('69)
A-B/A	Here Comes My Girl('79)
A5-B5	Mississippi Queen('70)
Aadd9-Badd9	Reelin' In The Years('73)
AM7-B	Dreams('77)
A-B-E-G#+	Everybody Plays The Fool Sometime('72)
A-B-E-G#7	Imagine('71)
A-B7-E-F#m7	Come Back When You Grow Up('67)
AM7-B-E-B	Wear Your Love Like Heaven('67)
AM7-B7-EM7-C#7	I Just Want To Be Your Everything('77)
A-B-G#m-C#m	Cruel To Be Kind('79)
A-B-A-E	Ride The Wild Surf('64); When Will I Be Loved('75)
A-B-A-G	Unchained Melody('55)
A-B-C#m	Forever Man('85)
A-B-C#m-A	Prove It All Night('78)
AM7-B-C#m7	Maniac('83)
A-B7-C#m	Daydream Believer('67)
A-B-C#m-B	Wishing You Were Here('74)
A/E-B/D#-F#m-F#m/C#	Wish You Were Here('75)
AM7-B6-AM7-G#m	Just Remember I Love You('77)
AM7-B7-G#m7-C#m7	Almost Like Being In Love('47)
AM7-B/A-G#m7	I'd Really Love To See You Tonight('76)

AM7-B/A-G#m7-G#m7/C#	Too Much, Too Little, Too Late('78)
AM7-B/A-G#m7-C#m7	How Am I Supposed To Live Without You('90)
AM7-B/A-A-EM7	Arthur's Theme('81)
AM9-Bsus-B-D7#11	My Cherie Amour('69)
Aadd9-Bsus-C#m7-E	Round Here('93)
A7-B7-C#m-F#m7	Tell Me Why('64)
Am-B7-Am-B7#5	You Don't Own Me('64)
Am/B-B11-E/B-F#7/B	Takin' It To The Streets('76)
A-C	Journey To The Center Of The Mind('68)
A-C-E-F#	Oh! Darling('69)
A-Cadd9-Gadd9-D	Do You Feel Like I Do('76)

The following progression is an example of a Reverse Basic("C#m" Substitution).

A-C#m	(If Loving You Is Wrong)I Don't Want To Be Right('72); That Smell('77)
A-C#m-F#m-C#m	You're The One('65)
A-C#7-F#7-Bm	Kodachrome('73)
AM7-Am9-C#9-AM7	Reminiscing('78)
A7-C#m-F#7-C7	I Call Your Name('63)

The "A-D-A-E" progression is an example of a Reverse Classic Rock(Borrowed "D")Progression. The "A-D" progression is an example of a Partial Reverse Classic Rock(Borrowed "D")Progression.

A-D	Walk Like A Man('63); Five O'Clock World('65); You're In My Heart('77)
[G-G#]-A-[C-B]-A-[C#]-D	What's Your Name('78)
A-D-A-E	The Last Time('65); Do You Want To Make Love('77)
A7-D9-G13-C9	Shining Star('80)
Am-Am7-D7-G	You Don't Have To Say You Love me('66)
Am7-D7-G-Em7	Lady Madonna('68)
Am7-D7-G-C	Arthur's Theme('81)
Am7-D7-GM7-Em7	Even The Nights Are Better('82)

"A#" Chord Progressions

Only The Doors 1969 hit *Touch Me* shown below has a chorus that begins with an "A#" chord.

Chronological Listing

    Date/Song Title   *Chord Progression*

1969

    Touch Me(C)   C=A#-Am-A#-C-F-F6-F-A#-Am-A#-C-A#-F-F5-C#m-C#m9

"B" Chord Progressions

Sometimes songwriters will begin a verse, chorus, or bridge with a "B" Chord Progression to differentiate and contrast it with a corresponding verse, chorus, or bridge that is built around an "E" Chord Progression.

The most frequent progressions that begin with a "B" chord are as follows:

Reverse Folk   B7-E

Reverse Rock   B-A-E

The "B7-E" Reverse Folk Progression is, as the name implies, the reverse of the "E-B7" Folk Progression. The Reverse Folk Progression was used in The Everly Brothers' 1957 *Bye Bye Love* and The Beach Boys' 1963 *Surfin' U.S.A.*

The "B-A-E" Reverse Rock Progression is the reverse of the "E-A-B" Rock Progression. The Reverse Rock Progression has been used to create the Beatles' 1964 *Love Me Do*, Steppenwolf's 1968 *Magic Carpet Ride*, and Rod Stewart's 1971 *Maggie May*.

In addition to the most frequent progressions already discussed, there are a number of other "B" Chord Progressions that mainly continue to the "E", "A", and "C#m" chords. Although not used as frequently as the above progressions, the following four progression types are also employed:(1)"B-A" Reverse Partial Rock;(2)"B-C#m-E" Reverse Partial Rock Ballad; "B-C#m" Reverse Folk("C#m" Substitution); and(4)"B7-EM7-C#m7-F#m7" Standard("B7" First).

Below is a chronological listing of songs with verses and/or choruses that begin with the "B" Chord followed by a listing of chord progressions by type.

Chronological Listing

Date/Song Title   *Chord Progression*

1580

Greensleeves	C=B-C#m-G#7-B-C#m-G#7-C#m

1946

Anything You Can Do	V=B7-E(4x)

1947

Too Fat Polka	C=B7-E-Fo-B7/F#-B7-E(2x)-A6-B7-E-B7-E

1956

I Walk The Line	V=B7-E(2x)E7-A-E-B7-E

1957

Rock And Roll Music(A)	V=B7-E-A7-B7
Bye Bye Love(A)	V=B7-E(2x)E7-A-B7-E-E7

1958

Sweet Little Sixteen(Db)	V=B7-E(2x)A-E-B7-E

1960

You're Sixteen	B=B7-E-F#7-B7

1961

Never On Sunday	V=B7-E(4x)

1962

Ring Of Fire(G)	C=B-A-E(2x)B-E(2x)
Ramblin' Rose	V=B7-E-F#7-B7-E7-A-E-B7

1963

I'm Leaving It(All)Up To You	V=B7-E(2x)A-E
Surfin' USA(Eb)	V=B7-E(2x)A-E-B7-E

1964

Memphis, Tennessee(G)	V=B-E(2x)
I Want To Hold Your Hand(G)	B=Bm7-E7-A-F#m7-Bm7-E7-A-B(3x)
Save It For Me	V=B-G#m-E-F#7-D#-Cm-G#m-B7
Love Me Do(G)	C=B-A-E(2x)
It's All Over Now(G)	C=B-A-E(2x)
I'll Follow The Sun(C)	V=B7-A7-E-F#-E-E/D#-F#-B-E
Tobacco Road	V=B-C#m

1965

Turn, Turn, Turn(D)	V=B7-E(3x)A-G#m-F#m-B7-E-Esus-E
Help Me Rhonda(Db)	C=B-E(2x)A-C#m-E-F#m-B-E
For Lovin' Me	V=B7-E-B7-C#m-B-E-C#m-F#-B7-E
Yes It Is(E)	B=Bm-E-A-F#m-Bm-E-C#m-C#m7/E-F#-B7
The Night Before(D)	B=Bm-E7-A-C#m-F#7-B7
Flowers Never Bend With The Rainfall	C=B-A-E-C#m-A6-C#m-F#-A-E

Eight Days A Week(D)	B=B-C#m-F#-A-B

1966

Working In The Coal Mine	V=B-E(3x)B
Doctor Robert(D)	V=B7-E5/B(8x)A
Workin' My Way Back To You	C=Bm7-E-A-D-A-E-F#m(2x)B7-E-E7-A-E-E7-A-E(2x)
Look Through Any Window(E)	V=B-A-E-A-B(2x)C#m-E-B-E-B-(2x)F#-B-E-F#(2x) I=B-Bus-B-A-Asus-A(2x)
Yellow Submarine(Gb)	V=B-A-E-C#m-F#m-A-B7-E(4x)
Help Me Girl(Eb)	C=B-AM7(2x)G#sus-G#

1967

White Rabbit	B=B-E(2x)C#m-D(2x)
New York Mining Disaster	C=B-E(2x)A-G#7-C#m
Let's Spend The Night Together(G)	C=B7-E-G#m/D#-B-B7
Don't You Care(E)	V=Bm9-EM7(4x)
Light My Fire(D)	V=Bm-G#m(4x) Solo=Bm-C#m
I Dig Rock And Roll Music(D)	V=B7(G#m-E)2x-C#-F#7sus4
A Little Bit Me, A Little Bit You	V=B-A(8x)E-A-E-A-B7(7x)
Respect(C)	V=B-A(3x)
Strawberry Fields Forever(Bb)	V=B-B7-C#m-C#m/B-A-B-

E-C#m-A-B-A-E

1968

Sympathy For The Devil(E) C=B-A-E-A/E-E-B-E/B-B-A-E-Esus-E

1969

Magic Carpet Ride(G) V=B-A-E(16x)-E-G-A-E7

Rock Me(F) V=B-A-E(8x)E7

Ramblin' Gamblin' Man V/C=B-A-E-B

Proud Mary C=B-C#m-E

Touch Me(C) V=B-D#m-E-G-D-F#m7-G-A#-F

1970

Reach Out And Touch (Somebody's Hand) C=B7-EM7-C#m7-F#m7-B7-E C#m7-B7-EM7-C#m7-F#m7-B7-G#m7

No Time(C) C=B5-F#-C#m-F#(3x)-E-D#m(4x)

The Tears Of A Clown(C#) C=B-G#/C-C#m-AM7-E

Lookin' Out My Back Door(Bb) C=B-A-E-C#m-B

See Me, Feel Me(E) V=B-A-C-A-E-A-C-G-D-B-B7sus—A-C-A-E-A-C-G-D-B

1971

Brown Sugar(C) C=B-E(2x)

The Man Who Sold The World(A) C=B-E-Am-E-B-E-Am

Maggie May(D) V=B-A-E(2x)A-E-A-B-F#m-G#m-F#m-Esus/B-F#m-B(3x)E

Signs(G) C=B-A-E-B-E-B-F#-A

1972

Honky Cat(G) V=B7-E(2x)G#7-C#7-B7-E

1973

Drift Away C=B-F#-E(2x)B

Love Train(C) V=B-A(2x)B-C#m-B/C#-C#m-F#m7-B7-B/A-B7/G#-B7/F#

Shambala(A) V=B-A-E(8x)E-A(4x)E

Chevy Van C=B-A-E-B-F#7-A-B-E-Esus(2x)

Turn The Page C=B-C#m(2x)B-F#-A-B-C#m

1974

Rock 'N' Roll Heaven V=Bm7-E7-A-F#m-Bm7-E7-A-Bm7-E7-A-F#m7-Bm7-A/C#-F#m-B

Help Me(D) V=B-F#m7-AM7-GM7-DM7-AM7-DM7-Badd9-DM7-EM7
I=Badd9

Sweet Home Alabama(G) V=B-A-E(3x)

Don't Let The Sun Go Down On Me V=B-B7-A/E-E-A/E-E-A-B-E/B-B-E/B

Whatever Gets You Through The Night V=B-D-A(2x)F#m-E-D-A

B=B7-E(3x)D-A

1975

Thank God I'm A Country Boy	C=B-E(2x)E-A-E-B-E
Blackwater(D)	V=Bm7(4)-E5(8x)
Sister Golden Hair(E)	C=B-A-E(2x)F#m-G#m-Aadd9
Killer Queen	C=B-(D#m-G#m)2x-D#m7-G#7-C#-B

1976

New Kid In Town(E)	B=B7-E-B7-C#m-F#-Am7-D11-D7
She's Gone	V=B11-B(3x)G#m7-C#m7-B11
Let 'Em In	B=Bm-E(3x)Bm-B-BM7-B-B6-B
This Masquerade	B=Bm7-E7b9-AM7(2x)A#m7-D#13-D#7#5-G#M7-D#m7-D#13-D#7#5-G#9sus-D13#11
Strange Magic	C=Bm7-C#m(3x)F#m7-B7-E

1978

Baker Street	V=B-E(4x)B-F#m7 A-E(2x)Em7-Bm7(2x)D-A-E
Copacabanna	V=Bm7-E11-AM7-D#m7b5-G#7-C#m(M7)-C#m7-C#m6-C#m-G#7/C-E7/B

1979

What A Fool Believes	V=B7-Aadd9-E/G#-F#m9-B/C#-Ao-C#m

Head Games	C=B5-C#5-C#11-C#m7-F#/C#

1980

Never Be The Same	V=B/E-E(2x)C#11-C#m7(2x)-E/F#-F#m7(2x)B11-B-A-B-A/C#-B/D#
September Morn	V=B11-B9-E/B-EM7-B-F#m7/B
All Out Of Love	C=B-F#/A#-E/G#-E-F#

1981

Celebration	V=B11-E/B-B

1982

My City Was Gone(E)	V=Bm-A-A5 C=B5-E5
Eye Of The Tiger	C=B-C#m7-F#m-E/G#-B-C#m7

1984

Pride(In The Name Of Love)(E)	V/C=B-E-A-F#
Dancing In The Dark(C)	C=B-A-F#m-A-F#m-E-E6(2x)

1985

The Heat Is On	V=B7-E7-B7
Everybody Wants To Rule The World	V=B/E-A/E(4x)F#m-G#m-A-G#m-F#m-G#m-A-B

1986

All I Need Is A Miracle	C=B-E/G#-B/F#-E(3x)C#11

These Dreams(B)	C=B/D#-A/C#-E/B-F#m7-E/G#-B/D#-A/C#-E/B-Asus2-E/G#

1987

I Still Haven't Found What I'm Looking For(D)	C=B-A-E5(2x)
I Wanna Dance With Somebody	V=B-C#m(2x)F#m-B-E/G#-A-F#m7-E/G#-B/C#-A-B

1989

Save The Best For Last	V=B-A-E/G#-A-B-C#m

1991

She Talks To Angels(Open E)	C=B-A-E-A(6/9)/E-E-A(6/9)/E-E(2x)

1997

Candle In The Wind(E)	C=B-B7-E-A-E-A/E-E-B-Bsus-B

Listing By Progression Type

Chord Progression *Song Examples*

Reverse Folk

B-E	Memphis, Tennessee('64); Help Me Rhonda('65); Working In The Coal Mine('66); White Rabbit('67); New York Mining Disaster('67); Brown Sugar('71); Thank God I'm A Country Boy('75); Baker Street('78)
B7-E	Anything You Can Do('46); I Walk The Line('56); Bye Bye Love('57); Sweet Little Sixteen('58); Never On Sunday('61); Surfin' USA('63); I'm Leaving It(All)Up To You('63); Memphis, Tennessee('64); Turn, Turn, Turn('65); Honky Cat('72); Baker Street('78)
B7-E5/B	Doctor Robert('66)

Bm-E	Let 'Em In('76)
Bm7(4)-E5	Blackwater('75)
Bm9-EM7	Don't You Care('67)
B7-E7-B7	The Heat Is On('85)

Reverse Rock

B-A-E	Ring Of Fire('62); Love Me Do('64); It's All Over Now('64); Magic Carpet Ride('69); Rock Me('69); Maggie May('71); Shambala('73); Sweet Home Alabama('74); Sister Golden Hair('75)
B-A-E5	I Still Haven't Found What I'm Looking For('87)
B-B7-A/E-E	Don't Let The Sun Go Down On Me('74)
B7-A-E	Ring Of Fire('62)
B-A-E-B	Ramblin' Gamblin' Man('69); Signs('71); Chevy Van('73)
B-A-E-A	Look Through Any Window('66)
B-A-E-A/E	Sympathy For The Devil('68)
B-A-E-A(6/7)/E	She Talks To Angels('91)

Descending Bass Lines

B-E/G#-B/F#-E	All I Need Is A Miracle('86)
B-F#/A#-E/G#-E	All Out Of Love('80)

Static Bass Lines

B11-B	She's Gone('76)
B11-E/B-B	Celebration('81)
C#5-C#11-C#m7-F#/C#	Head Games('79)
B/E-E	Never Be The Same('80)
B/E-A/E	Everybody Wants To Rule The World('85)

Other "B" Progressions

The "Bm7-E7-A-D" progression follows the Circle of Fifths. The "B7-EM7-C#m7-F#m7" progression is an example of a Standard("B7" First)Progression.

B-E-A-F#	Pride(In The Name Of Love)('84)
B-E-Am-E	The Man Who Sold The World('71)
B-B7-E-A	Candle In The Wind('97)
B7-E-Fo-B7/F#	Too Fat Polka('47)
B7-E-F#7-B7	You're Sixteen('60); Ramblin' Rose('62)
B7-E-G#m/D#-B	Let's Spend The Night Together('67)
B7-E-A7-B7	Rock And Roll Music('57)
B7-E-B7-C#m	For Lovin' Me('65); New Kid In Town('76)
B7-EM7-C#m7-F#m7	Reach Out And Touch(Somebody's Hand)
Bm-E-A-F#m	Yes It Is('65)
Bm-E7-A-C#m	The Night Before('65)
Bm7-E-A-D	Workin' My Way Back To You('66)
Bm7-E7-A-F#m	Rock 'N' Roll Heaven('74)
Bm7-E7-A-F#m7	I Want To Hold Your Hand('64)
Bm7-E7b9-AM7	This Masquerade('76)
Bm7-E11-AM7-D#m7b5	Copacabanna('78)
B-F#m7-AM7-GM7	Help Me('74)
B-F#-E	Drift Away('73)
B5-F#-C#m-F#	No Time('70)
B-G#m	Light My Fire('67)
B-G#m-E-F#7	Save It For Me('64)
B-G#/C-C#m-AM7	The Tears Of A Clown('70)
B7-G#m-E-G#m	I Dig Rock And Roll Music('67)

The "B-A" progression is an example of a Reverse Partial Rock Progression. The "B-A-E-C#m" progression is an example of a Reverse Partial Rock & Partial Rock Ballad Combination Progression.

B-A	A Little Bit Me, A Little Bit You('67); Respect('67); Love Train('73)
B-A-E-C#m	Flowers Never Bend With The Rainfall('65); Yellow Submarine('66); Lookin' Out My Back Door('70)
B-A-E/G#-A	Save The Best For Last('89)
B-A-F#m-A	Dancing In The Dark('84)

B-A-C-A	See Me, Feel Me('70)
B-AM7	Help Me Girl('66)
B/D#-A/C#-E/B-F#m7	These Dreams('86)
B7-Aadd9-E/G#-F#m9	What A Fool Believes('79)
B7-A7-E-F#	I'll Follow The Sun('64)
Bm-A-A5	My City Was Gone('82)

The "B-C#m" progression is an example of a Reverse Folk("C#m" Substitution)Progression. The "B-C#m-E" progression is an example of a Reverse Partial "E-C#m-B" Rock Ballad Progression.

B-C#m	Tobacco Road('64); Turn The Page('73); I Wanna Dance With Somebody('87)
B-C#m-E	Proud Mary('69)
B-C#m-F#-A	Eight Days A Week('65)
B-C#m-G#7-B	Greensleeves(1580)
B-C#m7-F#m-E/G#	Eye Of The Tiger('82)
B-B7-C#m-C#m/B	Strawberry Fields Forever('67)
Bm7-C#m	Strange Magic('76)
B-D-A	Whatever Gets You Through The Night('74)
B-D#m-E-G	Touch Me('69)
B-D#m-G#m-D#m	Killer Queen('75)

"C" Chord Progressions

Hit songs whose verses or choruses begin with the "Borrowed C" chord are relatively rare. The Leaves' 1966 Hey Joe, Deep Purple's 1968 Hush, and Paul McCartney's 1977 Maybe I'm Amazed all begin with the "C" chord and then move forward following the Circle Of Fifths in a counter clockwise movement.

Below is a chronological listing of songs with verses and/or choruses that begin with a "C" chord followed by a listing of chord progressions by type.

Chronological Listing

Date/Song Title   *Chord Progressions*

1966

Hey Joe   V=C-G-D-A-E

1968

Hush   C=C-G-D-A-E-
                               A-D-A-E-A-D-A

1970

Didn't I(Blow Your Mind
This Time)(A)   C=CM7-Am7-Dm7-Dm9/G(2x)

Hand Me Down World(B)   C=C-A#-F-[A#-B]-C(2x)

Rock And Roll Hootchie Koo(A) C=C-D-E(3x)

1974

Free Man In Paris(A) C=C/G-G/D-A/E-Eadd9(2x)

1977

Maybe I'm Amazed(D) V=C-G/B-D/A-A/C#-C-G/B-D-C-G/B-D-A-C-G/B-A#-F/A-D

Barracuda(E) C=C5-E5(2x)D-A-E5-F#5-G5

Listing By Progression Type

Chord Progression	*Song Examples*
C5-E5	Barracuda('77)
C-G-D-A	Hey Joe('66); Hush('68)
C-G/B-D/A-A/C#	Maybe I'm Amazed('77)
C/G-G/D-A/E-Eadd9	Free Man In Paris('74)
CM7-Am7-Dm7-Dm9/G	Didn't I(Blow Your Mind This Time)('70)
C-A#-F-[A#-B]-C	Hand Me Down World('70)
C-D-E	Rock And Roll Hootchie Koo('70)

"C#" Only Chord Progressions

As discussed in the "E" Only Chord Progressions chapter of this book, the instances of one chord progressions for an entire verse and/or chorus are not very common. As shown below, "C#" Only Chord Progressions are not unheard of, but not as frequent as the "E" Only Chord Progressions.

Frankie Goes To Hollywood's 1985 *Relax* and the 1973 *Ridin' The Storm Out* are examples of Static Bass Lines built around the "C#11" chord which is contrasted against the "C#m" chord.

Below is a chronological listing of songs with verses and/or choruses that start with just the "C#" chord followed by a listing of chord progressions by type.

Chronological Listing

Date/Song Title	*Chord Progressions*
1967	
I'm A Man(Eb)	V=C#m7
1968	
In-A-Gadda-Da-Vida	V=C#m7(Riff)
Chain of Fools	V=C#m-C#m7
1969	
Undun(G)	B=C#m(add2)/G#-C#m(add2)/A-C#m(add2)/A#-C#m(add2)/A(4x)
1971	
Treat Her Like A Lady(A)	V=C#m

1972

Do It Again	V=C#m7

1973

Show Biz Kids	V=C#m7
Ridin' The Storm Out	V=C#m-C#11(14x)C#m

1978

Double Vision	V=C#m(no3)-Riff

1985

Relax	V=C#m-C#11
Shout	V=C#m-C#m/A-C#m/F#-C#m
	B=C#m/E-C#m/F#

Listing By Progression Type

Chord Progression — *Song Example*

"C#m" One Chord Progressions

C#m	Treat Her Like A Lady('71)
C#m(no3)	Double Vision('78)
C#m7	I'm A Man('67); In-A-Gadda-Da-Vida('68); Do It Again('72); Show Biz Kids('73)

Static Bass Lines

C#m-C#11	Ridin' The Storm Out('73); Relax('85)
C#m-C#m7	Chain Of Fools('68)

Other "C#" Only Progressions

C#m-C#m/A-C#m/F#-C#m   Shout('85)
C#m(add2)/G#-C#m(add2)/A-
C#m(add2)/A#-C#m(add2)/A   Undun('69)

"C#-E" Chord Progressions

The most frequent "C#-E" Chord Progressions are as follows:

Reverse Partial Rock Ballad   C#m-E

Descending "C#-B-A-G#"
Bass Lines   C#m-E/B-A-G#

The "C#m-E" Reverse Partial Rock Ballad Progression is, as the name implies, the reverse of the Partial "E-C#m" Progression. Examples of songs that use the "C#m-E" Progression include the 1898 *When Johnny Comes Marching Home* and Paul Simon's 1970 *El Condor Pasa*.

The "C#-B-A-G#" Descending Bass Line was used to create The Three Dog Night's 1971 *An Old Fashioned Love Song* and Bobby Hebb's 1966 *Sunny*. The "C#-B-A-G#" Descending Bass Line is the same bass line used to produce the Money Chords discussed in the "C#-B" Chord Progression chapter of this book.

In addition to the progressions already discussed, there are a number of other "C#-E" Progressions that mainly continue to move to the "F#" and "B" chords. Several of these progressions can be transformed into Descending Bass Line Progressions by playing other chord notes as the bass note.

Below is a chronological listing of songs with verses and/or choruses that use the "C#-E" sequence followed by a listing of chord progressions by type.

Chronological Listing
Date/Song Title   *Chord Progression*

1898

When Johnny Comes
Marching Home   V=C#m-E(2x)E-B-C#m-G#m-E

1961

(Ghost)Riders In The Sky(C)   V=C#m-E-C#m-(A-C#m)2x

1963

Greenback Dollar   V=C#m-E(2x)A7-Em-B-C#m-B-C#m

All My Loving(E)   C=C#m-C+-E(2x)

Out Of Limits(G)   V=C#m-E-F#-G#(3x)E-G#

1964

House Of The Rising Sun(C)   V=C#m-E-F#-A-C#m-E-G#-C#m-E-F#-A-C#m-G#-C#m

Thank You Girl(D)   B=C#m-E-B7-F#m-B7-E-A-B7-A-B7

1965

For Your Love(G)   V=C#m-E-F#-F#m(5x)
B=C#-G#-F#(2x)A#m-G#

Heart Full Of Soul(F)   C=C#-E-F#-C#-A-E-C#-G#7-F#7-C#m

Tell Her No(E)   C=C#m-E-C#m-EM7-F#m9-B13-EM7

1966

Lil' Red Riding Hood   V=C#m-E-F#-A-G#7-C#m-G#7

Sunny   V=C#m-E7/B-A7-G#7(2x)

Bus Stop   V=C#m-E-B-C#m-F#m-G#m-C#m

Wouldn't It Be Nice(F)	C=C#m/G#-E11-C#m/G#-G#m7-F#m7-B7

1967

Let's Live For Today(E)	V=C#m-E(5x)C#m

1968

I Love You	V=C#m-E7-F#-G#7(2x)A I=C#m-AM7-G#7
Sunday Morning	V=C#m-E7/B-A-G#7-C#m-C#7-F#m7-B7-E-D-G#7

1969

One	V=C#m-E-A#m7b5-AM7(7x)

1970

El Condor Pasa	V=C#m-E(2x)-C#m-A-A/G#-A/F#-E
Let It Be(C)	C=C#m-E/B-A-E-B-A-E
25 Or 6 To 4(C)	V=C#m-E/B-A#m7b5-AM7-G#(4x)A-E-B-A
Ohio(F)	V=C#m-E-B(4x)F#m7-B(4x)

1971

Treat Her Like A Lady(A)	B=C#m-E-F#m-C#m(4x)
I'd Love To Change The World(G)	V=C#m-E-F#m-A-G#7
Superstar	V=C#m-E/B-A-E/G#-F#7-A-G#-(2x)

An Old Fashioned Love Song	V=C#m-E/B-A-G#(4x)-C#-C#/B-A-G#
The Night They Drove Old Dixie Down(C)	V=C#m-E/B-A-A/G#-F#m(2x)-C#m/G#-A-E-A-C#m/G#-A-E-F#m-F#
If(A)	B=C#m-C+-E/B-A6-G#m7b5-C#7-F#m7-B7
Bangla Desh(C)	I=C#m-Co-E/B-A-G#+-G#7-C#m-F7/C-E/B-A-G#+-G#7
Locomotive Breath(G)	V=C#m-E-B(2x)G#-B C=E-F#-G#-B
Behind Blue Eyes(G)	V=C#m-E-B-Bsus-Aadd9-F#add9-(2x)

1972

Stairway To Heaven(C)	V1=C#m-C#m9/C-E/B-F#9/A#-AM7-B/D#-C#m
Pappa Was A Rolling Stone	V=C#m-E5-B5
Doctor My Eyes(F)	C=C#m-E-C#m-B-A/E-E
Summer Breeze	V=C#-E-B-F#-C#-F#m7-C#-E-B-F#-C# I=C#m7-F#m7(6x)

1974

W.O.L.D.	I=C#m-C+-E/B-A#m7b5 AM7-C#m/G#-F#m7-E-D-C#m

1976

Crazy On You(C)	V=C#m-E-F#m-G#7(2x)

Break=C#m-D#m/G#

1977

Slip Slidin' Away   V=C#m7-E6-A-B-A-A7-E-C#m7-E-B-A-B-E

1978

Da Ya Think I'm Sexy(F)   C=C#m7-E(2x)

We Are The Champions(Eb)   V=C#m-C#11(4x)E-E/A(2x)

1980

Call Me   C=C#m-E-F#-A(2x)

Refugee(A)   V=C#m-E-B(4x)A-F#
                           C=C#m-E-B(2x)

1984

Cover Me(D)   V=C#m-E-B(4x)-
                           F#m-F#m11(2x)F#m-
                           C#m-E-B(2x)A-B-
                           C#m-E-B(2x)

1989

What I Am   V=C#add9-Eadd9-Badd9

1991

To Be With You   V=C#m-E-Aadd9-E(2x)

Listing By Progression Type

Chord Progression   *Song Examples*

Reverse Partial Rock Ballad

C#m-E	When Johnny Comes Marching Home(1898); Greenback Dollar('63); Let's Live For Today('67); El Condor Pasa('70)
C#m7-E	Da Ya Think I'm Sexy('78)
C#m-E-C#m-EM7	Tell Her No('65)
C#m-C+-E	All My Loving('63)

Descending Bass Lines

C#m-E/B-A-E	Let It Be('70)
C#m-E/B-A-E/G#	Superstar('71)
C#m-E/B-A-G#	An Old Fashioned Love Song('71)
C#m-E/B-A-A/G#	The Night They Drove Old Dixie Down('71)
C#m-E7/B-A-G#7	Sunday Morning('68)
C#m-E7/B-A7-G#7	Sunny('66)
C#m-E/B-A#m7b5-AM7	One('69); 25 Or 6 To 4('70)
C#m-C+-E/B-A6-G#m7b5	If('71)
C#m-Co-E/B-A	Bangla Desh('71)
C#m-C+-E/B-A#m7b5	W.O.L.D('74)

Yes, the following Descending Bass Line has been so overplayed that many guitar shops post signs requesting that customers please refrain from playing this progression while in their stores.

C#m-C#m9/C-E/B-F#9/A#	Stairway To Heaven('72)

Static Bass Lines

C#m-C#11	We Are The Champions('78)

Other "C#m-E" Progressions

The following progression can be transformed into a Descending "C#-B-A-G#" Bass Line Progression by playing the B note of the "E" chord as the bass note and by playing the A note of the "F#m" chord as the bass note creating the "C#m-

E/B-F#m/A-G#7" progression. In the same manner, the "C#m-E-F#-G#7" progression can be transformed into the "C#m-E/B-F#/A#-G#7" progression.

C#m-E-F#m-G#7	Crazy On You('76)
C#m-E-F#m-A	I'd Love To Change The World('71)
C#m-E-F#m-C#m	Treat Her Like A Lady('71)
C#m-E-F#-F#m	For Your Love('65)
C#m-E-F#-G#	Out Of Limits('63)
C#m-E-F#-G#7	I Love You('68)
C#m-E-F#-A	House Of The Rising Sun('64); Lil' Red Riding Hood('66); Call Me('80)
C#m-E7-F#-G#7	I Love You('68)
C#-E-F#-C#	Heart Full Of Soul('65)
C#m-E-Aadd9-E	To Be With You('91)
C#m-E6-A-B	Slip Slidin' Away('77)
C#m-E-B	Ohio('70); Locomotive Breath('71); Refugee('80); Cover Me('84)
C#m-E5-B5	Pappa Was A Rolling Stone('72)
C#m-E-B-Bsus4	Behind Blue Eyes('71)
C#m-E-B-C#m	Bus Stop('66)
C#m-E-B7-F#m	Thank You Girl('64)
C#-E-B-F#	Summer Breeze('72)
C#add9-Eadd9-Badd9	What I Am('89)
C#m-E-C#m-A	(Ghost)Riders In The Sky('61)
C#m-E-C#m-B	Doctor My Eyes('72)
C#m/G#-E11-C#m/G#-G#m7	Wouldn't Be Nice('66)

"C#-F#" Chord Progressions

The most frequent "C#-F#" Chord Progressions are as follows:

Minor Basic   C#m-F#m

Minor Basic("F#" Substitution)   C#m-F#

Standard("C#m" First)   C#m-F#m-B7-E

Ragtime("C#7" First)   C#7-F#7-B7-E

Minor Blues   C#m-F#m-C#m-G#m-F#m-C#m

Static Bass Lines   C#m-F#/C#

The "C#m-F#m" Minor Basic Progression is related to the "E-A" Basic Progression where the "C#m" chord has been substituted for the "E" chord and the "F#m" chord has been substituted for the "A" chord. Examples of the Minor Basic Progression include The Stories' 1973 *Brother Louie* and The Rolling Stones' 1978 *Miss You*.

The "C#m-F#" Minor Basic("F#" Substitution)Progression is similar to the above Minor Basic progression except that the "F#m" chord has been substituted by the harder sounding "F#" chord. This progression has produced numerous Rock hits over the years including Jefferson Airplane's 1967 *Somebody To Love*, Shocking Blue's 1970 *Venus*, Santana's 1970 *Evil Ways*, and Linda Ronstadt's 1975 *You're No Good*.

The "C#m-F#m-B7-E" Standard("C#m" First)Progression is similar to the Standard "E-C#m-F#m-B7" Changes except that it begins with the "C#m" chord instead of the "E" chord. Both progressions follow the Circle of Fifths movement. The "C#m-F#m-B7-E" progression was used in such diverse songs as Hammerstein & Kern's 1939 Standard *All The Things You Are*, Bart Howard's 1954 *Fly Me To The Moon*, and Gloria Gaynor's 1979 *I Will Survive*.

The "C#7-F#7-B7-E" Ragtime("C#7" First)Progression is similar to the Ragtime('E-C#7-F#7-B7")Progression, except that it begins with the "C#7" chord instead of the "E" chord. Both progressions follow the Circle of Fifths movement. Popular "C#7-F#7-B7-E" progression songs include the 1925 *Sweet Georgia Brown*, Simon & Garfunkel's 1968 *Mrs. Robinson* and Blood and Sweat & Tears' 1969 *Spinning Wheel*. The Ragtime("C#7" First)song, the 1938 *You Must Have Been A Beautiful Baby*, uses an interesting Descending Bass Line "E7-D#7-D7-C#7" turnaround.

The "C#m-F#m-C#m-G#m-F#m-C#m" Minor Blues Progression has not been used anywhere as often as the Standard Twelve-Bar Blues form. The definitive Minor Blues song is B.B. King's 1970 *The Thrill Is Gone*.

"C#m-F#/C#" Static Bass Line Progressions combine the use of the "C#m-F#" progression with a Static "C#" Bass Line. Examples of "C#m-F#/C#" Static Bass Line Progressions include Gary Lewis' 1965 *This Diamond Ring* and Steve Miller Band's 1977 *Fly Like An Eagle*.

In addition to the most frequent progressions already discussed, there are a number of other "C#-F#" Progressions that mainly continue to move to the "E", "G#", "A", "B", and "C#m" chords. Also, several progressions follow the Circle of Fifths movement and others represent various Combination Progressions.

Below is a chronological listing of songs with verses and/or choruses that begin with the "C#-F#" chord sequence followed by a listing of chord progressions by type.

Chronological Listing

Date/Song Title   *Chord Progression*

1908

Shine On Harvest Moon   C=C#7-F#7-B7-E-F#m7-Go-E/G#

1913

Ballin' The Jack   V=C#7-F#7-B7-E-G#7-A7-G#7

1925

Sweet Georgia Brown   V=C#7-F#7-B7-B+-E-B+-E-G#7

1931

Lazy River   V=C#7-[C#9-C9-B9-C#7]-F#7-

[G7]-F#7-B7-[F#m7-B9-C9-B9]

1938

You Must Have Been
A Beautiful Baby   V=C#7-F#7-B7-E-[E7-D#7-D7-C#7]

1939

All The Things You Are   V=C#m7-F#m7-B7-EM7-AM7-
                               D#7-G#M7-G#m7-C#m7-F#7

1941

Besame Mucho   V=C#m-F#m-C#m-F#sus-F#m

1954

Fly Me To The Moon   V=C#m7-F#m7-B7-EM7-AM7-
                               D#m7b5-G#7b9-C#m7

1955

Sixteen Tons   V=C#m-F#m-A7-C#m-F#m-C#m

1958

All Your Love(I Miss Loving)(A)   V=C#m-F#m-C#m-G#m-F#m-C#m

1960

A Taste Of Honey   V=C#m-C#m(M7)-C#m7-F#6(2x)-
(Beatles Version)   A-G#m7-C#m-F#m6-C#m

1962

Quiet Nights Of Quiet Stars(C)   V=C#m6-F7#9/C-Bm7-E7b5/A#-AM7-
                                 A6-Am7-Am6-G#m7-C#7(#5/b9)F#9-F#m9-B7

1963

Pipeline(G)	V=C#m-F#m-G#7-A-G#7-A-G#7-F#m-G#7-C#m
Chim Chim Cheree	V=C#m-C#m(M7)-C#m7-F#-F#m-C#m-D#7-G#7
More	B=C#m-C#m(M7)-C#m7-C#m6-F#m7

1964

I'm Happy Just To Dance With You(E)	V=C#m-F#m-G#7(3x)-A6-B6-E6-B7
She's Not There(C)	V=C#m-F#-C#m7-F# C#m-A-C#m-F# C#m7-F#(2x)C#m-A-C#
The Warmth Of The Sun(C)	C=C#M7-C#m7-F#9-BM7-B-B+

1965

A Taste Of Honey(A) (Herb Alpert Version)	V=C#m-F#(2x)C#m-E-G#7-C#m-F#m-C#m C=C#m7-F#-C#m-F#-A-G#m-C#m-F#m-C#m
Love Potion Number Nine	V=C#m-F#7(2x)E-F#7-G#-C#m O=C#m-F#7-G#7
Heart Full Of Soul(F)	V=C#m-F#-A-E(4x) I=C#m(Riff)
Killing Floor(C)	V=C#m7-F#m7-C#m7-G#m7-F#m7-C#m-G#7#9
Wait(A)	V=C#m7-F#/C#-F#m/C#-C#m-G#7-C#m(2x)

This Diamond Ring(Eb)	V=C#m-C#m7-F#/C#-C#m

1966

Red Rubber Ball(A-Bb)	C=C#m-F#m-B-A-E
Secret Agent Man(G)	V=C#m-F#m-C#m-G#7-C#m-F#m(2x)C#m
Lies(D)	V=C#m-F#7(3x)C#m-G#-F#-G#
Harlem Nocturne(G)	V=C#m(M7)-C#m-F#m-F#m(M7)-G#7-C#m
Sunny Afternoon(F)	C=C#7-F#7-B7-E-G#7-C#m-F#-C#m-F#7-E-G#7-C#m-C#m/B-C#m/A#-C#m/A-G#-G#/F#-G#/E-G#/D#

1967

Somebody To Love	V=C#m-F#(2x)C#m
I Heard It Through The Grapevine(F) (CCR Version)	C=C#m-F#(2x)
I Had Too Much To Dream(F)	C=C#m-F#(3x)C#m-G#-C#-B-A-B
People Are Strange(G)	V=C#m-F#7-G#-C#m(2x)
Friday On My Mind	V=C#m-F#m-B(2x)E-G#-C#7-F#m-F#-Bm-A-C#-F#-D#m-G#m-C#7
I Say A Little Prayer For You	V=C#m7-F#m7-B-E-D#m7-G#7 (2x)A-B/A-G#m7
New York Mining Disaster(C)	V=C#m-F#7-B-C#m-F#7

Incense And Peppermint	V=C#m-F#-C#m-A(4x) C#m-Cm-B-F#(2x) O=C#m-Cm-B-C#

1968

Love Is Blue	V=C#m-F#7-B-E-C#m-A-B-E
Those Were The Days	V=C#m-C#m6-C#m7-C#m6-C#7- F#m-F#6-F#m-F#m6-C#m-C#m6-D# C=C#m-F#m-B7-E- F#m-C#m-G#7-C#m-C#7
Spooky	V=C#m7-F#9(5x)C#o
Stormy(G)	C=C#m9-F#13(2x)A6-G#m7 C#m9-F#13 O=C#m9-F#13
Rocky Raccoon(C)	V=C#m7-F#sus-F#-B7-E-E/D#
Mrs. Robinson(A)	V=C#7-F#7-B7-E-A-F#m-C#-B7

1969

You Showed Me(Eb)	V=C#m-F#(2x)C#m A-B-C#m(2x)-A-B-AM7
Cold Turkey	V=C#m7-F#7(x)E-F#
You Never Give Me Your Money(C)	V=C#m7-F#m7-B7-E-AM7- D#m7b5-G#7-C#m
Wooden Ships(G)	V=C#m7-F#m9-D/A(4x)
Undun(G)	V=C#m7-F#7-E-D#m7-G#-D#m7 F#m7-E T/A=A9-G#9

Coming Into Los Angeles(C)   V=C#m-C#m/B-F#7/A#-A-E-G#

Spinning Wheel(G)   V=C#7-F#7-B7-E(3x)B7-B7#9
V2=C#7#9-F#13-B7#9-E(2x)-
B7-B7#9
I=B7#9

1970

Venus(G)   V=C#m-F#(7x)C#m
F#m-B(2x)C#m-F#(2x)
A-D#m7/G#-G#7-

C#m-F#(2x)

Evil Ways(Bb)   V=C#m-F#(12x)G#7-
C#m-F#(4x)

Solitary Man(G)   V=C#m-F#m-E-C#m-E-F#m-E-
F#m(2x)

Gypsy Woman(B)   V=C#m-F#m-G#m-F#m-G#m-
G#m7-F#m-B7

Share The Land(D)   V=C#m-F#-A-B-E-G#(2x)

Green-Eyed Lady   V/C=C#m-C#m7-F#7-A6-C#m(2x)

No Matter What(A)   C=C#m7-F#7-B7-E7-
A7-F#m-E-C#m7-F#7-B7-E7-
A7-F#m-D-B

The Thrill Is Gone(D)   V=C#m-F#m-C#m-AM7-G#7-C#m

1971

Legend In Your Own Time   V=C#m7-F#m7(6x)G#7-C#6-
C#m7-D#m-G#7-D#7-G#7
C=C#m7-F#m7(3x)F#9-G#7-
C#m7-F#m7
T/A=G#-A#m7-B6-G#7

	I=G#7+
It's Too Late	V=C#m7-F#6(2x)C#m7-Bm7-AM7 I=C#m7-F#6(2x)
Oye Como Va(C)	V=C#m7-F#9(8x)
Gypsys, Tramps And Thieves	V=C#m-F#7sus-A-E-C#m7-F#-F#m-F#m7-E-A-E
Lonely Days	V=C#m-F#m-B-EM7-E7-A-F#m-B-Co
Don't Pull Your Love(G)	V=C#m7-F#7-B-G#m(2x)
Wild World	V=C#m-F#7-B-E-A-F#m-G#-G#7
Riders On The Storm(G)	V=C#m-F#m-C#m-B-A-C#m
Love Her Madly(C)	V=C#m-F#-C#m-E-A-F#-C#m-G#-C#m(2x)-F#-G#-C#m-G#-C#m
I Feel The Earth Move	V=C#m7-F#-C#m7/F#-F#-C#m7-F#/C#-B-EM7-E6-AM7-A6-F#m7-B11-EM7-E6-AM7-F#m7-B11-F#/G#

1972

Rocket Man	V=C#m7-F#9(2x)A-E/G#-F#m-F#m/E-B/D#
Saturday In The Park	V=C#m7-F#9-F#m7/B-E(2x) D#m7-G#m7-F#M9
From The Beginning(C)	V=C#m9-F#add4/C#-E-B/D# Aadd9-B-F#m7

Tight Rope	V=C#m7-F#m7-A-E-D#m7b5 I=G#7+
Claire	V=C#m-F#m7-B7-G#m7-C#m7-F#m7-B7(2x)

1973

Brother Louie	V=C#m-F#m(3x)G#m-F#m-C#m
Hummingbird(F)	V=C#m7-F#-C#m7-C#m9-F#-C#m7(F#m7-C#m7)4x
I'm Just A Singer	V=C#m-F#m-G#7
Time In A Bottle(F)	V=C#m-C#m(M7)/C-C#m/B-C#m/A#-F#m/A-G#7-C#m-C#m(M7)/C-F#m/A-C#m-F#m/A-G#7 C=C#-C#/C-C#/A#-C#/G#-F# F#/F-D#m7-G#7(2x)
Crocodile Rock(G)	C=C#m-F#-B-E- C#m-F#-B-A- E-C#m-A-B
Dancin' In The Moonlight	V=C#m7-F#m7-B7-E
Long Train Runnin'(Bb)	V=C#11-C#m7(4x)C#11- F#m7-F#m6- C#11-C#m7(2x)C#11- A7-C#m/G#-G#7- C#11-C#m7(2x)C#11
Jesus Is Just Alright(C)	V=C#m-F#-C#m-G#7#9-C#m-F#-C#m-E-C#m-G#7#9-A9-G#7#9
Night The Lights Went Out In Georgia	V=C#m-C#11-C#m-F#/C#-C#m-G#7-C#m(4x)

1974

Angie Baby   V=C#m7-F#m7-B7-EM7-AM7
                          G#7sus4-G#7-C#m7

1975

You're No Good   V-C#m-F#(4x)A-B-
                          E-C#m-F#-G#
                          C=C#-F#

Lady Marmalade   V=C#m-F#(2x)F#m7-G#m7-
                          C#m-F#(3x)F#m-C#m

Fame   V=C#7-F#7-C#7

Feelings   V=C#m-C#m(M7)-C#m7-C#m6-
                          F#m-B7-E-F#m7-G#7(2x)

1976

Dream On   V=C#m-C#m/B-C#m/A#-F#m6/A(4x)

New Kid In Town(E)   C=C#m-F#(3x)F#m7-B7

(Shake, Shake, Shake)
Shake Your Booty   V=C#m7-F#7(2x)A-B-C#m(2x)

Low Down(G)   V=C#m9-F#13

Isn't She Lovely   V=C#m7-F#9-B11-E(2x)-
                          AM7-G#7b9-G#7

This Masquerade   V=C#m-C#m(M7)-C#m7-F#13-
                          C#m-A7-G#7-G#7+
                          I=C#m7-F#13

1977

Fly Like An Eagle   V=C#m7-F#/C#-A/C#-C#m7

So Into You	V=C#m7-F#m7-C#m7-C#7sus
1978	
Grease	V=C#m-F#(2x)C#m-G#m7-F#m7-E-D
Night Fever(E)	C=C#m7-F#m7-EM7-F#m7(2x)
Miss You(C)	V=C#m-F#m(4x)A-G#m-F#m(2x)G#7
1979	
I Will Survive	V=C#m-F#m-B-EM7-AM7-D#m7b5-G#sus-G#
Double Trouble(F)	V-C#m-F#m-C#m-G#7-F#m-C#m
Take The Long Way Home	V=C#m7-C#11-F#/C#-C#-C#11-C#(2x)
1980	
Woman In Love	V=C#m-F#m(2x)AM7-B-E-Bm-A-C#m7-F#m7-G#7
Give Me The Night(G)	V=C#m7-F#m7-G#m7-AM7(4x)-F#m7-B11-C#m7-F#m7-G#m7-AM7(2x)
Lady	V=C#m-F#m/C#-C#11-C#m(4x)-F#m-G#m-C#
1982	
Abracadabra	V=C#m-F#m-G#7#9-C#m
1983	
Say, Say, Say	V=C#m-C#m7-F#-F#m7(2x)

1985

    Power Of Love(Eb)   V=C#m-F#(4x)B-F#-C#m7-F# C=C#-F#(3x)B-F#-G#

    Everything She Wants(Gb)   V=C#7sus-C#7-F#m-B9(6x)

    Money For Nothing   V=C#m-F#-C#m-E-F#-C#m-B-C#m

1986

    Holding Back The Years   V=C#m9-F#

    These Dreams(B)   V=C#5-F#m11-G#m C#7sus-F#m11-G#m-Asus9-C#11-A-E/G#-F#m7-C#5-E/G#

1987

    Smoking Gun(G)   V=C#m7(9)-F#sus2-C#m7(9)-F#m-C#m7(9)

1990

    More Than Words(G)   C=C#m-C#m/G#-F#m7-B-Bsus2-B-E7-E7/G#-A-Am-E

Listing By Progression Type

    Chord Progression   *Song Examples*

Minor Basic

    C#m-F#m   Brother Louie('73); Miss You('78); Woman In Love('80)
    C#m7-F#m7   Legend In Your Own Time('71)

    C#m-F#m-C#m-F#sus   Besame Mucho('41)
    C#m7-F#m7-C#m7-C#7sus   So Into You('77)

Minor Basic ("F#" Substitution)

C#m-F#	A Taste Of Honey('65); Somebody To Love('67); I Heard It Through The Grapevine('67); I Had Too Much To Dream('67); You Showed Me('69); Venus('70); Evil Ways('70); You're No Good('75); Lady Marmalade('75); New Kid In Town('76); Grease('78); Power Of Love('85)
C#m-F#7	Love Potion Number Nine('65); Lies('66)
C#m7-F#6	It's Too Late('71)
C#m7-F#7	Cold Turkey('69); Shake Your Booty('76)
C#m7-F#9	Spooky('68); Oye Como Va('71); Rocket Man('72)
C#m9-F#	Holding Back The Years('86)
C#m9-F#13	Stormy('68); Low Down('76)
C#m-F#-C#m7-F#	She's Not There('64)
C#m7-F#-C#m7-C#m9	Hummingbird('73)
C#m7-F#-C#m7/F#-F#	I Feel The Earth Move('71)

Standard ("C#m" First)

C#m-F#m-B-EM7	Lonely Days('71); I Will Survive('79)
C#m-F#m-B7-E	Those Were The Days('68)
C#m7-F#m7-B-E	I Say A Little Prayer For You('67)
C#m7-F#m7-B7-E	You Never Give Me Your Money('69); Golden Slumbers('69); Dancin' In The Moonlight('73)
C#m7-F#m7-B7-EM7	All The Things You Are('39); Fly Me To The Moon('54); Angie Baby('74)
C#m-F#-B-E	Crocodile Rock('73)
C#m-F#7-B-E	Love Is Blue('68); Wild World('71)
C#m7-F#7-B7-E7	No Matter What('70)
C#m7-F#9-B11-E	Isn't She Lovely('76)

Ragtime ("C#7" First)

C#7-F#7-B7-E	Shine On Harvest Moon('08); Balling The Jack('13); Sweet Georgia Brown('25); You Must Have Been A Beautiful Baby('38); Sunny Afternoon('66); Mrs. Robinson('68); Spinning Wheel('69);
C#7#9-F#13-B7#9-E	Spinning Wheel('69)–Verse 2

Minor Blues

C#m-F#m-C#m-G#m-F#m-C#m	All Your Love(I Miss Loving)('58)
C#m-F#m-C#m-G#7-F#m-C#m	Double Trouble('79)
C#m-F#m-C#m-AM7-G#7-C#m	The Thrill Is Gone('70)
C#m7-F#m7-C#m7-G#m7-F#m7-C#m7-G#7#9	Killing Floor('65)
C#m7(9)-F#sus2-C#m7(9)-F#m-C#m7(9)	Smoking Gun('87)

Descending Bass Lines

C#m-C#m/B-F#7/A#-A	Coming Into Los Angeles('69)
C#m-C#m/B-C#m/A#-F#m6/A	Dream On('76)

The following progression combines the use of the "C#m" Cliché with a Descending Bass Line.

C#m-C#m(M7)/C-C#m/B-C#m/A#	Time In A Bottle('73)
C#m6-F7#9/C-Bm7-E7b5/A#	Quiet Nights Of Quiet Stars('62)

Static Bass Lines

C#m-C#m7-F#/C#-C#m	This Diamond Ring('65)
C#m-C#11-C#m-F#/C#-C#m	Night The Lights Went Out In Georgia('73)
C#m7-C#11-F#/C#-C#-C#11	Take The Long Way Home('79)
C#m7-F#/C#-F#m/C#-C#m	Wait('65)
C#m7-F#/C#-A/C#-C#m7	Fly Like An Eagle('77)
C#m-F#m/C#-C#11-C#m	Lady('80)
C#11-C#m7-C#11	Long Train Runnin'('73)
C#m-C#m(M7)-C#m7	A Taste Of Honey('60); Chim Chim Cheree('63); This Masquerade('76)
C#m-C#m(M7)-C#m7-C#m6	More('63); Feelings('75)
C#m-C#m6-C#m7-C#m6	Those Were The Days('68)
C#m(M7)-C#m	Harlem Nocturne('66)

Other "C#-F#" Progressions

The "C#m-F#m-E-C#m" progression is an example of a Minor Basic & Partial Rock Ballad Combination Progression.

C#m-F#m-E-C#m	Solitary Man('70)
C#m7-F#m7-EM7-F#m7	Night Fever('78)
C#m7-F#7-E-D#m7	Undun('69)
C#m7-F#9-F#m7/B-E	Saturday In The Park('72)
C#m9-F#add4/C#-E-B/D#	From The Beginning('72)
C#m-F#m-G#m-F#m	Gypsy Woman('70)
C#m-F#m-G#7	I'm Just A Singer('73)
C#m-F#m-G#7-A	Pipeline('63)
C#m-F#m-G#7-A6	I'm Happy Just To Dance With You('64)
C#m-F#m-G#7#9-C#m	Abracadabra('82)
C#m-F#7-G#-C#m	People Are Strange('67)
C#m7-F#m7-G#m7-AM7	Give Me The Night('80)
C#5-F#m11-G#m-C#7sus	These Dreams('86)

The "C#m-F#m-A-E" progression is an example of a Minor Basic & Reverse Basic Combination Progression.

C#m-F#m-A7-C#m	Sixteen Tons('55)
C#m-F#-A-E	Heart Full Of Soul('65)
C#m-F#-A-B	Share The Land('70)
C#m-F#7sus-A-E	Gypsies, Tramps And Thieves('71)
C#m-C#m7-F#7-A6-C#m	Green-Eyed Lady('70)
C#m7-F#m7-A-E	Tight Rope('72)

The "C#m-F#m-B" progression is an example of a Partial Standard Progression.

C#m-F#m-B	Friday On My Mind('67)
C#m-F#m-B-A	Red Rubber Ball('66)
C#m-F#m7-B7-G#m7	Claire('72)
C#m-F#7-B-C#m	New York Mining Disaster('67)
C#m-C#m/G#-F#m7-B	More Than Words('90)
C#m7-F#7-B-G#m	Don't Pull Your Love('71)
C#m7-F#sus-F#-B7	Rocky Raccoon('68)
C#7sus-C#7-F#m-B9	Everything She Wants('85)

The "C#m-F#-C#m-A" progression is an example of a Partial Standard("F#" Substitution)& Basic("C#m" Substitution)Combination Progression. The "C#m-F#-C#m-E" progression is an example of a Partial Standard("F#" Substitution)& Reverse Partial Rock Ballad Combination Progression. The "C#m-F#m-C#m-G#7" progression follows the Circle of Fifths movement.

C#m-F#m-C#m-G#7	Secret Agent Man('66)
C#m-F#m-C#m-B	Riders On The Storm('71)
C#m-F#-C#m-E	Love Her Madly('71); Money For Nothing('85)
C#m-F#-C#m-G#7#9	Jesus Is Just Alright('73)
C#m-F#-C#m-A	Incense And Peppermint('67)
C#m7-F#m9-D/A	Wooden Ships('69)

"C#-G#" Chord Progressions

The most frequent "C#-G#" Chord Progressions are as follows:

Minor Folk	C#m-G#m
Minor Folk ("G#7" Substitution)	C#m-G#7
Descending "C#-B-A-G#" Bass Lines	C#m-G#m/B-AM7-G#m C#m-G#m/B-AM7-G#11

The "C#m-G#m" Minor Folk Progression is related to the "E-B7" Folk Progression where the "C#m" chord has been substituted for the "E" chord and the "G#m" chord has been substituted for the "B7" chord. The "C#m-G#m" progression was used to write Seals & Croft's 1973 *Diamond Girls* and more recently R.E.M's 1991 *Losing My Religion*. The "C#m7-G#m7-C#m7-F#m7-C#m7-G#m7-C#m7" progression for Santana's 1971 *Black Magic Woman* has a unique Minor Blues feel.

The "C#m-G#7" Minor Folk("G#7" Substitution)Progression is similar to the above Minor Folk Progression except that the "G#m" chord has been substituted by the harder sounding "G#7" chord. This progression has been used to create several hits over the years such as The Rolling Stones' 1966 *Paint It Black* and Carol King's 1971 *You've Got A Friend*.

The "C#-B-A-G#" Descending Bass Line was used to create Hall & Oats' 1976 *Sara Smile* and The Police's 1979 *Roxanne*. The "C#-B-A-G#" Descending Bass Line is the same bass line used to produce Money Chords discussed in the "C#-B" Chord Progression chapter of this book.

In addition to the most frequent progressions already discussed, there are a number of other "C#-G#" progressions that mainly follow the Circle of Fifths movement and others represent various Combination Progressions.

Below is a chronological listing of songs with verses and/or choruses that use the "C#-G#" sequence followed by a listing of chord progressions by type.

Chronological Listing

Date/Song Title *Chord Progression*

1857

We Three Kings Of Orient Are   V=C#m-G#7(2x)C#m

1927

Blue Skies   V=C#m-C+-G#7/C-E/B-A#m7b5-Am6/C-E/B-A9-B+-E

1932

Brother, Can You Spare A Dime(E)   V=C#m-G#7-C#7-F#-B7-E-G#7-F#m-G#7-C#m-A7-F#m-G#7-C#m

1935

Summertime   V=C#m6-G#7/D#(3x)

1958

Fever   V=C#m-G#7-C#m

1960

Take Five   V=C#m-G#m7(4x)

1963

Washington Square   V=C#m-G#-C#m-A-E-G#

1965

Girl(Eb)   V=C#m-G#7-C#m-C#m7-F#m-E-G#7-C#m-G#7-C#m-C#m7-F#m-

C#m

1966

Paint It Black(Ab)   V=C#m-G#7(2x)

1967

Let's Live For Today(E)   C=C#m-G#m(2x)A-B

I Heard It Through
The Grapevine(Gb)   V=C#m-G#-F#7(2x)A#m-F#7-
                                  C#m-F#7

Happy Together(A)   C=C#-G#m7-C#-E(2x)
                                  O=C#m-G#(8x)C#

1968

La La Means I Love You   C=C#m-G#m-F#m7-F#m7/B-
                                  EM7-G#m7-C#m-G#m-F#m7-
                                  F#m7/B-EM7

A Beautiful Morning(Eb)   B=C#m-C#m(M7)-C#m7-C#m6
                                  (2x)G#m7-C#m7-F#m7-F#m7/B

Happiness Is A Warm Gun(C)   V=C#m7-C#m6-G#m9-G#m(2x)-
                                  F#m6-C#m(4x)C#7-E-C#m(2x)-
                                  C#7-E-C#7-B7

Delilah   V=C#m-G#7(2x)C#-C#7-
                                  F#m-C#m-G#7-C#m-B7

Moon Dance(C)   V=C#m7-G#11(x)-
                                  C#m7-D#m7-G#m-
                                  C#m-F#m7-B7(3x)G7+

Just Dropped In   V=C#m7-G#7-C#m-F#m-C#m-
                                  G#7-C#m

The Look Of Love	V=C#m7sus-G#m7-A-A6-G#7sus-G#7-C#m7sus-C#7sus-C#7-A6-Am6-EM7-E7

1969

I Started A Joke(G)	C=C#m-G#m-A-E-G#m-C#m-C#m/B-F#m7-B7
Let The Sunshine In(D)	C=C#m-G#7-C#m-A-E

1970

Vehicle	V=C#m-G#7(2x)F#m7-G#-A G#sus-G#-F#m7-G#-A-G#7-C#m
A Song For You	V=C#m-G#7/C-E/B-A#m7b5-A G#m7-F#m7(2x)G#m7-A-E-G#7
The Long And Winding Road	V=C#m-G#m-B11-E-E/D-A E/G#-C#m-F#m7-B7-E7sus-E7
Share The Land(D)	C=C#-G#-F#-C#-G#-F#-C#

1971

You've Got A Friend(A)	V=C#m-G#7(2x)C#m7-F#m7-B7sus4-E-Esus-E
The Man Who Sold The World(F)	V=C#m-G#(2x)E-B-G#-C#m-B
Black Magic Woman(F)	V=C#m7-G#m7-C#m7-F#m7-C#m7-G#m7-C#m7
Ain't No Sunshine	V=C#m7-G#m7-G#m7/B-C#m7-(2x)G#m7-F#m7
Love Story	V=C#m-G#7-C#m-AM7-A6-G#7-G#11-G#7-G#7b9-C#m

If You Really Love Me	V=C#M7-G#7b9-C#M9-G#7b9-C#m7-C#m-C#m7-F#-Am-E-C#7-F#7-F#11-B7

1972

Superstition	V=C#m-G#-A7-G#-G7b5-F# G#7#5-C#m
Witchy Woman(Bb)	V=C#m6-G#9-[F#-E]-C#m7 C=C#m7-G#7-[F#-E]-C#m7(2x)
Layla(E)	V=C#m7-G#7-C#m7-C-D-E-E7-F#m-B-E-A(2x)

1973

Diamond Girl	V=C#m-G#m(2x)B-E/B-B-C#m-B-E/B-B-C#m7-F#m7-B-E-G#m7b5/D-C#7sus4-C#7-F#m7-B-G#7
Ain't No Woman	V=C#m7-G#m7(3x)C#m7-F#-EM7-D#m7-C#m7-G/B-F#/G#-E/G#
Angie(C)	V=C#m-G#7-Bsus-B-D-A-E-F#m-E-E/D#(2x)

1974

Don't You Worry 'Bout A Thing	V=C#m-G#+-C#m7-F#7-Bm7-E9-AM7-G#+/D-C#m-G#+-C#m7-F#7-Bm7-E9-AM7-G#+/D-E-E7-G#m-AM7-F#7-B11-EM7-G#+

1976

Sara Smile	V=C#m-G#m/B-AM7-G#11-G#-

(2x)A-B-Co-C#m-A-B-D7-
C#m-F#m7-
C=C#m-G#m-F#m7-B11-Co-
C#m-G#m-F#m7-B11

1977

Don't It Make My
Brown Eyes Blue(E)   B=C#m7-G#m-A-E(3x)F#m-
G#m-A-B7

Just A Song Before I Go   V=C#m7-G#m7-A-F#m7(2x)-
E-D-F#m7-G#m7-E-D-F#m7

Hotel California(D)   V=C#m-G#7-Badd9-F#9-A-E-
F#m7-G#7

1979

Roxanne   V=C#m-G#m/B-AM7-G#m-F#m-
Bsus-C#sus

1980

With You I'm Born Again   V=C#m-G#m-AM7-G#m-F#m7-
F#m/G#-G#7b9-C#sus2/4-C#

Fame   V=C#m-G#7-C#m-F#m7-B-F#-A

1981

In The Air Tonight   V=C#m-G#m/C#-A/C#-E/C#(2x)

Waiting For A Girl Like You   V=C#m-C#11(4x)G#m7-F#/G#-
(4x)

1982

You Can Do Magic   V=C#m-G#m7-A-B(7x)G#m7
C=C#m-G#m7-AM7-B(12x)

1984

That's All   V=C#m-G#m/C#(2x)C#m-A6/9-B6/9-C#m-(F#m7-B)3x C#m-E-F#m-B(2x)

1985

Don't Lose My Number   V=C#m-G#m7/C#-C#11-A/C#-(3x)C#m-G#m7/C#-F#m-A-B

1990

Black Velvet   V=C#m-G#7sus-G#7-F#7sus-F#7-E7sus-E7-Bsus

1991

Losing My Religion(C)   V=C#m-G#m(3x)[Gm]-F#m-B

Listing By Progression Type

Chord Progression   *Song Examples*

Minor Folk

C#m-G#m	Let's Live For Today('67); Diamond Girl('73); Losing My Religion('91)
C#m-G#m7	Take Five('60)
C#m7-G#m7	Ain't No Woman('73)
C#m7-C#m6-G#m9-G#m	Happiness Is A Warm Gun('68)
C#m7-G#m7-G#m7/B-C#m7	Ain't No Sunshine('71)

Minor Folk("G#7" Substitution)

C#m-G#	Happy Together('67); The Man Who Sold The World('71)
C#m-G#7	We Three Kings Of Orient Are(1857); Paint It Black('66); Delilah('68); Vehicle('70); You've Got A Friend('71)
C#m6-G#7/D#	Summertime('35)

C#m7-G#11	Moon Dance('68)
C#m-G#7-C#m	Fever('58)
C#m-G#7-C#m-C#m7	Girl('65)

Descending Bass Lines

C#m-G#m/B-AM7-G#m	Roxanne('79)
C#m-G#m/B-AM7-G#11	Sara Smile('76)
C#m-C+-G#7/C-E/B-A#m7b5	Blue Skies('27)
C#m-G#7/C-E/B-A#m7b5	A Song For You('70)

Static Bass Lines

C#m7sus-C#7sus-C#7	The Look Of Love('68)
C#m-C#11	Waiting For A Girl Like You('81)
C#m-C#m(M7)-C#m7-C#m6	A Beautiful Morning('68)
C#m-G#m/C#	That's All('84)
C#m-G#m/C#-A/C#-E/C#	In The Air Tonight('81)
C#m-G#m7/C#-C#11-A/C#	Don't Lose My Number('85)

Other "C#-G#" Progressions

The "C#m-G#m-F#m7-B7" progression is an example of a Minor Folk & Partial Standard Combination Progression.

C#m-G#m-F#m7-F#m7/B	La La Means I Love You('68)
C#m-G#m-F#m7-B11	Sara Smile('76)
C#m-G#-F#7	I Heard It Through The Grapevine('67)
C#m-G#7sus-G#7-F#7sus	Black Velvet('90)
C#m7-G#7-F#-E	Witchy Woman('72)-Chorus
C#m6-G#9-F#-E	Witchy Woman('72)–Verse
C#-G#-F#-C#	Share The Land('70)

The following progression is an example of a Minor Folk & Reverse Basic Combination Progression.

C#m-G#m-A-E	I Started A Joke('69)

C#m-G#m-AM7-G#m	With You I'm Born Again('80)
C#m-G#m7-A-B	You Can Do Magic('82)–Verse
C#m-G#m7-AM7-B	You Can Do Magic('82)-Chorus
C#m-G#-A7-G#	Superstition('72)
C#m7-G#m-A-E	Don't It Make My Brown Eyes Blue('77)
C#m7-G#m7-A-F#m7	Just A Song Before I Go('77)

The following progression is an example of a Minor Folk & Reverse Folk Combination Progression.

C#m-G#m-B11-E	The Long And Winding Road('70)
C#m-G#7-Bsus-B	Angie('73)
C#m-G#7-Badd9-F#9	Hotel California('77)

The "C#m-G#7-C#m-A" progression is an example of a Minor Folk("G#7" Substitution)& Basic("C#m" Substitution)Combination Progression. The "C#m-G#7-C#m-F#m" progression is an example of a Minor Folk("G#7" Substitution)& Minor Basic Combination Progression.

C#m-G#-C#m-A	Washington Square('63)
C#m-G#+-C#m7-F#7	Don't You Worry 'Bout A Thing('74)
C#m-G#7-C#m-A	Let The Sunshine In('69)
C#m-G#7-C#m-AM7	Love Story('71)
C#m-G#7-C#m-F#m7	Fame('80)
C#m-G#7-C#7-F#	Brother Can You Spare A Dime('32)
C#m7-G#m7-C#m7-F#m7	Black Magic Woman('71)
C#m7-G#7-C#m-F#m	Just Dropped In('68)
C#m7-G#7-C#m7-	Layla('72)
C#-G#m7-C#-E	Happy Together('67)
C#M7-G#7b9-C#M9-G#7b9	If You Really Love Me('71)

"C#-A" Chord Progressions

The most frequent "C#-A" Chord Progressions are as follows:

Basic("C#m" Substitution)	C#m-A
Rock("C#m" Substitution)	C#m-A-B
Descending "C#-B-A-G#" Bass Lines	C#m-C#m/B-A7-G#7
Descending "C#-B-A#-A" Bass Lines	C#m-C#m/B-C#m/A#-AM7
Static Bass Lines	C#m-A/C# C#m-C#m(M7)-C#m7-C#m6

The "C#m-A" Basic("C#m" Substitution) Progression is similar to the "E-A" Basic Progression except the "C#m" chord has been substituted for the "E" chord. The "C#m-A" progression has been used to create such hits as The Beatles' 1966 *Eleanor Rigby*, The Doobie Brothers' 1972 *Listen To The Music*, and Fleetwood Mac's 1978 *Rhiannon*.

The "C#m-A-B" Rock("C#m" Substitution) Progression is similar to the popular "E-A-B" Rock Progression except the "C#m" chord has been substituted for the "E" chord. Although not as widely used as the Rock Progression, the "C#m-A-B" progression was used to create Alice Cooper's 1971 *Eighteen* and Heart's 1976 *Crazy On You*.

The "C#-B-A-G#" Descending Bass Line was used to write such diverse songs as Duke Ellington's 1932 *It Don't Mean A Thing* and the Lovin' Spoonful's 1966 *Summer In The City*. The "C#-B-A-G#" Descending Bass Line is the same bass line used to produce the Money Chords discussed in the "C#-B" Chord Progression chapter of this book.

Another Descending Bass Line("C#-B-A#-A") was used in Elton John's 1970 *Your Song* and George Harrison's 1968 *While My Guitar Gently Weeps* both of which also combine the use of the "C#m"

Cliché. The "bluesy" 1953 *Cry Me A River* and Phil Collins' 1981 *In The Air* both utilize particularly effective Static Bass Lines built around the "C#m" and "A/C#" chords.

The 1937 Richard Rodgers and Lorenz Hart standard *My Funny Valentine* and Johnny Rivers' 1967 hit *Summer Rain* were both created around the "C#m-C#m(M7)-C#m7-C#m6" Minor Cliché Progression which is produced by using same Chord Quality Substitutions. The Minor Cliché is sometimes combined with a Descending "C#-C-B-A#" Bass Line creating the "C#m-C#m(M7)/C#-C#m7/B-C#m6/A#" progression.

In addition to the most frequent progressions already discussed, there are a number of other "C#-G#" Progressions which mainly represent various Combination Progressions.

Below is a chronological listing of songs with verses and/or choruses that begin with the "C#m-A" chord sequence followed by a listing of chord progressions by type.

Chronological Listing

Date/Song Title   *Chord Progression*

1932

It Don't Mean A Thing   V=C#m-C#m/B-A7-G#7-C#m
F#7/C#-C7#5-F#m7/B-E6-G#7#5

1937

My Funny Valentine   C=C#m-C#m(M7)-C#m7-C#m6-
A-F#m7-D#m7b5-G#7

1941

God Bless The Child(G)   B=C#m-C#m/C-C#m/B-A7-
G#m-G#m/F#-EM7-E/D#-
C#m-C#m/C-C#m/B-A7-
G#m7b5-C#7-F#m7b5-B7sus-B7

1947

Steppin' Out With My Baby   C=C#m-C#m/B-A6-G#7(2x)

1953

Cry Me A River   V=C#m-A/C#-C#m6-C#+7-
                        F#m7-B13sus-B+7-EM7

1958

Fever   C=C#m-A6-C#m-G#7-C#m

1959

My Favorite Things   V=C#m-AM7-F#m7-B9-
                        EM7-AM7(2x)D#m7b5-G#7

1964

I Should Have Known Better(G)   B=C#m-A-E-G#7-
                                C#m-E-E7-A-B7-E-C#m-A-B7-
                                E-B(2x)

Remember
(Walkin' In The Sand)(F)   V=C#m-A-F#m-G#7(2x)

1965

Drive My Car(D)   C=C#m-A7(2x)C#m-F#7-B7-
                        E-A-B

Just A Little(C)   V=C#m-A-F#-B(2x)E-B-A-B
                        E-B-A-G#-C#m

We Can Work It Out(D)   B=C#m-A-G#-
                        C#m-C#m/B-C#m/A-C#m/G#-
                        (2x)E7

Eight Days A Week(D)   C=C#m-A6-C#m-F#-E-F#-A-E

Ticket To Ride(A)   C=C#m-A7-C#m-DM7-C#m-B-E

1966

My World Is Empty Without You   V=C#m-A(2x)[G#m]-E-B-F#m-C#m-[F#m7-G#m7]

Eleanor Rigby(G)   V=C#m-A(2x)C#m
C=C#m7-C#m6-A/C#-C#m(2x)

Reason To Believe(G)   C=C#m-A-B-A-B-C#m-B-A-B-C#m-B

Help Me Girl(Eb)   V=C#m-C#m/B-AM7-G#7(2x)-C#-F#/C#(4x)

Summer In The City   V=C#m-C#m/B-AM7-C#m/G#-(2x)G#-G#7-C#m-C#-F#-B(4x)D#m-G#(4x)

Flowers On The Wall   C=C#-A-B-A-B

You Don't Have To Say You Love Me   C=C#-A#m-D#m7-G#7(2x)-C#-Fm-A#m-D#m7-G#

1967

San Francisco   V=C#m-A-E-B(2x)C#m-E-A-E-C#m-G#m-C#m7-B

The Letter   V=C#m-A-C#m7-F#7-C#m-A7-G#7-C#m(2x)

Standing In The Shadows Of Love(Db)   C=C#m-C#m/B-AM7-G#-G#7-(2x)

Ruby Tuesday(Db)   V=C#m-C#m/B-A-B-(Esus-E)2x-C#m-B6-A-E-B7-C#m-F#7-B(2x)E-B

Holiday(C)   C=C#m-[C#m/B]-A-C#m(2x)B

Ain't No Mountain High Enough(D)	V=C#m/B-A#m7b5-AM7-F#m7-(2x)G#m7
Your Mother Should Know(C)	V=C#m-AM7-C#7/G#-F#m-B7-E-E/D#-C#7-F#7-B7-E-G#7

1968

Summer Rain	V=C#m-C#m(M7)-C#m7-C#m6-(3x)A-E(2x)
Cry Baby Cry(G)	V=C#m-C#m(M7)-C#m7-C#m6-A7-E(2x)
While My Guitar Gently Weeps(C)	V=C#m-C#m/B-C#m/A#-AM7-C#m-B-F#-G#

1969

Time Of The Season	V=C#m-[C#m/B]-A(2x)C#m-E-C#m(2x)A-E/G#-F#m7-C#
Cowgirl In The Sand	V=C#m-A(2x)E-B-AM7-B(2x)
What Are You Doing The Rest Of Your Life	V=C#m-C#m(M7)-C#m7-C#m6-AM7-F#m7-G#m-D#m7

1970

Make Me Smile	V=C#m-A-E-D#m7-G#(2x)-C#m-B7-E-A-D#m7-G#
Southern Man(F)	V=C#m-A-F#m(3x)G# C=C#m-C#m/F#-EM7/B-A-F#-(2x)
Your Song	B=C#m-C#m/B-C#m/A#-A6-E/G#-A6-A-B-Bsus-B

1971

That's The Way
I've Always Heard It Should Be   V=C#m/E-AM7(2x)Em9-DM7-Bm7-A#M7-A

Eighteen(G)   V=C#m-A-B(2x)A-B-C#m-A-B

1972

Listen To The Music(E)   C=C#m-A(3x)F#7-A-Aadd9(4x)

Brandy   C=C#m7-AM7(2x)E-B7-A-E-A-B11

Take It Easy(G)   C=C#m-A-E-F#m-A-C#m-A-E(2x)F#m-A-E

Heart Of Gold(G)   V=C#m-A-B-E(3x)-(C#m-E-A [G#m-F#m-E])2x I=C#m7-B-C#m

School's Out(G)   V=C#m-A-B-C

You're So Vain   V=C#m-A-C#m(2x)A-B-G#m-C#m-A-E-B-A

Back Stabbers(Eb)   C=C#m-C#m/B-A-G#m7-F#m7-G#+(2x)

(If Loving You Is Wrong)
I Don't Want To Be Right(G)   V=C#m-C#m/B-[AM7-F#m7-G#m7-AM7-G#m7](2x)-F#m-C#m(2x)

1973

Wishing Well(G)   V=C#m-A-B(6x)

Wild Flower(F)   V=C#m-C#m/B-A#m7b5-AM7-

	F#m7/B-B7-EM7-G#7+5
Hello-Hurray	V=C#m-C#11-A/C#-C#11

1974

W.O.L.D	V=C#m-A-B-E- C#m-A-B-F#m-E- A-B-C#m-DM7-A-B-F#m7
The Lord's Prayer	C=C#m-A-B-E-G#m-C#m-F#m- C#m-G#7-C#m
Pretzel Logic(C)	V=C#m7-AM7-C#m7-F#m7-C#m7
Doctor Wu(G)	V=C#m-C#11-A-C#11-A-C#m7- F#m7-G#m7-F#m7

1976

Show Me The Way(D)	C=C#m-A(2x)B11
Rhiannon(C)	V=C#m-A(2x)E-A(2x)C#m C=C#m-A-C#m(4x) O=C#m9-C#m-A
Crazy On You	C=C#m-A-B(2x)C#m-B-A P/C=F#m-G#m-E-A-F#m-G#7

1977

Peace Of Mind(E)	C=C#5/G#-A-E5-B5(2x)A5
Cold As Ice	V=C#m(sus4)-C#m(2x)A6-A (2x) F#m-E-D#+-F#m/C#-A-B11
The Things You Do For Love(D)	V=C#m-A-E-E/D#-F#-[G#]-A- G#sus-G#-A-B-E-A-E
Go Your Own Way(F)	C=C#m-A-B(3x)

1978

Because The Night(D)   V=C#m-A-B-C#m(4x)

1979

This Is It   V=C#m7-A-F#m7-G#m7-AM7-A#o

The Logical Song   V=C#m-A-G#-B-A-A#o(2x)

Head Games   V=C#m-A/C#-C#11(4x)

1980

Call Me   V=C#m-A7(2x) F#-G#(2x)

Love On The Rocks   V=C#m-A-B-G#m7-A-D#7-G#

I Can't Tell You Why   C=C#m-C#11-AM7-G#7sus4-G#7-AM7-G#m7

1981

In The Air Tonight   C=C#m-C#11-A/C#-C#11(3x)-C#m

1982

Eye Of The Tiger   V=C#m-A/C#-C#11-C#m

1983

Sweet Dreams(E)   V=C#m-A-G#sus(8x)

1984

Boys Of Summer   V=C#m-A-B-A

I'm So Excited   C=C#m-A-B-C#m(2x)

What's Love Got To Do With It	V=C#m7-C#11(2x)AM7-B(3x)

1986

You Give Love A Bad Name	C=C#m-A-B(2x)E5

1993

Mr. Jones(C)	V=C#m-A-F#m-B-C#m-A-B(2x)

1999

Smooth(C)	V=C#m-A-G#7

Listing By Progression Type

Chord Progression   *Song Examples*

Basic("C#m" Substitution)

C#m-A	Eleanor Rigby('66); My World Is Empty Without You('66); Cowgirl In The Sand('69); Listen To The Music('72); Show Me The Way('76); Rhiannon('76)
C#m-[C#m/B-]-A	Time Of The Season('69)
C#m-A7	Drive My Car('65); Call Me('80)
C#m/E-AM7	That's The Way I've Always Heard It Should Be('71)
C#m7-AM7	Brandy('72)
C#m-A-C#m	You're So Vain('72)

Rock("C#m" Substitution)

C#m-A-B	Eighteen('71); Wishing Well('73); Crazy On You('76); Go Your Own Way('77); You Give Love A Bad Name('86)
C#m-A-B-C#m	Because The Night('78); I'm So Excited('84)

Descending Bass Lines

The AM7 chord has the same notes as the C#m/A chord.

C#m-C#m/B-A-G#m7	Back Stabbers('72)
C#m-C#m/B-A6-G#7	Steppin' Out With My Baby('47)
C#m-C#m/B-A7-G#7	It Don't Mean A Thing('32)
C#m-C#m/B-AM7-G#-G#7	Standing In The Shadows Of Love('67)
C#m-C#m/B-AM7-G#7	Help Me Girl('66)
C#m-C#m/B-AM7-C#m/G#	Summer In The City('66)

The A#m7b5 chord has the same notes as the C#m6 chords.

C#m-C#m/B-A#m7b5-AM7	Wild Flower('73)
C#m-C#m/B-C#m/A#-A6	Your Song('70)
C#m-C#m/B-C#m/A#-AM7	While My Guitar Gently Weeps('68)

The above two progressions use the "C#m" Cliché with a Descending Bass Line.

The C#m/C chord has the same notes as the C#m(M7) chord.

E-D#+-F#m/C#-A	Cold As Ice('77)
G#m-G#m/F#-EM7-E/D#	God Bless The Child('41)
C#m-C#m/B-AM7-F#m7	(If Loving You Is Wrong)I Don't Want To Be Right('72)
C#m-C#m/C-C#m/B-A7	God Bless The Child('41)
C#m/B-A#m7b5-AM7-F#m7	Ain't No Mountain High Enough('67)

Static Bass Lines

C#m(sus4)-C#m	Cold As Ice('77)
C#m-C#11	Doctor Wu('74); I Can't Tell You Why('80)
C#m7-C#11(2x)	What's Love Got To Do With It('84)
C#m-C#m(M7)-C#m7-C#m6	My Funny Valentine('37); Summer Rain('68); Cry Baby Cry('68); What Are You Doing The Rest Of Your Life('69)
C#m-C#11-A/C#-C#11	In The Air('81)
C#-C#11-A/C#-C#11	Hello-Hurray('73)
C#m-A/C#-C#11	Head Games('79)
C#m-A/C#-C#11-C#m	Eye Of The Tiger('82)

C#m-A/C#-C#m6-C#+	Cry Me A River('53)
C#m7-C#m6-A/C#-C#m	Eleanor Rigby('66)

Other "C#m-A" Progressions

The "C#m-A-E-F#m" progression is an example of a Basic("C#m" Substitution)& Basic("F#m" Substitution)Combination progression. The "C#m-A-E-B" progression is an example of a Basic("C#m" Substitution)& Folk Combination Progression.

C#m-A-E-E/D#	The Things You Do For Love('77)
C#m-A-E-F#m	Take It Easy('72)
C#m-A-E-G#7	I Should Have Known Better('64)
C#m-A-E-B	San Francisco('67)
C#m-A-E-D#m7	Make Me Smile('70)
C#5/G#-A-E5-B5	Peace Of Mind('77)

The "C#m-A-F#m-B" progression is an example of a Basic("C#m" Substitution)& Partial Standard("F#m" First)Combination Progression.

C#m-A-F#m	Southern Man('70)
C#m-A-F#m-G#7	Remember(Walkin' In The Sand)('64)
C#m-A-F#m-B	Mr. Jones('93)
C#m-A-F#-B	Just A Little('65)
C#m-AM7-F#m7-B9	My Favorite Things('59)
C#m7-A-F#m7-G#m7	This Is It('79)

The "C#m-A-G#7" progression is an example of a Partial Money Chords Progression.

C#m-A-G#-B	The Logical Song('79)
C#m-A-G#-C#m	We Can Work It Out('65)
C#m-A-G#7	Smooth('99)
C#m-A-G#sus	Sweet Dreams('83)
C#m-A-B-E	Heart Of Gold('72); The Lord's Prayer('74); W.O.L.D.('74)
C#m-A-B-G#m7	Love On The Rocks('80)
C#m-A-B-A	Boys Of Summer('84)
C#m-A-B-A-B	Flowers On The Wall('66); Reason To Believe('66)
C#m-A-B-C	School's Out('72)
C#m-C#m/B-A-B	Ruby Tuesday('67)

The "C#m-A-C#m7-F#7" progression is an example of a Basic("C#m" Substitution)& Minor Basic("F#7" Substitution)Combination Progression. The "C#m-A6-C#m-G#7" progression is an example of a Basic("C#m" Substitution)& Minor Folk("G#7" Substitution)Combination Progression.

C#m-A-C#m7-F#7	The Letter('67)
C#m-A6-C#m-F#	Eight Days A Week('65)
C#m-A6-C#m-G#7	Fever('58)
C#m-AM7-C#7/G#-F#m	Your Mother Should Know('67)
C#m-A7-C#m-DM7	Ticket To Ride('65)
C#m7-AM7-C#m7-F#m7	Pretzel Logic('74)
C#-A#m-D#m7-G#7	You Don't Have To Say You Love Me('66)

"C#-B" Chord Progressions

The most frequent "C#-B" Chord Progressions are as follows:

Money Chords	C#m-B-A-G#
Partial Money Chords	C#m-B-A
	C#m-B

The "C#m-B-A-G#" Money Chords Progression, which is based on a great Descending Bass Line, was so named because these sequence of chords were used to produce so many huge hit songs during the 1960s. The Venture's 1960 *Walk Don't Run*, Del Shannon's 1961 *Runaway*, Ray Charles' 1961 *Hit The Road Jack*, The Beach Boy's 1966 *Good Vibrations*, The Turtles' 1967 *Happy Together*, Zager & Evans' 1969 *In The Year 2525*, and Dire Straits' 1979 *Sultans Of Swing* among others are examples of songs written primarily around these Money Chords.

The "C#m-B-A" Partial Money Chords Progression, which is comprised of the first three Money Chords, has also been used to create many hit songs. Examples of the "C#m-B-A" progression include The Rolling Stones' 1966 *Under My Thumb* and Elvis Presley's 1972 *Burning Love*. A common variation of these Partial Money Chords is the C#m-B-A-B progression which is best exemplified in The Mamas And Papas' 1966 *California Dreaming*.

The "C#m-B" Partial Money Chords Progression, which is comprised of the first two Money Chords, has also been used numerous times to create memorable Rock songs. Examples of the "C#m-B" progression include such hits as Deep Purple's 1973 *Smoke On The Water*, Vicki Sue Robinson's 1976 *Turn The Beat Around*, Michael Jackson's 1983 *Beat It*, and The Miami Sound Machine's 1984 *Conga*.

In addition to the most frequent progressions already discussed, there are a number of other "C#m-B" Progressions that mainly continue to move to the "E", "F#", and "C#m" chords. Also, several other progressions represent various Combination Progressions.

Below is a chronological listing of songs with verses and/or choruses that begin with the "C#-B" chord sequence followed by a listing of chord progressions by type.

Chronological Listing

Date/Song Title   *Chord Progression*

1580

Greensleeves/What Child Is This?   V=C#m-B-C#m-G#7(2x)C#m

1740

Drunken Sailor   V/C=C#m-B-C#m-G#m-C#m

1959

Three Cool Cats   B=C#m-B-A-G#7(2x)

1960

Walk Don't Run(C)   V=C#m-B-A-G#-
                               C#m-A-B-E-B-E-G#

1961

Hit The Road Jack   V=C#m-B-A-G#

Runaway(C)   V=C#m-B-A-G#7(2x)

1964

Under The Boardwalk(G)   C=C#m-B(2x)C#m

Ballad Of Gilligan's Isle   V=C#m-B(3x)A-B-C#m

Yesterday's Gone   B=C#m-B-G#7-C#m-B-G#m-F#m-B7

I'll Be Back(C)   V=C#m-B6-AM7-G#-C#(2x)

Time Is On My Side(F)   V=C#m-B-C#m-F#-
                               B-A(3x)B

And I Love Her(E)	B=C#m-B-C#m-G#m(2x)B

1965

Don't Let Me Be Misunderstood(D)	V=C#m-B-A-G#(2x) I=C#m-F#m(2x)
Stop! In The Name Of Love(C)	V=C#m-B-A-B(2x)E-A(2x)-E-F#m-E
The Sounds Of Silence	V=C#m-B-C#m-E-A(3x)E-C#m-E-B-C#m

1966

Happenings Ten Years Time Ago	V=C#m-B
Bus Stop	I=C#m-B/D#(2x)
Paint It Black(Ab)	C=C#m-B-E-B(2x)F#-G#7
Sunny Afternoon(F)	V=C#m-B-E-B-G#-G#7/F#-G#/E-G#/D#(2x)
You Keep Me Hangin' On	V=C#m-B-G#m-A
Under My Thumb	V=C#m-B-A(2x)E-A-F#-C#m-B-A-E
A Hazy Shade Of Pale	V=C#m-B-A-G#m-B-C#m-B-A-G#7-C#m
Good Vibrations(F#)	V=C#m-B-A-G#(2x)B7
California Dreaming(E)	V=C#m-B-A-B-G#7sus4-G#7-A-E-G#7-C#m-A-G#7sus4-G#7
Break On Through(G)	V=C#m-B-C#m

1967

I Had Too Much To Dream(F)	V=C#m-B(2x)F#m-C#m(2x)F#-C#m-Cm-F#-E-D
When I Was Young(G)	V=C#m-B(4x)C#m
Happy Together(A)	V=C#m-B-A-G#(2x)
Ruby Tuesday(Db)	V=C#m-B-A-B7-E
We Ain't Got Nothin' Yet	V=C#m-B-C#m-F#(6x)C#m-B-A#m-G#-A#m-D#7-C#m

1968

White Room(F)	V=C#m-B5-F#/A#-A-B
Tales Of Brave Ulysses(F)	V=C#m-B-F#/A#-A
Long Time Gone(C)	C=C#m-B6-AM7(2x)C#m-B6-F#
All Along The Watch Tower(C)	V=C#m-B-A-B

1969

Wait A Million Years	V=C#m-B-A-G#
In The Year 2525	V=C#m-B-A-G#7
Come Together(D)	C=C#m-B-A-B
Hawaii Five-O(Eb-E)	V=C#m-B-C#m-E-C#m-B-E-G#7-C#m-F#-A-B-C#m-B-C#m-A7

1970

Lay Down(Candles In The Rain)	V=C#m-B(4x)C#m

I(Who Have Nothing)	V=C#m-B(2x)E-G#7-C#m-B-A-G#7
Paranoid(G)	V=C#m-B-E-B-C#m(2x)
The Long And Winding Road(Eb)	V=C#m-B11-E-E7/G#-A-G#m-C#m-F#m-B7-E11-A-G#m-C#m-F#m-B7-E
Love The One You're With(C)	C=C#m-B-A(3x)

1971

Mr. Bojangles	C=C#m-B(3x)
She's A Lady	V=C#m-B(2x) C=C#m-C#m/F#-B-C#m-C#m/F#-G#m
Working Class Hero(C)	V=C#m-B(3x)C#m C=C#m-B(2x)F#/C#-C#m
Duncan	V=C#m-B-E-F#-B-A-E(3x)B-C#m
Timothy	V=C#m-B/D#-F#7-AM7-BM7-F#m7-B-F#
Lonely Nights	C=C#-B-F#-B-C# C#-B-C#-B-F#

1972

Mother And Child Reunion	V=C#m-B(2x)C#m-A-B
Nights In White Satin(G)	V=[C#m-B(2x)A-E-D-C#m] 2x-F#-A(C#m-B)2x
Burning Love	C=C#m-B-A(3x)B-E

Layla(E)   C=C#m-B-A-B

1973

Smoke On The Water   V=C#m-B(4x)C#m
                            I=C#m-E-F#-C#m-E-G-F#-C#m-
                            E-F#-E-C#m

Turn The Page   V=C#m-B-F#(2x)C#m

No More Mr. Nice Guy(A)   C=C#m-B-A(2x)C#m-E

1974

Let It Ride(A)   V=C#m-B

Radar Love(A)   V=C#m-B-F#-C#-B-F#-G#

1975

Miracles   V=C#m-B-A-C#m-B-Aadd9-
                            F#m(addB)-E-B/D#-C#m

One Of These Nights(G)   V=C#m-B6-AM7-F#m-C#m-G#m-(2x)

1976

Turn The Beat Around   V=C#m-B
                            C=C#m-B-A-B-C#m

Dream Weaver   V=C#m-B-A(2x)E-B-A(2x)

Dream On(A)   C=C#m-B-A-B(2x)

Don't Fear The Reaper(C)   V=C#m-B-A6sus2-B(4x)

Kid Charlemagne(C)   V=C#m-B6-A6/9-D13(2x)-
                            A-B-C#m7-B6

1977

You Make Loving Fun(Bb)   V=C#m-B-A(2x)

Carry On Wayward Son   V=C#m-B6-AM7-B6(2x)
C=C#m-E-B-Aadd9-
C#m-E-B(2x)Aadd9-A

50 Ways To Leave Your Lover   V=C#m/E-B6-AM7-G#7b9-G#7-
C#m-Co-EM9#5-
C#m-B6-AM7-G#7b5-G#7-
C#m-F#m7-C#m

Stayin' Alive(Ab)   V=C#m7-B-C#m(2x)F#7-C#m-
B-C#m-G#m7-C#m7

1978

Da Ya Think I'm Sexy(F)   V=C#m-B(4x)

Josie(G)   V=C#m7-BM7-E/A-B/E-A/D-
C#m7-F#7-E/A-B/E-A/D-
C#m7-B/E-C#/F#-C#m7-A/D

Right Down The Line   V=C#m-B-G#m-E(3x)-
B-F#-G#m-F#-E

Macho Man   V=C#m-C7-B7

1979

Sultans Of Swing(F)   V=C#m-B-A-G#7(2x)E-B-A-
C#m-A-B

1980

Ride Like The Wind   V=C#m7-B(4x)AM7-G#m7(2x)

1982

Maneater(D)   C=C#m-B-A-G#-C#m-B-F#m7-A-B

Down Under   V=C#m-B-C#m-A-B(4x)

1983

Beat It   V=C#m-B(2x)A-B-C#m-B
C=C#m-B(6x)

1984

What's Love Got To Do With It   C=C#m-B-A-B

Girls Just Want To Have Fun   C=C#m-B-A-C#m-B-E

Caribbean Queen   V=C#m-B
C=C#m-B-AM7-C#m/G#-F#m7-A-B-C#-B

Hello   V=C#m-B6-AM7-B6-AM7(3x)

1985

I Want To Know What Love Is(G)   V=C#m-B-E-A-C#m(2x)

1986

Conga   V=C#m-B

Danger Zone   V=C#m-B(2x)A

1987

Shake Your Love   V=C#m-B

1989

I Won't Back Down   C=C#m-B-E(2x)C#m-B-A-C#m-B-E

Another Day In Paradise   V=C#m7-B-F#m7-C#m7-B-C#m7
                           C=C#m-B11-A/C#-B11

1997

My Heart Will Go On   C=C#m-B-A-B(4x)E

1999

Livin' La Vida Loca   C=C#m-B-C#m

Listing By Progresson Type

Chord Progression   *Song Example*

Money Chords

The "C#m-B-A-G#" Money Chords Progressions have Descending Bass Lines.

C#m-B-A-G#   Walk Don't Run('60); Hit The Road Jack('61); Don't Let Me Be Misunderstood('65); Good Vibrations('66); Happy Together('67); Wait A Million Years('69); Man Eater('82)

C#m-B-A-G#7   Three Cool Cats('59); Runaway('64); In The Year 2525('69); Sultans Of Swing('79)

C#m-B-A-G#m   A Hazy Shade Of Winter('66)

C#m-B6-AM7-G#   I'll Be Back('64)

C#m/E-B6-AM7-G#7b9   50 Ways To Leave Your Lover('77)

Partial Money Chords

C#m-B-A   Under My Thumb('66); Love The One You're With('70); Burning Love('72); No More Mr. Nice Guy('73); Dream Weaver('76); You Make Loving Fun('77); Girls Just Want To Have Fun('84)

C#m-B6-AM7   Long Time Gone('68)

C#m-B-A-B   Stop! In The Name Of Love('65); California Dreaming('66); All Along The Watch Tower('68); Come Together('69); Layla('72); Turn The Beat Around('76); Dream On('76);

	What's Love Got To Do With It('84); My Heart Will Go On('97)
C#m-B-A-B7	Ruby Tuesday('67)
C#m-B-A6sus2-B	Don't Fear The Reaper('76)
C#m-B6-AM7-B6	Hello('84); Carry On Wayward Son('77)
C#m-B11-A/C#-B11	Another Day In Paradise('89)
C#m-B-A-C#m	Miracles('75)
C#m-B6-A6/9-D13	Kid Charlemagne('76)
C#m-B	Under The Boardwalk('64); Ballad Of Gilligan's Isle('64); Happenings Ten Years Time Ago('66); I Had Too Much To Dream('67); When I Was Young('67); Lay Down(Candles In The Rain)('70); I(Who Have Nothing)('70); Mr. Bojangles('71); She's A Lady('71); Working Class Hero('71); Nights In White Satin('72); Mother And Child Reunion('72); Smoke On The Water('73); Let It Ride('74); Da Ya Think I'm Sexy('78); Beat It('83); Caribbean Queen('84); Conga('86); Danger Zone('86); Shake Your Love('87)
C#m7-B	Ride Like The Wind('80)
C#m-B-C#m	Break On Through('66); Livin' La Vida Loca('99)
C#m7-B-C#m	Stayin' Alive('77)

Descending Bass Lines

C#m7-BM7-E/A-B/E	Josie('78)
C#m-B6-AM7-F#m	One Of These Nights('75)
C#m-B-F#/A#-A	White Room('68); Tales Of Brave Ulysses('68)

Other "C#-B" Progressions

The "C#m-B-E-A" progression is an example of a Partial Money Chords & Basic Combination Progression. The "C#m-B-E-B" progression is an example of a Partial Money Chords & Folk Combination Progression.

C#m-B-E	I Won't Back Down('89)
C#m-B-E-A	I Want To Know What Love Is('85)
C#m-B-E-B	Paint It Black('66); Sunny Afternoon('66); Paranoid('70)
C#m-B-E-F#-B	Duncan('71)

C#m-B11-E-E/G#-A   The Long And Winding Road('70)

The "C#m-B-F#-C#" progression follows the Circle of Fifths movement.

C#m-B-F#   Turn The Page('73)
C#m-B-F#-C#   Radar Love('74)
C#m-B/D#-F#7-AM7   Timothy('71)
C#m7-B-F#m7-C#m7   Another Day In Paradise('89)
C#-B-F#-B   Lonely Nights('71)

C#m-B-G#m-E   Right Down The Line('78)
C#m-B-G#m-A   You Keep Me Hangin' On('66)
C#m-B-G#7-C#m   Yesterday's Gone('64)

The "C#m-B-C#m-E" progression is an example of a Partial Money Chords & Reverse Partial Rock Ballad Combination Progression. The "C#m-B-C#m-F#" progression is an example of a Partial Money Chords & Minor Basic("F#" Substitution)Combination Progression. The "C#m-B-C#m-A-B" progression is an example of a Partial Money Chords & Rock(C#m Substitution)Combination Progression. The "C#m-B-C#m-G#7" progression can be transformed into a Descending "C#-B-A-G#" Bass Line Progression by substituting an "A" chord for the second "C#m" chord creating Money Chords Progression.

C#m-B-C#m-E   Sounds Of Silence('65); Hawaii Five-O('69)
C#m-B-C#m-F#   Time Is On My Side('64); We Ain't Got Nothin' Yet('67)
C#m-B-C#m-G#m   Drunken Sailor(1740); And I Love Her('64)
C#m-B-C#m-G#7   Greensleeves(1680)
C#m-B-C#m-A-B   Down Under('82)

C#m-C7-B7   Macho Man('78)

"C#-D" Chord Progressions

A few hit songs in the 1960s had verses that began with a "C#m" chord and then moved to a "D" chord which is "Borrowed" from another key. The most noteworthy song is the Richard Harris' 1968 and Donna Summer's 1978 *MacArthur Park*.

Below is a chronological listing of songs with verses and/or choruses that begin with the "C#-D" progression followed by a listing of chord progressions by type.

Chronological Listing

Date/Song Title   *Chord Progression*

1966

Mother's Little Helper(G)   V=C#m-D-B-E-A-A/G#-F#m-B7-C#m

It Was A Very Good Year   V=C#m-D-C#m-E-D-C#-B-C#

1967

White Rabbit   V=C#m-D(2x)E-G-A-E

1968

MacArthur Park   V=C#m-C#m/B-D/A-F#m-A/E-(2x)G-A-B-BM7-F#m7/B-E-EM7-B/D#-C#m7-B/D#-EM7-D-Bm

1973

Free Ride(A)   C=C#m-D-E-

C#m-D-A(2x)

Listing by Progression Type

Chord Progression   *Song Examples*

The following progression is an example of a Partial Classic Rock("C#m" Substitution) Progression.

C#m-D   White Rabbit('67)
C#m-D-E   Free Ride('73)
C#m-D-B-E   Mother's Little Helper('66)
C#m-D-C#m-E   It Was A Very Good Year('66)
C#m-C#m/B-D/A-F#m-A/E   MacArthur Park('68)

"C#-D#" Chord Progressions

Several hit songs had verses that began with a "C#m" chord and proceeded to a "D#" chord. However, the "C#m-D#m" sequence produced several big hits including The Association's 1966 *Along Comes Mary* and Michael Jackson's 1983 *Billie Jean*.

The Bob Crew Generation's 1967 *Music To Watch Girls By* was written around the "C#m" Cliché.

Below is a chronological listing of songs with verses and/or choruses that begin with the "C#-D#" chord sequence followed by a listing of chord progressions by type.

Chronological Listing

Date/Song Title   *Chord Progression*

1928

Love Me Or Leave Me   V=C#m-D#7-G#7(2x)

1966

Eight Miles High(G)   V=C#m-D#m-E-B-A-E-B-A

Along Comes Mary(C)   V=C#m-D#m/C#-C#m7-D#m/C#(2x)

1967

Music To Watch Girls By   V=C#m-C#m(M7)-C#m7-C#m6-
                           D#7-F#m-D#7-G#7

Monterey(C)   V=C#m-D#m(6x)A-G#sus-G#

1968

Long Time Gone(C)   V=C#m-D#m/C#-E/C#-D#m/C#(2x)

1969

Because(E)   V=C#m-D#m7b5-G#7-A-C#m-A7-A13-D-Do

I Want You(She's So Heavy)(F)   C=C#m-C#m7/E-D#7b9-A7-G#

1973

Diamond Girl   C=C#m7-D#m7-F#-C#m7(4x)

1975

Could It Be Magic   V=C#sus-C#-D#sus-D#-EM7

1983

Billie Jean   V=C#m-D#m/C#-C#m7-D#m/C#

1984

Against All Odds(Take A Look At Me Now)   V=C#7sus-C#m7-D#m7-Eadd9

Listing By Progression Type

Chord Progression   *Song Example*

Static Bass Line

C#sus-C#   Could It Be Magic('75)

C#m-C#m(M7)-C#m7-C#m6   Music To Watch Girls By('67)

The "C#m7" chord and the "E/C#" chord share the same notes.

C#m-D#m/C#-E/C#-D#m/C#   Long Time Gone('68)

C#m-D#m/C#-C#m7-D#m7/C#   Along Comes Mary('66); Billie Jean('83)

Other "D#" Progressions

The "C#m-D#m" progression can be transformed into a Static Bass Line Progression by changing the quality of the "D#m" chord to a "D#m7" chord and then by playing the C# note as the bass note creating the "C#m-D#m/C#" Progression.

C#m-D#m   Monterey('67)

C#m-D#m-E-B   Eight Miles High('66)

C#7sus-C#m7-D#m7-Eadd9   Against All Odds(Take A Look At Me Now)('84)

C#m7-D#m7-F#-C#m7   Diamond Girl('73)

C#m-D#m7b5-G#7-A   Because('69)

C#m-D#7-G#7   Love Me Or Leave Me('28)

C#m-C#m7/E-D#7b9-A7-G#   I Want You(She's So Heavy)('69)

"D" Chord Progressions

A few hit songs in the 1960s and 1970s had verses or choruses that began with the "Borrowed D" chord. The "D-A-E" Classic Rock("D" First)Progression follows the Circle of Fifths and is similar to the Classic Rock "E-D-A" sequence with the last two chords played first.

In 1967, several hit songs used "D" progressions to create choruses to contrast with and provide variation from verses that begin with "E" chord progressions.

The Beatles' 1967 *Magical Mystery Tour* and Brian Wilson's 1966 *God Only Knows* verses were constructed around interesting "D" Chord Progressions combined with Descending Bass Lines while Bruce Springsteen's 1975 *Born To Run* bridge demonstrates the effectively use of Suspended Chords.

In addition to the progressions already discussed, there are a number of other "D" Chord Progressions that continue to move to the "B" and the "Borrowed" "G" chords. Although not used frequently, the following progression type is also employed: The "D-E" Reverse Partial Classic Rock Progression.

Below is a chronological listing of songs with verses, choruses, and/or bridges that begin with the "D" chord followed by a listing of chord progressions by type.

Chronological Listing

Date/Song Title   *Chord Progressions*

1961

Big Bad John   V=D-E

1962

The Lonely Bull   V=D-E(2x)D-C-B
                               E-F#m7-B7-E

1965

You've Got Your Troubles(A)	C=D-E(2x)B
Lemon Tree	C=D-A7(2x)D
Midnight Hour(E)	I=D-B-A-G-(E-A)2x

1966

Poor Side Of Town(E)	B=D-G-C-Bm C-Bm-Am7-GM7-B
God Only Knows(E)	V=D/A-Bm6-F#m-F#m7-F#m6/A-E/B-Co-E/B-A#m7b5-A-E/G#-F#m7-E

1967

How Can I Be Sure(D)	I=D-E(3x)G-F#m-E
Lucy In The Sky With Diamonds(A)	C=D-G-A(3x)
Penny Lane(B)	C=D-D/F#-G(2x)B7
Magical Mystery Tour(E)	V=D-D/C-G/B-Gm/A#-D/A-A I=D-A-E
(You Make Me Feel Like)A Natural Woman	V=D-A-[E/G#-F#m7]-E-B/D#-D-A-[E/G#]-F#m7-G#m7(3x)AM7-F#m7/B
With A Little Help From My Friends(E)	C=D-A-E(2x)A-E-C#m11-F#-E-D-A(2x)
Midnight Confession(F#)	B=D-A-E-B D-A-E-C#

Baby, I Need Your Loving   C=D-Bm7-A-F#m7-A

San Francisco   B=D-Bm(2x)E

Blackbird(G)   C=D-C#m-Bm-A-G-A-
                                  D-C#m-Bm-A-G-F#7-Esus/B

1968

Love Child   C=D-G-Em7-C-B-
                                  Em7-D-C-B(2x)

Hurdy Gurdy Man   C=D-A-E

1969

Easy To Be Hard(D)   V=DM7-B7(2x)-
                                  E-F#m-B7(2x)

Proud Mary   I=D-B(3x)A-G

[Note the similarity between the above Introduction and that of the 1965 *Midnight Hour*.]

Polythene Pam(E)   V=D/E-A-E(2x)G-B7-
                                  C-D-E(2x)

1970

Instant Karma   C=D-F#m-Bm(3x)A-B9

It Don't Matter To Me   B=DM7-GM7(4x)EM7-AM7

1971

It's Too Late   C=DM7-AM7(3x)F#m7-AM7-
                                  G#7sus-G#m7

Theme From Shaft   V=DM9-C#m

1972

I Need You(A)   C=D-Bm-F#m-Em-A

Layla(E)   C=Dm-Bb-C(3x)

1974

Rikki Don't Lose That
Number(E)   V=D-Aadd9-E(2x)-
                                 [C#5-B5]-D-A-E-F#m11-A-
                                 [B7#9]

1975

Born To Run(E)   B=Dsus-D(2x)Gsus-G(2x)
                                 Asus-A(2x)Csus-C(2x)

1977

Baby, What A Big Surprise   C=D-E-A-E/G#-F#-D-E-A-G-D

1978

Reminiscing   V=DM7-D9+11-C#9(2x)-
                                 AM7-C9-E-F#m/E-E

Listing By Progression Type

Chord Progression   *Song Examples*

Classic Rock("D" First)

D-A-E   With A Little Help From My Friends('67); Hurdy Gurdy Man('68)
D-Aadd9-E   Rikki Don't Lose That Number('74)
D/E-A-E   Polythene Pam('69)
D-A-E-B   Midnight Confession('67)

Static Bass Lines

"D" Chord Progressions

Dsus-D   Born To Run('75)

Descending Bass Lines

C⁰-E/B-A#m7b5-A   God Only Knows('66)
D-D/C-G/B-Gm/A#-D/A   Magical Mystery Tour('67)

Other "D" Chord Progressions

The following progression is an example of a Reverse Partial Classic Rock Progression.

D-E   Big Bad John('61); The Lonely Bull('62); You've Got Your Troubles('65); How Can I Be Sure('67)
D-E-A-E/G#   Baby, What A Big Surprise('77)

D-F#m-Bm   Instant Karma('70)

D-G-Em7-C   Love Child('68)
D-G-A   Lucy In The Sky With Diamonds('67)
D-G-C-Bm   Poor Side Of Town('66)
D-D/F#-G   Penny Lane('67)
DM7-GM7   It Don't Matter To Me('70)

D-A-[E/G#-F#m7]-E-B/D#   (You Make Me Feel Like)A Natural Woman('67)
D-A7   Lemon Tree('65)
DM7-AM7   It's Too Late('71)

D-B   Proud Mary('69)
D-B-A-G   Midnight Hour('65)
D-Bm   San Francisco('67)
D-Bm-F#m-Em   I Need You('72)
D-Bm7-A-F#m7   Baby, I Need Your Loving('67)
DM7-B7   Easy To Be Hard('69)

Dm-Bb-C   Layla('72)

D-C#m-Bm-A   Blackbird('67)
DM7-D9+11-C#9   Reminiscing('78)
DM9-C#m   Theme From Shaft('71)

"D#" Chord Progressions

Only a few songs have verses, choruses, or bridges that begin with a "D#" chord. *The Shadow Of Your Smile* follows the Circle of Fifths through six changes.

Chronological Listing

Date/Song Title　　　　　*Chord Progression*

1959

Three Cool Cats　　　　　V=D#7-G#7-C#m(5x)

1965

The Shadow Of Your Smile　　V=D#m7-G#7b9-C#m-F#m7-B7-EM7-AM7

1970

See Me, Feel Me(E)　　　　I=D#M7-Fsus-F-Fsus-F-G(4x)

1971

Aqualung(Ab)　　　　　　B=D#m-C#-A-Am-D#m-C#

1978

Josie(G)　　　　　　　　C=D#7#9-G#+7-C#m7-A/D-D#7#9-G#+7-C#m7-F#7-F#m7-B9-EM7-AM7-D#7#9-G#7#9-C#m7

Listing By Progression Type

Chord Progression *Song Examples*

D# Chord Progressions

D#M7-Fsus-F-Fsus See Me, Feel Me('70)

D#m7-G#7b9-C#m-F#m7 The Shadow Of Your Smile('65)
D#7-G#7-C#m Three Cool Cats('59)
D#7#9-G#+7-C#m7-A/D Josie('78)

D#m-C#-A-Am Aqualung('71)

Appendix

The "80" Most Popular Progressions

Basic   E-A

  F#m Substitution   E-F#m
  C#m Substitution   C#m-A
  Minor   C#m-F#m
  Minor(F# Subst.)   C#m-F#
  Reverse   A-E
  Partial   E

Folk   E-B7

  Minor   C#m-G#m
  Minor(G#7 Subst.)   C#m-G#7
  Reverse   B7-E

Rock   E-A-B7

  C#m Substitution   C#m-A-B
  A First   A-B-E
  Reverse   B-A-E
  Reverse(E First)   E-B-A

Rock Ballad   E-C#m-A-B7

  G#m Substitution   E-G#m-A-B7
  A First   A-B-E-C#m
  Partial   E-C#m
  Reverse Partial   C#m-E

Standard   E-C#m-F#m-B7

   G#m Substitution   E-G#m-F#m-B7
   F#m First   F#m-B-E-C#m
   F#m First/A Subst.   F#m-B-E-A
   C#m First   C#m-F#m-B7-E
   Partial   E-F#m-B7
   Partial(F#m First)   F#m-B-E
   Partial(F#m First)   F#m-B

Ragtime   E-C#7-F#7-B7

   C#7 First   C#7-F#7-B7-E
   Five Chord   E-G#7-C#7-F#7-B7

Diminished Cliché

   Fo Cliché   E-Fo-F#m7-B7
   F#m7 First   F#m7-B7-E-Fo
   Fo Cliché   E-Fo-F#m7-Go
                              E-Fo-B7/F#-B7
   Go Cliché   E-Go-F#m7-B7
                              E-E/G#-Go-B7/F#-B7

Classic Rock   E-D-A

   D First   D-A-E
   Partial   E-D
   Borrowed D   E-A-D-A
   Borrowed G   E-G-A-E

Blues

   Classic   E7-A7-E7-B7-A7-E7-B7
   Quick Change   E7-A7(2x)E7-B7-A7-E7-B7
   Minor   C#m-F#m-C#m-G#m-F#m-C#m

Ascending Bass Lines

E-E/G#-A-B
E-F#m-E/G#-A
E-F#m-G#m-A
E-F#m-A-B7
E-F#-A-B
E-G#m-A-B7

Descending Bass Lines

E-E/D#-C#m-C#m/B
E-G#m/D#-Bm/D-C#7
E-G#m/D#-C#m-E/B
E-G#7/D#-C#m-E7/B
E-B/D#-C#m-G#m/B
E-B/D#-C#m-A
E-B/D#-D-A/C#
C#m-E/B-A-G#
C#m-G#m/B-AM7-G#m
C#m-C#m/B-A7-G#7
C#m-C#m/B-C#m/A#-AM7

Money Chords   C#m-B-A-G#
Partial   C#m-B-A
                          C#m-B

Static Bass Lines

Chord Quality Substitutions   E-EM7-E6-EM7
                              E-E+-E6-E7
                              E-Esus
                              E-E11
                              C#m-C#11
                              C#m-C#m(M7)-C#m7-C#m6

Same Note Bass Lines   E-F#m/E
                              E-G/E

E-A/E
E-B/E
C#m-F#/C#
C#m-A/C#

Combinations

Basic & Folk   E-A-E-B7
Folk & Basic   E-B7-E-A

Circle of Fifths Progressions

Basic   E-A

  Reverse   A-E
  Minor   C#m-F#m
  Reverse Minor   F#m-C#m
  Minor(F# Subst.)   C#m-F#
  Reverse Minor(F# Subst.)   F#-C#m

Folk   E-B7

  Reverse   B7-E
  Minor Folk   C#m-G#m
  Reverse Minor   G#m-C#m
  Minor(G#7 Subst.)   C#m-G#7
  Reverse Minor(G#7 Subst.)   G#7-C#m

Standard   E-C#m-F#m-B7

  F#m First   F#m-B-E-C#m
  C#m First   C#m-F#m-B7-E
  Partial   E-F#m-B7
  Partial(F#m First)   F#m-B7-E
  Partial(F#m First)   F#m-B7
  A Substitution(F#m7 First)   F#m7-B7-EM7-AM7

Ragtime   E-C#7-F#7-B7

  C#7 First   C#7-F#7-B7-E
  Five-Chord   E-G#7-C#7-F#7-B7-E
  G#7 First   G#7-C#7-F#7-B7

Classic Rock   E-D-A

    D First   D-A-E
    Borrowed G   E-G-A-E
    Borrowed G&D   G-D-A-E
    Borrowed C&G   C-G-D-A-E

G# Variations

                                      G#m11-C#7b5/G-F#m11-B7b5/F
                                      G#7sus4-G#7-C#m-F#7-BM7-EM7-AM7

C# Variations

                                      C#m-F#m-B
                                      C#m7-F#m7-B7-EM7-AM7

D# Variations

                                      E-D#7-G#7-C#7-F#7-B7-E
                                    E-D#7-G#7-C#9-F#m7-B7
                                    D#7-G#7-C#m
                                    D#m7-G#7b9-C#m-F#m7-B7-EM7-AM7

Ascending Bass Lines

"E-F-F#-G" Bass Lines

    E-Fo-F#m7-Go   Ain't Misbehavin'('29); Bewitched('41); Orange Colored Sky('50)

"E-F#-G-G#" Bass Lines

E-F#m7-Go-E/G#	Don't Get Around Much Any More('42)
E-Eo-E-E+-F#m7-Go-G#m7	If I Loved You('45)

"E-F#-G#-A" Bass Lines

Many of the following progressions continue to move to a B chord.

E-F#m-E/G#-A	Uptown Girl('83)
E-F#m-E7/G#-A	Baby What A Big Surprise('77)
E-F#m7-E/G#-A	I'm Gonna Wash That Man Right Outa My Hair('49); It's The Same Old Song('65); Sunshine On My Shoulders('74); Slow Dancin'('77)
E-F#m7-EM7/G#-A	Longer('80)
E-F#m(addB)-E/G#-Aadd9	Heart Of The Matter('90)
E-F#m-G#m-A	Like A Rolling Stone('65); Daydream Believer('67); Getting Better('67); Girl Watcher('68); Love(Can Make You Happy)('69); Lean On Me('72)
E-F#m-G#m-AM7	Ain't Nothing Like The Real Thing('68)
E-F#m7-G#m7-A	The Patty Duke Theme('63); Here, There, And Everywhere('66)
E-F#m7-G#m7-AM7	Sexy Sadie('68)
E-F#-G#-A	Bad, Bad Leroy Brown('73)
E11-E-F#m7-G#m7-AM7	You've Lost That Lovin' Feelin'('78)

"E-F#-G#-B" Bass Lines

E-F#m-G#m-B	Ride The Wild Surf('64)
EM7-F#m7-G#m7-F#m7/B	La La Means I Love You('68)

"E-F#-A-B" Bass Lines

E-F#m-A-B	My Girl('65); It's My Life('66); I've Got To Get A Message To You('68); Reach Out In The Darkness('68); No Matter What('70); I'd Love You To Want Me('72); I Believe In Music('72)
E-F#m-A-B7	Love Is All Around('68); Vincent('72); Must Have Got Lost('75)
E-F#-A-B	As Tears Go By('66); Walk A Mile In My Shoes('70); Old Fashioned Love Song('71); American Girl('76)
E-F#-A-B7	She'd Rather Be With Me('67)
E-F#7-Am-B9	You've Got Your Troubles('65)
E-F#9-A-AM7/B	Love Train('73)
EM9-F#m-A-B11	Key Largo('82)

"E-G-A-B" Bass Lines

E-E7-G-A-B11	I Am The Walrus('67)
E-G-A-B	Knock On Wood('66)

"E-G-A-C" Bass Lines

E-G-A-C	I'm Not Your Steppin' Stone('67); Gimme Some Lovin'('67)

"E-G-A-D" Bass Lines

E-G-A-D	Bend Me, Shape Me('68)

"E-G#-A-B" Bass Lines

E-E/G#-A-B	Expressway To Your Heart('67); My Life('79); Lady In Red('87)
E-E/G#-A-B-B11	Get Off Of My Cloud('65)
E-E/G#-A-B11	With A Little Luck('78)
E-E7/G#-A-B11	Take Me To The Pilot('69)

Eadd9-EM7/G#-AM7-B11	Somewhere Out There('87)
E-G#m-A-B	A Summer Song('64); Fun, Fun, Fun('64); You Baby('66); Different Drum('67); Georgy Girl('67); Woman, Woman('68); I Started A Joke('69); Crocodile Rock('72); Nice To Be With You('72); Ziggie Stardust('72); Every Time You Go Away('79)
E-G#m-A-B7	True Love Ways('58); I Feel Fine('64); Mister Lonely('64); A Lover's Concerto('65); I Go To Pieces('65); Hurdy Gurdy Man('68); Jean('69); Ballad Of Easy Rider('69)
E-G#m-A-B7-B7b9	Live And Let Die('73)
E-G#m-A-B11	You Didn't Have To Be So Nice('66); Key Largo('82)
E-G#m-AM7-B	Weekend In New England('76)
E-G#m-Am-B7	I Don't Want To See You Again('64)
E-G#m7-A-B	Sooner Or Later('71); Changes('71); Hard To Say I'm Sorry('82)
E-G#m7-A-B11	Right Time Of The Night('77); Have I Told You Lately('89)
E-G#m7-Aadd9-B	Goodbye Girl('78)
E-G#-A-B	Rock 'N' Roll Suicide('72)
E-G#7#5-A-B11	Build Me Up Butter Cup('69)

"E-G#-A-A#" Bass Lines

E-E7/G#-A-C/A#	Ask Me No Questions('71)

"F#-G#-A-B" Bass Lines

F#m-G#m-A-B	Rain, The Park And Other Things('67)
F#m7-G#m-A-B7	Younger Girl('65)
F#m7-G#m7-AM7-AM7/B	One Less Bell To Answer('70)

"F#-G#-A-C#" Bass Lines

F#m-G#m7-A6-C#m	Misunderstanding('80)

"A-B-C-C#" Bass Lines

A-B-Co-C#m	Sara Smile('76)

"A-B-C#-D#" Bass Lines

    A-B-C#m-B/D#   Somebody's Baby('82)

"B-C#-D#-E" Bass Lines

    B7-A/C#-B/D#-E   Tonight's The Night('76)

"C#-E-F#-G#" Bass Lines

    C#m-E-F#-G#   Out Of Limits('63)

Descending Bass Lines

"E-C#-C-B" Bass Lines

E-C#m-C7-B7	Sir Duke('77)
E-C#m7-CM7-B7	Free As A Bird('95)

"E-D-C-B" Bass Lines

E-Dadd9-C-B Bernadette('67)

"E-D-C#-A" Bass Lines

E-D-A/C#-A China Grove('73)

"E-D-C#-C" Bass Lines

The E/D chord has the same notes as the E7 chord. The E/C# chord has the same notes as both the E6 and C#m7 chords.

E-E/D-E/C#-E+/C	Dear Prudence('68); Lucy In The Sky With Diamonds('67)
E-E/D-E/C#-C6	Takin' It To The Street('76)
E-E/D-E/C#-CM7	Hand Me Down World('70)
E-E/D-A/C#-Am/C	Santa Claus Is Coming To Town('34)
E-E/D-A/C#-Am6/C	Theme From "The Andy Griffith Show"('60)
E-E/D-A/C#-C7	Short People('78)
E-E/D-C#m-Am/C	Celebrate('72)
Em-G/D-A7/C#-C	Temptation Eyes('71)

"E-D#-C#-A" Bass Lines

E-E/D#-C#m-A Not Enough Love In The World('85)

E-B/D#-A/C#-A	All Out Of Love('80)
E-B/D#-C#m-A	Baby, I Love Your Way('76); Slow Dancing(Swayin' To The Music)('77); Can You Feel The Love Tonight('94)
E-B/D#-C#m-AM7	Let It Be('70)
E-D#+-F#m/C#-A	Cold As Ice('77)

"E-D#-C#-B" Bass Lines

The E/D# chord has the same notes as the EM7 chord. The E/D# and EM7 chords have the same notes, except E, as the G#m/D# chord.

E-E/D#-E/C#-E/B	Changes('71); Everything I Own('72)
E-E/D#-C#m-E/B	America('68); All The Young Dudes('72)
E-E/D#-C#m-EM7/B	Aubrey('73)
E-E/D#-C#m-Bm	All The Young Dudes('72)-Chorus
E-E/D#-C#m-C#m/B	Something('69); Have You Ever Seen The Rain('71); Garden Party('72)
E-E/D#-C#m7-E/B	Hello Goodbye('67); Our House('70)
E-E/D#-C#m7-E7/B	Mr. Bojangles('71)
E-G#m/D#-F#m/C#-B11	Midnight Train To Georgia('73)
E-G#m/D#-C#m-E/B	Piano Man('74)
E-G#m/D#-C#m-E6/B	A Whiter Shade Of Pale('67)
E-G#m/D#-C#m-B	San Franciscan Nights('67); Runaway Train('92)
E-G#m/D#-C#m-B7	I'm So Lonesome I Could Cry('49)
E-G#m/D#-C#m-C#m/B	Can't Help Falling In Love('62);Yesterday Once More('73)
E-G#7/D#-C#m-E/B	Didn't I(Blow Your Mind This Time)('70)
E-G#7/D#-C#m-E7/B	'Taint Nobody's Business If I Do('23); Georgia On My Mind('30); Love Me Tender('56); Happy Birthday Sweet Sixteen('62); There's A Kind Of Hush('67)
E-B/D#-F#m/C#-B7	With A Little Help From My Friends('67)
E-B/D#-A/C#-F#m7/B	He Ain't Heavy, He's My Brother('70)
E-B/D#-A/C#-B	Wonderful Tonight('78)
E-B/D#-C#m-E/B	For No One('66); When Will I See You Again('74); Shower The People('76); Always On My Mind('82)
E-B/D#-C#m-E7/B	When A Man Loves A Woman('66)

E-B/D#-C#m-G#m/B	Let It Be Me('60); End Of The World('63); The Weight('68); I'll Be There('70); Don't Pull Your Love('71); Love Takes Time('90)
E-B/D#-C#m-B	Bridge Over Troubled Water('70); Dust In The Wind('78)
E-B/D#-C#m-C#m/B	I Got A Name('73); Tears In Heaven('92)
E-B/D#-C#m7-E/B	Your Smiling Face('77)
E-B/D#-C#m7-B	59th Street Bridge Song('66); Reelin' In The Years('73)
E-B/D#-C#m7-B6	I Got The Sun In The Morning('46)
E-B/D#-C#11-C#m7-B	All Cried Out('86)
E-B6/D#-C#m-E/B	Mind Games('73)
E-D#m-C#m-B	You're In My Heart('77)

"E-D#-C#-C" Bass Lines

E-G#m/D#-C#m-Am/C	Anytime At All('64)
E-B/D#-A/C#-Am/C	How Am I Supposed To Live Without You('90)
E-B/D#-C#m-G#/C	Star Spangled Banner(1814); Beach Baby('74)

"E-D#-D-A" Bass Lines

E-B/D#-D-A	(You Make Me Feel Like)A Natural Woman('67)
E-B/D#-D6-A	Give Me Just A Little More Time('70)

"E-D#-D-C" Bass Lines

E-B7/D#-D-Am/C	It Don't Matter To Me('70)

"E-D#-D-C#" Bass Lines

The B/D# chord has the same notes, except G#, as the G#m7/D# chord.

E-E/D#-D-D/C#	Hold On Loosely('81)
Eadd9-EM9/D#-E9/D-C#m11	If('71)
E-G#m/D#-Bm/D-C#7	Until It's Time For You To Go('72); All By Myself('76)

E-G#m/D#-Bm6/D-C#7	My Way('69); Rainy Days And Mondays('71)
E-G#m7/D#-C#m7b5/D-C#7b9	Together Again('97)
E-B/D#-Bm/D-F#m7/C#	I Hear A Symphony('65)
E-B/D#-Bm6/D-C#7	Homeward Bound('66)
E-B/D#-D-A/C#	Walk Away Renee('66); Never My Love('67); Three Times A Lady('78)
E6-B/D#-Bm/D-C#m	Blue Eyes('82)
Em-B+/D#-Em7/D-A9/C#	The Most Beautiful Girl('73)
E-D#+-Bm6/D-C#7	Try A Little Tenderness('32); It Won't Be Long('63)

"G-F#-E-D" Bass Lines

G-Bm/F#-Em-D	This Diamond Ring('65)

"G-F#-E-D#" Bass Lines

G#m-G#m/F#-EM7-E/D#	God Bless The Child('41)

"G#-G-F#-F" Bass Lines

The following progression combines the use of a Descending Bass Line with a Circle of Fifths chord movement.

G#m11-C#7b5/G-F#m11-B7b5/F	One Note Samba('61)

"A-G-F#-E" Bass Lines

A-G-B/F#-E	Something('69)–T/A

"A-G#-F#-E" Bass Lines

The A/F# chord has the same notes as the A6 chord. The A/G# chord has the same notes as the AM7 chord.

A-E/G#-B/F#-E	Signs('70)

A-G#m-F#m-E	Oh How Happy('66); Piece Of My Heart('68); Superstar('71)
AM7-G#m7-F#m7-EM7	Hey There Lonely Girl('70); Kid Charlemagne('76)
A-A/G#-F#m-F#m/E	Hey Jude('68)
A-A/G#-A/F#-A/E	Rescue Me('65)

"A-G#-G-F#" Bass Lines

The A/G chord has the same notes as the A7 chord.

A-E/G#-Em/G-F#m7	Maybe I'm Amazed('77)
A-A/G#-A/G-F#7	Back In The USSR('68)

"A#-A-G#-F#" Bass Lines

A#m7-A-A/G#-F#m	Sir Duke('77)

"A#-A-G#-G" Bass Lines

The A#m7b5 chord has the same notes as the C#m/A# and C#m6 chords.

A#m7b5-Am7-G#m7-Go-F#m11	Night And Day('32)

"B-G#-F#-E" Bass Lines

B-E/G#-B/F#-E	All I Need Is A Miracle('86)

"B-A-G#-F#" Bass Lines

The B/A chord has the same notes as the B7 chord. The B/G# chord has the same notes as the B6 and G#m7 chords.

E/B-A-E/G#-F#m	The Long And Winding Road('70)
B-B/A-B/G#-B/F#	You've Got To Hide Your Love Away('65)

"B-A#-G#-E" Bass Lines

B-F#/A#-E/G#-E	All Out Of Love('80)

"B-A#-A-F#" Bass Lines

The A#m7b5 chord has the same notes as the C#m/A# and C#m6 chords. The AM7 chord has the same notes as the C#m/A chord.

C#m/B-A#m7b5-AM7-F#m7	Ain't No Mountain High Enough('67)

"B-A#-A-G#" Bass Lines

E/B-A#m7b5-A-E/G#	God Only Knows('66)

"C#-B-A-E" Bass Lines

C#m-E/B-A-E	Let It Be('70)
C#m-BM7-E/A-B/E	Josie('78)

"C#-B-A-F#" Bass Lines

C#m-B6-AM7-F#m	One Of These Nights('75)
C#m-C#m/B-AM7-F#m7	(If Loving You Is Wrong)I Don't Want To Be Right('72)

"C#-B-A-G#" Bass Lines

The C#m/A chord has the same notes as the AM7 chord.

A/C#-E/B-A-E/G#	Way Down('77)
A/C#-EM7/B-AM7-G#m7	Tiny Dancer('71)

C#m-E/B-A-E/G#	Superstar('71)
C#m-E/B-A-A/G#	The Night They Drove Old Dixie Down('71)
C#m-E/B-A-G#	An Old Fashioned Love Song('71)

C#m-E7/B-A-G#7	Sunday Morning('68)
C#m-E7/B-A7-G#7	Sunny('66)
C#m-G#m/B-AM7-G#m	Roxanne('79); With You I'm Born Again('80)
C#m-G#m/B-AM7-G#11	Sara Smile('76)
C#m-B-A-G#m	A Hazy Shade Of Pale('66)
C#m-B-A-G#	Walk Don't Run('60); Hit The Road Jack('61); Runaway('61); Don't Let Me Be Misunderstood('65); Good Vibrations('66); Happy Together('67); Wait A Million Years('69); Man Eater('82)
C#m-B-A-G#7	Three Cool Cats('59); Runaway('61); In The Year 2525('69); Sultans Of Swing('79)
C#m-B-AM7-C#m/G#	Caribbean Queen('84)
C#m-B6-AM7-G#	I'll Be Back('64)
C#m-C#m/B-A-G#m7	Back Stabbers('72)
C#m-C#m/B-A6-G#7	Steppin' Out With My Baby('47)
C#m-C#m/B-AM7-G#-G#7	Standing In The Shadows Of Love('67)
C#m-C#m/B-AM7-G#7	Help Me Girl('66)
C#m-C#m/B-AM7-C#m/G#	Summer In The City('66)
C#m-C#m/B-A7-G#7	It Don't Mean A Thing('32)
C#m-C#m/B-C#m/A-C#m/G#	Expressway To Your Heart('67); We Can Work It Out('65)

"C#-B-A#-G#" Bass Lines

C#m-E7/B-F#/A#-G#7	I Love You('68)

"C#-B-A#-A" Bass Lines

The "A#m7b5" chord has the same notes as the "C#m/A#" chord.

C#m-E/B-F#/A#-A	House Of The Rising Sun('64); Lil Red Riding Hood('66); Call Me('80)
C#m-E/B-A#m7b5-AM7	One('69); 25 Or 6 To 4('70)
C#m-C#m/B-F#7/A#-A	Coming Into Los Angeles('69); Piano Man('74)
C#m-C#m/B-A#m7b5-AM7	Wild Flower('73)

C#m-C#m/B-C#m/A#-F#m6/A	Dream On('76)
C#m-C#m/B-C#m/A#-A6	Your Song('70)
C#m-C#m/B-C#m/A#-AM7	While My Guitar Gently Weeps('68)

The above "C#m" Cliché can have either a Static or Descending Bass Line.

C#-B-F#/A#-A	White Room('68); Tales Of Brave Ulysses('68)

"C#-C-B-A" Bass Lines

The C+ chord has the same notes, except C#, as the C#m/C and C#m(M7) chords.

C#m-C+-E/B-A6	If('71)
C#m-Co-E/B-A	Bangla Desh('71)
C#m-C#m/C-C#m/B-A7	God Bless The Child('41)

"C#-C-B-A#" Bass Lines

The E+/C and G#+/C chords have the same notes, except C#, as the C#m/C and C#m(M7) chords.

C#m-E+/C-E/B-A#m7b5	W.O.L.D.('74)
C#m6-F7#9/C-Bm6-E9b5/A#	Quiet Nights Of Quiet Stars('62)
C#m-G#+/C-G#7/C-E/B-A#m7b5	Blue Skies('27)
C#m-G#7/C-E/B-A#m7b5	A Song For You('70)
C#m-C#m/C-C#m/B-C#m/A#	Will You Love Me Tomorrow('60)
C#m-C#m9/C-E/B-F#9/A#	Stairway To Heaven('72)
C#m-C#m(M7)/C-C#m/B-F#9/A#	Something('69)
C#m-C#m(M7)/C-C#m/B-C#m/A#	Time In A Bottle('73)

"D-C-B-A#" Bass Lines

The D/C chord has the same notes as the D7 chord.

D-D/C-G/B-Gm/A#   Magical Mystery Tour('67)

"D-C#-B-A" Bass Lines

The Em/D chord has the same notes as the Em7 chord. The Em/C# chord has the same notes as the Em6 chord. The D/C# chord has the same notes as the DM7 chord. The Bm/A chord has the same notes as the Bm7 chord.

Em/D-Em/C#-Em7/B-A7   Fixin' A Hole('67)
D-D/C#-Bm-Bm/A   Cat's In The Craddle('74)

"D-C#-C-B" Bass Lines

E/D-A/C#-Am/C-E/B   Can't Find My Way Back Home('69)

Static Bass Lines

Two ways songwriters and performers have created memorable Static Bass Lines are to use Chord Quality Substitutions("5"/"6", "6"/"M7", Augmented & Suspended, "Add9," Dominant 7th, Eleventh, and Minor Cliché Variations) and Same Note Bass Lines("E","F#","G", "G#" "A","B","C", "C#", "D", an "D#" Chord Variations).

"5"/"6" Variations

E5-E6	Truckin'('71)
E5-E6-E5-E6	Blues/Rock Shuffle #1
E5-E6-E7	Born To Be Wild('68)
E5-E6-E7-E6	Blues/ Rock Shuffle #2

"6/"M7" Variations

E-E6	Ain't That A Shame('55); Call Me Irresponsible('62); I Guess The Lord Must Be In New York City('69); I Can Help('74); Dancing In The Dark('84)
E-E6-EM7	Mame('66)
E-E6-EM7-E	Love Train('73)
E-E6-EM7-E6	It Must Be Him('67); It's Impossible('68)
E-E6-EM7-E6-E-E6	A Wonderful Day Like Today('64)
E-E6-EM7-E6-EM7-E6	Walkin' My Baby Back Home('30); Sure Gonna Miss Her('66)
E-EM7	Lazy Day('67); These Eyes('69); Lyin' Eyes('75); Wildfire('75); Tomorrow(from "Annie")('77); Two Out Of Three Ain't Bad('78)
E-EM7-E	Just A Gigolo('85)
E-EM7-E6	Carolina In The Morning('22); I'm Gonna Sit Right Down And Write Myself A Letter('35)
E-EM7-E6-E	You Always Hurt The One You Love('44); I Remember It Well('57); Everybody Loves A Clown('65); Go Now('65); Have You Seen Her('71); After The Lovin'('77)
E-EM7-E6-EM7	Gentle On My Mind('68); Mandy('74)

E-EM7-E6-EM7-E	It Might As Well Be Spring('45); Jingle Bell Rock('57)
E-EM7-E6-EM7-E7	Harper Valley P.T.A('68)
E-EM7-E7	We'll Sing In The Sunshine('64);Hooked On A Feeling('68); Rain Drops Keep Fallin' On My Head('69); I Just Can't Help Believin'('70); You Are So Beautiful('75); Another Somebody Done Somebody Wrong Song('75); I'll Play For You('75); Maybe I'm Amazed('77); I Love The Night Life('78)
E-EM7-E7-E7#9	Kodachrome('73)
E-EM7-E9	Can't Take My Eyes Off Of You('67)
E-EM7-Eo	Cloudy('66)
E-EM9	Salvation('72)
EM7-E	The Best Of My Love('74); Still The Same('78)
EM7-E6	Bobby Sox To Stockings('59); Tell Her No('65); Honey('68); Alone Again Naturally('72); Let Em In('76); Emotion('78)
EM9-E	The Impossible Dream('65)
EM9-E6	So Far Away('71)
Em7-EM7	Goin' Out Of My Head('64)
G-GM7-G6-G	Love Train('73)
A-AM7-A6-AM7	You Didn't Have To Be So Nice('66)
A6-AM7-A	Holly, Holy('69)

Augmented & Suspended Variations

E-E+	Swanee('19); Kind Of A Drag('67); Strange Magic('76); Baby Hold On('78)
E-E+-E6	For Once In My Life('68)
E-E+-E6-E+	Match Maker('64)
E-E+-E6-E7	Because('64); Laughing('69); Stand Tall('76); The Greatest Love Of All('86)
E-E+-E6-E7-E6	Sentimental Journey('44)
E-E+-E6-E9	Maybe This Time('63)
E-Eo-E-E+	If I Loved You('45)
E-Esus	We Can Work It Out('65); Monday, Monday('66); Western Union ('67); Suite: Judy Blue Eyes('69); Chevy Van('73); Peaceful Easy Feeling('73); Anne's Song('74)

E-Esus-E	Born To Run('75); More Than A Feeling('76); Margaritaville('77); Hot Blooded('78)
E-Esus-Eadd9	Eve Of Destruction('65)
Esus-E	She's A Rainbow('68); Pinball Wizard('69); Hold Your Head Up('72); She Believes In Me('79)
E-Esus4/2	No Sugar Tonight('70)
E-E7sus-E	Anticipation('72)
E5-EM7(no3)-E6sus4-E	Big Yellow Taxi('75)
Asus-A	Darling Be Home Soon('67)
C#m(sus4)-C#m	Cold As Ice('77)
C#m7sus-C#7sus-C#7	The Look Of Love('68)
C#sus-C#	Could It Be Magic('75)
Dsus-D	Born To Run('75)

"Add9" Variations

Eadd9-E	Lost In Love('80)
Eadd9-EM7	Touch Me In The Morning('73)
Aadd9(add D#)-Aadd9	Sailing('80)

Dominant 7th Variations

E-E7	Get Back('69)
E-E7-E	It Takes Two('67)
E7-E	Little Sister('61)

The following three progressions are called Harmony Shuffles.

E-E7sus4/6-E	Swlabr('69)
E-E7sus4/6-E7(no3)-E7sus4/6-E	Change The World('96)
E7-E7sus4/6-E7(no3)-E7sus4/6-E7	The Pusher('64)
E7-E7#9-E7	Taxman('66)

Eleventh Variations

E-E11	On Broadway('63); The In Crowd('64); 19th Nervous Breakdown ('66); Tomorrow Never Knows('66); 98.6('67); Gimme Some Lovin'('67); Listen To The Music('72); It's Gonna Take Some Time('72); I Won't Last A Day Without You('74); Got To Get You Into My Life('76); Rhythm Of The Night('85)
E-E11-E	If I Needed Someone('65)
E11-E	You've Lost That Lovin' Feeling('78);(I've Had)The Time Of My Life('87)
E-E11-A/E	Take Me To The Pilot('69); Country Road('71)
EM7-E11	Never Can Say Goodbye('71)
E11-E	Suite: Judy Blue Eyes('69); Rocky Mountain Way('73)
A11/E-E	Wild Thing('66)
B11-B	She's Gone('76)
C#m-C#11	Ridin' The Storm Out('73); Doctor Wu('74); We Are The Champions('78); I Can't Tell You Why('80); Waiting For A Girl Like You('81); Relax('85)
C#m-C#11-A/C#-C#11	What About Love('85)
C#m7-C#11	What's Love Got To Do With It('84)
C#11-C#m7-C#11	Long Train Runnin'('73)

Minor Cliché

Em-Em(M7)-Em7-Em6	Michelle('66); How Can I Be Sure('67)
F#m-F#m7-F#m7b5	Seasons In The Sun('74)
F#m-F#m(M7)-F#m-F#m(M7)	I Just Called To Say I Love You('84)
F#m-C#+/F#-F#m7	The Guitar Man('72)
F#m-F#m(M7)-F#m7	Elenore('68)
F#m-F#m(M7)-F#m7-F#m6	That's Amore('53); Y.M.C.A('79)
G#m-G#m(M7)-G#m7	And Your Bird Can Sing('66)
G#m-G#m(M7)-G#m7-G#m6	Got To Get You Into My Life('76)
Bm/E-Bm(M7)/E-Bm7/E-E7b9	God Bless' The Child('41)

C#m-C#m6-C#m7-C#m6	Those Were The Days('68)
C#m-C#m(M7)-C#m7	A Taste Of Honey('60); Chim Chim Cheree('63); Cabaret('66); This Masquerade('76)
C#m-C#m(M7)-C#m7-C#m6	My Funny Valentine('37); More('63); Music To Watch Girls By('67); Summer Rain('68); A Beautiful Morning('68); Cry Baby Cry('68); What Are You Doing The Rest Of Your Life('69); Time In A Bottle('73); Feelings('75); She Believes In Me('79)
C#m(M7)-C#m	Harlem Nocturne('66)
C#m(M7)-C#m7-C#m6-C#m	Copacabanna('78)

"E" Chord Variations

E/F#-F#	What's Love Got To Do With It('84)
E/B-F#m7/B	Rainy Days And Mondays('71)
Am/B-B11-E/B-F#7/B	Takin' It To The Streets('76)
B-E5/B	Doctor Robert('66)
B11-E/B-B	Celebration('81)

"F#" Chord Variations

E-F#m/E	Oh How Happy('66); Only The Strong Survive('69); Rock 'N' Roll Heaven('74)
E-F#m/E-Em7-F#m/E	Living In The City('73)
E-F#m/E	The Sun Ain't Gonna Shine Anymore('66); Hurting Each Other('72); Laughter In The Rain('75)
E-F#m/E-E-Bm7/E	Sing('73)
E-F#m/E-EM7	Baby, I'm-A Want You('71)
E-F#m/E-E11-F#m/E	Precious And Few('72)
E-F#m/E-G/E-F#m/E	Whipping Post('70)
E-F#m11/E-EM7-F#m11/E	Melissa('74)
E-F#/E	The Lights Are On('79)
E-F#/E-F#m/E-E	Only Women Bleed('75); Evergreen('76)
E-F#/E	Temptation Eyes('71)
E-F#/E-Aadd9/E-E	Wedding Song(There Is Love)('71)
E-F#/E-Am6/E-E	Can't Take My Eyes Off Of You('67)
E-E11-F#m/E	Lightnin' Strikes('66); Feels Like The First Time('77)
E6-F#m/E	Fool On The Hill('68)

E6-F#o/E	Nights Are Forever Without You('76)
EM7-F#m7/E	Leaving On A Jet Plane('69); Make It With You('70); Day By Day('71); Beginnings('71)
EM7-F#/E	You Are Everything('72)
EM7-Em7-F#/E-F/E-E	Never Can Say Goodbye('71)
Eadd9-F#/E-A6/E-Eadd9	Eight Days A Week('65)-Intro
Eadd9-F#9/E	Tonight('56)
Eadd9-EM9-E9-F#m/E	If('71)
F#m-F#m7	Little Green Apples('68)
F#m/B-G#m/B-F#m/B	I'll Play For You('75)
F#m/E-E-Bm7/E-A/E	Hurting Each Other('72)
F#m7/B-B	Uncle Alber/Admiral Halsey('71)
F#m7/B-B7	Spill The Wine('70)
F#m7/B-B9	Welcome Back('76)
F#-F#m	Sealed With A Kiss('62); She's Not There('64)
F#-F#m7-F#m7/B-B	My Little Town('75)
F#-B/F#	Closer To You('76)
F#-Bm/F#	You Are Everything('72)
F#/C#-A#m/C#	What Becomes Of The Broken-Hearted('66)
C#m-F#m/C#-C#11-C#m	Lady('80)
C#5-C#11-C#m7-F#/C#	Head Games('79)
C#m-C#11-C#m-F#/C#-C#m	The Night The Lights Went Out In Georgia('73)
C#m-C#m7-F#/C#-C#m	This Diamond Ring('65)
C#m7-F#/C#-F#m/C#-C#m	Wait('65)
C#m7-F#/C#-A/C#-C#m7	Fly Like An Eagle('77)
C#m7-C#11-F#/C#-C#	Take The Long Way Home('79)

"G" Chord Variations

E-G/E-A/E-E	I Can See For Miles('67)
E-G/E-A/E-G/E	Wake Up Little Susie('57);(I Know)I'm Losing You('66)
E-GM7/E-A/E-E	No Time('70)
Em-G/E-A/E-[D]-Em	School's Out('72)

"G#" Chord Variations

C#m-G#m/C#-A/C#-E/C#	In The Air Tonight('81)
C#m-G#m7/C#-C#11-A/C#	Don't Lose My Number('85)

"A" Chord Variations

E-A/E — Side By Side('27); Mona Lisa('49); Mystery Train('55); April Come She Will('65); I Got You Babe('65); She's Just My Style('66); Gimme Some Lovin'('67); Cry Like A Baby('68); Everday People('69); I've Got A Feeling('70); I Just Can't Help Believin''('70); Baby Don't Get Hooked On Me('71); Tiny Dancer('71); Jet('74); Then Came You('74); Send In The Clowns('75); Lyin' Eyes('75); Desiree('78); Little Jeannie('80); Start Me Up('81); Like A Rock('86)

E-A/E-E — I Got You Babe('65); I Am A Rock('66); Rain('66); Mother Nature's Son('68); Both Sides Now('68); In The Ghetto('69); Bridge Over Troubled Water('70); Listen To The Music('72); Operator(That's Not The Way I Feel)('72); Longfellow Serenade('74); Junior's Farm('74); Don't Go Breaking My Heart('76); The Gambler('78); Footloose('84); Forever Young('88)

E-A/E-E-F#m/E — Love The One You're With('70)

E-A/E-Eadd9-A/E — Come Sail Away('78)

E-A/E-E7-E — Baby You're A Rich Man('67)

E-A/E-E7-A/E — Boy From New York City('65); Mercy, Mercy, Mercy('67)

E-A/E-Em7-A/E — Lonesome Loser('79)

E-A/E-F#m/E-E — (Your Love Keeps Lifting Me)Higher And Higher('67)

E-A/E-Am6/E-E — Lonely Stranger('92)

E-A/E-B/E-E — Goodbye To Love('72); Closer To You('76); Sometimes When We Touch('78)

E-A/E-B/E-A/E — Your Song('70)

E-A/E-B/E-A/E-Am/E — Up Where We Belong('82)

E-A/E-B7/E-E — You Needed Me('78)

E-A/E-D/E-B/E — We Built This City('85)

E-A6/E — Come See About Me('64); Laughter In The Rain('74)

E-A6/E-E — Boom, Boom('62)

E-A6/E-E6 — What Now My Love('66)

E-A(6/9)/E — She Talks To Angels('91)

E-AM9/E-Am9/E-E	I Just Can't Help Believin'('70)
E-Am/E	You Make Me Feel Brand New('74); Even The Nights Are Better ('82)
E-Am/E-E	All By Myself('76)
E-EM7-A6/E	I Just Can't Help Believing('70)
E-Em7-A/E-E	Mother Nature's Son('68)
E5-A/E-E5-Aadd4/E	All Right Now('70)
E5-A/E-D/E-E5	Hollywood Nights('78)
EM7-A/E	How Can You Mend A Broken Heart('71); I'll Play For You('75)
EM7-E11-A6/E-E	Diary('72)
Eadd9-A/E	Free Man In Paris('74)
Eadd9-EM7-A/E	Imagine('71)
A/E-E	Running On Empty('78); All Out Of Love('80); Boulevard('80)
A6/E-E	Blue On Blue('63)
A11/E-E	Wild Thing('66)
C#m-A/C#-C#m7-C#+	Cry Me A River('53)
C#m-A/C#-C#11	Head Games('79)
C#m-A/C#-C#11-C#m	Eye Of The Tiger('82)
C#m-C#11-A/C#-C#11	In The Air Tonight('81)
C#m7-C#m6-A/C#-C#m	Eleanor Rigby('66)
C#-C#11-A/C#-C#11	Hello-Hurray('73)

"B" Chord Variations

E-B/E	Looks Like We Made It('77); Jack And Diane('82)
E-B/E-A/E	Babe('79)
E-B/E-A/E-E	Substitute('66); You Don't Bring Me Flowers('78); Time Passages('78)
E-B/E-A/E-Am6/E	Up Where We Belong('82)
E-B/E-A/E-B/E	Can't Get It Out Of My Head('75); We've Got Tonight('78); The One That You Love('81)
E-B7/E-E	Groovy Kind Of Love('66)
E-Bm/E	Taxi('72); Vision Of Love('90)

F#-B/F#	Closer To You('76)
A-B/A	Here Comes My Girl('79)
B/E-E	Never Be The Same('80)
B/E-A/E	Everybody Wants To Rule The World('85)

"C" Chord Variations

A-C/A-D/A	You Ain't Seen Nothin' Yet('74)

"C#" Chord Variations

E-E+-C#m/E-E+-E	(Just Like)Starting Over('80)
E/C#-D#/C#-D/C#-C#m	Wishing You Were Here('74)

"D" Chord Variations

E-D/E-A/E	Get Back('69)
E-E11-E-DM7/E	The Way You Make Me Feel('88)
E-Dadd9/E	Helplessly Hoping('69)

"D#" Chord Variations

The "E/C#" and "C#m7" chords share the same notes.

C#m-D#m/C#-E/C#-D#m/C#	Long Time Gone('68)
C#m-D#m/C#-C#m7-D#m/C#	Along Comes Mary('66); Billie Jean('83)

Substitute Chord Progressions

Any of the common chord progressions listed below can be used in place of the other listed chord progression. Let your ears tell you which substitute chord progression sounds best for use with any particular song. Examples of how substitute chord progressions may be used are shown after the Substitution Chord Progression listing.

Chord Progression	*Progression Type*
E-A E-F#m E-E+-A-A#o E-G#7#5-A-A#o	Basic
E-B7	Folk
E-A-B7	Rock
E-C#m-A-B7 E-G#m-A-B7	Rock Ballad
E-C#m-F#m-B7 E-E6-F#m-B7 E-G#m-F#m-B7 E-G#m-Gm-F#m-B7 E-G#m-Go-F#m-B7 E-F#m-B7	Standard
E-C#7-F#7-B7 E-F#7-B7	Ragtime
E-Fo-F#m-B7 E-Fo-F#m-Go E-G7-F#m-B7	Fo Cliché

E-Go-F#m-B7   Go Cliché

Substitute Chord Progression Examples

E———B7	Original Progression for *Auld Lang Syne*
E-C#m-F#m-B7	Substitute Chord Progression for the first two bars of the verse
E———A	Original progression for *Dixieland*
E-C#m-F#m-Go	Substitute chord progression for the first two bars of the verse
E———F#7-B7	Original progression for *Oh Susanna*
E-C#m-F#m-B7	Substitute chord progression for the first two bars of the verse
EM7-F#m7-G#m7-C#m7	
E-C#m-F#m7-B11	Substitute chord progression similar to James Taylor's recording in the early 1970's.
E-E6—-F#m-B7	Original progression for *I Got Rhythm*
E-C#m-F#m-B7	Common Substitution for the first two bars of the verse
E———A—-B	Substitute chord progression similar to The Happenings 1967 hit recording
E-G#m-Go-F#m-B7	Original progression for *Smoke Gets In Your Eyes*
E-C#m——F#m-B7	Substitute chord progression for first two bars of the verse
E-C#m-F#m-B7	Original progression for *Ain't Misbehavin'*
E-Fo——F#m-Go	Similar to Luther Henderson's Substitution for the first two bars of the verse
E-C#m—-F#m—-B7	Original progression for *Heart And Soul*
E-C#m7—F#m7--B7	Chord Quality Substitution for the first two bars of the verse
E-G#m-Gm-F#m-B7	Substitute chord progression for the first two bars of the verse
E————F#m-B7	Another substitute chord progression
E-E6————F#m-B7	And another substitute chord progression

Turnarounds

Blues Turnarounds

The last two bars of a Blues Chord Progression are known as the Turnaround. Twelve common Turnarounds shown below may be substituted for each other based on the preference of the song-writer or performer. As with any chord progression, the quality of any of the chords in these Turnarounds may be changed to their Major, Minor, or Dominant 7th quality. The most common substitutions in Blues Progressions are to change the "E" and "A" chords to "E7","E9","A7", or "A9." Also, any of the first or last bars shown below can be substituted for each other. For example, you could combine the "E-E7-A-Am" first bar with the "E-A#7-B7" last bar.

```
E                                       E       B7
/       /       /       /               /       /       /       /
E                                       E       C7 B7
/       /       /       /               /       /       /       /
E                                       E       A#7 B7
/       /       /       /               /       /       /       /
E                                       E       A7 A#7 B7
/       /       /       /               /       /       /       /
E       E7/D    E6/C#   E+/C            E/B     B7
/       /       /       /               /       /       /       /
E               A                       E       B7
/       /       /       /               /       /       /       /
E               A                       E       B+
/       /       /       /               /       /       /       /
E       E7      A       Am              E       B7
/       /       /       /               /       /       /       /
E       E7/D    A/C#    Am/C            E/B     B7
/       /       /       /               /       /       /       /
E       E7      A       C7              E       B7
/       /       /       /               /       /       /       /
E       E7/G#   A       C/A#            E/B     B7
/       /       /       /               /       /       /       /
E       E7/D    A/C#    C7              E       B7
/       /       /       /               /       /       /       /
```

Jazz/Standard Turnarounds

The last two bars of a phrase or verse before it is repeated are referred to as the Turnaround. A sampling of interchangeable Turnarounds are shown below. The most common Turnarounds are the "E-C#m7-F#m7-B7" and "E-F#m7-B7" progressions and their substitute chord progressions as shown in the Substitute Chord Progression section of the Appendix. Remember that each chord in the turnaround can be substituted for its Major, Minor, or Dominant 7th quality. The most frequent chord substitutions are the "M7" and "m7". Twelve examples of Basic and Embellished Jazz/Standard Turnarounds are shown below.

Basic Turnaround   *Embellishment Examples*

E-   C#m- F#m-B7   EM7-C#m7-F#m7-B7   E6-Fo-F#m7-B7b5
                       EM7-E6-F#m7-F#m6   E6-Go-F#m7-B7b5
                       EM7-C#m7-F#m7-F7b5   E-Go-F#m7-B9
/ /   / /   / /   / / E-C#m-A-B11   E-G#o-F#m7-B7

E-   C#7- F#m-B7   EM7-C#7-F#m7-B7
                       E6-C#7#9-F#m7-B7   E-G13-F#m7b5-B7#9
/ /   / /   / /   / / E6-C#9-F#m7-B7b9   EM7-G9-F#m7-B7#5b9

E-   C#7- F#7- B7   E-G7-C7-B7   E-C#7-F#9-B7
/ /   / /   / /   / / E-G7/D-C7-B7   EM7-GM7-CM7-B7
                       EM7-G13-CM7-B13   EM7-G13-CM7-FM7
                       E-G13-CM7-B7sus4   E-G13-F#m7-B7b5/F

E-   F#m- B7   E-A6-C7-B7   E-EM7-F#m7-B11
/ /   / /   / /   / / E-F#m11-F7b5

E-   F#7- B7
/ /   / /   / /   / /

E-   B7   E-B9
/ /   / /   / /   / / E-B+

E7- D#7- D7- C#7   E9-D#9-D9-C#9
 /   /   /   /   E13-D#13-D13-C#13

GM7-CM7-FM7-F#m7-B7
/ /   / /   / /   /   /

G#m-C#m-F#m-B7
/ /   / /   / /   / /

G#m-C#7- F#m- B7
/ /   / /   / /   / /

G#7-C#7- F#m- B7
/ /   / /   / /   / /

G#7- C#7- F#7- B7
/ /   / /   / /   / /

G#m7-C#m7-F#m7-B7
G#m-Gm7-F#m7-B7

G#m-C#7-F#m-B9
G#m-G7-F#m-F7

G#7-C#7-F#m7-B7

G#7#5-C#9-F#7#5-B9
G#7b13-C#9-F#7b13-B9

G#m-Go-F#m-F7
G#o/D-C#m7-F#7-B7

G#m7-G7-F#m7-B7
G#m7-C#7-F#m7-F7

Endings

There are two commonly used Endings. The first, the Fade Out, is generally only available for pre-recorded music. The second is to end cold on a specific chord or sequence of chords giving the feeling of finality. Several examples of this type of ending which are appropriate for live performances are shown below.

E
C7-B7-E

E6
E-F#m7-Fo-E6

EM7
E-EM7
FM7-EM7
G6-F#7-FM7-EM7

E6/9
E-CM7-FM7-E6/9

E7
E-E7-A-Am-E-E7(Blues)
E-A7-C7-E-E7(Blues)

E9
F9-E9
E-D#9-E9
E-D9-Eb9-E9

E13

F#

C#

F#-EM7-D#

Transposing

In order to play a particular song in a different key it is necessary to transpose the individual chords in a progression from the key they are written in to the new key. An easy way to change chords from one key to another is to use the Transposing Chart shown below.

The first step in transposing is to determine the key of the song you want to change. All the chord progressions in this book are presented in the key of "E". Otherwise, to determine the key a song was written in you need to look at the beginning of the written music to determine the number of sharps(#) or flats(b) that are shown. The chart directly below tells you the key the song was written in by the number of sharps or flats shown in the sheet music. If there are no sharps or flats, the song is in the key of "C". If for example the written music shows two flats, the song is in the key of "Bb".

Key of F=one flat   Key of G=One Sharp

Key of Bb=two flats   Key of D=Two sharps

Key of Eb=Three flats   Key of A=Three sharps

Key of Ab=four flats   Key of E=Four sharps

Key of Db=five flats   Key of B=Five sharps

Key of Gb=Six flats   Key of F#=Six sharps

Key of Cb=Seven flats   Key of C#=Seven sharps

By way of an example, let's transpose the Standard "E-C#m-F#m-B7" Changes in the key of "E" to the key of "C." First you need to find the "E" in the far left hand column. This row lists all the chords in the key of "E." Now find the "C" in the same far left hand column. This row has all the corresponding chords in the key of "C." Now find the "E" chord in the key of "E" row and the corresponding chord in the same column in the key of "C" row. So, the "E" chord in the key of "E" is transposed to a "C" chord in the key of "C." Next find the "C#" in the key of "E" column and the corresponding chord in the key of "C" which is "A." So a "C#m" chord in the key of "E" transposes to an "Am" chord in the key of "C." Continuing the process you will see that the "E-C#m-F#m-B7" progression in the key of "E" transposes to the "C-Am-Dm-G7" progression in the key of "C".

Transposing Chart

I	IIm	IIIm	IV	V7	VIm	VIIm
E F	F#	G G#	A A#	B C	C#	D D#
F F#	G	G# A	A# B	C C#	D	D# E
G G#	A	A# B	C C#	D D#	E	F F#
A A#	B	C C#	D D#	E F	F#	G G#
C C#	D	D# E	F F#	G G#	A	A# B
D D#	E	F F#	G G#	A A#	B	C C#

A quick and easy way to change the key of a song on a standard tuned guitar is to use a capo. As all the progressions in this book are in the key of "E", a capo across the first fret of the guitar will change the key to "F". Below is a quick reference chart to determine which fret the capo would need to be placed across to change to that key:

Fret	Key
1	F
2	F#
3	G
4	G#
5	A
6	A#
7	B

Guitar Chord Chart

The suggested guitar chord fingerings are those commonly used for rhythm guitar. The six numbers and/or letters represent the finger location to be used to play the chord indicated by the Chord Symbol on a Standard Tuned guitar(E-A-D-G-B-E). The common first position "C" chord would be indicated as x32010 while the "C" Bar Chord would be shown as 8aa988. The "x" means do not play that string and "0" means play the open string. The tenth fret is indicated as "a", the eleventh as "b", the twelfth as "c", and so on up the fret board. All chords, unless indicated by a slash, are chords with the Root on the lowest string played.

Major "E" Chords

Symbols	*Notes*	*Fingerings*			
	1 3 5 6 7 9				
E	E-G#-B	022100	076454	x7999x	076400
		0x999x			
E/G#	E-G#-B	4x2400	4x245x	xb999x	
E/A	E-G#-B-A	x02100	x0999x		
E/B	E-G#-B	x22100	7x999x		

The E5 chord is referred to as a Power Chord.

E5	E- B	022x00	02245x	022400	079900
		0x9900	022xxx		

The E6 chord has the same notes as the C#m7 chord. The E6 chord is sometimes referred to as E/C#.

E6	E-G#-B-C#	022120	04210x	0x6600	0x9999
		cxbdcx			
E/C#	E-G#-B-C#	x42100	x46454	9x999x	

Chord	Notes			Fingerings			
E6/G#	E-G#-B-C#			4x242x			

The EM7 chord has the same notes, except C#, as the C#m9 chord and the same notes, except E, as the G#m.

Chord	Notes			Fingerings			
EM7	E-G#-B-	D#		021100	022444	02x144	0x6444
				076444	066400	076800	079897
				0x9890	0x999b	0x6800	
EM7/G#	E-G#-B-	D#		4x2444			
EM7/B	E-G#-B-	D#		x22444			
E/D#	E-G#-B-	D#		xx1100	x66454		

The G#m7 chord has the same notes, except E, as the EM9 chord.

Chord	Notes			Fingerings		
EM9	E-G#-B-	D#-F#		0x4444	099800	x7687x

The "E+" chord has the same notes as the "G#+" and the "C+" chords and has the same notes as C#m(M7) chord except C# and G#7#5 chord except F#.

Chord	Notes		Fingerings		
E+	E-G#-C		03211x	x7655x	0x655x
E+/C	E-G#-C		x3211x	x3x554	

The Esus chord is also referred to as Esus4.

Chord	Notes			Fingerings			
Esus	E-A- B			022200	002200		
Esus4/2	E-A- B-		F#	022252			
Eadd9	E-G#-B-		F#	024100	09999x	0x4454	0x2102
				022102			
E/F#	E-G#-B-		F#	2x2100			
Eadd#9	E-G#-B-		G	076000			
E6/9	E-G#-B-C#-		F#	0x6677	02x122		
E(6/9)/G#	E-G#-B-C#-		F#	4x2422			

Dominant 7th "E" Chords

	1 3 5 b7 9 11 13				
E7	E-G#-B- D	022130 x79797	020100 0x999a	022434	x7675x
E7/G#	E-G#-B- D	4x0430	4x0400		
E7/B	E-G#-B- D	x20100	x22434	7x675x	
E/D	E-G#-B- D	xx0100	ax999x	x5x454	
E7(no3)	E- B- D	050400			
E7sus4	E-A- B- D	020200 x797ax	020230 0x99aa	02223x	077700
E7sus4/6	E-A- B- D-C#	0402xx			

The E7b5 chord has the same notes as the A#7b5 chord.

E7b5	E-G#-Bb- D	0x2334	6x6750		
E7#5	E-G#-C- D	0x011x			
E7#5/b9	E-G#-C- D-F	0x0111	x76768		
E7#5/#9	E-G#-C- D-G	x76788			

The Do, Fo, G#o, and Bo chords have the same notes, except E, as the E7b9.

E7b9	E-G#-B- D-F	x7676x	02x131	0x6767	0x676x
E7b9/#11	E-G#-B- D-F-A#	x76766	0x6766		
E7#9	E-G#-B- D-G	x7678x	02x133		

The Bm6 chord has the same notes, except E, as the E9 chord.

E9	E-G#-B- D-F#	02x132 0x6777	020102	024130	x76777

Chord	Notes		Fingerings			
E9/G#	E-G#-B-	D-F#	4x2432	4x6777		
E9b5	E-G#-Bb-	D-F#	x7x776	x76776		

The G#7b5 and D7b5 chords have the same notes, except E, as the E9#5 chord.

Chord	Notes		Fingerings			
E9#5	E-G#-C-	D-F#	x76778			
E9#11	E-G#-B-	D-F#-A#	01x332	0x6776	x7x776	

The E11 chord is the same as the Bm7/E chord.

Chord	Notes		Fingerings			
E11	E-G#-B-	D-F#-A	077777	022232		
E13	E-G#-B-	D-F#-A-C#	x76779	0x6779		
E13b9	E-G#-B-	D-F-A-C#	1x0120	0x6769		
E13(b5/b9)/Bb	E-G#-Bb-	D-F-A-C#	68x799			

Minor "E" Chords

1 b3 5 6 b7 9 11

Chord	Notes		Fingerings			
Em	E-G-B		022000 x79987	022003	075000	0x5450
Em/B	E-G-B		x22000			
Em(add2)/B	E-G-B-	F#	x24000			
Em/C	E-G-B C		x32000			
Em(add2)/C	E-G-B- C F#		x34000			
Em(add2)/C#	E-G-B-	F#	x44000			

The Em6 chord has the notes as the C#m7b5 chord and has the same notes, except A, as the A9 chord.

Chord	Notes	Fingerings			
Em6	E-G-B-C#	022020 0xbccc	04545x	045000	042000
Em/C#	E-G-B-C#	x42000			

Em6/9	E-G-B-C#- F#	022022	0abb00		

The Em7 chord has the same notes as the G6 chord.

Em7	E-G-B- D	020000	022030	055000	020030
		022033	0x2433	x79787	0xcccc
		0acc00	075700		

Em7/G	E-G-B- D	3x0000	3x243x		

Em7/B	E-B-G- D	x20000	7x575x		

Em/D	E-G-B- D	x55430	x55400		

The Em7b5 chord has the same notes as the Gm6 chord.

Em7b5	E-G-Bb- D	0x2333	01203x	x7878x	0x878x

The GM7 chord has the same notes, except E, as the Em9 chord.

Em9	E-G-B- D-F#	020002	022032	024000	024030
		054000	0x5777	x75777	

Em(M7)	E-G-B- D#	021000	0x2443	065000	x79887

Em11	E-G-B- D- A	022233	x7x785		

Diminished "E" Chords

1 b3 5 b7

The Eo chord has the same notes as the Go, the A#o, and the C#o chords.

Eo	E-G-A#-C#	012020	0x2323	x7x686

Eo/G	E-G-A#-C#	3x232x		

Major "F#" Chords

1 3 5 6 7 9

F#	F#-A#-C#	244322	x98676	x9bbbx

F#/A#	F#-A#-C#	6x467x			
F#5	F#- C#	244xxx			

The F#6 chord has the same notes as the D#m7 chord.
F#6	F#-A#-C#-D#	24x342	2x132x	

The F#M7 chord has the same notes, except D#, as the D#m9 chord.
F#M7	F#-A#-C#- F	2x332x	24x366	x98666
F#M9	F#-A#-C#- F-G#	x96666	x98a9x	

The A#m7 chord has the same notes, except F#, as the F#M9 chord.
F#+	F#-A#-D	xx4332	x9877x

The F#+ chord has the same notes as the D+ and A#+ chords.
F#sus	F#-B-C#	2444xx	24x422	224422
F#add9	F#-A#-C#- G#	xx4324		
F#6/9	F#-A#-C#-D#- G#	211122	24x344	x98899

Dominant 7th "F#" Chords

                                        1 3 5 b7 9 11 13

F#7	F#-A#-C#-E	242322	242352	2x232x	xx4320
F#/E	F#-A#-C#-E	044320			
F#7/C#	F#-A#-C#-E	x44320			
F#7sus4	F#-B- C#-E	242422			

The F#7b5 chord has the same notes as the C7b5 chord.
F#7b5	F#-A#-C-E	2x2310	
F#7#5	F#-A#-D-E	2x233x	

The C#o, A#o, Eo, and Go chords have the same notes, except F#, as the F#7b9 chord.

F#7b9	F#-A#-C#-E-G	x9898x
F#7(b9/#11)	F#-A#-C#-E-G-C	x98988
F#7#9	F#-A#-C#-E-A	24x355

The C#m6 chord has the same notes, except F#, as the F#9 chord.

F#9	F#-A#-C#-E-G#	242324	x98999
F#9/A#	F#-A#-C#-E-G#	6x8999	
F#9b5	F#-A#-C-E-G#	x98998	

The A#7b5 and E7b5 chords have the same notes, except F#, as the F#9#5 chord.

F#9#5	F#-A#-D-E-G#	2x2334	
F#9#11/E	F#-A#-C#-E-G#-C	cxbddx	
F#9#11/G#	F#-A#-C#-E-G#-C	444556	
F#11	F#-A#-C#-E-G#-B	2x2100	x99999
F#13	F#-A#-C#-E-G#-B-D#	2x2344	x9899b
F#13b9/G	F#-A#-C#-E-G-B-D#	3x234x	x9898b
F#13(b5/b9)/C	F#-A#-C-E-G-B-D#	8ax9bb	

Minor "F#" Chords

1   b3   5   6   b7   9   11

F#m	F#-A-C#	244222	x979ax	x9bba9
F#m/A	F#-A-C#	x0x222	x04222	5x46xx

The F#m6 chord has the same notes as the D#m7b5 chord and has the same notes, except B, as the B9 chord.

F#m6	F#-A-C#-D#	2x1222

F#m6/A	F#-A-C#-D#	5x464x			

The F#m7 chord has the same notes as the A6 chord.

F#m7	F#-A-C#- E	2x2222	242222	2xx220	x9b9a9
F#m/E	F#-A-C#- E	0x2222	0x7670		
F#m7/A	F#-A-C#- E	5x465x			

The F#m7b5 chord has the same notes as the Am6 chord.

F#m7b5	F#-A-C- E	2x2210	x9x9a8

The AM7 chord has the same notes, except F#, as the F#m9 chord.

F#m9	F#-A-C#- E-G#	2x2224	242224	x97999
F#m(M7)	F#-A-C#- F	243222		
F#m11	F#-A-C#- E- B	2x2200		
F#m11/E	F#-A-C#- E- B	044200		

The F#m7/B chord has the same notes, except D#, as the B11 chord.

F#m7/B	F#-A-C#- E- B	x22222

Diminished "F#" Chords

1 b3 5 b7

The F#o chord has the same notes as the Ao, the Co, and the D#o chords.

F#o	F#-A-C-D#	2x121x	
F#o/C	F#-A-C-D#	x3x242	x3424x

Major "G#" Chords

1 3 5 6 7 9

G#	G#-C-D#	466544	43111x

G#/C	G#-C-D#	x3111x	

G#5	G#- D#	466xxx	

The G#6 chord has the same notes as the Fm7 chord.

G#6	G#-C-D#-F	46x564	4x354x

The G#M7 chord has the same notes, except F, as the Fm9 chord.

G#M7	G#-C-D#- G	4x554x	46x588

The Cm7 chord has the same notes, except G#, as the G#M9 chord.

G#M9	G#-C-D#- G-A#	xb8888

The G#+ chord has the same notes as the C+ and E+ chords.

G#+	G#-C-E	xx6554

G#+/C	G#-C-E	x3211x

G#sus	G#-C#-D#	4666xx	446644

G#add9	G#-C#-D#- A#	xx6546

G#6/9	G#-C-D#-F- A#	46x566

Dominant 7th "G#" Chords

                                                                   1   3   5   b7   9   11   13

G#7	G#-C-D#-F#	464544	46x57x	4x45xx

G#7/D#	G#-C-D#-F#	x64544

G#7sus4	G#-C#-D#-F#	464644

The G#7b5 chord has the same notes as the D7b5 chord.

G#7b5	G#-C-D-F#	4x453x

The E+ chord has the same notes, except F#, as the G#7#5 chord.

G#7#5	G#-C-E-F#	4x455x

The F#o, D#o, Ao and Co chords have the same notes, except G#, as the G#7b9 chord.

G#7b9	G#-C-D#-F#-A	4x45x5 4x4545 xbabax
G#7(b9/#11)	G#-C-D#-F#-A-D	xbabaa
G#7#9	G#-C-D#-F#-B	46x577

The D#m6 chord has the same notes, except G#, as the G#9 chord.

G#9	G#-C-D#-F#-A#	xbabbb
G#9b5	G#-C-D-F#-A#	xbabba

The C7b5 and F#7b5 chords have the same notes, except G#, as the G#9#5 chord.

G#9#5	G#-C-E-F#-A#	4x4556
G#9#11/A#	G#-C-D#-F#-A#-D	666778
G#11	G#-C-D#-F#-A#-C#	4x432x
G#13	G#-C-D#-F#-A#-C#-F	4x4566
G#13b9	G#-C-D#-F#-A-C#-F	xbabad
G#13b9/A	G#-C-D#-F#-A-C#-F	5x456x

Minor "G#" Chords

                       1 b3 5 6 b7 9 11

G#m	G#-B-D#	466444

The G#m6 chord has the same notes as the Fm7b5 chord and the same notes, except C#, as the C#9 chord.

G#m6	G#-B-D#-F	4x3444

The G#m7 chord has the same notes as the B6 chord.

G#m7	G#-B-D#- F#	4x4444 464444

G#m7/D#	G#-B-D#- F#	x64444	

The G#m7b5 chord has the same notes as the Bm6 chord.

G#m7b5	G#-B-D- F#	4x443x	
G#m7b5/D	G#-B-D- F#	x5443x	
G#m7#5	G#-B-E- F#	4x445x	

The BM7 chord has the same notes, except G#, as the G#m9 chord.

G#m9	G#-B-D#- F#-A#	4x4446	464446
G#m(M7)	G#-B-D#- G	465444	4x544x
G#m11	G#-B-D#- F#- C#	4x442x	

Diminished "G#" Chords

1 b3 5 b7

The G#o chord has the same notes as the Bo, the Do, and the Fo chords.

G#o	G#-B-D-F	4x343x
G#o/F	G#-B-D-F	1x010x

Major "A" Chords

1 3 5 6 7 9

A	A-C#-E	x02220	577655		
A/C#	A-C#-E	x4222x			
A/E	A-C#-E	0x222x	04222x	0x765x	

The A/D chord has the same notes, except F#, as the DM9 chord.

A/D	A-C#-E-D	x57655	xx0220		
A5	A- E	577xxx	x022xx	x022x0	x02255

Chord	Notes	Fingerings			
A(b5)/E	A-C#-E-D#	x7764x			

The A6 chord has the same notes as the F#m7 chord.

Chord	Notes	Fingerings			
A6	A-C#-E-F#	x02222	x0465x	5x465x	57x675
A/F#	A-C#-E-F#	2x222x			

The AM7 chord has the same notes, except F#, as the F#m9 chord and the same notes as the C#m/A chord.

Chord	Notes	Fingerings			
AM7	A-C#-E-G#	x0212x	x066x0	5x665x	x06654
		x0ede0	X02224		
A/G#	A-C#-E-G#	4x222x			

The C#m7 chord has the same notes, except A, as the AM9 chord.

Chord	Notes	Fingerings			
AM9	A-C#-E-G#-B	x02100	x09999	5x6600	x06600
AM9/B	A-C#-E-G#-B	x22224			

The A+ chord has the same notes as the C#+ and the Fo+ chords.

Chord	Notes	Fingerings		
A+	A-C#-F	x0322x	x0766x	
Asus	A-D-E	x02230	5777xx	557755

The Aadd9 chord is sometimes referred to as Asus2 or Aadd2.

Chord	Notes	Fingerings		
Aadd9	A-C#-E-B	x02200	x07600	577600
Aadd9(D#)	A-C#-E-B-C#	x07800		
A6/9	A-C#-E-F#-B	x22222	57x677	
A6/9/E	A-C#-E-F#-B	044200	022222	
A6(no3)	A-E-F#-B	x04200		

Dominant 7th "A" Chords

1 3 5 b7 9 11 13

Chord	Notes	Fingerings			
A7	A-C#-E-G	x02020	x02023	575655	57x68x

Chord	Notes	Fingerings			
A/G	A-C#-E-G#	3x222x			
A7(no3)	A- E-G	x05050			
A7sus4	A-D-E-G	x02030	x05x30	575755	
A7sus4/6	A-D-E-G-F#	x04030	x02032		

The A7b5 has the same notes as the D#7b5 chord.

Chord	Notes	Fingerings			
A7b5	A-C#-D#-G	5x564x			
A7#5	A-C#-F-G	x03223	5x566x		
A7(#5/b9)	A-C#-F-G-A#	5x5666			

The A#o, C#o, Eo, and Go chords have the same notes, except A, as the A7b9 chord.

Chord	Notes	Fingerings			
A7b9	A-C#-E-G-A#	5x5656	x05656		
A7#9	A-C#-E-G-C	57x688			
A9	A-C#-E-G-B	x02000	x05600	5x5600	575657
		x0bccc			
A9/E	A-C#-E-G-B	075600			
A9b5	A-C#-D#-G-B	x0bccb			

The C#7b5 and G7b5 chords have the same notes, except A, as the A9#5 chord.

Chord	Notes	Fingerings			
A9#5	A-C#-F-G-B	5x5667	x0bccd		
A9#11	A-C#-E-G-B-D#	x02443			
A9#11/B	A-C#-E-G-B-D#	777889			
A11	A-C#-E-G-B-D	x00000	5x543x	x0cccc	
A13	A-C#-E-G-B-D-F#	x05677	5x5677		
A13b9	A-C#-E-G-A#-D-F#	x05676			

Minor "A" Chords

      1 b3 5 6 b7 9 11

Chord	Notes	Voicings
Am	A-C-E	x02210 577555
Am/C	A-C-E	x32210 x3x555

The Am6 chord has the same notes as the F#m7b5 chord and has the same notes, except D, as the D9 chord.

Chord	Notes	Voicings
Am6	A-C-E-F#	x02212 5x4555 x04555
Am6/E	A-C-E-F#	0x4555

The Am7 chord has the same notes as the C6 chord.

Chord	Notes	Voicings
Am7	A-C-E- G	x02010 575555 5x5555 x05555

The Am7b5 chord has the same notes as the Cm6 chord.

Chord	Notes	Voicings
Am7b5	A-C-D#- G	5x554x x05543

The CM7 chord has the same notes, except A, as the Am9 chord.

Chord	Notes	Voicings
Am9	A-C-E- G-B	5x5500 5x5557 575557 x05557
		x0acc0 x0accc x07500
Am(M7)	A-C-E- G#	x02110 x0655x
Am11	A-C-E- G- D	5x5530 x05530

Diminished "A" Chords

      1 b3 5 b7

The Ao chord has the same notes as the Co, D#o, and F#o chords.

Chord	Notes	Voicings
Ao	A-C-D#-F#	5x454x x04545
Ao/F#	A-C-D#-F#	2x121x

Major "B" Chords

      1 3 5 6 7 9

B	B-D#-F#	x2444x	799877		
B/E	B-D#-F#-E	0x444x	0x987x		
B/D#	B-D#-F#	xx1x02	x6444x		
B/F#	B-D#-F#	22444x			
B5	B- F#	x244xx	x2440x	799xxx	

The B6 chord has the same notes as the G#m7 chord.

B6	B-D#-F#-G#	x24444	7x687x	79x897
B/G#	B-D#-F#-G#	4x4444		

The BM7 chord has the same notes, except G#, as the G#m9 chord.

BM7	B-D#-F#- A#	x24342	7x887x	79x8bb

The D#m7 chord has the same notes, except B, as the BM9 chord.

BM9	B-D#-F#- A#-C#	x2132x	x24322

The B+ chord has the same notes as the D#+ and G+ chords.

B+	B-D#-G	x2100x
Bsus	B-E-F#	x24400 7999xx 779977
Badd9	B-D#-F#- C#	x24422 xx9879
B6/9	B-D#-F#-G#- C#	x21122 79x899

Dominant 7th "B" Chords

1 3 5 b7 9 11 13

B7	B-D#-F#-A	x21202	x24242	7x78xx	797877
		79x8ax			
B/A	B-D#-F#-A	5x444x	x0444x		

B7sus4	B-E-F#-A	x24455	x22202	x24200	x24252
		797977			

The B7b5 has the same notes as the F7b5 chord.

B7b5	B-D#-F-A	x2324x	7x786x
B7#5	B-D#-G-A	x21203	7x788x

The Co, D#o, F#o and Ao chords have the same notes, except B, as the B7b9 chord.

B7b9	B-D#-F#-A-C	x2121x	
B7#9	B-D#-F#-A-D	x2123x	79x8aa

The F#m6 chord has the same notes, except B, as the B9 chord.

B9	B-D#-F#-A-C#	x21222	7x754x
B9b5	B-D#-F-A-C#	x21221	

The D#7b5 and A7b5 chords have the same notes, except B, as the B9#5 chord

B9#5	B-D#-G-A-C#	x21223	7x7889
B9#11/C#	B-D#-F#-A-C#-F	999aab	

The F#m7/B chord has the same notes, except D#, as the B11 chord.

B11	B-D#-F#-A-C#-E	x22222	x2x220	7x7655
B13	B-D#-F#-A-C#-E-G#	x21224	x2x244	7x7899
B13sus	B-E-F#-A-C#-G#	x22224		
B13b9/C	B-D#-F#-A-C-E-G#	8x789x		

Minor "B" Chords

	1 b3 5 6 b7 9 11		
Bm	B-D-F#	x24432	799777
Bm/D	B-D-F#	x5x777	

The Bm6 chord has the same notes as the G#m7b5 chord and has the same notes, except E, as the E9 chord.
Bm6   B-D-F#-G#   x20102   7x6777

Bm6/D   B-D-F#-G#   x56777   xx0102

The Bm7 chord has the same notes as the D6 chord.
Bm7   B-D-F#- A   x24232   x2x23x   7x7777   797777

Bm/A   B-D-F#- A   x04432   x07777

Bm7(4)   B-D-E-   A   7x7700

The Bm7b5 chord has the same notes as the Dm6 chord.
Bm7b5   B-D-F-   A   x2x231   7x776x

The DM7 chord has the same notes, except B, as the Bm9 chord.
Bm9   B-D-F#- A-C#   x20222   7x7779

Bm(M7)   B-D-F#- A#   x2433x   798777

Bm11   B-D-F#- A-   E   x20230   7x775x

Bm11/A   B-D-F#- A-   E   x04430

Diminished "B" Chords

$$1 \quad b3 \quad 5 \quad b7$$

The Bo chord has the same notes as the Do, Fo, and G#o chords.
Bo   B-D-F-G#   x2x131   7x676x

Major "C#" Chords

$$1 \quad 3 \quad 5 \quad 6 \quad 7 \quad 9$$

C#   C#-F-G#   x43121   x4666x   9aab99

C#5   C#- G#   x466xx   9aaxxx

The C#6 chord has the same notes as the A#m7 chord.
C#6   C#-F-G#-A#   x4332x   x46666   9bxabx   9x8a9x

The C#M7 chord has the same notes, except A#, as the A#m9 chord.
C#M7   C#-F-G#-C   x43111   x46564   9xaa9x   9bxadd

The Fm7 chord has the same notes, except C#, as the C#M9 chord.
C#M9   C#-F-G#-C-D#   x4354x   x41111   x46544

The C#+ chord has the same notes as the F+ and the A+ chords.
C#+   C#-F-A   x4322x

C#sus   C#-F#-G#   x4667x

C#add9   C#-F-G#-D#   x46644

C#6/9   C#-F-G#-A#-D#   x43344

Dominant 7th "C#" Chords

                         1 3 5 b7 9 11 13

C#7   C#-F-G#-B   x4342x   x4646x   9x9axx

C#7sus4   C#-F#-G#-B   x4647x   9b9b99

The C#7b5 chord has the same notes as the G7b5 chord.
C#7b5   C#-F-G-B   9x9a8x

C#7b5/G   C#-F-G-B   3x342x

C#7#5   C#-F-A-B   9x9aax

The G#o, Bo, Do, and Fo chords have the same notes, except C#, as the C#7b9 chord.
C#7b9   C#-F-G#-B-D   x4343x

C#7#9   C#-F-G#-B-E   x4345x   x43100

The G#m6 chord has the same notes, except C#, as the C#9 chord.

C#9	C#-F-G#-B-D#	x43444		
C#9b5	C#-F-G-B-D#	x43443	x4x443	

The F7b5 and B7b5 chords have the same notes, except C#, as the C#9#5 chord.

C#9#5	C#-F-A-B-D#	x43445	9x9aab	
C#9#11/B	C#-F-G#-B-D#-G	7x688x		
C#11	C#-F-G#-B-D#-F#	x44444	9x987x	
C#13	C#-F-G#-B-D#-F#-A#	x43446	9x9abb	
C#13b9/D	C#-F-G#-B-D-F#-A#	ax9abx		
C#13(b5/b9)/G	C#-F-G-B-D-F#-A#	35x466		

Minor "C#" Chords

                1 b3 5 6 b7 9 11

C#m	C#-E-G#	x46654	9bb999	
C#m(add2)/G#	C#-D#-G#	4x664x		
C#m(add2)/A	C#-D#-G#-A	5x664x		
C#m(add2)/A#	C#-D#-G#-A#	6x664x		

The C#m6 chord has the same notes as the A#m7b5 chord and has the same notes, except F#, as the F#9 chord.

C#m6	C#-E-G#-A#	9x8999	x4x354	
C#m/A#	C#-E-G#-A#	6x665x	6x8999	

The C#m7 chord has the same notes as the E6 chord.

C#m7	C#-E-G#-B	x4645x	x4245	9x9999
C#m/B	C#-E-G#-B	7x9999	x2x120	7x665x

The C#m7b5 chord has the same notes as the Em6 chord.
C#m7b5   C#-E-G- B   x4545x   9x998x

C#m7#5   C#-E-A- B   x4x455   9x99ax

The EM7 chord has the same notes, except C#, as the C#m9 chord.
C#m9   C#-E-G#- B-D#   x42444   9x999b

The C#m(M7) chord has the same notes, except C#, as the E+ chord.
C#m(M7)   C#-E-G#- C   x4x554   9xa99x

C#m/C   C#-E-G#- C   x3x554

C#m11   C#-E-G#- B- F#   x44454   x4x452   9x997x

Diminished "C#" Chords

$1\ b3\ 5\ b7$

The C#o chord has the same notes as the Eo, Go, and A#o chords.
C#o   C#-E-G-A#   x4x353   9x898x   x4535x

Major "D#" Chords

$1\ \ 3\ 5\ \ 6\ 7\ \ 9$

D#   D#-G-A#   x65343   x6888x   bddcbb

D#5   D#- A#   x688xx   bddxxx

The D#6 chord has the same notes as the Cm7 chord.
D#6   D#-G-A#-C   x6554x   x68888   bxacbx

D#M7   D#-G-A#- D   xx1333   x65333   x68786   bxccbx

The Gm7 chord has the same notes, except D#, as the D#M9 chord.
D#M9   D#-G-A#- D-F   x63333   x6576x

The D#+ chord has the same notes as the G+ and B+ chords.

D#+	D#-G-B	xx100x	x6544x
D#sus	D#-G#-A#	x6889x	
D#add9	D#-G-A#-F	x68866	
D#6/9	D#-G-A#-C-F	x65566	

Dominant 7th "D#" Chords

                                   1   3   5   b7   9   11   13

D#7	D#-G-A#-C#	x6564x	x656x6	x68686	xx1323
D#7sus4	D#-G#-A#-C#	x6869x			

The D#7b5 chord has the same notes as the A7b5 chord.
D#7b5	D#-G-A-C#	x6768x
D#7#5	D#-G-B-C#	bxbccx

The Go, A#o, Eo, and C#o chords have the same notes, except D#, as the D#7b9 chord.
D#7b9	D#-G-A#-C#-E	x6565x
D#7#9	D#-G-A#-C#-F#	x6567x

The A#m6 chord has the same notes, except D#, as the D#9 chord.
D#9	D#-G-A#-C#-F	x65666
D#9b5	D#-G-A-C#-F	x65665
D#9#11	D#-G-A#-C#-F-A	x65665

The G7b5 and C#7b5 chords have the same notes, except D#, as the D#9#5 chord.
D#9#5	D#-G-B-C#-F	x65667	
D#11	D#-G-A#-C#-F-G#	x66666	
D#13	D#-G-A#-C#-F-G#-C	x65668	axabcc

D#13b9/E	D#-G-A#-C#-E-G#-C	cxbcdx			
D#13(b5/b9)/A	D#-G-A-C#-E-G#-C	57x688			

Minor "D#" Chords

1 b3 5 6 b7 9 11

D#m	D#-F#-A#	x6467x	x68876	bddbbb	

The D#m6 chord has the same notes as the Cm7b5 chord and has the same notes, except G#, as the G#9 chord.

D#m6	D#-F#-A#-C	x6x576	bxabbb		

The D#m7 chord has the same notes as the F#6 chord.

D#m7	D#-F#-A#- C#	x68676	xx1322	x6x67x	bxbbbb

The D#m7b5 chord has the same notes as the F#m6 chord.

D#m7b5	D#-F#-A- C#	xx1222	x6767x	x6x675	

The F#M7 chord has the same notes, except D#, as the D#m9 chord.

D#m9	D#-F#-A#- C#-F	x64666	bxbbbd		
D#m(M7)	D#-F#-A#- D	xx1332	x6x776		
D#m11	D#-F#-A#- C#- G#	x6x674	bxbb9x		

Diminished "D#" Chords

1 b3 5 b7

The D#o chord has the same notes as the F#o, Ao, and Co chords.

D#o	D#-F#-A-C	xx1212	x6757x	x6x575

Common "Borrowed" Chords (Chords "Borrowed" from Keys other than "E")

F7	131211	13x241
Fo	1x010x	

Appendix

G	3x0033	320003	355433	
G6	355400			
G/E	05543x			
GM7/E	0x5777	0x4430		
G7	353433	35x46x		
G13	3x3455			
Go	3x232x			
A#7	464544	4x45xx		
A#m7b5	6x665x			
A#m7#5	6x667x			
C	x32010	x32013	x3555x	8aa988
C/E	0x555x			
C/A	x0555x			
CM7	x32000	x35400	x35453	8x998x
	8aa900	89x8cc	x35500	
D	xx0232	x5777x		
D/F#	2x023x			
DM7	xx0222			
Dadd9	xx0230	x5775x